REIMAGINING *A RAISIN IN THE SUN*

REIMAGINING
A RAISIN IN THE SUN

FOUR NEW PLAYS

Edited by Rebecca Ann Rugg
and Harvey Young

NORTHWESTERN UNIVERSITY PRESS
EVANSTON, ILLINOIS

Northwestern University Press
www.nupress.northwestern.edu

Printed in the United States of America

10   9   8   7   6   5   4   3   2   1

Library of Congress Cataloging-in-Publication Data

Reimagining A raisin in the sun : four new plays / edited by Rebecca Ann Rugg and
    Harvey Young.
        p. cm.
    ISBN 978-0-8101-2813-2 (pbk. : alk. paper)
    1. American drama—21st century. 2. African Americans—Social conditions—Drama.
3. United States—Race relations—Drama. 4. Hansberry, Lorraine, 1930–1965—
Influence. I. Rugg, Rebecca Ann. II. Young, Harvey, 1975–
PS634.2.R45 2012
812'.608—dc23
                                                                    2011038718

∞ The paper used in this publication meets the minimum requirements of the
American National Standard for Information Sciences—Permanence of Paper
for Printed Library Materials, ANSI Z39.48-1992.

For
Zora Charles, Rosalind Wilder, and Mark Ezekiel

CONTENTS

INTRODUCTION: THE PEOPLE NEXT DOOR

Rebecca Ann Rugg and Harvey Young

In January 2009, a black family moved not only to town but also into a house that had never previously seen a black occupant (but plenty of black servants). The arrival of the Obamas, recently inaugurated President Barack Obama, his wife, Michelle, and daughters Malia and Natasha (Sasha), prompted a variety of pundits with widely contrasting political ideologies and affinities to openly ponder, "Should we continue to call it the 'White House'?" if black people now live there.[1] This recurring question was at its best playful—gesturing to the many African and Afro American cultural centers on college campuses that are affectionately referred to as "the Black House," a safe haven from a world in which race-based discrimination frequently targets people on the basis of the color of their skin. At its worst, the phrase was intended to conjure fears of decay and decline popularly associated with the arrival of a black family into a white neighborhood. Is the presence of a black man in the White House a harbinger of the end of U.S. prominence in the world?

Fifty years earlier, in January 1959, the national conversation centered on the topic of neighborhood integration, particularly black families moving into white neighborhoods. The discussion which had been triggered by a series of earlier court battles (*Hansberry v. Lee*, 1940; *Brown v. Board of Education of Topeka, Kansas*, 1954; et al.)—and which, perhaps, dates back to community discussions and zoning laws designed to prevent African American freemen from living "next door" throughout the eighteenth and nineteenth centuries—was given new energy by playwright Lorraine Hansberry and her play *A Raisin in the Sun*. The play concerns an African American family, the Younger family, whose matriarch Lena is set to inherit $10,000 in life insurance from her late husband's policy. The family of five—Lena's daughter Beneatha, her son Walter Lee, and Walter Lee's wife Ruby and son Travis—live on Chicago's South Side in a tiny apartment, with a shared bathroom down the hall. Through the promise of the imminent inheritance, Hansberry creates a dramatic structure that is almost the reverse of the traditional mortgage melodrama, in which the regular catalyst of the drama is the protagonist's not having enough money to pay the rent. In this play, the family is about to have more money than they've ever known, and the prospect of it engenders a furious storm of hopes, dreams, and impatient accusations. The family's competing dreams allow Hansberry to explore in depth crucial questions of race politics and materialism—questions at the intersections of race, gender, class, and nation. In playing out the reverse mortgage melodrama, the family ultimately uses the money to buy a home in a white neighborhood of the city, and the play ends as they move out of their too-small apartment into a home with a yard in an unwelcoming, potentially hostile community.

A Raisin in the Sun was an immediate critical and commercial success. Theater critics praised the 1959 production, cited its broad appeal, and frequently compared it to canonical theatrical works. As Brooks Atkinson observed in his *New York Times* review, "You might, in fact, regard 'A Raisin in the Sun' as a Negro 'The Cherry Orchard.'"[2] Audiences, of all colors, flocked to the Ethel Barrymore Theatre on Broadway and demonstrated through their presence and dollars that people were interested in seeing and hearing African American experiences portrayed on the stage. The play established Lorraine Hansberry as a *major* playwright and a leading voice of the American Theater in the 1960s, enhanced the already lustrous reputation of film actor Sidney Poitier, and launched the careers of a series of individuals who would actively reshape the look and sound of American theater over the next generation, including director Lloyd Richards and actors Ruby Dee, Ossie Davis, Glynn Turman, and Douglas Turner Ward. Over the years, *A Raisin in the Sun* maintained its popularity, and with every remount, revival, and adaptation, it catalyzed a discussion of race in the United States by drawing attention to the tensions and anxieties related to neighborhood integration. In 1961, the original cast reunited to appear in a film version of the play. Twelve years later, *A Raisin in the Sun* was adapted into a musical, *Raisin,* which ran for two years on Broadway and received the Tony Award for Best Musical. Since then, Hansberry's play has seen numerous productions, the most recent being the Tony Award–nominated 2004 Broadway revival with Sean Combs, Phylicia Rashad, and Audra McDonald as headliners. In his review of the production, theater critic Ben Brantley reminded contemporary audiences of how forward-thinking Hansberry was: "'Raisin' was remarkably prescient in identifying issues that would continue to shape African American life: black men's struggles for self-assertion in households dominated by strong women; the movement to separate African from American identities; Christianity as both an oppressive and redemptive power; the restlessness of women imprisoned by domesticity."[3]

Not only is *A Raisin in the Sun* a classic, but it's also something of a sacred text. As the play that opened the doors of Broadway and, later, regional theaters to African American directors, designers, actors, and critics, *A Raisin in the Sun* has become a source of reverence.[4] So it was quite shocking when, in 1986, George C. Wolfe's breakout hit *The Colored Museum* took direct aim at Hansberry's play in one of its satiric interludes, titled "The Last Mama-on-the-Couch Play." In what the *New York Times* called a "wild new evening of black black humor at the Public Theater" over which Wolfe would later come to preside, *The Colored Museum*, according to lead critic Frank Rich, "says the unthinkable, says it with uncompromising wit and leaves the audience, as well as a sacred target, in ruins."[5] Rich continues:

Ms. Reynolds and Mr. Montgomery provide stinging parodies of both the lines and performances of Claudia McNeil and Sidney Poitier in "Raisin"—with Mama forever instructing the angry son to let God settle his grievances with "the Man." But if Mr. Wolfe is merciless in mocking the well-made plays, "shattering" acting and generational conflicts of a 1950s black American drama preoccupied with "middle-class aspirations," he doesn't stop there. "The Last Mama-on-the-Couch Play" eventually satirizes a more pretentious, latter-day form of black theater (blamed on Juilliard in this case)—and finally turns into an all-black Broadway musical that spirals into a nightmarish indictment of the white audience's eternal relationship to black performers. By then, Mr. Wolfe, too, has torn "at the very fabric of racist America"—but not before he has revealed the cultural blind spots of blacks and whites alike. Although the letter of Miss Hansberry's work has been demolished, the spirit of its political punch is upheld.[6]

Critiquing the structure of the well-made play, melodrama, and 1970s (American) theatrical realism, Wolfe champions a form, theatrical satire, in which the "political punch" of *A Raisin in the Sun* can be appreciated by new, younger audiences who live in a different cultural moment and, perhaps, are less interested in the popular theatrical conventions of the past. In so doing, Wolfe inspired a wave of playwrights to engage with Hansberry and, by extension, U.S. racial politics—not by merely restaging *A Raisin in the Sun* but by wrestling with its themes, issues, politics, familiar storyline and reimagining them within their own uniquely original productions. Through *The Colored Museum*, Wolfe demonstrated that *A Raisin in the Sun* is not and should not be treated as an untouchable relic.

This history serves as a background to the subject of this anthology, which is concerned with the topic of neighborhood integration and the social themes of *A Raisin in the Sun* as they intersect with a contemporary theater landscape. The plays contained here—Bruce Norris's *Clybourne Park,* Robert O'Hara's *Etiquette of Vigilance,* Gloria Bond Clunie's *Living Green,* and Branden Jacobs-Jenkins's *Neighbors*—make the case for a revitalized preoccupation of American domestic drama: the lives of people living in proximity, in a word: neighbors. In the new millennium, domestic interiors are home to families working out their relationships to each other, as they long have been, and also to families and individuals in homes nearby. Recent theater seasons have seen a small eruption of plays on the subject of how Americans live side by side—or don't—and how they navigate across lines of class, culture, and race. *Caroline or Change* by Tony Kushner, *Well* by Lisa Kron, *Detroit* by Lisa D'Amour, *Palmer Park* by Joanna McClelland Glass, and *Mary* by Thomas Bradshaw are just a few plays that may productively be read through this lens. These works are in conversation with each other, with their cultural moment, and with American history. In particular, this collection considers the implications and meanings of one small but important branch of this new family tree: a group of four new "neighbor plays" that explicitly reimagine the 1959 classic *A Raisin in the Sun*. In discovering the convergence of these plays, questions proliferate: are they borne of a generational moment based on the classic play's anniversary and legacy; and if so, what was the moment and what is the legacy? What do these plays and their preoccupations have to do with the contemporary American political and racial landscape and with Obama's presidency?

NEIGHBORLY DRAMA

The subject of American neighborliness has long been a fascination of American drama—from what's been called the very first American play, *Metamora, or the Last of the Wampanoags* (1829) through two mid-twentieth-century theatrical high points: *Oklahoma!* (1943) and *Death of a Salesman* (1949). Written by John Augustus Stone as a star vehicle for American tragedian Edwin Forrest, *Metamora* centered on a Native American chieftain who struggled to protect his people from the encroachment of white (English) Puritan settlements. Eventually and predictably, Metamora and the Wampanoags are defeated—evicted from their own lands—by the white man's military superiority. By the time that *Oklahoma!* arrived, Native Americans had been dispossessed of their lands and relocated to Indian Territory (the modern-day state of Oklahoma), while the majority of their former landholdings were transformed into farms tended by white farmers. In light of this history, it is more than ironic that the popular musical offers the lyrical directive that the "Farmer and the Cowman should be friends." Neighborliness occurs only after racial difference has been eradicated.

The rapid expansion and increasing (and increasingly diverse) population of American cities became the de rigueur subject matter of American playwriting. The encroachment of the city and neighbors on a person's property and, consequently, lifestyle provide dramatic tension. We recall the scene in Arthur Miller's *Death of a Salesman* when Willy and Linda Loman lament how the growth of the city and the arrival of neighbors have "boxed [them] in."

> WILLY: The way they boxed us in here. Bricks and windows, windows and bricks.
> LINDA: We should've bought the land next door.

Just a moment later, Willy expostulates, "Population is getting out of control! Smell the stink from that apartment house! And another one on the other side."[7]

The proximity of neighbors—the intrusion of others—is what motivates the action of *A Streetcar Named Desire* (1947), where Stanley and Stella Kowalski split a house divided into two one-bedroom units with upstairs neighbors and also briefly share their cramped space with Stella's sister Blanche. Domestic abuse and sexual assault surface as by-products of the claustrophobic conditions. Similar space-related tensions exist within *A Raisin in the Sun.* The Youngers have outgrown their tenement apartment. What used to be a place that held only two people (Lena and her husband) became increasingly crowded with the birth of Walter Lee and Beneatha, the arrival of Ruth, the birth of Walter Lee and Ruth's son Travis. At the start of the play, the two-bedroom household that used to accommodate two people now barely holds five. Out of bedrooms, Travis sleeps on the couch. Beneatha bunks with Mama (Lena). Lacking an en suite bathroom, they share the bathroom down the hall with the residents of, presumably, equally overstuffed units. The sense of being boxed in is palpable and the Youngers' longing for an escape—from subsistence, from the tenement building—understandable.

What separates *A Raisin in the Sun* from its contemporaries is the way in which the tensions resulting from the encroaching city and the longing for more space are escalated by the presence of racial difference. The only white character in Hansberry's play and a representative of the Clybourne Park Improvement Association, Karl Lindner offers to buy the Youngers' recently acquired home back from them to prevent specifically black new neighbors from moving into the white community. His efforts are motivated by a desire for a very specific type of population control. Although the offer is initially rebuffed by Walter Lee, an unfortunate investment that results in Walter's being swindled of half of his father's insurance money prompts Hansberry's protagonist to consider accepting Lindner's money and, in so doing, to tacitly accept the Clybourne Park Improvement Association's racist views.

> I'll look that son-of-a-bitch right in his eye and say—"All right, Mr. Charlie. All right, Mr. Lindner—that's *your* neighborhood out there! You got a right to keep it like you want! You got a right

to have it like you want! Just write the check and the house is yours." And—and I am going to say—"And you—you people just put the money in my hand and you won't have to live next to this bunch of stinking niggers!"[8]

With these words, Walter places a spotlight on the intersection of race and community. He gestures to the logic that supported six decades of Jim Crow legislation that enabled "separate but equal" to exist—justifying the abuse of black bodies when they inadvertently crossed the invisible line that separated "their" and "our" sections of town, beach, bus, diner, store. He reveals the bias that lies at the heart of efforts to prevent African Americans from ever becoming neighbors to white homeowners.

In the wake of *A Raisin in the Sun,* a number of plays followed that directly addressed the experience of segregation from an African American perspective. Although the continued reverence for (or deliberate distancing from) Hansberry's drama prevented an engagement with the particular issue of neighborhood integration, these new works indirectly addressed the topic of neighborliness. Amiri Baraka's *Dutchman* (1964) stages black-white tension by locating it on a subway car, beneath and between segregated neighborhoods. Douglas Turner Ward's *A Day of Absence* (1965) places a spotlight on the African American presence even within white neighborhoods by scripting a drama premised on what would happen if all black people disappeared. Ward's *Happy Ending* (1965) centers on a black female domestic and, slowly, through the narrative reveals how closely intertwined black and white households are. Charles Fuller's Pulitzer Prize–winning *A Soldier's Play* (1981) emphasizes the destructive effects of internalized prejudice and institutional racism on a company of African American soldiers. Each play is indebted to *A Raisin in the Sun.*

The plays in this collection move beyond the writings of Baraka, Ward, Fuller, and others by returning to the intersection of race and neighborliness. Norris, O'Hara, Clunie, and Jacobs-Jenkins revisit and restage aspects of Hansberry's signature work. Rather than attempting to revive Hansberry's politics within the twenty-first century, they radically reenvision her play, insert their own voices, and present original works for a contemporary audience. Norris directly engages with *A Raisin in the Sun* by staging the play at the same address to which the Youngers are destined at the close of Hansberry's drama. He also creates a space for a Hansberry character, Karl Lindner, within his play. In *Clybourne Park*, Lindner is not redeemed. His campaign to prevent the black family—they are never referred to by name—from moving to the neighborhood falls on both figurative and literal deaf ears. Although Norris suggests racial disharmony and miscommunication, his characterization of the racism of Clybourne Park residents lacks the vitriol that Hansberry allows her reader to imagine. Both *An Etiquette of Vigilance* and *Living Green* present the experiences of black families who have moved to white neighborhoods within Chicago. O'Hara introduces his audience to an aged Travis, who bears the psychological scars of having watched his parents combat racism within their neighborhood. A bus driver and an alcoholic, Travis invests his hopes and dreams into his daughter Lorraine, whose ambitions differ from her father's. In contrast to Travis, Clunie's Freemans are highly successful, white-collar, African American professionals. The drama of *Living Green* hinges on the parents' concerns that their children, raised in a predominantly white neighborhood and school, are becoming increasingly detached from black history and are "headed for a . . . white life." This sense of losing black culture inspires them to consider moving back to their old, primarily African American, neighborhood, which has declined since they left. The psychological effects of not only moving to a white neighborhood but also being disconnected from black history provides the structure for Jacobs-Jenkins's *Neighbors*. Richard Patterson, a successful African American man, experiences a personal crisis when a blackface minstrel troupe moves in next door and becomes friendly—perhaps overly friendly—with his white wife and mixed-race daughter. Part of his anxiety rests in a concern that his new neighbors' blackness will rub off on his family.

SUBURBIA

Though suburbia seems to sidle up so naturally to a post–World War II cultural aesthetic, the concept of the suburb first emerged in the medieval ages to discuss the areas that existed outside of a literally fortified city's walls.[9] The suburb was the region just below (and beyond) the main gates and, perhaps, on the other side of the moat. To live in the suburbs was to have space unparalleled within the city. It also meant always being vulnerable and at risk. When cities were attacked by marauders, the suburbs were consistently ravaged—their storehouses looted, their residents abused. Suburban existence, for decades, was neither desirable nor something to envy. The outlook on suburban life changed as the walls came down and crime began to increase within (as opposed to outside) densely populated urban centers.

Dolores Hayden's comprehensive *Building Suburbia* describes several evolving patterns of suburban development in the U.S.: The building of individual estates in borderlands around cities began in 1820, primarily for an affluent elite who wanted and were able to escape the noxious industry of city life. While at the time these borderlands were rural, now they are part of the urban core: Brooklyn Heights, Staten Island, Boston's Back Bay, Chicago's Hyde Park. Landscape gardening also became a profession at this time, linked to Christian ideals of the creation of beauty in home and garden. By the 1850s, this impulse had developed into a communitarian ideal of the "picturesque enclave," in which groups of country homes were built with nearby common space, often featuring natural aspects of the landscape, such as a waterfall, to promote community life. Frederick Law Olmsted's 1869 plan for Riverside, Illinois, aimed to promote "the harmonious association and co-operation of men in a community . . . The families dwelling within a suburb enjoy much in common, and all the more enjoy it because it is in common . . . that they are Christian."[10] To enshrine the ideal of shared beliefs, developers and residents began limiting access to communities on the basis of ethnicity, race, and class. Pricing was the clearest way to ensure an affluent community, but other means to guarantee exclusivity were codified over time. The conflict over segregation in housing is, of course, one of the most infamous parts of America's built history, and the one which *A Raisin in the Sun* explicitly engages. Redlining of mortgages for certain groups along lines of race and class became a common practice in the twentieth century, followed by more formal restrictive local covenants.

Within Northern and Midwestern cities, the combination of redlining coupled with the neighborhood preferences of "Great Migration" settlers, African Americans who moved from the South, created racially homogenous communities. In response to the increasing population and the decreasing availability of real estate in black neighborhoods, white homeowners, frightened by the prospect of African Americans moving into *their* communities, established improvement societies, block clubs, and community associations. In Chicago, real Karl Lindners actively worked to maintain the whiteness of their block. The limited housing options available to African Americans resulted in overcrowding: apartment buildings were divided into smaller units and transformed into tenements; rents were substantially higher for smaller, substandard units than elsewhere in the city (in the white areas); and enrollments were higher and class sizes larger in black public schools.[11] Despite problems resulting from population density of primarily African American neighborhoods, these segregated communities possessed beneficial qualities. They were relatively self-sufficient, filled with African American entrepreneurs, professionals, teachers, preachers, and politicians, among others who existed as everyday role models for the people living in those communities. In addition, neighbors not only served as protective shields insulating fellow residents, particularly children, from the daily stings of prejudice but also promoted self-confidence and racial pride by offering seemingly endless encouragement. Gloria Bond Clunie, who grew up in the African American section of Henderson, North Carolina, recalls, "Though there were outside forces that may have been very challenging, you had a cocoon that nurtured. Someone would say, you are wonderful but you've got to be twice as good."[12] George C. Wolfe, who was raised in segregated Frankfort, Kentucky, similarly remembers, "I grew up in this very protected, celebration of self environment."[13] Beginning in the 1940s with the successful lawsuit of Hansberry's father and gaining momentum throughout the 1950s, redlining and other segregationist policies were barred, and African Americans—particularly those with greater financial resources—left black communities and integrated other regions of the city as a result.[14] In response, white homeowners, who could afford a house in the suburbs, packed up their belongings and moved.

From the "white flight" from urban centers of the 1950s and 1960s to today's redevelopment of the urban core as desirable, high-end real estate, the lives and fortunes of cities and the people who live in them have long been intertwined with how people live just outside metropolitan zip codes and school districts. The architecture of first-ring suburbia in the post–World War II period was made immortal by the TV sitcom. *Father Knows Best, Make Room for Daddy, The Dick Van Dyke Show,* and *Bewitched* (with its interesting difference) dramatized a particular family ideal that can look bizarre from a contemporary perspective. June Cleaver never takes off her string of pearls—not even when cleaning house. In watching reruns, it's hard not to see *Leave It to Beaver* as a dated fantasy based on postwar philosophical views of family and culture. Now that commonly held views of family have expanded to include single-parent units and two–working parent families—among other variations—the midcentury sitcom family comes across as extremely particular rather than universal. The desire for this fantasy could account for the continued popularity of Thornton Wilder's play *Our Town*, which waxes nostalgic about a way of life (including a homogenous community) that was already in the rearview mirror when the play premiered in 1937.

In a 1997 article in the *New York Times*, famed architecture critic Herbert Muschamp describes how the building materials of the first-ring suburbs—subdivisions of single-family homes built around metropolitan cores from the post–World War II period through the mid-1970s—are wearing out. The literal glue along with the social glue of these communities is wearing thin. Muschamp declares a state of emergency in the suburbs, where what historian Dolores Hayden calls a "Triple Dream," of house plus land plus community, has long failed to materialize as residents had hoped.[15] Muschamp notes that "some planners believe that the recycling of the first ring is the key to determining the way that Americans will live in the next 50 years."[16] He asserts that the reinvention of the first ring is crucial to the health of the cities they border. By extension, the health of the suburbs can also be seen as crucial to the health of the nation as a whole and its lifeblood, this triple-faceted American Dream.

The delicate line separating "wearing thin" and the promise of reinvention is staged in *Clybourne Park, Etiquette of Vigilance, Living Green,* and *Neighbors*. The contemporary suburb seems almost as tired and worn as the Youngers' apartment in Hansberry's play. The memory of a dead son haunts the house in *Clybourne Park*. A few decades later, the same neighborhood, within O'Hara's *Etiquette of Vigilance*, has lost its luster and appeal. Its promise has not been realized. Neither has the Youngers' dream of having a doctor in the family. The Freemans, in *Living Green*, are prompted to move *back* to the city when a move to the suburbs has not brought them any closer to the happiness they desire. The drama of *Neighbors* rests on a similar level of dissatisfaction, as the play's protagonist realizes that his suburban environment complicates his and his child's relationship to race.

ON CITIES AND CITIZENSHIP

Before there were nations, there were cities—a location of identity and residence and a locus of citizenship. Although one project of nation-building is to dismantle the historic primacy of urban citizenship and to replace it with the national, anthropologists James Holston and Arjun Appadurai argue that cities remain the strategic arena for the development of citizenship.[17] As modern nations have developed criteria for citizenship on a large scale, there have long been disjunctions between the form and substance of citizenship—between the promise and the lived reality. One reactionary response to this disjunction aims for even greater exclusivity on the substantive level. This leads to exactly the kinds of legislation we see today in local communities, or in any gated housing complex, and which allowed for the restrictive neighborhood covenants of America's urban north in the mid-twentieth century. As Holston and Appadurai note, "around the world, it is all too common to find home-owner associations using these powers and privileges of democratic organization to exclude, discriminate, and segregate."[18]

The anthropologists write that the basis for the idea of a nation of citizens is a liberal compact that imagines the nation less as a "neutral framework for competing interests than . . . as a community of shared purposes and commensurable citizens."[19] They continue:

> The working assumption is that this national community is committed to constituting a common good and to shaping a common life well-suited to the conditions of modernity. This notion requires a set of self-understandings on the part of citizens which lies at the core of the liberal compact of citizenship: it requires that people perceive, through a kind of leap of faith, that they are sufficiently similar to form common purpose . . . This liberal compact is now under tremendous strain. With the unprecedented growth of economic and social inequalities during the last few decades in so many nations, the differences between residents have become too gross and the areas of commonality too few to sustain this

compact. As a result, the social imaginary of a nation of commensurable citizens disintegrates . . . In the breach, the idea of a shared culture seems implausible.[20]

This large question of common purpose, the viability of the liberal compact, is what is being worked out in these contemporary plays about neighbors. One reason that *A Raisin in the Sun* is such a common touchstone in the twenty-first century, particularly during the Obama presidency, must be that with a black family in the White House, there is a question for many Americans about the ongoing disjunction between the form and substance of citizenship. If in the moment of Obama's election, the American creed seemed to be rejuvenated, the country's sins cleansed, and its promise symbolically fulfilled, then what of the abilities of everyday people to make common purpose together across lines of race, culture, and class? And where better to look for an answer and a way to engage than to one of the most famous theatrical meditations on the liberal compact's failure: *A Raisin in the Sun.* Theater works ideas about national affiliation out in private interactions, more often today than in courtroom dramas, because ideas about privacy and community are at the very heart of the history and creed of this country.

As the four plays within this collection all demonstrate, cities and our built environments remain crucial sites of the dialogue about our liberal compact. *Clybourne Park, Etiquette of Vigilance, Living Green,* and *Neighbors* are attempts to revitalize the dialogue about what it means to live together as citizens. Through their use of irony, postmodern recycling of history, realism, and satire, each of these plays stands as an attempt to contribute to the offstage possibility of doing so. In this capacity, they take on one of the most ancient functions of theater, as a place of civic discourse.

If that seems a bit grand, for plays set in domestic interiors, scholars have long argued that in *A Raisin in the Sun*, Hansberry proposes that the oppressive nation, or "house," that has withheld from African Americans their "birthright of full citizenship" is to be forcibly stormed.[21] The house of Hansberry has a particular metaphoric and landmark status in the theater, as a rich metaphor for the American Dream—of freedom and community, and for the liberal compact as a whole. Its inhabitation now by other dramatists creates opportunities to see how Hansberry's call, in a 1964 *Village Voice* article, for the reconstruction of this divided house has turned out.[22] And each of these plays uses the house of Hansberry as a means to take the pulse of how Americans speak to each other now—how we fashion ourselves in public and private, in the places we choose, and those we inhabit, online and off. In short, how does citizenship live in our neighborhoods, our living rooms, our backyards?

THE PLAYS

Bruce Norris's play *Clybourne Park* begins in 1959 as the white family is moving out of their house in Chicago's (fictional) Clybourne Park neighborhood, and their neighbors come over to ask them not to sell to the incoming Youngers. Norris has spoken of his impulses in writing the play—one being that he was exposed early to the film and musical versions of *A Raisin in the Sun,* and loved them, and another, that one of his reactions to the play and the musical *Raisin* was that, as a white actor, he couldn't be in them, except as Karl Lindner.[23] Since the opportunity never came for him to play that role, he says he decided as a writer to give Lindner more to do. After a scathing act 1, which reveals, among other things, a family tragedy at the heart of why the house was sold so cheaply, the play moves to the current day, where a white family, moving into the city from the suburbs, is meeting with the neighborhood committee about their plans to build a new structure on the Clybourne Park property, which now sits in a black neighborhood in the midst of gentrification.

The play, which was commissioned by Playwrights Horizons and produced in 2010, takes no prisoners as it exposes the hypocrisies of white liberalism in particular, but also domestic partnerships, ideas about disability, community support, and, of course, black and white relationships. Norris's signature rapid-fire overlapping dialogue and group scenes are particularly suited to a driving buildup of shocking revelations and interactions in both acts. The play, in production, frequently prompts audible gasps from its audiences at certain things characters say to each other—in particular, an exchange of racist jokes that flies fast and furious toward the end of act 2. Critically acclaimed, *Clybourne Park* has been described by Ben Brantley in the *New York Times* as being "spiky and damningly insightful."[24] Peter Marks, writing for the *Washington Post,* observed, "It's the dramatist's sophisticated take on the treacherousness of language—

the way we eventually unmask ourselves through words, no matter how hard we try to prettify them—that prompts 'Clybourne's' big laughs."[25]

Robert O'Hara's *Etiquette of Vigilance* begins in the present day with Travis, Hansberry's ten-year-old who sleeps on the couch—now a middle-aged Chicago Transit Authority bus driver, living in the home his parents fought so hard to keep in Clybourne Park. He's in shock from some kind of incident on his bus, which we later discover was a fatal bombing, recalling the midcentury violence of neighborhood integration and the period of civil rights struggles. Travis and his daughter Lorraine examine their relationship in a series of scenes which move in time from the 1980s to the current day, each period marked by the image of a famous black politician on the mantel. As the story unfolds, Lorraine's decision to drop out of medical school to become a playwright is complicated by the discussion of their shared family legacy of dreams deferred, drinking, and depression.

In O'Hara's play, Travis repeatedly watches the 1967 film *Guess Who's Coming to Dinner* on television. Linked by the presence of Sidney Poitier, *A Raisin in the Sun* and *Guess Who's Coming to Dinner* might be said to present a double portrait of America's reimagining of racial and interracial domesticity in the 1960s. At one point the white father, played by Spencer Tracy, asks his prospective black son-in-law, played by Sidney Poitier, whether the young couple has given any thought to the problems their children will have. To this question the black doctor replies that he knows the children will face difficulties but that Joey, his young bride-to-be, feels that all of their children will be presidents of the United States. The timing is perfect: Barack Obama could be the son of the couple in *Guess Who's Coming to Dinner*—which couple, incidentally (or not), met and began their whirlwind romance in Hawaii, just as Obama's parents did in the early 1960s. Certainly the conversation between Travis and his daughter Lorraine under the portrait of Obama with the logo HOPE is resonant with a history external to the family.

Etiquette began its life as a commission from La Jolla Playhouse, which asked O'Hara to consider the state of African Americans at this point in history. In a recent interview, O'Hara commented on his disavowal of La Jolla's directive:

> It seemed to me to be too big of a question to tackle and not really that interesting a play for me to write . . . But I've always wanted

to do something with *A Raisin in the Sun* . . . I was always struck
by how people think the play's ending is uplifting. A broken family moving into a house they CANNOT afford (they only have
enough for a down payment). Why on earth would anyone think
that this fucked-up family would make it through the sixties segregated Chicago suburbs intact . . . ? And what of the young boy
. . . ? Travis is ten at the end of *Raisin* . . . He has slept all those
ten years on the couch in a living room of chaos . . . And at the
end of the play he is thrust into one of the most brutally racist and
violent points in our history in one of the most brutally racist cities
in our country.[26]

With this play, O'Hara refuses the mandate to speak for his race, and in
this play, he speaks instead on behalf of the little boy growing up, sleeping on the couch, absent for much of *Raisin*, wondering how he would
learn to be a man, an adult, a father. Rather than premiering in San Diego
at La Jolla, *Etiquette of Vigilance* first appeared onstage in Chicago—the
explicitly named setting of *A Raisin in the Sun, Etiquette of Vigilance,* and
Living Green—at the Steppenwolf Theatre Company in fall 2010.

The third play, *Living Green,* by Chicago playwright Gloria Bond
Clunie, centers on an affluent, African American family who reside in
a primarily white, Clybourne Park–like suburb of Chicago. Angela and
Frank Freeman are successful in business and take pride in their ability to
pay for the private school tuition of their children, Carol and Dempsey,
without having to rely upon financial aid or scholarships. They live the
dream that Lena Younger has for her children and grandchildren. Set
in the mid-1990s, against the backdrop of the ex–football player O. J.
Simpson's murder trial and Louis Farrakhan's Million Man March, the
Freemans are horrified when they learn that their daughter Carol has
trashed her school's bathroom and that Mr. Parks, a friend from their
former, primarily black neighborhood and the school's janitor, has to
clean up her mess. Concerned that their children are losing their connections to the black community and the historical struggles of the black
community, Angela and Frank consider selling their house and moving
back to their old neighborhood.

Living Green premiered in winter 2009 at Victory Gardens, where
Clunie serves as a member of the Tony Award–winning company's

esteemed playwriting ensemble. The play proved to be both a critical and commercial success. *Chicago Tribune* senior theater critic Chris Jones praised it as a "gutsy piece of writing" and "a compassionate look at the dilemma faced by many urban families with children who must weigh the appeal of a flight to safety versus the moral imperative to make a difference in a community and teach their kids what's right."[27] Consistently, reviewers identified *Living Green* as an "homage" to *A Raisin in the Sun* and gestured to some of the more apparent influences of Hansberry. For example, the plays share a similar structure. Both begin with the protagonists racing to gain access to a single bathroom and end with the family's matriarch, surrounded by moving boxes, picking up a plant before exiting toward an uncertain future in a new neighborhood.

Neighbors, by Branden Jacobs-Jenkins, caused quite a stir in a spring 2010 workshop production at the Public Theater in New York. Patrick Healy, reviewing the play for the *New York Times,* deemed it "one of the most sustained shocks of the theater season," and Adam Hetrick, in an article for *Playbill,* described it as "explosive."[28] This provocative and incendiary play investigates a relationship between an interracial middle-class suburban couple, living in an otherwise white neighborhood, and their new neighbors, an uncouth family of blackface minstrel performers. The narrative tension in the play roots itself in the racial insecurities and anxieties of Richard Patterson, which prompt him to become increasingly critical of the relationships that his wife and daughter are forming with the new neighbors. The play takes breaks from the narrative for parodic and yet virtuosic minstrel interludes. For instance, one calls for the character named Mammy, while smoking at the washboard, to, among other things, midwife a white woman's birth of twins, which the mother abandons. The stage directions then call for the following:

> MAMMY goes bug-eyed. She runs around in circles, as before, miming like she's screaming. Eventually . . . she stops. She notices her breasts hanging out. She takes her huge breasts and attaches one baby to each nipple. They suckle. They start to hurt her. She tries to pry them off, but they're stuck. She lets go and they sort of hang there. She tries to shake them off, but they hang there. This shaking gets more and more extreme until eventually she is doing a Matahari-esque belly dance, putting her hands behind her head

and twirling the babies clamped to her nipples like tassels on a bra. She does jazz hands.

Racial stereotypes, the history of black performance, and its audiences are under scrutiny throughout this play. Just as clearly, Branden Jacobs-Jenkins, an emerging African American playwright with a reputation as a provocateur, is having a lot of fun imagining this crazy racial pantomime. Even without the interludes and the blackface, the play, like *Living Green,* would question the effect of life in the suburbs on a person's racial identity and conception of blackness.

First produced within two years of one another, *Clybourne Park, Etiquette of Vigilance, Living Green,* and *Neighbors* are clearly part of a cultural moment—perhaps evidence of the "Age of Obama," in which ideas of race and the politics of race and racism are being explored anew. This "moment" seems increasingly evident when we consider that the plays are being written by playwrights who differ quite strikingly from one another in terms of writing style, politics, and audience. The race politics in *Clybourne Park* are biting, and, in Norris's usual style, there's excessive provocation, but formally, it is realism. *Etiquette of Vigilance* and *Neighbors* are fractured narratives in which time moves in peculiar ways, the audience is addressed directly, and there is explicit, meta-theatrical engagement with cultural modes such as blackface minstrelsy and classic black Hollywood film. In comparison, *Living Green* seems the most conservative in approach, borrowing the structure and feel of the well-made play and bearing an uncanny structural similarity to *A Raisin in the Sun.* None of these frameworks proves better at inviting a conversation than the others. However, the accumulation of these approaches and audiences who appreciate each approach offers multiple perspectives in which to consider the intersection of race and community.

Following each play within this collection, an interview with the playwright appears in which the author is given an opportunity to reflect on her or his play and a chance to consider the legacy of Hansberry's *A Raisin in the Sun.* None of these interviews has been previously published. Conducted specifically for this collection, they offer a glimpse into the motivations for each play and reveal that the playwrights are aware of the other dramatists working on and thinking about similar issues within the same cultural moment. For example, Jacobs-Jenkins has this to say about *Clybourne Park*:

It was actually running in New York at the same time as *Neighbors*, and there was a certain amount of comparison happening among audiences, and when I finally skipped my show one night to see it, I lost my mind. I thought the two plays were eerily in conversation with each other and overlapped in all sorts of odd ways—like even down to certain gentrification jokes, many of which have been consequently written out of *Neighbors*—but maybe I'm just flattering myself. Basically all I wanted to do after the show was stalk Bruce Norris everywhere and eat the things he ate and read the things he was reading and wear his clothes when he wasn't looking and try to figure out how he pulled it off. In fact, I still do.[29]

The authors featured within this collection are familiar with one another. They know theater history. They speak about each other's work in nuanced and generous ways. In presenting their words, this collection promotes and stages a dialogue among them. Concluding this collection of plays and interviews is a transcribed conversation with George C. Wolfe. A quarter century after the premiere of *The Colored Museum*, he reflects on the play's intervention, his politics, and the writings of the next generation of authors who followed along the path blazed by Hansberry and, later, by himself.

BLUEPRINTS

The plays within this collection are presented in an order designed to highlight their engagement with themes evident not only in *A Raisin in the Sun* but also with one another. Opening this anthology, *Clybourne Park* stages the race and real estate conversations that are occurring elsewhere within the Chicagoland area, away from Lena, Walter Lee, Ruth, Beneatha, and Travis Younger. Chronologically, it opens only minutes after Karl Lindner, representing the Clybourne Park Improvement Association, has returned from the Youngers' home after having informed them that the "overwhelming majority" of the neighborhood association feels that "for the happiness of all concerned that our Negro families are happier when they live in their own communities." With its second act set in the present day, Norris's play demonstrates how the neighborhood changed from exclusively white to primarily black within a generation. He also gives Lena, the great-niece of Hansberry's character Lena (Mama)

Younger, an opportunity to voice her understanding, appreciation, and respect for the racism that her uncle and aunt, presumably Walter Lee and Ruth, endured in order to provide their family with an environment that could nurture greater possibilities for future generations. Robert O'Hara's *Etiquette of Vigilance* dovetails with *Clybourne Park*. The play opens with an adult Travis, much like Lena, still living in the Younger home. The sense of promise and possibility that ends *A Raisin in the Sun* has disappeared, and the lasting impression is that, despite the move to a new (and now declining) neighborhood, the family's hopes and dreams remain deferred. Even with the passing of years and the sense of possibility made evident through the presence of political portraits of Martin Luther King Jr., Jesse Jackson, and Barack Obama, hope remains just beyond the grasp of Travis and his daughter Lorraine. In Gloria Bond Clunie's *Living Green,* the playwright demonstrates that a (white) community does not deteriorate with the presence of a black family. She also reveals that African Americans can achieve their professional aspirations. The question that she raises and interrogates with her play is whether a person can maintain her connection to—and self-perception as being a part of—the black community when she no longer resides within one. Branden Jacobs-Jenkins wrestles with a similar question. In addition, through his inclusion of the interludes, he asks his audience if we're ready, capable, and comfortable confronting the United States' charged and complicated racial history even within the present cultural moment.

Despite this arrangement, a number of other critical reading strategies could be employed. To read the interviews beginning with George C. Wolfe followed by the other playwrights featured in this collection reveals an engaging conversation of artists actively thinking about the construction of race within today's society and the ongoing legacy of Lorraine Hansberry. To explore the plays after encountering the voices of the playwrights, in interviews, offers an opportunity to detect the influences and politics of the playwrights that reside beneath or between the words of their characters. There are other equally insightful strategies: to pick plays at random, to begin with *Neighbors* and work your way backward (toward the beginning). All are worthwhile strategies that will result in unique discoveries. Regardless of the reading choice selected, the most important thing to remember is that the words contained within this collection—whether play texts or interviews—were meant to be embodied. Read them aloud. Share them with friends. Join the conversation.

NOTES

1. John Ensslin, "Joke Leaves 'em Gasping: Obama Quip Stuns Citizen of West Banquet Crowd," 17 January 2008, http://www.rockymountainnews.com/news/2008/jan/17/joke-leaves-em-gasping/.
2. Brooks Atkinson, "A Raisin in the Sun," *New York Times,* 12 March 1959.
3. Ben Brantley, "A Breakthrough 50's Drama Revived in Suspenseful Mood," *New York Times,* 27 April 2004.
4. Although not the first African American play produced on Broadway, *A Raisin in the Sun*—thanks to its commercial appeal—encouraged producers to invest in black theater at unprecedented levels and, therefore, opened the doors to Broadway.
5. Frank Rich, "'Colored Museum' Satire by George C. Wolfe," *New York Times,* 3 November 1986.
6. Ibid.
7. Arthur Miller, *Death of a Salesman* (New York: Penguin, 1977), 17.
8. Lorraine Hansberry, *A Raisin in the Sun* (New York: Vintage, 1986), 144.
9. John R. Stilgoe, *Borderland: Origins of the American Suburb* (New Haven: Yale University Press, 1988), 1.
10. Dolores Hayden, *Building Suburbia: Green Fields and Urban Growth, 1820–2000* (New York: Vintage, 2004), 62.
11. St. Clair Drake and Horace Cayton, *Black Metropolis: A Study of Negro Life in a Northern City* (Chicago: University of Chicago Press, 1993); and Philip T. K. Daniel, "A History of Discrimination against Black Students in Chicago Secondary Schools," *History of Education Quarterly,* 20:2 (Summer 1980), 147–62.
12. Harvey Young, "Interview with Gloria Bond Clunie," published in this collection.
13. Harvey Young, "Interview with George C. Wolfe," published in this collection.
14. The effect of segregation, integration, and, most recently, gentrification on communities originally formed by the "Great Migration" has been the subject of numerous sociological studies. Mary Pattillo's recent writings on black Chicago are particularly exemplary sources. See Mary Pattillo, *Black on the Block: The Politics of Race and Class in the City* (Chicago: University of Chicago Press, 2008); and Mary Pattillo-McCoy, *Black Picket Fences: Privilege and Peril Among the Black Middle Class* (Chicago: University of Chicago Press, 2000).
15. Hayden, 8.
16. Herbert Muschamp, "The Nation: Becoming Unstuck On the Suburbs," *New York Times,* 19 October 1997, http://www.nytimes.com/1997/10/19/weekinreview/the-nation-becoming-unstuck-on-the-suburbs.html.
17. James Holston and Arjun Appadurai, "Cities and Citizenship," *Public Culture,* 8:2 (Winter 1996), 188.
18. Ibid., 191.

19. Ibid., 192.
20. Ibid.
21. Kristin Matthews, "The Politics of 'Home' in Lorraine Hansberry's 'A Raisin in the Sun,'" *Modern Drama,* 51:4 (October 2008), 569.
22. Hansberry, referring to integration, noted in a 1964 letter to the *Village Voice* that "the Negro people would like to see this house rebuilt." See Lorraine Hansberry, "Miss Hansberry on 'Backlash,' *Village Voice,* 23 July 1964, 10.
23. Bruce Norris, "Bruce Norris on Clybourne Park," RoyalCourtTheatre.com, 11 August 2010, http://www.royalcourttheatre.com/news/articles/bruce-norris-on-clybourne-park/; Henry Haun, "What Inspired *Clybourne Park?*, *PlayBlog,* 26 February 2010, http://www. playbill.com/playblog/2010/02/what-inspired-clybourne-park/.
24. Ben Brantley, "Good Defenses Make Good Neighbors," *New York Times,* 22 February 2010, http://theater.nytimes.com/2010/02/22/theater/reviews/22clybourne.html.
25. Peter Marks, "Peter Marks Reviews Bruce Norris's 'Clybourne Park' at Woolly Mammoth Theatre," *Washington Post,* 25 March 2010, http://www.washingtonpost.com/wp-dyn/ content/article/2010/03/24/AR2010032402981.html.
26. Rebecca A. Rugg, "Interview with Robert O'Hara," published in this collection.
27. Chris Jones, "Family Struggles with Community, Identity in Memorable 'Living Green,'" *Chicago Tribune,* 3 February 2009, http://leisureblogs.chicagotribune.com/the_theater_ loop/2009/02/living-green.html.
28. Patrick Healy, "New Play Puts an Old Face on Race," *New York Times,* 2 February 2010, http://www.nytimes.com/2010/02/03/theater/03neighbors.html; Adam Hetrick, "Jacobs-Jenkins *Neighbors* Will Move to Los Angeles in August; Casting Announced," *Playbill,* 29 July 2010, http://www.playbill.com/news/article/141616-Jacobs-Jenkins-Neighbors-Will-Move-to-Los-Angeles-in-August-Casting-Announced.
29. Rebecca A. Rugg, "Interview with Branden Jacobs-Jenkins," published in this collection.

REIMAGINING *A RAISIN IN THE SUN*

CLYBOURNE PARK

Bruce Norris

PRODUCTION HISTORY

Clybourne Park was first presented by Playwrights Horizons at the Playwrights Horizons Mainstage Theater in New York City in February 2010. It was directed by Pam MacKinnon, with set design by Daniel Ostling, costume design by Ilona Somogyi, lighting by Allen Lee Hughes, and sound by John Gromada. C. A. Clark was the production stage manager. Cast was as follows:

Francine/Lena	Crystal A. Dickinson
Jim/Tom/Kenneth	Brendan Griffin
Bev/Kathy	Christina Kirk
Albert/Kevin	Damon Gupton
Betsy/Lindsey	Annie Parisse
Karl/Steve	Jeremy Shamos
Russ/Dan	Frank Wood

The play was subsequently produced by Woolly Mammoth Theatre Company in Washington, D.C., in March 2010. It was directed by Howard Shalwitz, with set design by James Kronzer, costume design by Helen Huang, lighting by Colin K. Bills, and sound by Matt Otto.

Francine/Lena	Dawn Ursula
Jim/Tom/Kenneth	Michael Glenn
Bev/Kathy	Jennifer Mendenhall
Albert/Kevin	Jefferson A. Russell
Betsy/Lindsey	Kimberly Gilbert
Karl/Steve	Cody Nickell
Russ/Dan	Mitchell Hebert

The play premiered in London at the Royal Court Theatre in September 2010 and transferred to the Wyndham's Theatre (West End) in January 2011. It was directed by Dominic Cooke, with set by David Innes Hopkins, sound by David McSeveney, and lighting by Paule Constable.

Francine/Lena	Lorna Brown
Jim/Tom	Sam Spruell
Kenneth	Michael Goldsmith
Bev/Kathy	Sophie Thompson
Albert/Kevin	Lucian Msamati
Betsy/Lindsey	Sarah Goldberg
Karl/Steve	Martin Freeman
	(succeeded by Stephen Cambell Moore)
Russ/Dan	Steffan Rhodri
	(succeeded by Stuart McQuarrie)

Note: In the original production, the actor playing Jim and Tom also played the role of Kenneth. In some subsequent productions a separate actor was hired to play the role of Kenneth alone.

CHARACTERS

Act 1 (1959)

Russ, white, late forties
Bev, married to Russ, white, forties
Francine, black, thirties
Jim, white, late twenties
Albert, married to Francine, black, thirties
Karl, white, thirties
Betsy, married to Karl, late twenties

Act 2 (2009)

Tom (played by the actor who played Jim)
Lindsey (played by the actor who played Betsy)
Steve, married to Lindsey (played by the actor who played Karl)
Kathy (played by the actress who played Bev)
Kevin, married to Lena (played by the actor who played Albert)
Dan (played by the actor who played Russ)
Kenneth (played by the actor who played Jim and Tom)
Lena (played by the actor who played Francine)

The set is the interior of a modest, three-bedroom bungalow, 406 Clybourne Street, in the near northwest of central Chicago. There is a sitting room with front-door access, a fireplace with an oak mantelpiece, and a separate dining area with built-in cupboards. At the rear of the dining area, a swinging door leads to a kitchen. A staircase leads up to a second floor, and beneath it, another door leads down to a basement. There is a hallway and a bathroom door as well.

ACT 1

[*September 1959. Three o'clock, Saturday afternoon. The house is in disarray. Cardboard boxes are stacked in corners. Some furniture has been removed, shelves emptied. Pictures have been removed from the walls, and carpets have been rolled and stood on end. Not far from the fireplace,* RUSS *sits alone reading a copy of* National Geographic. *He is dressed in pajama top and chinos, socks, no shoes. On a table next to him sits a carton of ice cream into which, from time to time, he dips a spoon. Music plays softly on a radio next to him. After some time,* BEV *descends the stairs carrying linens to place in a cardboard box. As she packs, she stops to look at* RUSS.]

BEV: You're not going to eat all of that, are you?

[RUSS *turns down the radio.*]

RUSS: [*with his mouth full*] Whaddya say?
BEV: What ice cream is that?
RUSS: Um. [*with a look at the carton*] Neapolitan.
BEV: Well, don't feel compelled to eat that.
RUSS: [*shrugs, barely audible*] Going to waste.

[*He turns the radio back up, and* FRANCINE *enters from the kitchen, wearing a maid's uniform.* RUSS *remains in the foreground as* BEV *joins her.*]

FRANCINE: [*to* BEV] So, if it's all right I'm just going to put these candlesticks here in the big box with the utensils.
BEV: That is what I would do, yes, but you do mean to wrap them first?
FRANCINE: Oh, yes, ma'am.
BEV: Oh. Now: Francine: I was wondering about this chafing dish, which we have practically never used.
FRANCINE: Yes, ma'am.
BEV: Do you own one of these yourself?
FRANCINE: No, I sure don't.
BEV: Because I do love to entertain though for the life of me I can't remember the last time we did. But still, it does seem a shame to give it away because it's just such a nice thing, isn't it?
FRANCINE: Oh, yes it is.

BEV: And it just looks so lonely sitting there in the cupboard *so:* I was wondering if this might be the sort of thing that would be useful to you?

FRANCINE: Ohhhh, thank you, I couldn't take that.

BEV: [*re: the chafing dish*] See how sad he looks?

FRANCINE: You don't want to be giving that to me.

BEV: Well, nonetheless I'm offering.

FRANCINE: No, I don't think I should.

BEV: Well, you think about it.

FRANCINE: But thank you for offering.

BEV: You think about it and let me know.

FRANCINE: Yes, ma'am.

BEV: And do put some paper around those.

FRANCINE: Yes, ma'am.

[FRANCINE *goes into the kitchen.* BEV *returns with more to pack, passing* RUSS.]

BEV: That's a funny word, isn't it? Neapolitan.

[RUSS *turns off radio.*]

RUSS: Funny what way?

BEV: What do you suppose is the origin of that?

RUSS: Uhhh . . . Naples, I imagine.

BEV: *Naples?*

RUSS: City of Naples?

BEV: Noooo.

RUSS: Of or pertaining to.

BEV: That would not be my first guess.

RUSS: Yup.

BEV: *I* would think it had something to do with *neo,* as in something *new,* and then there's the *-politan* part which to me would suggest a *city,* like *metropolitan.*

RUSS: Could be.

BEV: Meaning *new city* or something to that effect.

RUSS: [*shrugs*] Told you what *I* think.

BEV: Because a person from Naples, I mean they wouldn't be called, well, not *Napoleon,* obviously. I guess that was already taken! [*Laughing, then serious*] On the other hand, you *do* say *Italian.* But *cities,* though, and specifically ones that end in *S,* because there must be a rule of some sort, don't you think? Help me think of a city other than *Naples* that also ends in *S.*

[*Pause.*]

RUSS: Uhhh—

BEV: Oh, fiddle. Um.

RUSS: Des Moines.

BEV: Not a *silent* S.

RUSS: Brussels.

BEV: All right. There you go. And how do we refer to them?

RUSS: Belgians.

BEV: But, the people from the *city.*

RUSS: Never *met* anyone from Brussels.

BEV: But there has to be a word.

RUSS: Look it up.

BEV: Where?

RUSS: Dictionary?

BEV: But it's not going to say this is the capital of Belgium and by the way the people who live there are called—

RUSS: Give Sally a call.

BEV: She won't know that.

RUSS: She and Ray went to Paris.

BEV: So?

RUSS: *Close* to Brussels.

BEV: Sally never knows those sort of things.

RUSS: Oh. Oh.

BEV: What?

RUSS: Parisians.

BEV: What about them?

[FRANCINE *returns with more packing.*]

RUSS: Paris ends in S.

BEV: But—it's not *Brusselsians.*

RUSS: Or Nice.

BEV: I'm serious.

RUSS: Got the "S" *sound*.

BEV: But not *Nicians*. Like *Grecians*.

RUSS: No, no. *Niçoise*.

BEV: I know that, but—

RUSS: Know that salad your sister makes?

BEV: But that's *French*.

RUSS: It's a French *city*.

BEV: I understand, but, I'm saying how would we say, in *Eng*—? Well, now I don't remember the original question.

RUSS: Brussels.

BEV: No no.

RUSS: Des Moines?

BEV: *No.*

RUSS: Naples.

BEV: *Naples*. And I don't think *Neopolitan*. How would that become *Neopolitan?*

RUSS: Muscovites.

BEV: What?

RUSS: People from Moscow.

BEV: Well, I give up, because that's just *peculiar*.

RUSS: [*chuckles at the word*] Muscovites.

BEV: [*the same*] I wonder if they're *musky*.

RUSS: [*savoring the sound*] Musss-covites.

BEV: [*coming up with one*] Cairenes!

RUSS: *That* is a strange one.

BEV: I'm telling you, that's what they're called!

RUSS: I'm not disputing.

BEV: But why *Cairenes?*

RUSS: [*shrugs*] Dated a girl named *Irene*.

[FRANCINE *exits again*.]

BEV: Or *Congolese?*

RUSS: That, too, is correct.

BEV: So why don't we say *Tongalese?*

RUSS: Or *Mongolese*.

BEV: No, Mongol-*oid*.

RUSS: No no, that's different.

BEV: Oh, you're right.

RUSS: That's uhhh, you know, that's—

BEV: No, I know.

RUSS: [*taps his finger on his temple*] The thing with the—

BEV: [*does the same*] Like the Wheeler boy.

RUSS: Right. The one who—

BEV: Bags the groceries.

RUSS: Right.

[*Beat, then:*]

BEV: But that's nice, isn't it, in a way? To know we all have our place.

RUSS: There but for the grace of God.

BEV: Exactly.

[*Pause.* RUSS *breaks it with:*]

RUSS: [*pronouncing grandly, with a sweep of his hand*] Ulan Bator!

BEV: What?

RUSS: [*an exact repeat*] Ulan Bator!

BEV: What are you doing?

RUSS: [*once again*] Ulan—!

BEV: Stop it. Tell me what you're doing.

RUSS: Capital of Mongolia.

BEV: Well, why would I know that?

RUSS: [*shrugs*] *National Geographic.*

BEV: Oh oh. Did you change the address like I asked you?

RUSS: What do you mean?

BEV: For the *National Geographic.*

RUSS: The address?

BEV: Oh, *Russ!*

RUSS: Me?

BEV: I *asked* you.

RUSS: You did?

BEV: I asked you *fifteen times.*

RUSS: When?

BEV: I said don't forget the change of address for the magazine and you promised me that you would, you promised me *specifically*—[*cont'd.*]

RUSS: [*overlapping*] I did it last week.

BEV: [*continuous*]—that you would see to it so I—Oh.

RUSS: Pulling your leg.

BEV: I see.

RUSS: [*a gentle imitation*] Oh, *Russ*!!

BEV: Maybe people don't *like* having their leg pulled.

RUSS: I was just—I was—Okay.

[*Pause.*]

BEV: And are you going to bring that trunk down from upstairs?

RUSS: Yup.

BEV: Thought you said after lunch.

RUSS: Sort a two-person job.

BEV: And you really want to wear those clothes all day?

RUSS: Hadn't really thought about it.

[*A silence passes between them.* RUSS *scratches his elbow.*]

BEV: But you know, you *are* a funny person. I was telling Francine—I ran into Barbara Buckley at Lewis and Coker's and Barbara said that Newland told her a funny joke that you told at Rotary last year.

RUSS: That *I* told?

BEV: About a man with a talking dog?

RUSS: [*shakes his head*] Thinking of Don Lassiter.

BEV: No, it was you.

RUSS: Don's the one with the jokes.

BEV: You know jokes. You tell jokes.

RUSS: A talking *dog*?

BEV: And Barbara said does Russ not go to Rotary anymore? Apparently they all keep saying where's Russ? [*Beat, then:*]
Not that I care one way or the other but it does seem that you used to enjoy going and I don't see why that, of all things, should have to change—[*cont'd.*]

[RUSS *shifts in his chair.*]

[*continuous, quickly*]—and please don't say *what's the point*, Russ. I hate it when you say that. Because for that matter—[*cont'd.*]

RUSS: [*overlapping*] I wasn't going to say—[*cont'd.*]

BEV: [*continuous*]—what's the point of *anything* enjoyable, really?—[*cont'd.*]

[*The phone rings.* FRANCINE *enters.*]

[*continuous*]—Why not just sit in a chair all day and wait for the end of the world but *I* don't intend to live the remainder of my life like that and I think you could take notice of the fact that talking that way *frightens* me.

FRANCINE: [*phone*] Stoller residence?

RUSS: [*quietly, to* BEV] Not trying to frighten you.

FRANCINE: Who may I say is calling, please?

RUSS: [*to* BEV *quietly*] Ulan Bator.

FRANCINE: Excuse me, Miz Stoller?

BEV: Who is it?

FRANCINE: Mister Lindner wanting to talk to you.

RUSS: [*with a groan*] Ohh for the love of—

BEV: [*to* FRANCINE] Tell him I'll call him back.

RUSS: Not one thing it's another.

FRANCINE: [*phone*] Mister Lindner, she wonders if she can call you back?

BEV: [*overlapping* FRANCINE, *to* RUSS] I only mean that people are concerned about you—[*cont'd.*]

RUSS: [*overlapping*] Well, what's the *nature* of the concern?

BEV: [*continuous*]—and I don't see the point of *spurning* their good intentions.

RUSS: Gee whiz, I'm just reading a magazine.

FRANCINE: [*to* BEV] Says he's calling from a pay phone.

RUSS: [*to* FRANCINE] Just say we're occupied.

BEV: No, I'll take it, thank you, Francine. [*To* RUSS, *as she crosses*] I'm just repeating what Barbara said. [*phone*] Hello?

RUSS: [*to himself*] Barely know the woman.

BEV: [*phone*] No no no, it's just, we're in a state of disarray, Karl.

RUSS: Somehow I *spurned* her.

[*As* FRANCINE *returns to the kitchen, the front door opens and* JIM *sticks his head in. He is a youthful minister—wears a clerical collar under his jacket.*]

JIM: Ding dong?

RUSS: [*seeing* JIM, *not rising*] Oh. Uh, hey, Bev?

JIM: May one intrude, he politely asked?

RUSS: [*to* BEV] Jim's at the door.

BEV: [*seeing* JIM, *she mouths silently to him*] Oh, oh, oh! *Come in!! Come in!!* [*phone*] Karl, I can't hear what you're saying.

JIM: Russ, my friend, I am crossing the threshold!

RUSS: Hey, Jim.

JIM: [*looking around*] Holy Toledo Jiminy Christmas.

RUSS: Bev's on the phone.

JIM: Hate to be the one to break it to ya, buddy, but somebody made off with yer stuff!

RUSS: Kinda discombobulated.

BEV: [*phone*] Oh, Karl, I don't think so, not today.

JIM: [*to* RUSS] S'not the big day, is it?

RUSS: [*to* JIM] No no. Monday.

BEV: [*phone*] No, it's just, Russ is a little under the weather.

JIM: Piece of advice. Watch out when you start lifting things. Learned that the hard way last month.

RUSS: [*preoccupied with* BEV] Izzat right?

JIM: [*to* RUSS] Ohhhh *yeah*. Judy says Jim, I gotta have me this spinet piano, a task which naturally falls to *me*—[*cont'd.*]

BEV: [*phone, overlapping*] Well, if it's absolutely necessary.

JIM: [*continuous*]—and there I am with this thing halfway up the front steps and me *underneath*. And of course, it's not the *weight*, you know. It's the *angle*—[*cont'd.*]

BEV: All right, Karl.

[BEV *hangs up.*]

JIM: [*continuous*]—which is why they tell ya to bend the knees.

BEV: [*to* JIM] Well, will you look what the cat dragged in?

RUSS: [*to* BEV, *re: phone call*] What was that about?

JIM: Bev, I am *trying* to bestow the pearls of my wisdom upon this man.

RUSS: [*to* JIM] No no, I was listening.

BEV: Oh, isn't it just a *jumble* in here, all of this?

JIM: S'what I was saying to Russ, said somebody cleaned ya out!

RUSS: Not coming here, is he?

BEV: Oh, I don't know. You know Karl.

JIM: Karl Lindner?

RUSS: Bev?

JIM: Ohmigosh. Ya got a look at Betsy lately?

BEV: [*eyes wide*] Oh, I *know.*

JIM: Give that girl a *wide berth.*

BEV: Jim, can I get you some iced tea?

RUSS: [*to* BEV] Maybe call back and ask him to come later.

BEV: It was a pay phone. [*To* JIM] Oh oh oh oh oh! I know! Now wait. Now Jim: I am going to ask you a question:

JIM: Huh-oh!

BEV: [*to* RUSS] And don't help him. [*To* JIM] Now: I want you to tell Russ what you think the word *Neapolitan* means.

RUSS: [*to* JIM] She thought—

BEV: *Shhhhhhh!!!* You're not allowed to say.

JIM: Well, that'd be your basic vanilla, strawb—

BEV: No no. The *derivation.*

RUSS: I *told* her what I th—

BEV: [*to* RUSS] *Shhhhh!!!*

JIM: Uh, think it's *Naples,* isn't it?

BEV: Ohhhhh *phooey.*

JIM: Or *Napoli,* as we like to say.

[FRANCINE *enters.*]

BEV: You two are *cheating.* And then—well, Russ's in a funny mood. He keeps going [*trying to do what* RUSS *did*] Oo-lan Ba-tor!

JIM: Whatzat, capital of Nepal?

RUSS: Mongolia.

JIM: Mongolia. So then what's the *Nepalese*—Do ya say *Nepalese?*

BEV: [*chuckles, slaps* RUSS'*s arm*] I hope it's not Ne-*politan!*

RUSS: Kathmandu.

BEV: Oh, well, I don't even know why you two know these things.

FRANCINE: Miz Stoller?

JIM: Knowledge is power, Bev.

BEV: Then I choose to remain *powerless.* [*To* RUSS] Do it again.

RUSS: Do what?

BEV: How you said it.

RUSS: No.

BEV: *Do* it, Russ.

RUSS: No.

BEV: Do it for Jim.

RUSS: Bev?

BEV: Why *not*?

RUSS: Sorry, Jim.

BEV: Why for me but not for him?

RUSS: Well, for one thing, 'cause it's not *funny*.

FRANCINE: Excuse me, I'm fixing to go, so if you need something else?

BEV: Oh. Yes. One thing. Francine, you remember that big trunk that's upstairs?

RUSS: No no no no. Bev?

BEV: She doesn't mind.

RUSS: Just told you I'm doing it.

BEV: You said it's a two-person job, and here's two of you right here.

RUSS: Well, what's the emergency?

JIM: [*to* BEV] I *would* offer my services—[*cont'd.*]

BEV: [*overlapping*] Oh no no no no no.

JIM: [*continuous*]—but I am under doctor's orders, believe it or not.

FRANCINE: Well, I'm just needing to leave by three thirty.

BEV: [*resigned*] All right.

RUSS: Francine? *I* am going to move the gol-darned trunk.

FRANCINE: Yes, sir.

BEV: [*to* JIM, *mock-private*] That's what I get for trying.

[FRANCINE *exits. Discomfort.*]

JIM: [*to* RUSS] Soooo—

BEV: Did you get any lunch, Jim? Do you want some—?

JIM: No no no no no.

BEV: Since I guess we're *cleaning out the larder* and Russ seems to be eating every last thing in the icebox, so you'll have to fight him for the ice cream.

JIM: Not for me.

RUSS: [*shrugs*] Well, ya know. Can't pack ice cream in a suitcase.

[BEV *finds this hilarious.*]

BEV: *In a suitc—*[*To* JIM] *Did you hear what he just said?*

JIM: [*chuckling as well*] Man's got a point!

BEV: [*slapping* RUSS's *shoulder*] *How do you think of those things?* Ice cream in a—

JIM: Not unless you're moving to the North Pole!

[BEV *laughs harder.*]

BEV: Thank goodness we're not moving *South*!

JIM: *That'd* be a mess. No question.

[BEV *and* JIM *stop laughing, sigh. More discomfort.*]

No question.

BEV: [*jumping up*] Well, I'm going to see what we *do* have.

[BEV *exits into the kitchen, leaving* RUSS *and* JIM *alone.*]

JIM: Whaddya, coming down with something?

RUSS: Who?

JIM: Bev said "under the weather."

RUSS: Me?

JIM: And here ya sit in your PJs—

RUSS: No no no no no. I'm—Took the day to—Truck coming, so—

JIM: I gotcha.

RUSS: Coupla days off.

JIM: Playing hooky.

RUSS: No no.

JIM: Bev's your alibi.

RUSS: Just giving her a hand with stuff.

JIM: And you are hard at work, as I see.

RUSS: [*smiles a little*] No. I just.

JIM: Kidding you.

RUSS: I know. I—I—Yup.

JIM: Woulda come to your aid there, only I'm dealing with a little, uh, issue.

RUSS: Oh yeah?

JIM: Piano I told ya about?

RUSS: Right?

JIM: Didja ever . . . [*lowers voice*] . . . ever need a *truss*? Have to wear one of those?

RUSS: Uhhhh . . . Don't recall.

JIM: Oh, you'd recall it if you did.

RUSS: Guess not, then.

JIM: Then you are a *fortunate* man.

RUSS: I hear you.

JIM: Bend the knees or suffer the consequences.

RUSS: Yup.

[*Brief pause.*]

JIM: So, *Monday,* you said.

RUSS: Yup.

JIM: Off to the hinterlands.

RUSS: Monday it is.

BEV: [*calling from off*] Jim, was that a yes or a no on the iced tea?

JIM: [*calling back to her*] Uhhh, I would not say no to that.

BEV: [*same*] Russ?

[RUSS *shakes his head.*]

JIM: [*same*] I believe Russ is declining your gracious offer.

BEV: [*same*] I thought as much.

[*Pause.*]

JIM: *Monday.*

RUSS: Indeed.

JIM: Head 'em up. Move 'em out.

RUSS: Yup.

JIM: And when ya start that Glen Meadows office?

RUSS: Monday after.

JIM: How about that.

RUSS: Yup.

JIM: And how's that shaping up?

RUSS: Oh, boy, now. That's a nice setup.

JIM: I betcha.

RUSS: And *spacious,* that's the thing. And *carpeted*? And I got a look at
that office they're putting me in. Tell you what I thought to myself,
I thought what the heck do ya do with all this space? *Corner* office.

Windows two sides. But the space is the primary—That is just an . . . *extravagant* amount of space.

JIM: Elbow room.

RUSS: Other thing is, once we get situated up in the new place. The time it takes? Driveway to the parking lot? Know what that's gonna take me?

JIM: Five minutes.

RUSS: Six and a half.

JIM: Close enough.

RUSS: Timed it. Door to door.

JIM: Roll outa bed and *boom*.

RUSS: And Tom Perricone. I don't know if you know Tom. Colleague of mine. Now, he's going to relocate to that same office and they live right down here offa Larabee. You know what *that's* gonna take him on the expressway?

JIM: That's a drive.

RUSS: Thirty-five minutes. And that's no traffic.

JIM: Well, Judy and I are sure gonna miss having you two around.

RUSS: Well . . . Yeah.

[*Awkward pause.*]

JIM: [*lowers voice, secretively*] And how's Bev doing?

RUSS: Oh, you know. Bev loves a project.

JIM: Keep her occupied.

RUSS: The *mind* occupied.

JIM: What, does she worry a lot?

RUSS: No. No more than—

JIM: About you?

RUSS: Me? No.

JIM: Ya seem good to me.

RUSS: I meant—you know how she gets.

JIM: Sure.

RUSS: Overexcited.

JIM: I can see that.

RUSS: Worked up over things. Minor things.

JIM: Things like?

RUSS: Oh, you know.

JIM: Not calling yourself a *minor thing*, are you?

RUSS: [*slightly irritated*] No, I didn't—I meant things like—

JIM: [*chuckles*] Do *you* consider yourself a *minor thing*?

RUSS: Jim, I didn't—Well, actually, in the grand scheme of things I don't think any one of us is, uh . . . particularly—did Bev *ask* you to come over?

JIM: Nope.

RUSS: I mean, good to see you. Great to see you.

JIM: I mean, we *ran into* each other coupla days ago. Got to talking.

RUSS: Uh-huh.

JIM: Little about you. Since she cares about you.

RUSS: Right. Right.

[RUSS *looks for* BEV.]

'The heck's she's doing in there?

JIM: Everybody cares about you, Russ.

RUSS: Uh-huh. Uh-huh. Yup. Well. Tell ya what I think. And I'm not a psychiatrist or anything but I do think a lotta people today have this tendency, tendency to *brood* about stuff, which, if you ask me, is, is, is—well, short answer, it's *not productive.* And what *I'd* say to these people, *were* I to have a degree in psychiatry, I think my advice would be maybe, get up offa your rear end and *do* something.

JIM: Huh.

RUSS: Be my solution.

JIM: Uh-huh.

RUSS: Of course, what do I know?

JIM: I think you know plenty.

[*Pause.* RUSS *looks toward the kitchen.*]

RUSS: [*calling*] Hey, Bev?

JIM: Like, I think you know your son was a good man, no matter what. Hero to his country. Nothing changes that.

RUSS: Yup yup yup.

JIM: And I also think you know that sometimes talking about things that happen, painful things, maybe—

RUSS: Uh, you don't happen to have a degree in psychiatry *either,* do you, Jim?

[JIM *stares*.]

No? Just checking.

JIM: We all suffer, you know. Not like you and Bev, maybe, but—

RUSS: But, see, since what *I'm* doing here is, see, since I'm just minding *my own* business—[*cont'd*.]

JIM: [*overlapping*] But it doesn't hurt—

RUSS: [*continuous*]—sorta seems to *me* you might save yourself the effort worrying about things you don't need to *concern* yourself with and furthermore—[*cont'd*.]

JIM: [*overlapping*] He's in a better place, Russ.

RUSS: [*continuous*]—if you *do* you keep going on about those things, Jim, well, I hate to have to put it this way, but what I think I might have to do is . . . uh, politely ask you to uh, [*clears his throat*] . . . well, to go fuck yourself.

[*Pause*.]

JIM: Not sure there's a polite way to ask that.

[RUSS *rises to exit*.]

RUSS: [*embarrassed*] Okay? So.

JIM: I just can't believe Kenneth would've wanted his own father to—

RUSS: [*maintaining calm*] Yup. Yup. So, you can go fuck yourself, okay?

[BEV *enters with* JIM's *iced tea*.]

BEV: So wait. So if it's *Napoli* in Italian, then wouldn't adding an E before the A just seem superfluo—What's happening?

JIM: Bev, I believe I will hit the road.

BEV: What are you—? Russ?

RUSS: Going upstairs.

BEV: What happened?

JIM: Not to worry.

BEV: [*to* RUSS] What did you do?

JIM: Another time.

BEV: [*to* RUSS] Come back here.

JIM: [*overlapping, to* BEV] No no. Russ made his feelings clear in—[*cont'd*.]

BEV: [*overlapping, quietly to* RUSS] Why are you being like this?

JIM: [*continuous*]—no uncertain terms.

RUSS: [*to* BEV] Going up, now.

JIM: Terms maybe more appropriate for the *locker room* than the—

BEV: [*to* JIM] I *told* you so. I *told* you what it's like. And he uses these ugly words in other people's presence [*to* RUSS] and I'm not some kind of *matron*, but what in the world is wrong with *civility*?

RUSS: Honey? I am not going to stand here with you and Jim and dis-cuss—[*cont'd.*]

BEV: [*overlapping*] Well, you're being *ugly,* and I don't like *ugliness.*

RUSS: [*continuous*]—*private* matters, matters that are between me and the memory of my son—[*cont'd.*]

BEV: [*to* JIM, *overlapping*] I think his *mind* has been affected, I really do.

RUSS: [*continuous, overlapping*]—and if the two of you want to talk about Kenneth on your *own* time, if that gives you some kind of *comfort*—

BEV: And what's wrong with *comfort*? Are we not *allowed* any comfort anymore?

RUSS: Well, Kenneth didn't get a whole lotta comfort, did he?

BEV: He was *sick,* Russ! And for you to use nasty words to Jim—

JIM: Nothing I haven't heard before.

RUSS: [*moving upstairs*] Changing my shirt.

JIM: I was in the service, too, you know.

RUSS: [*bitter laugh*] Oh, right. And tell me again. How many people did *you* kill?

BEV: *Oh, for God's sake, stop it!!*

RUSS: Sat behind a *desk,* didn'tcha? Goddamn *coward.*

[*The doorbell rings. All stand in silence.* BEV *covers her mouth. At the front door, we can see* ALBERT *peer through a small window.*]

ALBERT: [*from off*] Hello?

[*And still no one moves.*]

Anybody home?

[BEV *looks at* JIM, *who moves to open the door.*]

JIM: Afternoon.

ALBERT: [*to* JIM] Uh, how d'you do? I'm just here to—

BEV: *Francine? Albert's here.*

FRANCINE: [*calling from off*] Yes, ma'am. I'm coming.

BEV: She's on her way.

ALBERT: Thank you, ma'am.

[JIM *does not know whether to invite* ALBERT *in or not. He turns to* BEV. RUSS *turns and exits up the stairs.* BEV *turns back to* ALBERT.]

BEV: Albert, would you like to wait inside?

ALBERT: Uh. All right, thank you, ma'am.

BEV: I bet it's warm out there, isn't it?

ALBERT: Ohhh, yes it is.

BEV: Can I offer you some iced tea?

ALBERT: No. Thank you, though.

BEV: Well, I'm sure she'll be right along.

ALBERT: Thank you.

[ALBERT *sits near the door but within earshot of* JIM *and* BEV.]

JIM: [*whispering because of* ALBERT] I think maybe it's time for me—

BEV: [*rapidly whispering*] Oh, please don't go, please don't, I just don't want to be alone with him right now. It makes me feel so alone—[*cont'd.*]

JIM: [*overlapping*] You're not alone.

BEV: [*continuous*]—the way he sits up all night long. Last night he was just sitting there at three in the morning—[*cont'd.*]

JIM: [*overlapping*] I know. I do.

BEV: [*continuous*]—and I say to him say don't you feel sleepy? Do you want to take a Sominex, or play some cards maybe, and he says *I don't see the point of it* as if there has to be some grand justification for every single thing that a person—

[*And now* BEV *notices* ALBERT *rising and heading for the door.*]

 [*to* ALBERT]—Wait. Yoo-hoo?

ALBERT: [*having overheard*] S'all right.

BEV: Something wrong?

ALBERT: No no.

BEV: She said she's on her way.

ALBERT: I can wait outside.

BEV: [*calling off*] Francine?

FRANCINE: [*from off*] I'm coming.

BEV: There she is.

[FRANCINE *enters in street clothes, with two large bags of hand-me-downs. She stops to put on her earrings.*]

FRANCINE: I'm sorry. I guess I'm moving a little slower than usual.

BEV: And here's Albert waiting so patiently. If only I had *door-to-door service like Francine!*

FRANCINE: So, I'll see you Monday, then.

BEV: Albert, isn't this place just a *catastrophe?*

ALBERT: Oh, yes it is.

BEV: [*to* ALBERT] I tell you, I don't know *what* I would do without a friend like Francine here, and on a *Saturday,* I mean she is just a treasure. What on earth are we going to do up there without her?

ALBERT: Well, I trust y'all can sort things out.

BEV: [*to* FRANCINE] Oh, and maybe Monday we can see about that big trunk, why don't we?

FRANCINE: We'll make sure and do that.

BEV: I'd do it myself but I'm not a big strapping man like Albert here.

JIM: Afraid I've gotta exempt myself—

BEV: Oh no no no no no. Francine and I can manage.

ALBERT: What's it, a trunk, you said?

FRANCINE: [*with a shake of the head to dissuade* ALBERT] A footlocker.

ALBERT: Where's it at?

BEV: No no no no no we just need to bring it down the stairs.

ALBERT: I don't mind.

BEV: Oh, thank you, but no.

FRANCINE: [*to* BEV] But definitely Monday.

ALBERT: These stairs, here?

BEV: Oh no no no—I mean, it wouldn't take but two minutes.

FRANCINE: [*to* BEV, *re: her bags*] It's just I got these things here to take care of.

ALBERT: I can put them in the car.

JIM: Oh, got yourself a car?

ALBERT: Yes, sir.

JIM: [*looking out*] Whatzat, a Pontiac?

ALBERT: Yes, sir.

FRANCINE: [*significantly, to* ALBERT] It's just that I'm afraid we're going to be late.

ALBERT: [*not getting it*] Late for what?

FRANCINE: The place we gotta be?

ALBERT: The *place*?

FRANCINE: Remember?

ALBERT: [*to* FRANCINE] The—What're you—?

FRANCINE: [*to* BEV] I'm sorry.

ALBERT: [*to* FRANCINE] Said two minutes is all.

FRANCINE: [*quiet, pointedly*] Well, I've got my *hands* full.

ALBERT: I just said I can put them in the—

FRANCINE: [*testily, as they start to go*] *I* can put them in the car. *I* can do that.

BEV: Did you get the chafing dish?

FRANCINE: No, ma'am, thank you, though.

ALBERT: [*to* BEV *and* JIM] Be right back.

[ALBERT *opens the door to reveal* KARL LINDNER, *about to ring the bell. He is oddly formal and uncomfortable-seeming.*]

KARL: Ah. Unexpected. Uhhh . . . ?

BEV: Hello, Karl.

KARL: [*relieved*] Ah, Bev. Voila.

ALBERT: [*to* KARL, *squeezing past*] Excuse us, if you don't mind?

KARL: [*to* ALBERT, *formally*] Not at all. After *you*, sir.

[KARL *makes way for* ALBERT *and* FRANCINE *to pass.*]

ALBERT: [*to* FRANCINE, *as they exit, barely audible*] What is the *matter* with you?

KARL: [*from the door, seeing* JIM] Ah. Jim, too. Hello, lad.

JIM: Karl.

BEV: [*unenthusiastically*] Come on in, Karl.

KARL: Uhhh . . . [*as if working out a puzzle*] Yes. *Could* do that. However, you'll recall, Bev, that Betsy currently happens to be, uh, how shall we say—?

BEV: Ohhh, is it almost that time?

KARL: Uh, point *being*, that she did accompany me.

BEV: What do you—you mean she's in the *car*?

KARL: She is.

BEV: Well, for heaven's *sake*, Karl! Don't leave her out in a hot *car*.

KARL: Well, that was my thinking.

BEV: Bring her *in* with you.

KARL: Will do.

BEV: Of all *things*.

KARL: [*as he goes*] Back in a flash.

[*As* KARL *exits again,* RUSS *descends the stairs in a clean shirt and shoes.* BEV *and* JIM *allow him to silently pass by them. He walks to the chair and collects the ice cream carton.*]

BEV: You changed your shirt.

[RUSS *continues into the kitchen without responding. Beat.*]

JIM: [*quietly*] Bev.

BEV: [*whispering*] I know I'm being silly. I know I am, but—[*cont'd.*]

JIM [*overlapping*]: Not at all. Not in the least.

BEV: [*continuous whisper*]—it's just that after two and a half *years* you'd think that with *time*, because that's supposed to be the thing that helps, isn't it? A little bit of time—[*cont'd.*]

JIM: [*overlapping*] A great healer.

BEV: [*continuous whisper*]—and I thought with the new job and the move I thought somehow he would start to let go of—

[RUSS *returns from the kitchen.* BEV *goes silent. He goes to a door beneath the stairs, opens it, pulls a string to turn on a light, and exits.*]

[*calling after him*] Where are you going, the basement?

RUSS: [*from off*] Yup.

BEV: Are you looking for something?

RUSS: [*farther*] Yup.

[*The front door opens.* KARL *escorts his wife,* BETSY, *who is eight months pregnant and who also happens to be totally deaf.*]

KARL: Here we are, then.

BEV: Oh, *there she is*!

BETSY: Hehhyoooh, Behhhh. [Hello, Bev.]

BEV: [*overenunciating for* BETSY's *benefit*] Well just *look* at you! My *good-ness*. You are just the biggest *thing*.

BETSY: Ah nohhh! Eee toooor. Ah so beee!!! [I know! It's true. I'm so big!!!]

KARL: Took the liberty of not ringing the bell.

BEV: Betsy, you know Jim.

JIM: Indeed she does.

BETSY: Hah, Jeee. [Hi, Jim.]

[JIM *shows off his sign language skills to* BETSY, *finger-spelling the last word.*]

BEV: Oh, well, now look at *that*. Look at them go. What is that about? Somebody translate!

BETSY: [*laughing to* KARL] Huhuhuuh!! *Kaaaaa!!*

JIM: [*chuckling along*] Uh-oh! What did I do? Did I misspell?

[BETSY *signs to* KARL.]

KARL: [*chuckles*] Uh, it seems, Jim, that you, uh, told Betsy that she was expecting a *storm*!!

BEV: *No!* He meant stork! You meant *stork*, didn't you?

BETSY: [*pantomimes umbrella*] Ahneemah-umbrayah! [I need my umbrella!]

[*All laugh.*]

BEV: Her *umbrella!* [*To* BETSY] I understood that!

KARL: Have to check the weather report!

BEV: A *storm*, I'm going to tell that to Russ.

JIM: Must have rusty fingers!!

[*All chuckle.*]

BETSY: [*to* KARL, *asking for translation*] Kaaaah?

KARL: [*speaks as he signs*] Uh, Jim says *his fingers are rusty.*

[BETSY *laughs and covers her mouth.*]

BEV: See? She understands.

BETSY: [*to* JIM, *pantomimes washing hands*] Jeee, mehbbe yew neeee sooohh!! [Jim, maybe you need soap!!]

[*More polite laughing.*]

BEV: [*explaining to* JIM]   JIM: [*to* BEV]
Soap. For the *rust* on your—   No, I understood.

[RUSS *emerges from the basement, carrying a large shovel.*]

KARL: And there's the man himself! Thought he'd absconded!
BEV: [*to* RUSS] The Lindners are here.
BETSY: Hehhyoooo, Ruuuuhhh. [Hello, Russ.]
RUSS: Betsy. [*To* BEV] Ya seen my gloves anywhere?
KARL: [*re: the shovel*] Tunneling to China, are we?
RUSS: [*to* BEV] Pair of work gloves?
BEV: [*to* KARL] Do you know I just got through saying how Russ and I
   never entertain and here it is a regular neighborhood social!
KARL: Well, we shan't be long.
BEV: Karl, do you suppose Betsy would like a glass of iced tea?

[BETSY *does not see* KARL.]

KARL: Bets—? [*To* BEV] Point to me.
BEV: [*to* BETSY, *overenunciated*] *Betsy, look at Karl.*

[BETSY *looks at* KARL.]

KARL: [*to* BETSY, *signing simultaneously*] *Bev wants to know if you want
   some iced tea to drink?*
BETSY: Ohhh, yehhhpeee. Dahhnyoo, Behhh. [Yes, please. Thank
   you, Bev.]
RUSS: [*to* BEV] Know the gloves I'm talking about?
BEV: Well, Karl's here. I thought you were going to talk to Karl.

[FRANCINE *and* ALBERT *have entered and started up the stairs.*]

RUSS: [*seeing* ALBERT *and* FRANCINE] 'The heck's going on?
BEV: Nothing. Now, we two girls are going to the refreshment stand, so
   you boys'll have to manage on your own.
KARL: Have no fear.
BEV: [*while exiting, as before*] *So how are you feeling, Betsy? Are you tired?*
BETSY: Noooo, ahhhh fiiieee, Behhhh, reeeee. [No, I'm fine, Bev,
   really.]

[BETSY *and* BEV *exit to the kitchen.*]

KARL: Now, Russ, Bev tells me you're indisposed, and normally I'd— [*realizing*] Ah. Not *contagious*, is it?

RUSS: Is what?

KARL: Hate for Betsy to, uh, come into contact with any—

RUSS: Not contagious.

KARL: Can't be too careful. Or possibly one can. Anyway, hate to commandeer your Saturday afternoon here, *a man's home,* as they say, but, as we haven't seen your face at Rotary of late I thought I might— [*cont'd.*]

RUSS: [*overlapping*] What's on your mind, Karl?

KARL: [*continuous*]—intrude upon the sanctity of—what'd you say?

RUSS: What's on your mind?

KARL: Ah. Well. Firstly—May I sit?

RUSS: Yeah, yeah.

JIM: Karl, I will be taking my leave.

KARL: Not on my account?

JIM: Parish business.

KARL: Uh, well, truth to tell, Jim, we might actually benefit from your insight, here.

JIM: [*looking at watch*] Uhhhhh—

KARL: If it's not pressing?

JIM: Actually—

KARL: Not to usurp your authority, Russ. Your castle. You are the king.

RUSS: What's on your mind?

KARL: [*as he sits on a box*] Is this safe?

RUSS: Anywhere.

KARL: No breakables? And Jim?

[JIM *sits, looking at* RUSS.]

JIM: Uhh . . . minute or two.

KARL: Good. Good good good. So.

[BEV *opens the kitchen door.*]

BEV: Iced tea for you, Karl?

KARL: Ah. Problem *being* that I *do* have some sensitivity to the cold beverages, so my question would be is the tea *chilled,* by which I mean has it been *in* the Frigidaire?

BEV: [*enduring him*] No, Karl.

KARL: Then, if I might have a serving *minus* the ice? That would suit me fine.

BEV: All right, Karl.

[BEV *closes the door.*]

KARL: Anyway, Russ, if you don't mind, I will proceed directly to, dare I say, *the crux*. So. First and foremost, as far as matters of *community* are concerned, I've always maintained—

[BEV *and* BETSY *enter from the kitchen with glasses of iced tea.*]

BEV: All right, you boys.

KARL: [*panicky about* BETSY] What's—? Is something—?

BEV: [*handing* KARL *his tea*] She's *fine*, Karl.

KARL: Is that tea she's drinking?

BEV: Yes, Karl.

KARL: Slow sips. Small sips.

BEV: All right, Karl.

[BETSY *and* BEV *sit at the dining table, away from the men. They begin to communicate via pad and pencil.*]

RUSS: You were saying?

[KARL *takes his glasses off and mops his brow.*]

KARL: Tad overwrought, I suppose. [*Lowers voice*] What with Betsy's condition, but . . . well, given our history of two years ago, I don't know, Russ, if you knew the details of that.

RUSS: Some, yup.

KARL: And Jim: Source of great comfort for us during all of that. [*Beat, then to* RUSS] It was the umbilical cord. Nature of the problem.

RUSS: I knew that.

KARL: Wrapped around the . . . [*Indicates his neck*] Exactly. So, no one at fault. No one to *blame*. But these tragedies do come along. As you and Bev well know.

JIM: What're you hoping? Boy or girl?

KARL: Ah, no. Touch wood. No tempting fate.

JIM: There you go.

KARL: [*back to* RUSS] Not to compare *our* little . . . setback . . . to what the two of you endured, but—

RUSS: Something about a *crux*?

KARL: Right you are. Well: To backtrack. I take it, Russ, you're aware that the Community Association meets the first Tuesday of each month? And as I'm sure you know, Don Skinner is part of the steering committee. And somehow it came to Don's attention at this late juncture that Ted Driscoll had found a buyer for this house and I have to say it *did* come as something of a shock when Don told us what sort of people they were.

RUSS: What sort of people are they?

[*Beat.* KARL *stares at* RUSS.]

KARL: Well. [*Chuckles*] Uhh . . . Huh. I suppose I'm forced to consider the possibility that you actually don't *know*.

RUSS: Don't know *what*?

KARL: Well, I mean. That they're colored.

RUSS: Who are?

KARL: The family. It's a colored family.

[*Pause.*]

So: I contacted the family—

JIM: Wait wait wait.

KARL: [*to* RUSS] You're saying Ted never bothered to tell you?

RUSS: We, uhh . . . sort of gave Ted free rein on the—

JIM: I don't think you're right on this one, Karl.

KARL: Oh, but I am. Oh, I've spoken with the family.

RUSS: Bev?

JIM: On the *telephone*?

KARL: Oh, no. As a matter of fact, Betsy and I've just come directly from . . . [*Beat, for effect.*] Well, from *Hamilton Park*.

BEV: [*to* RUSS] What is it?

RUSS: C'mere a second.

KARL: Now, Russ: You know as well as I do that this is a progressive community.

BEV: [*to* RUSS, *as she joins them*] What's he talking about?

KARL: If you take the case of Gelman's grocery: That's a fine example of how we've all embraced a different way of thinking—

RUSS: Slow down a second. Bev, get Ted Driscoll on the phone.

BEV: [*to* RUSS] What for?

RUSS: Karl says. Karl is *claiming*—

KARL: Russ, I have met *personally* with the family, and—

BEV: What family?

RUSS: He claims this family. The family to whom Ted sold the house.

KARL: It's a colored family.

[*Pause.* JIM *shakes his head.*]

JIM: [*to* KARL] Sorry, don't we say *Negro,* now?

KARL: [*irritated*] I *say* Negro—[*cont'd.*]

JIM: [*overlapping*] Well, it's only common courtesy, and I'm—

KARL: [*continuous*]—I say them *interchangeably*—[*cont'd.*]

JIM: [*overlapping*]—not trying to tell you how to conduct your business.

KARL: [*continuous*]—and of course I said *Negro* to them—No I think we both know what you're doing.

JIM: And furthermore, I don't think Ted would pull a stunt like that.

KARL: Yes. We all admire Ted. But I don't think any of us would accuse him of putting the community's interests ahead of his own.

BEV: Oh, this is ridiculous.

KARL: And I don't think any of us have forgotten what happened with the family that moved onto Kostner Avenue last year. Now, Kostner Avenue is *one* thing, but *Clybourne* Street—

BEV: Waitwaitwait. Karl, are you *sure?*

KARL: I was sitting with them not two hours ago.

BEV: But isn't it possible that they're . . . I don't know, *Mediterranean,* or—?

KARL: Bev, they are *one hundred percent.* And I don't know how much time any of you have spent in Hamilton Park, but Betsy was waiting in the car and I can tell you, there are some *unsavory* characters.

RUSS: Karl?

KARL: But, in the case of Gelman's: I think there was some mistrust at first, having been Kopeckne's Market for such a long time, but in the end of all Murray Gelman found a way to *fit in.*

BEV: And they hired the Wheeler boy.

JIM: Is he the one with the—?

[JIM *taps his finger on his temple.*]

BEV: He's the—you know.

[BEV *does the same.*]

KARL: And *fitting into* a community is really what it all comes down to.

[*A very loud THUMP from upstairs is heard.*]

RUSS: 'The heck is going *on* up there?

KARL: Now, some would say change is inevitable. And I can support that, if it's change for the better. But I'll tell you what I *can't* support, and that's disregarding the needs of the people who *live* in a community.

BEV: But don't they have needs, too?

KARL: Don't who?

BEV: The family.

KARL: Which family?

BEV: The ones who—

KARL: The *purchasers?*

BEV: I mean, in, in, in, in *principle,* don't we *all* deserve to—shouldn't we *all* have the opportunity to, to, to—

KARL: [*chuckles with amazement, shakes his head.*] Well, *Bev.*

JIM: In *principle,* no question.

KARL: But you can't *live* in a principle, can you? Gotta live in a *house.*

BEV: And so do they.

KARL: Not in *this* house, they don't.

JIM: But here's the real question:

KARL: And what happened to *love thy neighbor?* If we're being so principled.

BEV: They would *become* our neighbors.

KARL: And what about the neighbors you already *have,* Bev?

BEV: I care about them, too!

KARL: Well, I'm afraid you can't have it both ways.

RUSS: Okay. Assuming—

BEV: Wait. Why not?

KARL: Well, do the boundaries of the neighborhood extend indefinitely? Who shall we invite next, the *Red Chinese*?

[ALBERT *has tentatively come to the bottom of the stairs, jacket off.*]

JIM: But the key question is this:

BEV: No. Why *not* have it both ways?

KARL: Darling, I came to talk to Russ.

ALBERT: [*having come down the stairs*] 'Scuse me, ma'am?

BEV: Why not, if it would *benefit* someone?

JIM: But *would* they benefit?

BEV: If we could make them our *neighbors*.

KARL: But they won't be *your* neighbors, Bev. *You're* the ones moving *away*!

JIM: The question is, and it's one worth asking:

ALBERT: Sorry to bother you?

RUSS: [*taking charge*] Okay. Let's *assume* your information is correct.

[*Then suddenly, a large green Army footlocker comes sliding down the stairs with a noisy thumpeta-thumpeta-thumpeta-thump.* ALBERT *jumps out of the way.*]

ALBERT:	FRANCINE:	BEV:	RUSS:
Sorry, sir, my my fault! That was me. That was all my my doing.	[*from top of the stairs*] *That was my fault! I'm sorry!*	Oh oh oh. What happened? Is everyone all right?	*Aw, for crying out loud!* What the heck is the matter with people? *Bev, darn it all!*

BEV: [*to* RUSS] Why are you shouting? Everything's *fine*, so—[*cont'd.*]

RUSS: [*overlapping*] Well, what did I *tell* you? [*cont'd.*]

BEV: [*continuous*]—please don't do that, they're just trying to *help*.

RUSS: [*continuous*] I *told* you I'd do it. You heard me plain as day.

BETSY: Eeeen *ahhhh* hurrrrhhh daaaaaa! [Even *I* heard that!]

KARL: [*to* RUSS *and* BEV] Little *mishap*, is it?

ALBERT: Little trouble making the corner, is all.

FRANCINE: [*now downstairs*] I'm sorry. It's heavy and I lost my gr—

RUSS: [*to* ALBERT] Just leave the darn thing where it is.

BEV:	KARL:	JIM:	ALBERT:
We can't leave it there.	May one be of assistance?	Lend you a hand, if I could, but—	What should we—? Would you prefer it if I—?

RUSS: [*to* ALBERT] Just, just, just, just *leave* it.

BEV: But it's blocking the way.

FRANCINE: No, ma'am, I can step over.

ALBERT: It's all right. I got her.

[ALBERT *helps* FRANCINE *climb over the box that now blocks the stairs.*]

KARL: Anyway, let's not drag this out ad infinitum.

[RUSS, *fed up, rises and exits to the basement, slamming the door behind him.*]

BEV: [*overlapping, as* RUSS *exits*] Russ, *don't.*

JIM: [*to* KARL] One second, if I might? [*To* FRANCINE] Sorry. Uh, *Francine,* is it?

FRANCINE: Yes, sir?

JIM: Francine, we've just been having a little conversation here, and I was wondering if maybe you could spare us a couple of minutes of your time?

KARL: What good does that do? Go next door. Talk to the Olsens. Talk to those who stand to lose.

JIM: [*ignoring him, to* FRANCINE] I want to pose a little hypothetical to you. What if we said this: let's imagine you and your husband here, let's say that the two of you had the opportunity to move from your current home into a different neighborhood, and let's say that neighborhood happened to be this one.

FRANCINE: Well, I don't think that we would, financially—

JIM: But for the sake of argument. Say you had the wherewithal. Would this be the sort of neighborhood you'd find an attractive place in which to live?

[FRANCINE *hesitates.*]

BEV: Oh, this is so sil—

FRANCINE: It's a very nice neighborhood.

JIM: [*to* FRANCINE] No, I'm asking, would the two of you—Would your fam—I assume you have children?

FRANCINE: Three children.

JIM: Oh, super. So, with your children, might this be the sort of place, bearing in mind that they, too, would stand to be affected—?

BEV: This is confusing things! It's confusing the issue!

FRANCINE: [*to* JIM] It's a *very lovely* neighbor—

JIM: No, be honest. We want you to say.

BEV: [*to* FRANCINE] I think what Jim is asking, in his way—

ALBERT: He means living next to white folks.

BEV: I—I—I—I—well, yes.

[*Pause.*]

FRANCINE: Well—

BEV: Francine and I have, over the years, the *two of us* have shared so many wonderful—[*To* FRANCINE] Remember that time the *squirrel* came through the window?

FRANCINE: [*smiling, indulging* BEV] Yes, I do.

BEV: That was just the silliest—the two of us were just *hysterical*, weren't we?

KARL: [*pressing ahead, to* FRANCINE] Think of it this way.

BEV: [*to the others*] We still laugh about that.

KARL: I think that you'd agree, I'm assuming, that in the world, there exist certain *differences*. Agreed?

FRANCINE: What sort of differences?

KARL: That people *live* differently.

FRANCINE: [*unsure*] . . . Yes?

KARL: From one another.

FRANCINE: I agree with that.

KARL: Different customs, different . . . well, different *foods*, even. And those diff—here's a funny—my wife, Betsy, now, Betsy's family happens to be Scandinavian, and on holidays they eat a thing known as *lutefisk*. And this is a dish, which I can tell you . . . [*he chuckles*] is *not* to my liking *at all*. It's . . . *oh* my goodness, let's just say it's *gelatinous*.

BEV: [*indicating for him to stop*] Karl?

BETSY: [*to* BEV] Whaaaaa sehhhhh? [What did he say?]

BEV: [*overpronouncing for* BETSY] *Lutefisk*.

BETSY: Whaaaaaa?

BEV: *Lutefi*—Karl, can you tell her?

KARL: [KARL *holds up a finger to* BETSY.] In a moment.

BEV: [*taking up her pad*] I'll write it down.

KARL: [*to* FRANCINE] So, certain groups, they tend to *eat* certain things, am I right?

FRANCINE: I've never had that dish.

KARL: But, for example, if Mrs. Stoller here were to send you to shop at Gelman's. Do you find, when you're standing in the aisles *at* Gelman's, does it generally strike you as the kind of market where you could find the particular foods *your* family enjoys?

FRANCINE: It's a *very* nice store.

JIM: [*interposing*] What if we were to say *this:*

FRANCINE: Mr. Gelman's a nice man.

[BEV *hands* BETSY *the pad of paper.*]

KARL: But, I mean, your *preferred* food items, would such things even be *available* at Gelman's?

ALBERT: Do they *carry* collards and pig feet?

[FRANCINE *shoots a look at* ALBERT.]

'Cuz I sho couldn't shop nowhere didn' sell no pig feet.

[*Pause. All stare at* ALBERT.]

JIM: Well, I think Albert's being *humorous* here, but—

BETSY: [*having deciphered* BEV's *handwriting*] Ohhhh, *loo-feee!* [Oh, *lutefisk!*]

[*To* BEV] Ah *lye* loofee! [I *like lutefisk!*]

JIM: But I will say this—

FRANCINE: [*to* KARL] I like spaghetti and meatballs.

[KARL *quiets* BETSY.]

JIM: You do find differences in modes of *worship.* If you take First Presbyterian. Now, that's a church down in Hamilton Park and I've taken fellowship there and I can tell you, the differences are notable.

BEV: Jim?

JIM: Not a *value* judgment. Apples and oranges. Just as how we have our organ here at Saint Thomas, for accompaniment, whereas at First Presbyterian, they prefer a piano and, occasionally . . . [*chuckles*] well, *tambourines.*

BEV: What's wrong with tambourines?

JIM: Nothing *wrong.*

BEV: I *like* tambourines.

JIM: I like tambourines as much as the next person.

[RUSS *returns from the basement carrying his work gloves. He is calmer.*]

KARL: Well, let me ask this. [*To* BEV] Excuse me. [*To* FRANCINE] Francine, was it?

FRANCINE: Yessir.

KARL: Francine, may I ask? Do you *ski?*

FRANCINE: Do I—?

KARL: Or your husband? Either of you?

FRANCINE: Ski?

KARL: Downhill skiing?

FRANCINE: We don't ski, no.

KARL: And this is my point. The children who attend St. Stanislaus. Once a year we take the middle-schoolers up to Indianhead Mountain, and I can tell you, in all the time I've been there, I have not *once* seen a colored family on those slopes. Now, what accounts for that? Certainly not any deficit in ability, so what I have to conclude is that, for some reason, there is just something about the pastime of skiing that doesn't appeal to the Negro community. And feel free to prove me wrong.

RUSS: Karl.

KARL: But you'll have to show me where to find the skiing Negroes!

RUSS: *Karl!*

BEV: Can we all modulate our voices?

RUSS: It's sold, Karl. The house is sold.

KARL: I understand that.

RUSS: The ink is dry.

KARL: And we all understand your reasons and no one holds that against you.

RUSS: Truck's coming on Monday.

KARL: Fully aware.

RUSS: And that's all there is to that.

KARL: *However.* [*Beat.*] There is *one* possibility.

RUSS: Nope. Nope.

KARL: If you'll hear me out.

RUSS: Don't see the point.

KARL: Because we went ahead and made a counteroffer to these people.

BEV: Who did?

KARL: The Community Association.

BEV: An offer on *this* house?

KARL: Very reasonable offer.

BEV: [*baffled*] But, but, but, they just *bought* it, Karl!

KARL: As opposed to the amount for which *you* offered the property, Russ, which was *far* below the assessor's value—[*cont'd.*]

RUSS: [*overlapping*] Well, we're entitled to *give* it away if that's our prerogative.

KARL: [*continuous*]—for this type of residence, all of which is neither here nor there, since the family *rejected* our offer. However:

BEV: [*to* RUSS] Why are we even *talking* about this?

KARL: Tom *has* pointed out to me that, as the seller of the property, you do have a sixty-day option to place it in receivership with the transacting bank to indemnify yourself against liability. Now, that's generally with *commercial* properties, but in this instance—[*cont'd.*]

RUSS: [*slowly, overlapping*] Nope. Nope. Nope. Nope. Nope.

KARL: [*continuous*]—I think that, inasmuch as Ted *deceived* you about the buyers, that the bank *could* still halt the sale and it would be a simple—[*cont'd.*]

RUSS: [*overlapping*] Karl?

KARL: [*continuous*]—matter of a signature, if I could finish?

RUSS: Prefer it if you didn't.

BETSY: Kaahhhh?

BEV: And for all we know this family could be perfectly lovely.

KARL: Well, that's hardly the point, is it?

BEV: Maybe it's a point to consider.

KARL: [*with a chuckle*] Bev, I'm not here to solve society's problems. I'm simply telling you what will happen, and it will happen as follows: first one family will leave, then another, and another, and each time they do, the values of these properties will decline, and once that process begins, once you break that egg, Bev, all the king's horses, etcetera—[*cont'd.*]

BETSY: [*overlapping*] Kaahhh?

KARL: [*continuous*]—and *some* of us, you see, those who *don't* have the opportunity to simply pick up and move at the drop of a hat, then *those* folks are left holding the bag, and it's a fairly *worthless* bag, at that point.

BEV: I don't like the tone this is taking.

RUSS: [*to* KARL] Okay. Tell you what.

KARL: And let's imagine if the tables were turned. [*Re:* FRANCINE *and* ALBERT] Suppose a number of *white* families started marching into *their* commun—? Well, actually that might be to their *advantage*, but—[*cont'd.*]

RUSS: *Karl.*

KARL: [*continuous*]—you do see my point.

RUSS: Need you to stop now.

KARL: Sorry. [*Beat.*] Maybe not handled with the—[*cont'd.*]

RUSS: It's all right.

KARL: [*continuous*]—utmost delicacy.

RUSS: But maybe time to let it drop.

KARL: Didn't mean to turn it into a public referendum. [*Beat.*] But you do understand—

RUSS: No no no no no. That's it. You hear me? Done. All done.

[*Pause. In the near distance a church bell begins to ring.*]

JIM: [*quietly looking at his watch*] Is it four o'clock?

KARL: Well, Russ, if I might—

RUSS: Nope. Nope.

KARL: If I could just say this:

RUSS: No. Karl?

KARL: Well, if you'd let me—

RUSS: No. No more.

KARL: Uhhh . . . [*chuckling*] Bev? I get the impression your husband is telling me I'm not permitted to *speak.*

RUSS: Don't think it's a good idea.

KARL: Well, Russ, I'm going to ask you at least to keep an open—

RUSS: *Karl!* What'd I just ask you?

KARL: Well, I think you're being a tad unreasonable.

RUSS: Well, *I* think we've reached the end of this particular discussion.

KARL: Is that right?

RUSS: Afraid it is.

KARL: Just like that.

RUSS: Just like that.

[*Another pause.*]

KARL: Then what about this:

RUSS: *Karl!?*

KARL: Well, I believe the Constitution endows me with a *right* to speak.

RUSS: Well, then you can go and do that in your own home.

[RUSS *crosses and opens the front door for* KARL *to exit.*]

KARL: Bev . . . ? [*Laughs*] He's not being serious, is he?

RUSS: Karl?

KARL: [*laughs*] Am I being *silenced*?

RUSS: Not going to ask you again.

KARL: Well, this is a new experience for me.

RUSS: So be it.

KARL: Bit like the Soviet Union. [*Laughs*] I am truly surprised.

RUSS: Well, *surprise.*

KARL: And a little disappointed.

RUSS: Sorry to disappoint you.

KARL: [*shakes his head*] A real shame. For all concerned.

RUSS: Well, that's the way things go sometimes.

KARL: Apparently so.

RUSS: Anyway. Appreciate you stopping by.

KARL: I see.

RUSS: Betsy, too.

KARL: Very well.

BETSY: Kaaaaahhhh?

RUSS: Okay, then? Okay.

[*Silence.* KARL *stands and looks to* BETSY. *The two of them slowly exit through the open door,* RUSS *quietly closing it as they go.*]

BETSY: [*quietly, before the door is closed*] Kaahhh, whaah happaaahh? [Karl, what happened?]

FRANCINE: [*carefully*] Miz Stoller, if we're done talking here?

JIM: [*rising*] Yes, you know, I think *I* will take this opportunity—

[*But* KARL *abruptly returns,* BETSY *following.*]

KARL: However:

JIM: [*quietly*] Karl, don't.

KARL: [*very slowly*] I *don't* imagine that . . . this particular family are *entirely* aware of *why* they've found such an agreeable price for the property. Don't suppose they know *that* aspect of it, do they? And let's say someone was to *inform* them of those facts. Let's say *that* was to happen.

RUSS: [*chuckles dangerously*] Really don't know when to quit, do ya?

KARL: Because I think that might be an interesting conversation to have.

FRANCINE: [*to* BEV] So I'll be seeing you on Mon—

RUSS: [*maintaining control*] Well, Karl? You go ahead and do what you think is right, but I'll tell you one thing. What you're going to do right *now* is—[*cont'd.*]

KARL: [*overlapping*] Well, I have a responsibility to the community as a whole. I can't afford to—[*cont'd.*]

RUSS: [*continuous*]—you're going to take yourself right through that door and out of this house.

KARL: [*overlapping, continuous*]—simply pursue my own selfish interests.

RUSS: [*maintaining calm*] Man, what a son of a bitch.

BEV: Russ, *don't.*

RUSS: [*to* KARL] If you honestly think I give a rat's ass about the god-damn—[*cont'd.*]

JIM: [*overlapping*] Okay. Okay.

RUSS: [*continuous*]—what, ya mean the *community* where every time I go for a haircut, where they all sit and stare like the goddamn grim reaper walked in the barber shop door? *That* community? [*cont'd.*]

KARL: [*overlapping*] My wife is two weeks away from giving birth to a *child.*

RUSS: [*continuous*] Where Bev stops at Gelman's for a quart of milk and they look at her like she's got the goddamn plague? That the community I'm supposed to be looking out for?

KARL: A community with *soon-to-be children.*

JIM: The Apostle Matthew—

RUSS: [*to* JIM] Oh no no no. *I'm* talking now.

BEV: [*to* FRANCINE *and* ALBERT] I am ashamed of every one of us.

BETSY: [*tugging at* KARL's *sleeve*] Kaaaaaah?

KARL: Betsy, wait in the car.

RUSS: Well, you go right ahead and you tell those folks whatever you want, Karl. And while you're at it why don't you tell 'em about everything *the community* did for my son. I mean *Jesus Christ,* Murray Gelman even goes and hires a goddamn *retarded* kid, but *my* boy? Sorry. No work for *you,* bub.

JIM: People were frightened, Russ.

RUSS: [*contemptuous*] Ahh, of *what?* He was gonna *snap?* Gonna go and kill another bunch of people? Send him off to defend the goddamn country, he does like he's *told* only to find out the kinda sons-of-bitches he's defending?

BEV: [*forthright*] He did not do the things they claimed he did. He would never—

RUSS: *Ah, Jesus, of course he did, Bev! He confessed to what he did!* Sit around all day with your head in the sand, it doesn't change the facts of what he *did.*

BEV: Not to innocent people in that country. And not to women or children. I mean, maybe he lost his temper in a—

RUSS: *Ah, for Christ's sake. What do you think happens in a goddamn war?* They told him to *secure the territory,* not go knocking on doors asking *permission.* And if he was man enough to admit what he did, maybe you oughta have the decency to do the same damn thing.

BEV: [*turning to* FRANCINE *for support*] You remember. Francine remembers what he was like.

[RUSS *makes a sound of disgust and goes to the footlocker. Under the following, he unlocks and opens the lid.*]

How he loved to read and think. That's just the kind of boy he was, wasn't it?

FRANCINE: Yes, ma'am.

BEV: [*to* FRANCINE] And the drawings? The most realistic drawings. I think a lot of people didn't realize—

KARL: Bev, it was never my intention to stir up—[*cont'd.*]

BEV: [*overlapping*] Ohhh, no, I think maybe it was.

KARL: [*continuous*]—such acrimonious feelings, but there is a situation, which—

BEV: Well, maybe if you had known my son a little better. If anyone had taken the time, the way that Francine took the time—

[RUSS *has produced an envelope from the footlocker. He steps forward removing the letter—on yellow legal paper.*]

RUSS: Here you go, Karl. Let's all read a little something, shall we?

BEV: What are you—?

RUSS: [*reading*] *Dear Mom and Dad.*

BEV: [*realizing*] *Stop it!!!*

RUSS: [*reading*] *I know you'll probably blame yourselves*—

BEV: [*standing, losing it completely*] *Russ, stop it stop it stop stop stop it!!!!*

JIM:	KARL [*to* RUSS]:
Russ. Don't.	I think you're unstable, Russ. I really do.

BEV: [*turning back to* JIM] *You see what this is like? You see?* [*To* RUSS] *Well, I refuse to live this way any longer!!*

[BEV *goes into the bathroom and slams the door behind her.*]

RUSS: [*starting over, calmly*] *Dear Mom and Dad.*

JIM: Russ?

RUSS: *I know you'll probably blame yourselves for what I've done*—

JIM: Need you to calm down.

RUSS: And *you* can go fuck yourself.

KARL: Well, *that* is over the line, mister. That is not language I will tolerate in front of my wife.

RUSS: [*beat, then*] She's *deaf*, Karl!! Completely—[*Waving to* BETSY, *fake-jolly*] Hello, Betsy! Go fuck yourself!

[BETSY *smiles, waves back.*]

So here's what I'll do for you, Karl: Make ya ten copies of this you can hand 'em out at Rotary. Or better yet. Put it in the newsletter. Rotary news: Kid comes back from Korea, goes upstairs and wraps an extension cord around his neck. Talk *that* over at the lunch buffet next week.

BETSY: [*barely audible*] Kaahhh?

RUSS: And Francine walking in at nine in the morning to find him there. You be my guest, Karl. You go ahead and tell those people what kind of house they're moving into and see if *that* stops 'em, because I'll tell you what, I don't care if a hundred Ubangi tribesmen with a bone through the nose overrun this goddamn place, 'cause I'm *through with all of you,* ya motherfucking sons of bitches. *Every one* of you.

[*All stand in silence. We can hear* BEV *crying from behind the bathroom door.* RUSS *slowly folds the letter.*]

JIM: Maybe we should bow our heads for a second.
RUSS: [*advancing on him*] Well, maybe I should punch you in the face.

[RUSS *moves toward* JIM, *who, in backing away, inadvertently tumbles backward over a box, toppling a floor lamp as he goes.*]

ALBERT:	KARL:	BETSY:	FRANCINE:
Whoa whoa	Easy now.	Kaahh!!	What in God's name
whoa whoa	Easy does	Waaahhhh	is *wrong* with alla you
whoa!!	it . . . careful—	happneee!?	people? [*To* ALBERT]
	Betsy, go!	[Karl!! What's	Stay out of it. Don't.
	Betsy?	happening!?]	Just stay out—

[BETSY *runs out the front door.* ALBERT *puts his hand on* RUSS's *shoulder.*]

ALBERT: Hang on. Let's be civilized, now.
RUSS: [*whirling on* ALBERT] Ohoho, don't you touch *me.*
ALBERT: Whoa whoa whoa.
RUSS: Putting your hands on *me*? No, *sir.* Not in *my* house, you don't.
JIM: [*gritting his teeth as he copes with his hernia*] I'm all right.
FRANCINE: [*to* ALBERT] What the hell d'you think *you're* doing?
ALBERT: Who're you talking to?
FRANCINE: Who do you *think*?
KARL: [*to* RUSS, *while helping* JIM *to his feet*] Very manly, Russ. Threatening a *minister.*
ALBERT: [*to* FRANCINE] Why're you talking to me like th—?
KARL: [*to* RUSS] Very *masculine.*

[KARL *and* JIM *exit out the front door.*]

FRANCINE: [*to* ALBERT] I think they're *all* a buncha idiots. And who's the biggest idiot of all to let yourself get dragged into the middle of it? Whatcha gonna be now, the big *peacemaker* come to save the day?

[KARL *sticks his head back in.*]

KARL: [*through the open door*] You're mentally unstable, Russ!

FRANCINE: [*to* ALBERT] Let 'em knock each other's *brains* out, for all *I* care. I'm done working for these people two days from now, and you never worked for 'em at *all*, so what the hell do you care *what* they do? And now I am going to the goddamn *car*.

[FRANCINE *exits. During the marital squabble,* RUSS *has returned the letter to the footlocker and dragged it out through the kitchen.* ALBERT *is now left alone in the middle of the room. He stands idly for a moment then moves to right the overturned floor lamp. As he does,* BEV *enters from the bathroom, blowing her nose.*]

ALBERT: [*seeing* BEV] It's all right. Nothing broken.

BEV: [*trying to be composed*] Oh oh oh don't mind that. But thank you so much.

ALBERT: No trouble.

BEV: And do let me offer you some money for your help.

ALBERT: Oh no, ma'am, that's all right.

BEV: Ohhh, are you sure?

ALBERT: Yes, ma'am.

BEV: [*finding her purse*] Well, here, then. Let me at least give you fifty cents.

ALBERT: No, now you keep your money.

BEV: Or, how about a dollar? Take a dollar. I don't care.

ALBERT: Ma'am?

BEV: Or take two. It's just money.

ALBERT: Happy to help.

BEV: Or take something. You have to take something.

ALBERT: No, ma'am. But—

BEV: What about this chafing dish? Did you see this dish?

ALBERT: Well, we got plenty of dish—

BEV: Not one of these. Francine told me—[*cont'd.*]

ALBERT: [*overlapping*] Well, that's very kind of you, but—

BEV: [*continuous*]—She said you didn't have one and somebody should take it and—[*cont'd.*]

ALBERT: [*overlapping*] But we don't *need* it, ma'am.

BEV: [*continuous*]—make use of it, so if you let me just wrap it for you.

ALBERT: *Ma'am, we don't want your things. Please. We got our own things.*

[*Pause.* BEV *is shocked.*]

BEV: *Well.*

ALBERT: [*gently*] Trying to *explain* to you.

BEV: Well, if *that's* the attitude, then I just don't know what to say anymore. I really don't. If that's what we're coming to.

ALBERT: Ma'am, everybody's sorry for your loss.

BEV: [*holding back tears, nobly righteous*] You know, I would be . . . so *proud*. So *honored* to have you and Francine as our neighbors. *And* the two children.

ALBERT: Three children.

BEV: Three chil—We would . . . Maybe we should *learn* what the other person eats. Maybe that would be the solution to some of the—If someday we could all sit down together, at one big table and, and, and, and . . .

[BEV *trails into a whisper, shakes her head.*]

ALBERT: Evening, ma'am.

[ALBERT *goes.* BEV *is left alone. After a moment,* RUSS *enters to fetch the shovel. He carries a pair of work gloves. Seeing* BEV, *he stops, unsure of what to say.*]

BEV: Where'd you find the gloves?

RUSS: Under the sink.

BEV: And where are you going to dig the hole?

RUSS: Under the, uh . . . What's that big tree called?

BEV: The crepe myrtle.

RUSS: Under that.

BEV: Kind of late now, isn't it?

RUSS: [*shrugs*] Do it tomorrow.

[RUSS *leans the shovel against the wall. Pause. He stands idly, apologetically.*]

Kinda lost my temper.

BEV: [*nods*] Well, that's what happens. As we know.

[RUSS *slowly moves to sit in the chair he sat in at the start of the act, then looks back at* BEV.]

RUSS: Know what I did the other day? Up there at the house?

BEV: What?

RUSS: Driveway to the office. Timed it. Know how long that's gonna take me now?

BEV: Five minutes?

RUSS: Six and a half.

BEV: Well, you'll have a leisurely breakfast.

RUSS: Read the paper. Cup of coffee and *bang.*

BEV: Hmm.

RUSS: Five-oh-seven, right back at your doorstep.

BEV: And what'll I do in between?

[RUSS *is caught off guard.*]

RUSS: I, I, uhhh . . . Well, gee, I guess, whatever you . . . Any number of . . .

BEV: Things.

RUSS: Projects.

BEV: Projects.

RUSS: To keep ya occupied.

BEV: I suppose you're right.

[RUSS *turns on the radio. Music. He looks back at* BEV, *who stares into space.*]

RUSS: [*feebly, with a little sweep of the arm*] Ulan Bator!

[BEV *smiles vaguely. The lights slowly fade.*]

ACT 2

[*September 2009. Three o'clock, Saturday afternoon. There is an overall shabbiness to the place that was not the case fifty years earlier. The wooden staircase railing has been replaced with a cheaper metal one. The oak mantelpiece and most of the woodwork have been painted over several times; the fireplace opening is bricked in; linoleum covers large areas of the wooden floor and plaster has crumbled from the lath in places. The kitchen door is now missing, and we can see through to an exterior door. The front door stands propped open. Lights rise to find six people facing each other in a rough circle. To one side,* STEVE *and* LINDSEY *with* KATHY, *and to the other* KEVIN *and* LENA *with* TOM, *all dressed in generic casual clothes for a weekend afternoon. It is warm, and some have iced drinks.* LINDSEY *is visibly pregnant. They sit upon improvised seating crates, abandoned furniture, etc.* STEVE, LINDSEY, *and* KATHY *study Xeroxed documents while the others watch. Finally:*]

TOM: Everybody good?

LINDSEY: I'm good.

STEVE: Good by me.

KATHY: Go for it.

TOM: So, I guess we should start right at the top.

STEVE: Question?

TOM: And I know we all got questions.

STEVE: The terminology?

TOM: So let's go one at a time: Steve.

STEVE: The term *frontage*?

TOM: Right.

STEVE: *Frontage* means?

LINDSEY: Where are we looking?

STEVE: First page.

TOM: *Frontage* means—[*Deferring to* KATHY] Did you want to—?

KATHY: [*to* STEVE] Means the portion facing the street.

TOM: Thus, *front*.

STEVE: [*to* TOM] Portion of the *property*?

KATHY: [*to* STEVE] Of the structure.

STEVE: [*to* TOM] Or portion of the *structure*?

TOM: The *facade*.

LINDSEY: [*to* STEVE] I'm not seeing it.

KATHY: [*to* LINDSEY] Second paragraph.

TOM: [*to* LINDSEY] Bottom of the page.

STEVE: [*to* LINDSEY] Where it says "minimum recess of frontage"?

TOM: Meaning, distance *from.*

KATHY: [*to* TOM] From the edge of the *property.*

TOM: Exactly.

STEVE: Is what?

TOM: Is the "recess."

STEVE: Not the *frontage.*

TOM: [*to* STEVE] The frontage is what you're measuring *to.*

LINDSEY: Got it.

STEVE: I'm confused.

LINDSEY: And "edge of the property" means as measured from the *curb?*

KATHY: Correct.

TOM: Not from the *sidewalk?*

KATHY: From the curb.

TOM: Uhh—I'll check, but I don't think that's right.

KATHY: Up to and including.

TOM: But the sidewalk falls under the easement.

KATHY: Right?

TOM: So if it's part of the easement then it can't be part of the property, *per se.*

KATHY: [*shaking her head*] By definition the property is inclusive of the easement. The easement is legal passage *across* the property.

TOM: I don't think you're right.

KATHY: So, my understanding has always been—

KEVIN: Sorry, but—does any of that really *matter?*

STEVE: It might.

KEVIN: I mean, I don't see how any of that really—[*cont'd.*]

STEVE: [*overlapping*] The language?

KEVIN: [*continuous*]—impacts the outcome of the specific problem that—

STEVE: But *I* don't want to get in a situation where we *thought* we found a solution only to have it turn out we're screwed because of the *language.*

TOM: Wait.

LINDSEY: [*to* STEVE] The language is clear to *me.*

TOM: [*easily*] And who's being *screwed*?

STEVE: No no no.

TOM: No one's *screwing* any—

STEVE: I didn't mean like *screwed over*, I meant like maybe we *screwed ourselves*.

KEVIN: But how does that address the *height* issue?

TOM: The elevation.

STEVE: [*to* TOM] But if the elevation is *conditional* on the perimeter, right?

TOM: That's the idea.

STEVE: If I'm reading correctly?

LINDSEY: But the perimeter isn't changing.

STEVE: But we're saying if it *could*.

LINDSEY: But we've established that it can't.

STEVE: But let's say it *did*.

LINDSEY: But I'm saying it won't.

STEVE: But I'm saying *what if*?

LINDSEY: But I'm saying *what did we discuss*?

[KATHY's *cell phone rings*.]

STEVE: [*to* LINDSEY, *with an easy laugh*] Okay, but do you have to *say* it like that?

LINDSEY: Like what?

STEVE: In that *way*?

LINDSEY: What *way*?

KATHY: [*looking at her phone*] It's Hector. I'd better—

STEVE: [*apologizing to* KEVIN *and* LENA *for* LINDSEY] Sorry.

LINDSEY: [*to* KEVIN *and* LENA] Did I say something in a *way*?

LENA: Not that I noticed.

KATHY: [*answering phone*] Hi, Hector.

STEVE: [*explaining to* KEVIN *and* LENA] The architect.

LINDSEY: Who really oughta be here.

KATHY: [*into phone*] No, we're doing it now. No, we're here at the house.

KEVIN: [*to* LINDSEY] Well, if you'd rather wait and do this when he *can* be?

STEVE: No no no.

LINDSEY: [*to* STEVE] Well, I think we both know what's going to happen—[*cont'd.*]

LINDSEY:
[*continuous*] He's going to go completely ballist—I'm just telling you what to expect.

STEVE:
I don't give a—And, I believe he's working for *us*, right? Not the other way around.

KATHY: [*phone*] No, we're here with—[*To* TOM] Tom, I forgot your last name.

TOM: Driscoll.

KATHY: [*back to phone*] Driscoll. So, Tom Driscoll and the people from the neighborhood thing. Property owners . . . thing.

LINDSEY: [*to* STEVE *and* LENA] And can I just say? I am in *love* with this neighborhood.

KEVIN: Great neighborhood.

LINDSEY: *Totally* great.

KATHY: [*phone*] Well, that's what we're trying to prevent.

LINDSEY: And the thing for me is? My current commute? Which is slowly eroding my soul?

KEVIN: [*to* LINDSEY] How far ya coming from?

LINDSEY: [*pointedly*] *Glen Meadows?*

KEVIN: [*wincing*] Ooof.

LINDSEY: Exactly. And if you work downtown?

KEVIN: Where downtown?

LINDSEY: [*do you know it?*] Donnelly and Faber?

KEVIN: On Jackson, right? Donnelly and—?

LINDSEY: Yeah, Jackson east of—

KEVIN: Yeah, I'm across the street.

LINDSEY: Where?

KEVIN: You know the big red building?

LINDSEY: I eat lunch in that building.

KEVIN: Capital Equities?

STEVE: You're kidding me.

KEVIN: I kid you not.

LINDSEY: [*to* KEVIN] And from *here* to downtown is like, what, five minutes?

STEVE: [*to* KEVIN] Ya ever meet Kyle Hendrickson?

KEVIN: I *work* with Kyle Hendrickson.

KATHY: [*phone*] No, but I do think you're being a *little* paranoid, because we're not going to let that happen.

LINDSEY: [*to* KATHY] Lemme talk to him.

KATHY: *I'm* not going to let it happen.

LINDSEY: Kathy.

KATHY: Wait. Lindsey wants to—

LINDSEY: Lemme do it. [*taking the phone.*] Hector?

KATHY: [*rolling her eyes*] I'm obviously not equipped to deal with—

LINDSEY: [*phone*] I thought you were in Seattle.

STEVE: [*to* KATHY] What's the problem?

KATHY: Tell you later.

LINDSEY: [*soothing*] No no no no. Kathy's here. Kathy's not going to let that—

[LINDSEY *rolls her eyes at the others.*]

STEVE: [*to the others*] Spaniards.

LINDSEY: [*whispering to the others*] Two seconds.

[LINDSEY *exits out the front door. Pause. The others wait.*]

KEVIN: [*to* STEVE] Spaniards?

STEVE: Architect, ya know.

KEVIN: Spanish.

STEVE: Temperamental.

KEVIN: Toro toro.

STEVE: Exactly.

TOM: Seemed cool to me.

STEVE: You talked to him?

TOM: On the phone, yeah.

STEVE: He's a good guy.

[*Little pause. Then small talk.*]

KATHY: We were in Spain last year.

KEVIN: S'that right?

KATHY: Me, my husband. Spain, Morocco.

STEVE: [*explaining to* KEVIN] I just meant—with all the paperwork and everything? And then we add *him* into the mix?

KEVIN: I hear you.

STEVE: Cooler heads, ya know.

KEVIN: Prevail.

STEVE: Right.

[*Little pause. Then more small talk.*]

KATHY: Spain's fantastic. We did four days in Barcelona. Saw the what's-it-called? The cathedral? Big, crazy—?

TOM: Sagrada Família.

KATHY: That. Which I loved. Likewise the food. Which I would happily eat every day for the rest of my life.

KEVIN: Paella.

KATHY: Then Morocco. To whatsit. To Marrakech. Which—I don't know how you feel about *heat*? But oh my God. And they keep giving you *hot tea.* Like, how refreshing. And some theory about how you're supposed to *sweat* in order to feel *cool,* which you'll have to explain to me sometime.

TOM: [*to himself*] Hot in *here.*

LENA: *Very* hot.

KATHY: *And.* To top it off. I don't want to bore you with the whole ugly saga *but:* When they tell you not to eat the produce? Take heed.

KEVIN: Like Mexico.

KATHY: Because if you ever need to know where to find a doctor at two in the morning in the capital of Morocco when your husband is doubled over with *dysentery*—?

KEVIN: Whoa.

KATHY: Gimme a call.

[*Little pause. All look at the door.*]

TOM: [*re:* LINDSEY's *absence*] Said two seconds.

KEVIN: [*to* KATHY, *indicating himself and* LENA] Went to *Prague* last April.

KATHY: [*to* LENA] Oh, I *love* Prague. Prague is beautiful.

KEVIN: Very pretty.

KATHY: The architecture?

KEVIN: That bridge?

KATHY: And it's small, is what's nice. So you can do it all in a couple of days.

KEVIN: And then from there to Zurich.

KATHY: Never been to Switzerland. [*With a laugh*] But I like the cheese!

LENA: [*formally*] Can I—? I'm sorry. I didn't mean to—but I was hoping I could say something to everyone, if you don't mind?

[*All pause for* LENA.]

As long as we're stopped?

KATHY:	KEVIN:	TOM:
No. Do. By all means.	Go ahead.	Yeah yeah, please.

LENA: All right, well . . . [*Clears her throat*] Um, I just feel like it's very important for me to express, before we start getting into the details—

STEVE: Sorry, but—maybe we should wait for Lindsey? Don't you think? If it's something important? Otherwise—

KEVIN: [*to* LENA] Do you mind?

STEVE: Wind up repeating yourself.

TOM: [*to* LENA] That okay with you?

LENA: It's fine with me.

STEVE: But, hold that thought.

LENA: I will.

[*Little pause.* TOM *drums his fingers.*]

STEVE: Meanwhile—

TOM: Meanwhile maybe we should look at page three?

KATHY: Maybe we should.

TOM: Catch her up when she—[*To* STEVE] if that's cool with you guys?

STEVE: S'cool with me.

TOM: Good.

KEVIN: Let's do it.

TOM: Just 'cuz I gotta be outa here by like four.

STEVE: Forge ahead.

KATHY: Page three.

TOM: Middle of three.

KATHY: Section two.

TOM: Roman numeral two.

STEVE: [*aside to* KATHY, *quietly*] Rabat, by the way.

TOM: [*Beat.*] Whadja say?

STEVE: Nothing.

KATHY: Couldn't hear you.

STEVE: The capital.

TOM: Of what?

STEVE: Morocco. She said Marrakech.

KATHY: It *is* the capital.

STEVE: No.

TOM: I'd've said Marrakech.

STEVE: Rabat.

KATHY: I don't think you're right.

STEVE: No, it is.

KATHY: But possibly.

STEVE: Definitely. Anyway.

TOM: Anyway—

KATHY: Or, wait. Is it *Tangiers?*

STEVE: Nope.

KATHY: Why am I thinking Tangiers?

STEVE: Dunno.

KATHY: Maybe we just *landed* in Tang—Or wait, no we didn't.

KEVIN: [*to* STEVE] *What's* the capital?

KATHY: *I* know what it is. Tangiers was the *old* capital.

STEVE: Umm . . . no?

KATHY: The *historic* capital.

[LINDSEY *returns.*]

LINDSEY: *So* sorry.

KEVIN: Everything all right?

LINDSEY: [*returning* KATHY's *phone*] It's fine. It's just, he said he was going to be in Seattle so we went ahead and scheduled this without him and now he's feeling a little proprietary—Anyway. Blah blah.

TOM: So, we skipped ahead.

LINDSEY: Great.

TOM: To page three?

KATHY: Middle of three.

TOM: And since I think we'd all basically agree that—

STEVE: [*to* LINDSEY] Hey. [*To* TOM] Sorry. [*To* LINDSEY] What's the capital of Morocco?

LINDSEY: The what?

STEVE: The capital.

LINDSEY: What are you talking about?

STEVE: Of Morocco.

LINDSEY: Why?

STEVE: Quick. Just—

LINDSEY: I have no idea.

STEVE: Yes, you do.

KATHY: [*explaining to* LINDSEY] I said Marrakech.

STEVE: [*to* KATHY]	LINDSEY:
No no, let her—	Marrakech, yeah.

STEVE: No. *Rabat.*

LINDSEY: Whatever.

KEVIN: [*explaining to* LINDSEY] Trying to figure out what it was.

LINDSEY: *Why?*

STEVE: She said she went to the capital of Morocco—[*cont'd.*]

LINDSEY: So?

STEVE: [*continuous*]—and it's not the capital.

LINDSEY: [*with a shrug*] Maybe they changed it.

STEVE: Who?

LINDSEY: The Moroccans.

STEVE: To what?

LINDSEY: Whatever it is now.

STEVE: Which is *Rabat.*

LINDSEY: Okay.

TOM: So—

KATHY: Oh, wait. You know what it is? It's *Timbuktu.*

STEVE: . . . *nnnnnnno?*

KATHY: The old capital. The historic—[*Tapping her temple*] That's why I—because it was part of our package.

STEVE: Um. Timbuktu is in *Mali.*

KATHY: But the *ancient* capital.

STEVE: Yeah. Of *Mali.*

LINDSEY: I thought Mali was in the Pacific.

STEVE: [*baffled*] In—?

LINDSEY: Where do they have the shadow puppets?

STEVE: [*sputtering*] Are you talking about *Bali?*

KATHY: Same difference.

STEVE: Uhhhh, *no?* The *difference* . . . [*cont'd.*]

LINDSEY: And who *gives* a shit, any—?

[DAN *has entered through the kitchen door. Work clothes, mustache, chewing gum. He lingers at a distance.*]

STEVE: [*continuous*]	LINDSEY: [*continuous*]	LENA:
. . . is that they happen	Steve. Steven. It's	I'm sorry. I
to be *three distinct*	whatever you want	don't mean to
countries so, I guess	it to be, okay?	interrupt
I give a shit—[*cont'd.*]		anyone, but—

STEVE: [*continuous, lowering his voice, to* LINDSEY]—and could you possibly not talk to me like a *child*?

LENA: [*in the clear*] Excuse me?

[*All turn to* LENA.]

I was hoping to say something, if I could?

STEVE: [*remembering*] Oh oh oh.

TOM: Right. [*To* LENA] Sorry. [*To* LINDSEY] Lena had wanted to mention something and it sounded kind of important so—

KEVIN: [*to* LENA] But you don't gotta ask *permission*.

LENA: I'm trying to be polite.

LINDSEY: We're totally rude.

KEVIN: No, you're not.

LINDSEY: It's my family. Irish Catholic, you know? *Blarney.*

KATHY: [*raising a hand*] Please, my husband? Half-Jewish half-Italian.

KEVIN: Is that right?

KATHY: Get a word in edgewise.

KEVIN: I believe that.

KATHY: Anyway. Lena.

LENA: Thank you.

LINDSEY: Wait. *Lena*, right?

LENA: Lena.

KATHY: Short for Leonora?

LENA: No.

KATHY: I knew a Leonora.

LENA: It was my aunt's name.

LINDSEY: [*reminding herself*] Anyway. Lena, Kevin.

KATHY: [*raising hand*] Kathy.

LINDSEY: [*indicating*] Kathy, Lindsey, Steve.

STEVE: And Tom.

KEVIN: Don't forget Tom.

LINDSEY: Tom we know. So:

DAN: [*from across the room*] Ding dong?

[*All turn to* DAN.]

STEVE: Hey.

DAN: Hey.

STEVE: How's it goin'?

DAN: S'there a Steve anywhere?

STEVE: Yeah?

DAN: You Steve?

STEVE: Yeah?

DAN: Hector said if there's a problem talk to Steve.

STEVE: That's me.

DAN [*to the others*]: How ya doing?

TOM:	KEVIN:	LENA:
Hey. Good.	Doing all right.	Fine, thank you.

DAN: Uhh . . . [*Lowers voice, crouches next to* STEVE] Quick question?

STEVE: [*a quiet sidebar*] Yeah?

DAN: [*privately*] So okay. So, we're, uh, digging that trench back there, ya know?

STEVE: Yeah?

DAN: Out in back?

STEVE: Yeah?

DAN: For the conduit line?

STEVE: Yeah?

DAN: Know what I'm talking about?

STEVE: Yeah?

DAN: 'Cuz before you hook up that line you gotta bury that conduit?

STEVE: Yeah?

DAN: And so in order to dig that trench we gotta take out that tree, right?

STEVE: Right?

DAN: Dead tree back there?

STEVE: Yeah?

DAN: 'Cause those roots, they go down like maybe eight feet?

STEVE: Yeah?

DAN: Which is why we're taking out that tree?

STEVE: Right?

DAN: Didja know that thing is *dead*?

STEVE: [*rising*] Hey. Maybe we should—[*To the others*] Sorry. You guys go ahead and—

DAN: Whoops.

STEVE: [*to* DAN] No no. It's just—two things at once.

KEVIN: We can wait.

STEVE: No no no. You guys keep—[*To* DAN] You wanna show me?

DAN: Lemme show ya.

STEVE: Lemme take a look.

DAN: Show ya what we're dealing with.

[DAN *and* STEVE *exit out the back door.*]

[*To* STEVE, *as they exit*] Tell ya one thing though, it is *hot* out here.

[LENA *fans herself. A little pause.*]

LINDSEY: Now I don't remember what we were—?

TOM: Page three.

LINDSEY: *Right.*

KATHY: Middle of three.

TOM: So. Knowing as we do that the height continues to be the sticking point—and by the way, the reason the petition was drawn up this way in the first place—I mean, nobody wants to be inflexible, but the idea was to set some basic guidelines whereby *if,* say, the height is the problem, like it is here, then one option would be to reduce the total exterior volume, like your husband was saying. And that's the rationale behind the table at the bottom of the page. So what those figures mean, essentially, is that with each additional foot of elevation beyond the maximum limit, there'd be a corresponding reduction in volume. And the numbers are based on the scale of the *original* structures, which is relatively consistent over the twelve-block radius, and of which this house is a fairly typical example. Now:

KATHY: Except we know they're *not.*

TOM: Not what?

KATHY: Not consistent.

TOM: Saying *relatively.*

KATHY: A lotta variables.

TOM: We know that.

KATHY: [*beginning a list*] The size of the lots, for starters?

TOM: Right, but—

KATHY: The year of construction?

TOM: Right, so the hope was that by establishing a couple of regula-
tions up front, hopefully we avoid this kinda situation in the future,
'cause, obviously, it's a pain in the ass for everybody. So, assuming the
Landmarks Committee passes this part of the petition next week—

KATHY: *Assuming.*

TOM: Safe assumption.

KATHY: And if the Landmarks Committee really wants to pick that
fight with the Zoning Department, that is *their* business, but that's a
matter of *if and when.*

TOM: [*to* LINDSEY] Why is this confrontational?

KATHY: Because somebody might've raised these issues when the plans
went to the Zoning Department five months ago.

LINDSEY: Kathy.

KATHY: I mean, no one had any objection back *then.*

LINDSEY: Can I say? We *talked* about renovation. We discussed it.
Because these houses are *so* charming and I know it's a shame—but
when you figure in the crack in the subfloor and the cost of the lead
abatement—and in a market like this one? It just made more sense to
start from scratch.

[TOM's *cell rings. He tries to ignore it.*]

TOM: Right. *But:* the Owners Association has a vested interest—Kevin
and Lena call me up last month, they say Tom, we've got this problem, these people are planning to build a house that's a full fifteen feet
taller than all the adjacent structures—[*cont'd.*]

LINDSEY:	KATHY:
Nooo . . . *fifteen?* Is that right?	It's exactly what the block is zoned for, Tom.

TOM: [*continuous*]—and I think we'd *all* agree that there's a mutual benefit to maintaining the integrity—[*glances at his phone*]—the *architec-
tural* integrity—[*cont'd.*]

LINDSEY: Wanna get that?

TOM: [*continuous*]—of a historically significant—god damn it—neighborhood. [*Answering phone*] Yeah?

[STEVE *returns, as* TOM *talks on the phone, leaving the kitchen door open.*]

[*phone*] Yeah, okay, but don't call *me* with that in the middle of a Satur—? Well, then give it to Marla. Because it's Marla's *account*. Well, where the fuck is Mar—? [*To the others*] Sorry.

[TOM *crosses the room to continue the call.*]

STEVE: What's happening?

LINDSEY: I don't know.

LENA: You know, it might be a good idea if we all turned off our phones.

LINDSEY: Excellent idea.

KEVIN: [*to* STEVE] Get your problem solved?

STEVE: Did what?

KEVIN: Out back.

STEVE: Yeah, I dunno. They hit something.

LINDSEY: What something?

STEVE: I dunno.

LINDSEY: Something dangerous?

STEVE: I dunno.

LINDSEY: Is it going to *explode*?

STEVE: It's not—[*To* KEVIN] We're putting in a koi pond, and there's a filtration system that has to hook into the municipal—anyway, they ran into some kind of—whatever. So whatzit, page three?

KEVIN: But maybe wait for Tom?

STEVE: [*with a shrug*] . . . Standing right *there*.

KEVIN: If we're getting into the legal stuff?

LINDSEY: I agree.

KEVIN: 'Cuz, I'm not a lawyer.

STEVE: I'm not a lawyer.

LINDSEY: But, Kathy's a lawyer.

STEVE: [*re:* TOM] And he's the one with the time issue.

KEVIN: Long as we're out by four.

STEVE: [*okay, but*] It's three thirty.

KATHY: We'll be done by four.

LINDSEY: [*to* KEVIN *and* LENA] Sorry about all this.

STEVE: Crazy.

[*All turn vaguely to* TOM, *who gestures apologetically and mouths, "Sorry."* LENA *sighs, fans herself.*]

KEVIN: [*small talk*] When's the baby due?

LINDSEY: Oh. Um, November.

KEVIN: In time for turkey.

LINDSEY: I know.

KEVIN: Boy or girl?

[STEVE *is about to answer.*]

LINDSEY: No no no. I don't want to know. Ask Steve. Steve saw the ultrasound. [*Fingers in ears, eyes closed*] La la la la la la la la la la la . . .

[STEVE *mouths the word "boy" then touches* LINDSEY's *knee.*]

    [*fingers out of her ears, eyes open*] . . . la la la—either way as long as it's healthy.

KEVIN: Knock wood.

LINDSEY: But something tells me it's a girl.

[*Pause. Feet tap.* KATHY *takes out her phone, dials a number, listens.*]

    [*To* LENA] You guys have kids?

LENA: Three.

LINDSEY: Wow.

LENA: Mmm.

LINDSEY: How great for you.

LENA: Yes.

LINDSEY: Congratulations.

LENA: Thank you.

[KATHY *starts to check messages. Beat.*]

STEVE: [*to* KEVIN] So Kyle Hendrickson?

KEVIN: [*remembering*] Kyle Hendrickson.

STEVE: Kyle Hendrickson—*who,* may I add, kicked my ass in the tenth grade?

LINDSEY: *Who* is this?

KEVIN: [*laughing*] Wait wait wait. *Little* Kyle Hendrickson—?

STEVE: Like the *one* solitary black dude in my entire high school.

KEVIN: Kicked *your* ass?

STEVE: *Publicly* kicked.

KEVIN: Kyle Hendrickson's like, what? Like five-*two*?

LINDSEY: Wait. *When?*

STEVE: [*to* KEVIN] Five-five. JV wrestling team. Tenth grade.

KEVIN: I think that might officially make you—?

STEVE: A pussy?

KEVIN: Think it might.

LINDSEY: [*to* STEVE] *Who* are you talking about?

STEVE: Okay. Remember I ran into a guy?

LINDSEY: No.

STEVE: Remember last week? I said a guy from middle school?

LINDSEY: No.

STEVE: I was meeting you downtown—oh, and he told me the *joke*?

LINDSEY: Right?

STEVE: The joke I told you?

LINDSEY: I don't remember.

STEVE: The joke about—well, neither do I, at the moment, but it was a joke we both thought was funny?

LINDSEY: Okay?

STEVE: Anyway. *That* guy: *that* is Kyle Hendrickson. Who *he* works with.

LINDSEY: [*to* LENA] Glad we cleared *that* up.

STEVE: Oh oh oh.

LINDSEY: What?

STEVE: Wait.

LINDSEY: What?

STEVE: Wait.

LINDSEY: *What?*

STEVE: The joke. It's about a guy? Remember? Guy who goes to jail?

LINDSEY: No.

STEVE: White-collar criminal goes to jail, remember? And and and they put him in a cell with—?

LINDSEY: [*realizing, privately to* STEVE] *Oh* Oh Oh. No.

STEVE: What?

LINDSEY: Hm-mm.

STEVE: *What?*

LINDSEY: Let's—[*Changing subject, to* LENA] How old are your kids?

STEVE: [*to* LINDSEY] Whatsamatter?

KEVIN: [*to* LINDSEY] Nine, ten, and twelve.

LINDSEY: *Wow.*

STEVE: [*to* LINDSEY] What's your problem?

LINDSEY: Steve.

STEVE: I was telling the joke.

LINDSEY: Later.

STEVE: You said remind me what joke—

LINDSEY: Okay.

STEVE: [*laughing*] But now I'm not *allowed* to tell it?

LINDSEY: [*quietly*] Stop a second.

STEVE: [*to* KEVIN] Anyway. Two guys stuck in a jail cell—

LINDSEY: *Steven?*

LENA: [*finally having had enough*] I'm sorry, and I don't mean to keep interrupting, but can somebody please explain to me what it is we're *doing* here?

[*Pause.* TOM *turns. All feel the chill from* LENA.]

TOM: [*quietly into phone*] Just send me the fucking document.

[KATHY *and* TOM *discreetly hang up.*]

LENA: I mean, I know I'm not the only person who takes the situation seriously and I don't like having to be this way but I have been sitting here for the last fifteen minutes waiting for a turn to speak—[*cont'd.*]

[*All overlap, quietly chastened.*]

TOM:	KEVIN:	LINDSEY:	KATHY:
Hey. Sorry 'bout that.	No one's taking *turns.*	I'm so sorry. I really am. I thought.	Well, Tom was on the phone.

LENA: [*continuous*]—and meanwhile it seems like nothing is even remotely getting accomplished.

LINDSEY: I agree.

[*A truck horn sounds outside.*]

KEVIN: [*to* LENA] So go ahead and say what you—

LENA: [*with a tense smile, to* KEVIN] And could you please not tell me when to—?

KEVIN: I'm not telling—

LENA: [*continuous*] They were having a conversation and—[*cont'd.*]

KEVIN: [*overlapping*] And now they stopped.

LENA: [*continuous*]—I try not to intrude—[*cont'd.*]

KEVIN: Just being friendly.

LENA: [*continuous*]—on other people's conversations when they're in the middle of them. [*To the others*] I'm not trying to be unfriendly.

LINDSEY: No, it's us.

KEVIN: No, it's not.

LINDSEY: No, it is.

KEVIN: You're being friendly.

LENA: *I'm* being friendly.

LINDSEY: [*to* KEVIN, *re:* LENA] She's being friendly.

STEVE: *I'm* being friendly.

KEVIN: If anybody's not being friendly—

LENA: Well, maybe the *friendly* thing to do would be for us to respect each other's time, would that be all right?

STEVE:	LINDSEY:	KATHY:	TOM:
Yeah. Sure.	*Yes.* Totally.	Was it me? Was it?	Sorry. Really.

LENA: Thank you.

[*All murmur quietly.*]

STEVE:	LINDSEY:	KATHY:	TOM:
[*to* KEVIN]	*So* glad someone	'Cuz, seriously,	No, you guys?
Was I	has the balls to	I thought	Was my fault.
disrespectful?	finally *say* it.	we'd stopped.	That was me.

[*Horn sounds again.*]

LINDSEY: [*to* LENA] Anyway.

LENA: Anyway. All right. [*Taking her time*] Well . . . I have no way of knowing what sort of connection you have to the neighborhood where *you* grew up?

[*Horn again.* STEVE *turns.*]

LINDSEY: [*to* STEVE, *rapid whisper*] *Just shut the door. Just shut the fucking—*

[STEVE *jumps up and exits to shut the kitchen door.*]

Sorry. [*Continuing* LENA's *last line*] The neighborhood where—?

LENA: And some of our concerns have to do with a particular period in history and the things that people experienced here in this community *during* that period—[*cont'd.*]

[STEVE *returns to the circle, sits.*]

STEVE: [*whispering to* LENA] Sorry.

LENA: [*continuous*]—both good and bad, and on a personal level? I just have a lot of *respect* for the people who went through those experiences and still managed to carve out a life for themselves and create a community despite a whole lot of obstacles?

LINDSEY: As well you should.

LENA: Some of which still exist. That's just a part of my *history* and my *parents'* history—and honoring the *connection* to that history—and, *no one,* myself included, likes having to dictate what you can or can't do with your own home, but there's just a lot of *pride,* and a lot of *memories* in these houses, and for some of us, that connection still has *value,* if that makes any sense?

LINDSEY: Total sense.

LENA: For those of us who have remained.

LINDSEY: Absolutely.

LENA: And *respecting* that memory; that has value, too. At least, that's what *I* believe. And that's what I've been wanting to say.

[*All nod solemnly for several seconds at* LENA's *noble speech.*]

STEVE: Um. Can I ask a—?

LINDSEY: [*to* STEVE]   STEVE: [*to* LENA]

Let her finish.   Sorry.

LENA: I was finished.

LINDSEY: [*to* LENA] Sorry.

STEVE: Right. So, um . . . Huh. [*How to say it?*] So, when you use the word *value,* um—?

LENA: Historical value.

TOM: You read the petition.

STEVE: Yeah.

TOM: Spelled out pretty clearly.

STEVE: Right. [*To* LENA] But, what I mean is—So, you don't literally mean . . . *monetary* value. Right?

[LENA *stares.*]

LENA: My great-aunt—[*cont'd.*]

STEVE: Or maybe you do.

LENA: [*continuous*]—was one of the first people of color to—in a sense, she was a pioneer—

STEVE: No, I understand—and correct me if—but *my* understanding was that the value of these properties had gone *up*.

KATHY: They have.

STEVE: [*to* KEVIN *and* LENA] Yours included.

KEVIN: That's true.

STEVE: *Way* up.

TOM: And we'd all like to *keep* it that way.

STEVE: But—You're not suggesting, are you, that, when we build *our* house—?

[LINDSEY *puts a hand on* STEVE.]

LINDSEY: [*to* LENA] Look, I for one—I am really grateful for what you said, but this is why we sometimes feel defensive, you know? Because we *love* this neighborhood.

STEVE: We do.

LINDSEY: We completely do, and we would never want to to to to carelessly—[*cont'd.*]

STEVE: Run roughshod.

LINDSEY: [*continuous*]—over anyone's—And I totally admit, I'm the one who was resistant, especially with the schools and everything, but once I stopped seeing the neighborhood the way it *used* to be, and could see what it is *now*, and its *potential*?

LENA: Used to be what?

LINDSEY: What do you mean?

LENA: What it "used to be"?

STEVE: [*helpfully, to* LENA] What *you* said. About the *history* of—?

LINDSEY: *Historically.* The changing, you know, demographic—?

STEVE: Although *originally*—[*to* LINDSEY] wasn't it German, pre-dominantly?

KATHY: German and Irish.

STEVE: Depending how far back you—

KATHY: It's funny, though. Even though my *father* was German—but back when *they* were living here—

LINDSEY: Wait, did I know this?

KATHY: I told you that.

LINDSEY: In this neighborhood?

KATHY: [*to* KEVIN *and* LENA] They went to church at St. Stan's! Isn't that crazy?

KEVIN: Is that right?

KATHY: [*to* KEVIN *and* LENA] This is the late fifties. [*Laughing*] My father was a "Rotarian"! But my *mother*—[*To* LINDSEY] She was deaf? I told you that?

LINDSEY: KEVIN:

That I knew.   Awwww, that's a shame.

KATHY: [*to* KEVIN] Thank you. It was congenital. But then she got pregnant with me and they moved out to Rosemont, anyway, *her* family, they were *Swedish*.

STEVE: [*to* KEVIN *and* LENA] There was a great article two weeks ago—I don't know if you saw this—about the history of the changing, uh, ethnic—[*cont'd.*]

LINDSEY: LENA:

Distribution.   Oh, I should read that.

STEVE: [*continuous*]—of the neighborhood and how in the seventies, eighties, how that was followed by a period of—of—of—of—of rapid—

KATHY: Decline.

LINDSEY: STEVE: KATHY:

No—Not—No   Of *growth*. A growing—   I don't mean *decline*—
                                           [*cont'd.*]

KATHY: [*continuous*]—I mean there was *trouble*.

LINDSEY: Not *trouble*, she didn't mean—

KEVIN: There was trouble.

LINDSEY: *Economic* trouble.

KEVIN: Drugs are trouble.

KATHY: That's what I'm saying.

KEVIN: Violence is trouble.

KATHY: [*vindicated*] Exactly.

LINDSEY: And the violence as an *outgrowth of* the criminalization of those drugs.

KEVIN: [*re: himself and* LENA] 'Cuz ya know, the two of us wuz both crackheads.

[*A frozen moment, then:*]

STEVE:	LINDSEY:	KATHY:	KEVIN: [*laughs*]
That's funny.	No, come on.	I know you're	I'm kidding
I know you're	Don't say that.	joking, but that	you. I'm just
kidding but	Really. Even	is exactly what	messing with
that *was* the per-	as a joke.	people *thought*.	you.
ception at the—			

STEVE: [*to* LINDSEY]—he's *being funny.*

LINDSEY: I know he was, and it *was* funny but when people are systematically *dehumanized*—If you've been placed in some faceless, institutional—[*cont'd.*]

KATHY: [*explaining to* KEVIN *and* LENA] The projects.

LINDSEY: [*continuous*]—I mean, like it or not, that kind of environment is not conducive to—to—to—to—

KEVIN: That's true.

LINDSEY: The formation of *community.*

KATHY: Horrible.

KEVIN: Tough place to grow up.

LINDSEY: With the effect on *children?*

KEVIN: On anyone.

LINDSEY: And to take what had been a pros—well, not prosperous, but a solidly middle-class, um—?

STEVE: Enclave.

LINDSEY: And then *undermine* the entire economic—[*cont'd.*]

STEVE: Infrastructure.

LINDSEY: [*continuous*]—by *warehousing* people inside of these—

STEVE: But that's the thing, right? If you construct some artificial *semblance* of a community, and then isolate people *within* that—I mean, what would be the definition of a *ghetto*, you know? A *ghetto* is a place where—[*cont'd.*]

LINDSEY: [*overlapping, to* STEVE] But who *uses* that word? I don't.

STEVE: [*continuous*]—where, where, where people are *sequestered*, right? [*To* LINDSEY, *defensively*] The *definition*, I'm saying.

LENA: Well, *my* family—

STEVE: Like Prague. If you think of—[*Pedagogically*] Okay: Prague had this ghetto, right? A Jewish ghetto?

LENA: [*thanks for the lecture*] We've been to Prague.

LINDSEY: Ohmigod. Prague is *beautiful*. [KEVIN *wiggles his hand*.] I loved Pr—You didn't love it?

KEVIN: Prague's *crowded*.

KATHY: And the food sucks. Or is that just me?

STEVE: But I'm saying, it's not like, one day all these Jews were sitting around Prague, looking at the real estate section, going, *"Hey here's an idea! Let's all go live in that ghetto!"* Right?

[*A beat where they all avoid* STEVE's *comment*.]

LINDSEY: [*to* LENA] When were you in Prague?

LENA: Last April.

KEVIN: First Prague, then Zurich.

LINDSEY: I want to go back.

KEVIN: [*to* STEVE] You ski?

[*A laugh erupts from* LINDSEY.]

LINDSEY: [*re:* STEVE] *Him?*

STEVE: You mean—like *downhill?*

LINDSEY: *That* I'd like to see.

KEVIN: Ever been to Switzerland?

STEVE: [*to* LINDSEY, *defensive*] I can *ski*. I *have* skied.

LINDSEY: Get that on video.

STEVE: Why is that funny?

LINDSEY: [*trying not to laugh, to* KEVIN] Sorry.

STEVE: Seriously. What is it about the idea of me skiing that you find so highly, uh—?

LINDSEY: Anyway.

STEVE: —*risible?*

KEVIN: [*to* STEVE] I just meant, you like to golf, you go to *Scotland*. And if you like to *ski?*

LINDSEY: [*still laughing*] Just trying to picture it.

STEVE: Gratuitous.

TOM: [*prodding the others*] Annnnnnyway.

LENA:	LINDSEY:	KATHY [*to* KEVIN]:
Yes. Maybe we should try to stick to the topic at hand.	Okay. Tom's right. Let's get it together.	I can't ski because I was born with weak ankles. Anyway.

LINDSEY: [*to* TOM] *Where* were we?

TOM: Page three.

LINDSEY: Uggh. You're kidding.

TOM: Nope.

LINDSEY: How can we still be—?

TOM: I dunno.

LINDSEY: How is that possible?

TOM: [*glancing at watch*] And it is now . . . quarter to four.

LENA: I'm sorry for taking time.

LINDSEY: No. What you said was *great*.

LENA: And I wasn't trying to *romanticize*.

LINDSEY: You didn't.

LENA: Nothing *romantic* about being poor.

LINDSEY: But, it was your *neighborhood*.

KATHY: [*to* LENA] Wait, what street?

LENA: Offa Larabee.

KATHY: My parents lived on Claremont!!

KEVIN: Ya'll would've been neighbors.

LENA: But I didn't mean to make it about my personal *connection* to the house. It's more about the *principle*.

KEVIN: But you can't *live* in a *principle*.

LINDSEY: You had a personal connection?

KEVIN: To the house.

LINDSEY: To *this* house?

KEVIN: [*to* LINDSEY] Her aunt.

LENA: I don't want to—let's not.

KEVIN: Lived here.

STEVE: Wait. *Who?*

LENA: Sort of beside the point, but yes.

KEVIN: *Great*-aunt.

LENA: On my mother's side.

LINDSEY: You don't mean *here,* here?

LENA: And this is fifty years ago.

LINDSEY: Here in this *house.*

LENA: For quite some time, actually.

LINDSEY: [*hand to her heart*]   STEVE:
Oh my G—! So so so wait, so—?   *Whoa.*

STEVE: [*clarifying*] This *exact house.*

LINDSEY: [*how weird*]—so, like, you've . . . *been in this room?*

LENA: I used to climb a tree in the backyard.

LINDSEY: STEVE:
Oh my *God.*   Whoa.

LENA: A crepe myrtle tree?

KATHY: Well, that is just bizarre.

KEVIN: Any rate, her great-aunt—and she had to save a long time to be able to afford a house like this.

LENA: She was a domestic worker.

KEVIN: And, a house isn't cheap.

LENA: Not *here,* anyway.

KEVIN: Here at *that* time.

LENA: At *that* time—well, when *I* was growing up I really don't remember seeing a single white face in the neighborhood for pretty much my entire—

KEVIN: Well, one, you said.

LENA: Who?

KEVIN: What's his name?

LENA: Mr. Wheeler?

KEVIN: Mr. Wheeler.

LENA: [*to the others*] I don't think anybody knew his first name.

KEVIN: He was a . . . what?

LENA: [*to* LINDSEY] At the grocery store.

KEVIN: Bagged the groceries.

LENA: At the Sup'r—Well, back then it was Gelman's but they tore down Gelman's.

KEVIN: And that became Sup'r Sav'r?

LENA: Well, then they tore down Sup'r Sav'r, so—

KEVIN: You know where the Whole Foods is?

STEVE: [*with a laugh*] And what happened to Mr. Wheeler?

KEVIN: Dead, probably.

LENA: He was, you know . . . [*taps her finger on her temple*] . . . developmentally . . . ?

LINDSEY:	STEVE:	KATHY:
Ohhhh.	Huh. Wow.	Ohhhh . . . you know why that
That's so sad.	Depressing.	upsets me? I have a niece with
		Asperger's syndrome.

LENA: But, given the makeup of the neighborhood at that time and the price of a home like this one, the question naturally arises as to whether it was the thing that happened here in the house—whether that in some way—

KEVIN: Played a factor.

LENA: In making a place like this affordable. For a person of her income.

[*All stare. Pause.*]

STEVE: The *thing.*

LENA: The sad—you know.

LINDSEY: I don't.

LENA: The tragic—

KEVIN: Thing that happened.

LINDSEY: What thing?

KEVIN: [*no big deal*] Well. Long time ago, but—

STEVE: In *this* house?

LENA: I'm just saying that, since she was one of the very first people of color—

LINDSEY: Wait. Something happened in the house?

STEVE: What, somebody *died,* or—?

KEVIN: S'not important.

LINDSEY: That we should be concerned about?

KEVIN: No no no no no.

LENA: Just that—there'd *been* a family. Who had a son who'd been in the Army.

KEVIN: Korea, maybe?

LENA: And who, well, a few years after he came back from the war—

KEVIN: Killed himself.

[*Beat.*]

LINDSEY: Oh my God.

KEVIN: Yeah.

STEVE: Wow.

LINDSEY: *Oh* my God.

KEVIN: Sad.

STEVE: Wow.

LINDSEY: Oh my God.

LENA: Which my great-aunt didn't know at the time.

LINDSEY: Oh my God, that is just—

LENA: Though I assumed *you* did.

STEVE: Umm, no?

LINDSEY: That is just—just—just—Wait. And they went ahead and *sold* the house to—?

LENA: Mm-hmm.

STEVE: Wow.

LINDSEY: Without *telling* her that? Because nobody ever told *us* that.

KATHY: Well, they *wouldn't*, would they?

KEVIN: [*dismissive*] Fifty *years* ago.

LINDSEY: [*to* KATHY] But *legally,* I mean, don't you have to *tell* people that?

KATHY: Not if you want to sell it.

LENA: It was something like he'd come back from the Army. And he'd been accused of something.

KEVIN: Killing people.

LENA: Innocent people.

KEVIN: Killing civilians.

LENA: And then—you know.

STEVE: But you don't mean, like like like like . . . [*laughs*] like *here in this very*—?

LENA: No—I mean, not *where we're sitting.*

KEVIN: Upstairs, wasn't it?

LINDSEY: [*freaking out*] I—I—I—I—

STEVE: [*touching* LINDSEY] Breathe.

LINDSEY: [*pushing* STEVE's *hand away*] Stop it.

LENA: I mean, the version *I* was told was, he went upstairs.

KEVIN: Hanged himself.

LINDSEY: [*standing, walking away*] Okay. *No.* No, I'm sorry, but that is *wrong.*

STEVE: [*following her*] Where are you going?

LINDSEY: That is just—*No.* To sell someone a—a—a *house,* where—?

STEVE: Whatsamatter?

[STEVE *and* LINDSEY *exit to the kitchen, from where we clearly hear:*]

LINDSEY: *No.* There should be a *law.* And I don't care *how,* okay? I don't want to know *how* he did it or in *what room*—Because I'm sorry, but that is just something that, from a legal standpoint, you should have to *tell* people!

KATHY: [*calling to* LINDSEY] It's not.

LINDSEY: [*sticking her head in, to* KATHY] *Well, it fucking well should be.*

STEVE: Hey. Hey.

LINDSEY: [*privately, to* STEVE] And now I have this horrifying *image* in my head?

STEVE: [*to* LINDSEY, *laughing*] But why d'you have to make such a big *deal* outa—?

LINDSEY: Uh, it *is* a big deal, Steve. If your *child*—if *our family* is going to *live* in a house where—?

STEVE: [*laughing, to the others*] I mean, it's not like he's still *hanging* up there!

LINDSEY: [*losing her shit, to* STEVE] *It's* not *funny, okay?!! It's not funny to me, so why are you acting like an asshole?!!*

[*The kitchen door bangs open and* DAN *noisily enters.*]

DAN: [*calling out*] Okay. Show ya whatcha got.

[*He drags a large trunk—the same trunk we saw in act 1, covered with mold and dirt—into the middle of the room.*]

So that's your problem right there. [*Coughs a couple of times*] S'cuse me. And I tell ya one thing: yank this up from down there, take a look at it, you know the first thing I'm thinking to myself? You know what I'm thinking? *Buried treasure.* Like Spanish doubloons or something and I know you're thinking Dan, ya crazy bastard but I tell ya what. I know a guy.

[DAN *joins the circle.*]

[*Coughs again*] S'cuse me. This guy. Last summer he's taking out a septic system—this house out in Mundelein. He's sitting on top of his backhoe. All of a sudden *clang.* And this guy's not exactly the sharpest tool in the box, if ya know what I mean, but he goes down in there about five, six feet with a chain and a winch—swear to God—ya know what he pulls out from down there? He stands back. He takes a look—[*Without stopping*] You're in the middle of something.

STEVE: Sorta.

DAN: My bad.

STEVE: No no.

DAN: Bull in a china shop.

STEVE: It's cool.

DAN: According to my wife.

STEVE: Oh yeah?

DAN: As well as a couple other names not suitable for mixed—Anyways.

STEVE: Thanks.

DAN: [*re: the trunk*] I'll just leave this here for ya.

STEVE: Thank you.

DAN: Need me to open it, you lemme know.

STEVE: Great.

DAN: Problem, though. [*Indicating the large padlock*] Problem's this puppy right here. Now the deal is: I got a saw. Take a hacksaw you could maybe saw it off but whatcha really want is a pair of bolt cutters and I don't think I got any bolt cutters, so.

STEVE: Ah, well.

DAN: 'Cause you never know. Turns out to be fulla Spanish doubloons we'll haveta split it six ways, huh?

LINDSEY: [*to* DAN, *taking over*] Sorry.

DAN: Whoops.

LINDSEY: I don't know your name.

DAN: [*extending hand*] Dan.

LINDSEY: Hi, Dan.

DAN: Dan or Danny.

LINDSEY: Great.

DAN: *Daniel* when the wife gets pissed.

LINDSEY: But listen—

DAN: No no no no no no I gotcha.

LINDSEY: If you wouldn't mind?

DAN: Middle of your thing and I come barging right into—

LINDSEY: Thank you.

DAN: But you find ya some bolt cutters you'll be in business.

LINDSEY: We will.

DAN: [*an idea*] Hey, ya know what? Hang on a second.

[DAN *heads to the back door.*]

TOM: So I'm just going to push ahead, if that's okay?

DAN: [*calling out the door, top of his lungs*] Ramirez!!!

TOM: 'Cause we still got seventeen pages to cover—

LINDSEY: [*to all*] And I'm sorry I lost my shit. No, I did. But I think we're both wound a little tight right now with the baby and the house and the money and everything—[*cont'd.*]

DAN: *Ramirez!!*

LINDSEY: [*continuous*]—and then to top it all off, we get sent this petition in the mail, you know, and suddenly our entire lives are thrown into chaos at the very same moment that—I mean, the demolition was scheduled to start on Monday and unless we get this resolved which I want as much as anyone then what do people expect?

DAN: *Ram*—!!! Ah, screw it.

[DAN *gives up, exits.*]

TOM: [*continuing*] So: Couple of options. One, as we said, is reducing the height—

KATHY: [*adamantly*] No. Tom, I'm sorry, but you can't just call an architect at the eleventh hour and snap your fingers and say can you completely redesign an entire—

LINDSEY: It's a little late in the day for that.

LENA: [*to* LINDSEY] I'm sorry you're upset.

LINDSEY: I'm not upset. I'm not.

KATHY: And may I remind everybody that these guys are under no obligation, legal *or* otherwise—

TOM: [*from a document*] Okay. Here's the wording from the city council, and I quote: "In recognition of the *historic* status of the Clybourne

Park neighborhood, and its distinctive collection of *low-rise single-family homes—[cont'd.]*

LINDSEY:	KEVIN:	TOM: [*continuous*]
Aren't *we* a	Hey. Hey.	*—intended to house a*
single family?	Everything's cool.	*community of working-class*
		families."

LINDSEY: And you know, the thing is? Communities change.

STEVE: They do.

LINDSEY: That's just the reality.

STEVE: It is.

LENA: And some change is inevitable, and we all support that, but it might be worth asking yourself who exactly is *responsible* for that change?

[*Little pause.*]

LINDSEY:	KEVIN:
I'm not sure what you—?	Wait, what are you trying to—?

LENA: I'm asking you to think about the motivation behind the long-range political initiative to change the face of this neighborhood.

[*Another little pause.*]

LINDSEY:	STEVE: [*to* LENA]	KEVIN:
What does that mean?	Wait, say that	The long-range
[*To* STEVE] Do you	again?	*what*?
know what—?		

LENA: I mean that this is a highly desirable area.

STEVE: Well, *we* desire it.

LENA: I know you do.

LINDSEY: Same as you.

LENA: And now the area is *changing*.

KATHY: And for the *better*, right?

LENA: And I'm saying that there are certain economic interests that are being served by those changes and others that are not. That's all.

STEVE: [*suspiciously*] And . . . *which* interests are being—?

LENA: [*systematically*] If you have a residential area, in direct proximity to *downtown*?

STEVE: Right?

LENA: And if that area is occupied by a particular *group*?

STEVE: LINDSEY: [*to* LENA]

Which group?   You know what? We're talking about *one house.*

LENA: [*to* LINDSEY] I understand that.

STEVE: Which group?

LINDSEY: A house for our *family*?

STEVE: Which group?

LENA: That's how it happens.

LINDSEY: In which to raise our *child*?

STEVE: No no. Which group?

LENA: It happens one house at a time.

STEVE: Whoa whoa whoa. Okay. Stop right there.

LINDSEY: What are you doing?

STEVE: No. I'm sorry, but can we just come out and *say* what it is we're actually—? Shouldn't we maybe *do* that? Because if *that's* what this is really about, then . . . Jesus, maybe we oughta save ourselves some time and and and and just . . . *say* what it is we're really *saying* instead of doing this elaborate little *dance* around it.

[*Dead stop. All stare at* STEVE.]

Never mind.

KATHY: *What* dance?

STEVE: I—I—I—I shouldn't have—whatever.

LENA: [*parsing his meaning*] So . . . you think I haven't been *saying* what I *actually*—?

STEVE: [*laughs*] Uhhh . . . Not to my way of thinking, no.

LENA: Well, what is it you *think* I'm—?

STEVE: I—I—I . . . [*laughs incredulously*] like we don't all *know*?

LINDSEY: *I* don't.

STEVE: Oh, *yes you do.* Of *course* you do.

KEVIN: Well, maybe you oughta *tell* us what *you* think she was saying.

STEVE: Oh oh, but it has to be *me*?

LENA: Well, you're the one who raised the question as to—[*cont'd.*]

STEVE: [*laughs, overlapping*] Oh, come on. It was *blatant.*

LENA: [*continuous*]—the sincerity of my speech.

LINDSEY: What the fuck, Steve?

STEVE: You know what? Forget I said it.

LINDSEY:	LENA:	STEVE:
You didn't *say* anything.	Oh no, I'm *interested*.	Let's forget the whole— [*cont'd.*]

STEVE: [*continuous*]—Okay. Okay. If you really want to—It's . . . [*tries to laugh, then, sotto*] . . . it's *race*. Isn't it? You're trying to tell me that that . . . [*To* LENA] That implicit in what you *said*—That this entire conversation . . . isn't at least *partly* informed—*am I right?* [*Laughs nervously, to* LENA] By the issue of . . . [*sotto*] of *racism?*

[*Beat.*]

LINDSEY: [*to* STEVE]	STEVE: [*to* LINDSEY]
Are you out of your—? [*To* LENA] I have no idea where this is coming from.	And *please* don't do that to me, okay? I've asked you repeatedly.

LENA: Well, the *original* issue was the inappropriately large *house* that— [*cont'd.*]

STEVE: [*to* LENA, *overlapping*] Oh, come *on.*

LENA: [*continuous*]—you're planning to build. Only, *now* I'm fairly certain that I've been called a *racist.*

STEVE: But I didn't say that, did I?

LENA: *Sounded* like you did.

STEVE: [*to* KEVIN] Did I say that?

KEVIN: Yeah, you kinda did.

STEVE: In what way did I say that?

KEVIN: Uh, *somebody* said racism.

STEVE: *-Cism! -Cism!* Not *-cist!!*

KEVIN: Which must originate from *somewhere.*

STEVE: And which we all find totally reprehensi—

KEVIN: So—are *you* the racist?

STEVE: Can I just—?

KEVIN: Is it your wife?

KATHY: Don't look at *me.*

STEVE: Look:

KEVIN: 'Cause, by process of elimination—

STEVE: Here's what I'm saying:

LINDSEY: What *are* you saying?!

STEVE: I'm saying: Was race *not* a factor—

LINDSEY: [*re:* STEVE, *exonerating herself*] I don't know this person.

STEVE: Were there *not* these differences—

LINDSEY: *What* differences!!? There's no—

STEVE: [*to* LINDSEY *re:* LENA] Okay: she walks in here, from the very beginning, with all these *issues*—[*cont'd.*]

LENA: [*overlapping*] About your *house*.

STEVE: [*continuous*]—and I'm only asking whether, were we not, shall we say—?

LINDSEY: You're *creating* an issue. *Where none exists.*

STEVE: Oh oh oh you *heard* what she *said*. She as much as claimed that there's some kind of, of, of *secret conspiracy*—

LENA: Oh, it's not a *secret.*

KEVIN: [*to* LENA]	LENA: [*to* KEVIN]	STEVE:
Ohh, *c'mon*. Are you *seriously*—?	Oh, please don't be purposely *naive*.	*There. Thank you. Now you see what I'm*—?

LENA: This has been under discussion for at least *four decades* now— [*cont'd.*]

KEVIN: [*overlapping, to* LENA] *You can't prove that.*

LENA: [*continuous*]—at the highest institutional levels of—[*To* KEVIN] *Oh, don't act like you don't know it's true.*

STEVE: [*to* LENA] What, and now we're the evil invaders who are— [*cont'd.*]

LINDSEY: [*to* STEVE] *She never said that!!!!*

STEVE: [*continuous*]—appropriating your *ancestral homeland*?

LINDSEY: [*to* STEVE] This, this, this—No. I'm sorry, this is the most asinine—[*To* LENA *and* KEVIN] *Half of my friends are black!*

STEVE: [*sputtering*] *What!!??*

LINDSEY: [*to* STEVE, *as to a child*] As is true for most *normal* people.

STEVE: Name *one*.

LINDSEY: *Normal* people? Tend to have *many* friends of a diverse and wide-ranging—

STEVE: You can't name *one!*

LINDSEY: Candace.

[*Beat.*]

STEVE: Name another.

LINDSEY: *I don't have to stand here compiling a list of—*

STEVE: You said *half.* You *specifically*—

LINDSEY: Theresa.

STEVE: *She works in your office!! She's not your "friend."*

LINDSEY: *She was at the baby shower, Steve! I hope she's not my enemy!!*

TOM: Well, this is all fascinating—

STEVE: [*to* LINDSEY] Name another.

TOM: And while I'd love to sit here and review *all* of American history *maybe* we should concentrate on the plans for your *property*—[*cont'd.*]

STEVE: [*overlapping*] Yes!! Yes!!—[*cont'd.*]

TOM: [*continuous*]—which *had* been the *original* topic of the convers—

STEVE: [*overlapping, continuous*] The history of America *is* the history of private property.

LENA: That may be—[*cont'd.*]

STEVE: Read De Tocqueville.

LENA: [*continuous*]—though I rather doubt *your* grandparents were *sold as* private property.

STEVE: [*to* KEVIN *and* LENA] Ohhhhh my *God.* Look. Look. Humans are *territorial,* okay?

LINDSEY: [*to* STEVE] Who *are* you?

STEVE: This is why we have *wars.* One group, one *tribe,* tries to usurp some *territory*—and now *you guys* have *this* territory, right? And you don't like having it *stolen away* from you, the way white people stole everything else from black America. *We get it,* okay? And we *apologize.* But what *good* does it do, if we perpetually fall into the same, predictable little euphemistic tap dance around the topic?

KEVIN: You know how to tap dance?

STEVE: *See? See what he's doing?!!*

LINDSEY: Maybe quit while you're ahead.

STEVE: *No.* I'm sick of—*No.* Every *single word* we say is—is—is *scrutinized* for some kind of latent—Meanwhile you guys run around saying n-word this and n-word that and *whatever.* We all know *why* there's a double standard but I can't even so much as repeat a fucking *joke* that *the one black guy I know told me*—

KEVIN: *So tell the goddamn joke.*

STEVE: Not *now!!*

KEVIN: If you feel so *oppressed,* either go ahead and *tell it*—[*cont'd.*]

LINDSEY: [*to* STEVE] Do *not.*

KEVIN: [*continuous*]—or maybe you could *move on.*

LINDSEY [*with finality*]: *Thank you!*

LENA: Well, I want to hear it.

KEVIN: [*to* LENA]	LENA: [*to* KEVIN]	LINDSEY:
Ohh, *don't.*	Why not? You're	No. Trust me.
	not interested?	It's offensive.

STEVE: [*to* LINDSEY] Of course it's *offensive*—[*cont'd.*]

LINDSEY: [*overlapping*] To *me.* Offensive to *me.*

STEVE: [*continuous*]—that's the whole point of the—How? How does it offend *you?*

LINDSEY: Because it's disgusting and juvenile and traffics in the worst possible type of obsolete bullshit stereotypes.

[*Beat.*]

LENA: Well, now I *gotta* hear it.

KEVIN:	STEVE:	LINDSEY:
No no no no no.	No. I can't.	Not while I'm
Aww, *c'mon.*		in the room.

LENA: [*to* KEVIN, *re:* LINDSEY] Well, she says it's so offensive, and I have no way of knowing if she's right, and if I don't ever *hear* it, how will I ever *know?*

[KEVIN *sighs, throws up his hands.*]

STEVE: Um, you know what? I don't even remember it now.

LENA: Two men in jail, you said.

KATHY: Oh, *I* know this one.

LINDSEY: [*a warning*] *Steven?*

LENA: Wasn't that it? Two men . . . ?

STEVE: I—Okay. So there's—*Look, it's not even my joke, okay?!!* It was told to me by Kyle Hendrickson, who, for what it's worth, happens to be—

LENA: Black.

STEVE: Right.

LENA: So the white man goes to jail.

LINDSEY: [*to* STEVE] *I can't believe you actually intend to*—!! Fine.

STEVE: Anyway.

LINDSEY: Knock 'em dead.

STEVE: Goes to jail for . . . you know. Embezzlement. Something. Little white guy. And he's put in a jail cell with this . . . uhhh . . .

LENA: With a black man.

STEVE: Big black guy.

LINDSEY: [*appalled*] And why "*big*"?—[*cont'd.*]

STEVE: [*overlapping, to* LINDSEY] I am repeating, *verbatim*, a joke— [*cont'd.*]

LINDSEY: [*continuous*]—Why does it have to be "big"? What does that reveal about your subconscious—?

STEVE: [*continuous*]—in the precise manner in which it was told to *me*.

LENA: Little white man.

LINDSEY: [*head in hands*] Oh God.

LENA: Big black man.

STEVE: In the . . . yeah, so they . . . um, slam the cell door . . . behind him, I guess, and the black guy turns to the white guy, black guy goes, "Okay, I'm gonna give you a choice. While you're in here with me, you can either be the mommy, or you can be the daddy." And the white guy thinks for a second and he goes, "Uh, well, um, I guess, if it's up to *me*, then, I guess I'd have to say *I'd* prefer to be the daddy." [*Clears his throat*] And, the black guy goes, "Okay, well then bend over 'cause Mommy's gonna fuck you in the ass."

[*Long pause. No one laughs or smiles. They simply nod or shake their heads.*]

KATHY: That's not the one I was thinking of.

STEVE: [*academically*] So: is that "*offensive*"?

LENA:	LINDSEY:
No.	*Are you ins*—?!?!!!

STEVE: [*to* LINDSEY] To *you*. How is it offensive to *you*?

LINDSEY: I don't think it's *me* you should be *asking*.

LENA: No, the problem with *that* joke, see, is that it's not *funny*.

LINDSEY: No shit.

STEVE: [*to* LINDSEY] *You laughed when I told it to you!!*

LENA: And had it been a *funny* joke—

STEVE: It *is* funny. Yes it is. And and and and the *reason* it's funny is, is, is that it plays upon certain latent fears of—of—of—of white people, vis-à-vis the—

TOM: Okay. I'd like to add: I'm *gay*.

STEVE:	KATHY:	LINDSEY:
I—I—I—I—well,	See? You never know.	Nice. Nice going,
I didn't know that.	You really don't.	Steven. Nice work.

TOM: So I guess you think sex *between men* is funny?

STEVE: *Oh, come on!!!*

TOM: Just *inherently* funny.

STEVE: And it's not even *sex,* it's *rape!*

LINDSEY: So *rape* is funny.

STEVE: N—*Yes!!!* In the context of the *joke.*

KATHY: My sister was raped.

STEVE: I quit.

KATHY: So it's offensive to *me.*

LINDSEY: *And* me!

STEVE: [*re:* TOM] *And* him. *And* them. *That's the point of the joke.* To permit the expression of—And what does it even *mean,* "offended"? I don't even know what it *means.*

KEVIN: How many white men does it take to change a lightbulb?

TOM:	LINDSEY:	KATHY:	STEVE:
Okay, I'm about	No. Can we	Aha. See?	*Fine!* Tell me
two minutes	please *not*?	Shoe's on the	the joke. I want
from leaving.	I'm asking	other foot now.	to hear it. I
So, *heads up.*	you as a favor.		do—[*cont'd.*]

STEVE: [*continuous*]—How many white men *does* it take to change a lightbulb?

KEVIN: All of 'em.

STEVE: And why is that?

KEVIN: One to hold the lightbulb while the rest of 'em screw the entire world.

STEVE: *So?!!* You think I'm *"offended"*? I can do this all day. What's long and hard on a black man?

LINDSEY: *How is this happening?!!*

KEVIN: I don't know, Steve. What *is* long and hard on a black man?

STEVE: First grade. Are you "offended"?

KEVIN: Nope.

STEVE: Neither am I.

LINDSEY: You *can't be* offended, you *moron*—[*cont'd.*]

STEVE: [*astonished laugh*] . . . I *can't*?

LINDSEY: [*continuous*]—because you've *never* been politically marginalized, unlike *the majority* of people in the world—[*cont'd.*]

STEVE: [*overlapping*] How can a *majority* be *marginal*?

LINDSEY: [*continuous*]—and, by the way, *all women, everywhere,* and it's your classic white male myopia that you're blind to that basic fact.

LENA: Why is a white woman like a tampon?

[*All turn to* LENA. *Pause.*]

LINDSEY: Why is what?

LENA: It's a joke.

KEVIN: No no no no no no—

LENA: *You* told a joke, now *I'm* telling one: why is a white woman—[*cont'd.*]

KEVIN: [*overlapping*] Baby, don't.

LENA: [*calmly, continuous, to* KEVIN]—and please don't *baby* me. You've got three babies at *home*—[*cont'd.*]

KEVIN: [*publicly, overlapping*] Good night. I wash my hands.

LENA: [*continuous, privately*]—if you need to *pacify* someone. [*To the others*] So:

STEVE: [*raising a finger*] Uhh . . . can you repeat the setup?

LENA: Why . . .

STEVE: . . . is a white woman, right . . . ?

LENA: . . . like a tampon?

[STEVE *looks around. No one else answers.*]

STEVE: Um, I don't know, why?

LENA: Because they're both stuck up cunts.

[*Pause. Again, no one laughs or smiles.* KEVIN *shakes his head.*]

LINDSEY: [*even*] Wow.

LENA: But I hope you're not *offended.*

STEVE: [*academically, not laughing*] See, *I* find that funny.

LINDSEY: Do you.

KATHY: Well, *I'm* offended.

STEVE: *Oh, you are not.*

LINDSEY: And how does it always come back around to *the women*?

LENA: [*innocently*] It was just a joke.

STEVE: *Exactly!!*

KATHY: An extremely *hostile* joke.

LINDSEY: Directed at me.

KATHY: And in what way am I *stuck up*, exactly? You mean, because I worked my ass off putting myself through law school, that makes me *stuck up*?

STEVE: It's a joke about a *tampon!!*

KATHY: And maybe there's a difference between being *stuck up* and being *intelligent*.

STEVE: [*to* KATHY] *You don't even know the fucking capital of Morocco!!!*

KATHY: [*insulted*] Ohhhhhhh . . . kay.

STEVE: And you know something? If there's anyone here who's being *marginalized* by the tide of history—You don't exactly see *me* sitting in the White House, do you?

LINDSEY: *Thank the Lord.*

STEVE: But you don't see *me* wetting my pants and acting all "offended."

KATHY: [*to* LINDSEY, *as she packs her things*] You know, I think maybe I'm *done*.

STEVE: No. You want to know what offends *me*? How about the neighborhood the two of us are living in right now? Bunch of white suburban assholes still driving around with the yellow ribbon magnets on their SUVs in support of some bullshit war. *That's* the kinda shit that offends *me*.

KEVIN: Why does *that* make them assholes?

[*Pause.*]

STEVE: Why does what?

KEVIN: Said assholes have yellow ribbons on their SU—

STEVE: I didn't say that.

KEVIN: Yeah, you did, you said—

STEVE: I said *"with"* the magnet, not, you know, *"by virtue of."*

KEVIN: So, it's not the *magnet* makes you the asshole?

LINDSEY: [*to* KEVIN] You have one on your car?

KEVIN: I have three of 'em.

STEVE: Three.

KEVIN: Three.

LINDSEY: Three?

LENA: Three.

STEVE: Three.

KEVIN: One for each member of my family serving overseas.

STEVE: Great.

[*Pause.*]

KATHY: I have the pink one for breast cancer.

KEVIN: So maybe I'm a *triple* asshole, but—

LINDSEY: [*fake-whisper to* KEVIN] *I think we know who the asshole is.*

STEVE: Wow.

LINDSEY: [*finishing off* STEVE] Well you're being an *idiot.* And in case you hadn't noticed, the rest of the world has begun a more sophisticated conversation about this topic than you apparently are qualified to participate in at this incredible moment in history. I mean, I used to *date* a black guy. *So what?* I mean, *seriously. Steve. Wake up.*

[*The same church bell that we heard in act 1 begins to ring. Pause.* TOM *looks at his watch, claps his hands together.*]

TOM: And it is now four o'clock.

STEVE: [*privately, to* LINDSEY] When did you date a black guy?

TOM: So: final thoughts? Lena?

LENA: No.

TOM: Kev?

KEVIN: I'm good.

TOM: Anybody?

KEVIN: Very informative.

LINDSEY: Well, I want to say this: I want to say I feel angry. And I'm basically kind of hurt by the implication that's been made that, just because we want to live as your neighbors and raise a child alongside yours, that somehow, in the process of doing that, we've had our ethics called into question. Because *that* is hurtful.

LENA: [*calmly*] No one has questioned your *ethics* at all.

LINDSEY: Well, I wish I could believe you.

LENA: No, what we're questioning is your *taste.*

[*The others rise to leave.*]

TOM: LINDSEY:
Kathy? I will call you when   Well, *that* was insulting.
the petition goes through.
KATHY: Thank you.
TOM: Tuesday at the latest.
LINDSEY: Wait, what's wrong with our *taste*?
TOM: [*putting on sunglasses*] Kev?
KEVIN: Right behind you.
LINDSEY: No. What is so *egregious* about the design of our *house*?
KEVIN: [*to* LENA, *who is about to respond*] No no no no no. Let it go.

[LENA *exits.*]

KATHY: [*to* LINDSEY] Sweetie, I've got a thing but I'll call you tomorrow.
TOM: [*to* LINDSEY *and* STEVE] And you guys got my number if you want
    to talk?
STEVE: Yep.

[TOM *is gone, with a thumbs-up.* KATHY *follows close behind. At the same time,* DAN *enters from the kitchen carrying a pair of bolt cutters. The others ignore him.*]

KEVIN: [*to* LINDSEY *and* STEVE] So, uhh . . . good luck with your house.
    And maybe y'all can just communicate with Tom from here on out.
    But, anyway, uhh . . . [*with a wave*] . . . y'all enjoy the rest of your
    evening.

[KEVIN *politely exits through the open front door.* STEVE *and* LINDSEY *stand silently for a moment.* DAN *holds up the bolt cutters.*]

DAN: Uhhhhh . . . ?
LINDSEY: [*quietly*] *Wow.*
STEVE: Wow is right.
LINDSEY: Amazing.
STEVE: [*but not quietly enough*] And for the record? *That woman* is the
    cunt.

[*And instantly* KEVIN *is back through the front door with* LENA *following.*]

KEVIN: [*advancing on* STEVE] Wait a second—*what'd* you say?

[*All hell breaks loose.*]

LENA:	KEVIN:	STEVE [*innocently*]:	LINDSEY:
Just leave it alone. Let 'em be. I don't care what kinda bullshit they think, all I want to do is go home now and take the longest shower of my life.	Whattya think I'm *deaf* or something? Standing right there on your front doorstep— Oh no, I *heard* you loud and clear. I'm just giving you the opportunity to repeat it to my *face* . . . [*cont'd.*]	What? What? What? I didn't . . . Hey, hey, hey, *whoa. Back off,* man. What is your fucking problem, dude? I didn't do anything to you *or* to her so why can't you *chill*? Please?	[*to* KEVIN] No no no no—I told you. It's the pressure. We're both under a huge amount of pressure and yes he acted like an idiot but could we all just maybe *step off.*

KEVIN: [*continuous, in the clear*] . . . and when you do? I will slap the taste outa your mouth.

STEVE:	LENA:
Oh oh oh good, *threaten me.*	Oh, *now* you're gonna stand up for me?

KEVIN: Don't you ever insult my wife, you hear me, *bitch*?

DAN: [*putting his hand on* KEVIN'*s shoulder*] Hey. Let's be civilized.

KEVIN: [*whirling on* DAN] Ohoho, don't you touch *me.*

DAN:	STEVE: [*to* DAN]	KEVIN: [*to* DAN]	LENA: [*to* KEVIN]
Whoa whoa whoa. Oh, That's cool. I'm just pass- ing through, is all.	Hey, do you *mind*, okay? We happen to be having a conversation.	Go putting your hands on *me*? Oh, no. Not in *this* neighbor—	For God's sake, are you coming—[*cont'd.*]

LENA: [*continuous*]—or are you too busy trying to make *friends* with everybody?

[DAN *backs off as two simultaneous arguments unfold.*]

LINDSEY: [*to* STEVE]
And why the fuck did you go and insult Kathy? We are *paying her,* I hope you realize?
STEVE:
Yeah, well you know what? I *agree* with them! *The house is too fucking big!*
LINDSEY:
Ohhhhhhhh do not *even*—
STEVE:
Very first time we saw the plans. What did I tell you? I told you that like *fifteen times!!*
LINDSEY:
Well, Steven, you're free to live wherever you want, but the baby and I will be here if you ever feel like visiting.

KEVIN: [*to* LENA]
What the hell is that supposed to—?
LENA:
Alllllllll afternoon. Always gotta be *every*body's friend. *Hi everybody! I'm Kevin!*
KEVIN: [*starting to exit*]
Oh gimme a fuckin'—So you want to fight with *me* now? Gotta pick a fight with *me?* You have had a bug up your ass from the moment we walked through this door.
LENA:
Yeah, well maybe some of us don't feel the need to constantly *ingratiate* ourselves with everybody.
KEVIN:
Well, maybe that's because some of us aren't *paranoid and delusional.*

[KEVIN *and* LENA *exit. By this point,* DAN *has succeeded in opening the trunk.*]

STEVE: [*continuous from above*] Fine by me.
LINDSEY: Do you have the keys?
STEVE: I mean, God forbid my needs should ever come before the *baby's.*
LINDSEY: You really want me to choose between you and the baby?
STEVE: Oh, I'm secondary.
LINDSEY: 'Cause that's an *easy* one.
STEVE: Correction: *tertiary.*

[*As* LINDSEY *and* STEVE *continue to argue, a bespectacled young man in a military uniform descends the stairs, unnoticed and oddly out of place. This is* KENNETH, *played by the actor who played* TOM. *He carries a yellow legal pad and a transistor radio. Oblivious to the scene around him, he takes a seat by a window near the front door as* DAN *removes a yellowed envelope from the trunk.* LINDSEY *and* STEVE *prepare to leave as the bickering continues.*]

LINDSEY: Or maybe you don't *want* the baby.

STEVE: Oh! That's funny. I didn't know I had a *choice*.

LINDSEY: Oh, you had a choice.

STEVE: If only I'd *known*.

LINDSEY: And you *chose*.

STEVE: And what were the options, again? Oh that's right. A) *Let's have a baby.*

LINDSEY: Which you *chose*.

STEVE: Or B) *I'm divorcing you.*

LINDSEY: But *you* chose *A.*

STEVE: A for *Arm-twisting.*

LINDSEY: Do you have the keys?

STEVE: B for *Blackmail.*

LINDSEY: [*from outside*] Do you have them or don't—?

STEVE: [*from the door*] YES! YES I HAVE THE GODDAMN—What, you think someone's gonna *rob* this place?

[DAN *turns to see them exit.*]

Help yourselves. Fuckin' shithole.

[STEVE *slams the door.* DAN *looks around with no acknowledgment of* KENNETH.]

DAN: [*to the empty house*] Hello?

[DAN *waits for a reply. Beat, then again:*]

Hello?

[DAN *sits on the trunk, opens the letter.*]

[*Reading to himself*] Dear Mom and Dad.

[*Lights change. Music begins to play from* KENNETH'S *transistor radio, not unlike the very beginning of the play. It is early morning, 1957. Dim light filters through the window, barely illuminating* KENNETH. *He bends over his legal pad, writing, as* BEV *slowly descends the stairs, dressed in her robe and slippers. She stops near the bottom.*]

BEV: [*bleary-eyed, confused*] Kenneth?

[KENNETH *turns down the volume on the radio.*]

KENNETH: Hmm?

BEV: What are you doing down here?

KENNETH: Writing a letter.

BEV: Oh. [*Beat.*] Did your father leave already?

[KENNETH *looks outside.*]

KENNETH: I don't see the car.

BEV: What time is it?

KENNETH: Don't know.

BEV: I overslept.

KENNETH: Yup.

BEV: [*yawning*] I don't know why I was up so late. I was up half the night and the house was so quiet and your father was sound asleep but for some reason my mind was just racing and it took forever to fall asleep.

KENNETH: Go back to bed.

BEV: [*finally focusing*] Oh look how you're dressed up. Why are you all dressed up like that?

[KENNETH *stares, doesn't answer.*]

    Kenneth?

KENNETH: Job interview.

[*A key turns in the front door. It opens and* FRANCINE *enters in her street clothes with a scarf tied around her head. She carries a wet umbrella.*]

FRANCINE: Morning.

KENNETH: Morning.

BEV: Morning, Francine.

FRANCINE: Morning.

BEV: Oh, is it *raining* out there?

FRANCINE: Sprinkling a little.

BEV: I didn't even notice. Well. It's good for the grass.

[BEV *stands at the bottom of the stairs, as* FRANCINE *crosses past her and up the hallway.* BEV *hesitates.*]

KENNETH: Aren't you going back to sleep?

BEV: [*pensive*] Oh, I will. I'm just about to.

[*For a moment, she stares into space then turns to* KENNETH.]

But you know, I think things are about to change. I really do. I know it's been a hard couple of years for all of us, I know they have been, but I really believe things are about to change for the better. I firmly believe that.

[KENNETH *waits.* BEV *turns and starts back up the stairs.*]

You have enough light, there?

KENNETH: Uh-huh.

BEV: [*as she ascends*] Well, don't hurt your eyes.

[*She is gone.* KENNETH *turns the radio back up, resumes writing.* DAN *continues to read. The lights slowly fade as the music concludes.*]

INTERVIEW WITH BRUCE NORRIS

Bruce Norris won the Pulitzer Prize for Drama and London's Olivier Award for Best New Play for Clybourne Park. *His other plays include* A Parallelogram, The Unmentionables, The Pain and the Itch, Purple Heart, *and* The Infidel. *He lives in New York City.*

Rebecca Rugg: The Royal Court production of *Clybourne Park* moved to the West End and won the Olivier for Best New Play. And then it won the Pulitzer Prize for Drama. Congratulations. How was your experience in London?

Bruce Norris: It's the weirdest experience, the play is in a theater I would have fantasized about as a child, a theater with plaster angels above the stage and box seats that were built in 1899. I would have really enjoyed it if I had been there for the experience, but I feel like I was sitting outside of myself watching this whole thing happen, feeling like it was happening to someone not me.

RR: Is that because of anxiety?

BN: I have a very complicated relationship to the entire notion of commercial productions. I'm very comfortable in the not-for-profit sector because there, people are coming to theater out of obligation, or because they have a subscription and they just have to dutifully go to the theater. I didn't imagine anyone would ever willingly pay for a product that I had created. Almost in kind of an adolescent way, I have an attitude that if someone likes what I do then that means by definition it is not good.

RR: So it's not insecurity, it's something else about the ambitions of what you're making?

BN: Yes, that if I do my job correctly I should outrage people and have rotten vegetables thrown at me, that that would be the only proof that I had done something successfully. Like I said, it's completely adolescent but that's the instinct that I have. So when people like something that I've done and they pay for it, it's very confusing to me. I don't understand why they would be paying for it if I wrote it to upset them.

RR: How is life different post-Pulitzer?

BN: The most important change is that now I have a very attractive glass paperweight with the profile of Joseph Pulitzer etched into it, so my papers remain securely in place on my desktop.

RR: I read an interview between you and Tim Sanford, Artistic Director at Playwrights Horizons. In it, you recall challenging him that he didn't want to do your plays because he believes in redemption. And after that come-on, he produced *Clybourne Park*. I'm really interested in this idea of redemption and where it fits into theater—

BN: You are?

RR: Because I think that the very act of making theater itself is a hopeful act.

BN: I've heard that over and over again but I don't necessarily think that at all. I think the act of making theater is an exhibitionistic act. It's an act of drawing attention to yourself for standing up in front of people and dropping your pants, essentially. It's getting attention. We've retroactively colored the history of theater with a kind of noble purpose. I think we've internalized that idea about theater from the history of the last fifty years or so, because it's an obsolete medium and we have to try and convince people to come see it. So we no longer sell theater as something you want but as something that is good for you, or virtuous, something that uplifts you and heals you. Everyone talks about it this way. But if that's what theater really is, then it's an obligation, it's not something people want. What people really want to watch is what's on TV. They'll sit there and watch it for hours and hours and you can't pry them away from it. That's what people really enjoy watching. Theater now is just a kind of fancy cultural vitamin that you have to take from time to time.

RR: So there's nothing redemptive in making it, we're just kidding ourselves.

BN: Well, let me ask this. If you thought, if you had to say, well I wasn't redeemed in any way, there was no virtue accrued to me from seeing this thing, I am not a better person from seeing it, I just saw it, would you feel bad about yourself? And would you feel bad about yourself because of how much money you spent?

You don't feel really bad if you go to see *Jackass: The Movie;* you just feel like, "Oh, well, that was just fun." There's a production of *Three Sisters* here in New York now. Now, you know, this is a play about some boring sisters in Moscow in the 1900s and their moaning, and tickets are $110. It's off-Broadway, a little theater off-Broadway. $110! For an off-Broadway play from 1900 about despair.

RR: Watching a bunch of Americans call each other "Protopopov."

BN: Right! I find it really preposterous, like buying jeans that have been predistressed. It's like, "I need something that looks painful and worn down in order to somehow make myself feel better." For all the privilege I have to go see something punishing in order to somehow deal with the fact that I'm privileged and healthy and safe.

RR: Okay, let's talk about *Clybourne Park*, because I'm trying to imagine it in the scenario you're painting, and I feel like it's too simple, this notion of just being punished. The experience of being in the audience of *Clybourne Park*, especially as a white person, it's not punishing; you know there are several more moods that are quite complicated.

BN: Well, I think the most interesting question that has been put to me about it was the one you put to me last time we talked, which was "Did you write this play for white people?" Remember?

RR: Yeah, and you said yes.

BN: And I said yes.

RR: And I was totally shocked. I was sure you were going to say no.

BN: No, I think it is a play for white people. It's definitely a play for white people. It's a play about white people. It's about the white response to race, about being the power elite, about being the people who have power in the race argument. And what that makes us in the present day, the contortions that makes us go through. Because on the left we really, really like to deny the power that we have. We don't want to seem like we're powerful and have the largest army in the world. We want to pretend that we don't. It is even better if there are a few black people in the audience because it makes it even more uncomfortable.

I was looking at the Goodman website this morning, and I noticed that they have a play by Regina Taylor and a play by Tanya Saracho, and they make this very concerted effort to try to do plays by people of color; *Chinglish*, by David Henry Hwang, is coming up. Obviously, they are trying to create this audience that does not currently go to the Goodman Theatre, or Steppenwolf, for that matter. That would be a black audience, a Hispanic audience, or an Asian American audience. So, now that they've produced these works, I'd really like to know if the numbers of people of color in the audience have gone up. Or if what they've got is just the parade of virtue, where the white audience, still a vast majority white audience, just dutifully attends these plays. And that's great in one sense because it provides great employment opportunities for people of color in the theater, but then we can't get embarrassed or ashamed suddenly when there are plays written specifically to address the whiteness of the people who are there. *Clybourne Park* is a play addressing whiteness.

RR: Let's talk about *A Raisin in the Sun*. The plays in this anthology are all inspired by *A Raisin in the Sun*. I've heard you say elsewhere that *Clybourne Park* is for Karl Lindner. Can you talk about your early experience of encountering *A Raisin in the Sun* in school?

BN: The first two plays I became seriously conscious of in my early teenage years were *Our Town*, which I went to see because I asked my parents to take me to see a play that had scenery, and they took me to see *Our Town*, which had no scenery. The other was *A Raisin in the Sun*, which I saw as a film in probably seventh grade in a social studies class. Interestingly our social studies teacher was showing it to a class of all white students who lived in an independent school district the boundaries of which had been formed specifically to prevent being, our being, integrated into the Houston school district and being bussed to other schools with black students.

So I don't know whether our teacher was just crafty and subversive, but she was showing us this movie that basically in the end—because Karl doesn't come in until the second act—is really pointing a finger at us and saying we are those people. So I watch it at twelve years old, and I could realize even then that I'm Karl Lindner. To see that when you're a kid and to realize that you're the villain has an impact.

For years I thought I wanted to be in the play *A Raisin in the Sun* and play Karl Lindner, but then as time went on I thought it's really an interesting story to think about the conversation that was going on in the white community about the Younger family moving into Clybourne Park. It percolated for many years, and that's how I ended up writing this play.

RR: In *Clybourne Park* the white people have a more expanded role relative to each other than the black people who work for them and are then later their neighbors.

BN: Right. It's a wholly different set of incidents. The black people in *Clybourne Park* bear no relation to the black people in *A Raisin in the Sun.* Actually, in the second act they do. But in the first act, Francine and Albert are no relation to them, but in the second act Lena is the great-niece of Lena Younger.

RR: The clarity of tension in the relationships between the people of different races in *Clybourne Park* is not something I've seen onstage before.

BN: I aimed to show the way that white people—specifically in the second act—who imagine themselves to be free of any psychological or verbal complication when talking to black people, the way we accidentally trip up ourselves over and over again, and how we reveal our lingering discomfort in conversations, historical discomfort, as we have those conversations.

RR: There's an inability to speak honestly.

BN: For me, I think my discomfort is always transparent. I was at the Olivier Awards, and when they announced the nominees for lead actor in a musical, I noticed that, for some stupid reason, I clapped the loudest for the lead actor from the musical *Fela!,* who, obviously, is black. Why did I clap louder? I've never seen that musical. I don't know that person. I just reflexively clapped louder for the black person, because . . . I don't know why. To show how *non*-racist I am? I tend to either go overboard, trying to show how strong my alliance is with someone black, or, if I know the black person well, I'll go 180 degrees in the opposite direction and try to make some irreverent joke (which more often than not backfires) to show how "comfortable" I am talking about race. In any case, whatever my conversational strategy is for dealing with the obvious injustices and unfairness that still persist, however I go about it, I can't avoid the conversation.

I'm trying now to write about gender and the way that gender conversations have changed in the last fifty years or so. For some reason it's easier for us as men to say to women, "Well you have all the power," or something like that, or fling accusations around and not feel like somehow it's socially destabilizing. But to have open and free conversations about race feels very threatening, especially to white people, because we will lose in those conversations. We know we have no rhetorical leg to stand on. And so we cling to a certain kind of conversational etiquette which we think will excuse us from losing the conversation. And so we have legitimate fear of entering into conversation honestly because we know we're wrong most of the time.

RR: Can we talk about theatrical realism a little bit? Is *Clybourne Park* part of a genealogy that you can trace? How does it fit into a larger history of form?

BN: Well, I tend to write in the "realistic" form because it limits what's possible and that gives a play a rigidity, a structure. A more freeform approach to writing a play feels loose and a little bit flimsy to me. I like the firm structure that's imposed by realism, not just realistic behavior, but realistic furniture and facts. If you want to demonstrate something about the way we behave and interact with each other, then it's really useful to have a concrete world there to interact with. I think when people want to write about dreams and magic onstage, they often don't have much they want to say about behavior. They want to talk about ideas and not behavior.

RR: So how come this play has a ghost in it? That's sort of outside the limits of the concrete world.

BN: Well, you know, that's a question, whether or not it's a ghost. We go back in time . . . In the script it says, "Kenneth descends the stairs," and then we kind of segue into the past, to early morning 1957. So . . .

RR: Okay, that's fair. But it still feels like there are ways in which this play, and your other work too, is inside the form of realism and also exceeds it.

BN: *Unmentionables* and *A Parallelogram* both break the fourth wall.

I think people are sophisticated enough in their theater language now that they understand both things. I think a great deal of pleasure is derived from realism. Like watching *Who's Afraid of Virginia Woolf,* it's nice to watch the curtain come up and we know it's pretend, we're pretending we're in this house and we're pretending these characters are these people, these people are these characters. But, once you allow that to happen, just as you would when watching a movie, you know, if you're watching *Star Wars,* you don't sit there and go, "I don't believe he's really Luke Skywalker, he's really Mark Hamill." There's a pleasure to be had in surrendering that, in suspending that disbelief. But because we're in the postmodern age, we also believe in being self-referential, so both things are pleasing. But I don't think it's just pleasing to take away realism; realism has great pleasure. It's fun to watch stories of other worlds, other people, and so forth.

RR: Realism is also extremely difficult to do well.

BN: To be snarky, I think we have a lot of playwrights now who come out of graduate school programs who have been encouraged to write in a kind of way that is innovative and form changing—formally innovative—and that's great to do that but I think you're swimming upstream. I feel like, why not talk to an audience in a language that they already have? I have no interest in educating an audience and teaching them a new language, because that's something for the future, and I'll be dead in the future. Since I'm doing a play now, I want to talk to them in the language they have now.

RR: In teaching this play, the subject of the jokes arose. Students wanted to know why the black woman is spared being the punch line of a joke, from a playwright who doesn't spare anyone.

BN: It's not formulaic, as though everyone in the room has to be the butt of a joke, one by one. It's a conversation, not a formula. But also, the black woman IS the person who everyone in that room would be most afraid of offending—the one person who would be off limits. All she has to do is say she's uncomfortable and everyone gets worried.

RR: With those same students we had a long conversation about the presence of the deaf woman in the first act. I wonder if you can talk about that character and the choice to include her.

BN: Well the first thing I'll say is that deaf is funny. And I defy anyone who tells me differently. But it's not that the deaf woman herself is funny, or her deafness that's funny, it's everyone around her and how they treat her and act toward her that's funny. And it makes it clear how awful everyone is around race, that there is this false CARE taken toward her deafness. It shines a light on race, by contrast.

RR: Why isn't there a disabled person in the contemporary scenes?

BN: Well, there wouldn't be. She's deaf, and I wanted to make the point that nobody who could HEAR Karl Lindner would marry him. Who else would marry him?

RR: In *Clybourne Park,* there is a running invocation of world capitals. People in this play have an imagination of elsewhere. Where did that come from? Thematically, what's it doing?

BN: Well, it happens in both acts, people talk about foreign countries. And I think that by virtue of us being the most economically powerful country—not for long maybe—and the most militarily powerful country in the world, really an empire, there's a kind of colonial impulse. Sometimes this manifests as the desire to know things about people outside of our empire. The bad colonial impulse is to go and put your tanks in their country and take over their government or take over the government by putting your business in and employing your workers, that's the bad colonial impulse. But there is a good part of the colonial impulse, which is to wonder, "What do they eat? What kind of houses do they live in? What do they speak?" I mean, there's a good kind of curiosity there.

RR: Curiosity is good.

BN: The problem is if you have power, it's almost impossible not to use it.

The play, to be reductive, the play is about territory. And it's about looking over the boundary of your territory into other territories and about people moving from one territory to another. And it's also why there's a framework in the play of war, I mean war is a big issue in the play because of Kenneth and then becomes a smaller issue in the second act because of an insult that happens around the Iraq war. Since it's all about territoriality and looking over borders in that way, naturally what the people in both acts speculate about is what the people in the other worlds do, and what's the capital of their country, and what are their countries like, and we travel there and visit them and they give us hot tea and we don't understand that. All that stuff is what people in a powerful empire speculate about.

RR: Do you think that these issues of territory are somehow more present in our contemporary world? You know there's this whole crop of plays that are somehow examining territorialism from the perspective of *A Raisin in the Sun*. I wonder why we're looking at it from inside this house that Lorraine Hansberry built, now.

BN: I don't know. There's a confluence of events, I suppose, that leads to that. We're at the tail end of ten years in which we invaded a sovereign country that had not attacked us. And we basically played out the Vietnam War a second time, and at the same time we suddenly have a black president in the White House and we're looking at why he's being vilified and viewed as a foreigner. Why are we looking at him— 50 percent of the country's looking at him and questioning whether or not he was actually born in America and has the right to be the president. So, we keep regarding each other suspiciously, and with good reason, because if we don't tread carefully across those borders, then we invade each other and kill each other. And I think we're afraid of invading each other and killing each other here at home, just like we do overseas.

RR: We want to congratulate ourselves that we're past that.

BN: Supposedly past that.

ETIQUETTE OF VIGILANCE

Robert O'Hara

PRODUCTION HISTORY

Etiquette of Vigilance was first presented in a workshop production by Steppenwolf Theatre Company, in the First Look Repertory of New Work series, at the Merle Reskin Garage Theatre in Chicago in November 2010. It was directed by Timothy Douglas, with set design by Scott Neale, costume design by Elizabeth Flauto, lighting by Marcus Doshi, sound by Rick Sims, and production dramaturgy by Rebecca Ann Rugg. Angela M. Adams was the production stage manager. Cast was as follows:

Lorraine . . . . Alana Arenas
Travis . . . . Alfred H. Wilson

Etiquette of Vigilance was originally commissioned by

La Jolla Playhouse, La Jolla, California
Christopher Ashley, Artistic Director & Steven Libman, Managing Director

CAST:
TRAVIS—60's.
LORRAINE—Early 40's (And various other Ages)

Setting: Clybourne Park Suburbs of Chicago, IL.
Time: Sooner or Later.

Author's Notes:
This play is a hybrid.

Scenes 1, 3, 5, and 7 are to be presented with a nod towards the spare, brutal, non-realistic works of Albee, Churchill, and Parks. These scenes move forward in time.

Scenes 2, 4, 6, and 8 are from a Play titled *The Crystal Stair*, written by the character, LORRAINE. They are to be presented with a nod towards the lush, verbal, naturalistic works of Hansberry, Wilson, and Williams. These scenes move backwards in time.

No Costume Changes. No Blackouts.

[My father] spent a small personal fortune, his considerable talents, and many years of his life fighting, in association with NAACP attorneys, Chicago's 'restrictive covenants' in one of this nation's ugliest ghettos. That fight also required our family to occupy disputed property in a hellishly hostile 'white neighborhood' in which literally howling mobs surrounded our house. My memories of this 'correct' way of fighting white supremacy in America include being spat at, cursed and pummeled in the daily trek to and from school. And I also remember my desperate and courageous mother, patrolling our household all night with a loaded German Luger [pistol] . . .
    —Lorraine Hansberry

ONE.

A Poster of **OBAMA** is hung **conspicuously.**

Its caption is **"HOPE"**

TRAVIS, Appears.

He wears a T Shirt and underwear.

He Holds a drink in one hand and Whispers into a cellphone in the other.

An Almost Darkness.

TRAVIS.
(whisper)
I'd like to report some suspicious
I don't know if I want to give my name at this point
I don't feel comfortable giving that information
Can you put something in a file or
I just wanted to do my part in trying
we're suppose to report
suspicious

LORRAINE, Appears in the Almost Darkness.

TRAVIS abruptly ends his phone call.

TRAVIS.
You liked ta' scared the bejesus out of me.
LORRAINE.
What is going on here?
TRAVIS.
Nuthin'.

LORRAINE.

Why haven't you been answering-

TRAVIS.

What are you doin' here?

LORRAINE.

Where is Mama?

TRAVIS.

Gone.

LORRAINE.

Gone where?

TRAVIS.

Gone.

LORRAINE.

Would you like for me to burn
this gatdamn house down?

TRAVIS.

No, I wouldn't like that.

LORRAINE.

Then answer my question.
Where is Mama?

TRAVIS.

Gone.

Silence.

LORRAINE takes out her cellphone,
dials, lets it ring out and then.

LORRAINE.
(into cell)

Aunt Kate. If Mama is there with you
call the house or call my cell.

She ends her phone call.

Silence.

LORRAINE.

. . . When was the last time you saw her?

TRAVIS.

When was the last time **you** saw her?

LORRAINE.

Daddy

TRAVIS.

We ain't seen hide nor hair of you—

LORRAINE.

Didn't you tell me
not to show my face
around here
until things cooled down—

TRAVIS.

If you cared so damn much—

LORRAINE.

Didn't you say
you didn't want them folks
asking me questions
having my face
all up
on the evening news

TRAVIS.

I'm talkin' about before all that—

LORRAINE.

How **long** has she been gone?!

TRAVIS.

A few days—

LORRAINE.

A few days?!

TRAVIS.

That's what I said.

LORRAINE.

And I'm just now
finding out about it?

TRAVIS.

What was I suppose to do?

Send smoke signals?

LORRAINE.

You have my number.
You know where I live.

Silence.

LORRAINE.
Did she take anything with her?

TRAVIS.
Anything like what?

LORRAINE.
Clothing, jewelry
money.

TRAVIS.
Nawl.

LORRAINE.
You check the bank?

TRAVIS.
Nawl.

LORRAINE.
You didn't check.

TRAVIS.
She didn't take nothing

LORRAINE is dialing cell.

LORRAINE.
(into cell)

. . . Yes
I would like to report
a Missing Person

TRAVIS.
She give me 3 days.

LORRAINE.
(to cell)

Hold on please

(to TRAVIS)

What?

TRAVIS.

3 days.

She abruptly ends phone call.

TRAVIS.

She give me 3 days
to deal with it.

LORRAINE.

What did she say is suppose
to happen
in 3 days?

TRAVIS.

That I better be
at the end of it.

LORRAINE.

Or what

TRAVIS.

That I better be
at the end of it all.

LORRAINE.

Or. What?

TRAVIS.

Or Else.

LORRAINE.

TRAVIS.

Silence.

LORRAINE.

So she should be back
anytime now.

TRAVIS.

I suppose.

LORRAINE.

Since she already been gone
a **few** days.

TRAVIS.

. . . I suppose.

Silence.

LORRAINE.

You come to
the end of it all?

TRAVIS.

I cain't come
to the end of it all.

LORRAINE.

Why not?

TRAVIS.

I cain't just sit up here
and be fine with it.

LORRAINE.

Why not?

TRAVIS.

It's not something you just
Get over in three days.

LORRAINE.

It's been a month.

TRAVIS.

I know how long
it's been
dammit.

LORRAINE.

Just go down there
and tell them what you know
about the bomb.

TRAVIS.

I don't know nuthin' 'bout no bomb.

LORRAINE.

It was your bus
You must know something

TRAVIS.

I don't

LORRAINE.

Then tell them that.

TRAVIS.

I did.

LORRAINE.

Then tell them again.

TRAVIS.

Why are you here?

LORRAINE.

You must have really lost your mind
for Mama to get up

TRAVIS.

What do you want?

LORRAINE.

Some man on TV
said you should be hunted down
dragged through the streets
Folks are making **threats** on **TV**, Daddy

TRAVIS.

Leave me be.

LORRAINE.

How much have you had to drink?

TRAVIS.

Not enough. Get out.

LORRAINE.

I'm not going anywhere.
I'm going to wait right here.

TRAVIS.

I want you out of this

LORRAINE.

Tough.

Silence.

LORRAINE.

If Mama
don't come back here

in an hour
I'm making a missing person's report.

TRAVIS.

She ain't missin'.

LORRAINE.

Then I'm calling
the ambulance
and having them put you up in
Cook County
for an evaluation

TRAVIS.

I'd like to see that.

LORRAINE.

See if I don't have them
cart you right on off
up to
Cook County—

TRAVIS.

They been making threats
calling my phone
for weeks now.
That ain't why you come here.

LORRAINE.

Yes it is.

TRAVIS.

You up to something

LORRAINE.

You up to something

TRAVIS.

You think you can make a fool out of me.

LORRAINE.

I'm not the one
in my underwear
whispering
into my cellphone
in the dark.

Silence.

TRAVIS.

I'm not
One of them gatdamn characters
From one of them gatdamn plays
You keep talking about you gonna write
But seem to never do
I know you Lorraine
You up to somethin' gatdammit

LORRAINE.

You got one hour daddy.

TRAVIS.

You ain't in charge of ALL gatdamn TIME.

LORRAINE.

I'm gonna have this whole damn place
lit up
with flashing red white
blue

TRAVIS.

Why don't you call up the evening news too
Make it interesting.

LORRAINE.

I just might.

TRAVIS.

Where would you like
For me to **stand**
For when they come
With my straight jacket??

LORRAINE.

Right there is fine.

TRAVIS.

I'm sure they're waiting by the phone.

LORRAINE.

What you drinking?

TRAVIS.

Bourbon.

Beat.

She makes herself a drink . . .

She notices for the first time, a
terrified trembling Man.

TRAVIS.
(soft)

It got a hold of me Lorraine
It got a hold of me good
try as hard as I can
can't seem to wrestle it loose.

Silence.

LORRAINE.
(smells blood)

One good **solid** hour, Daddy.
Then all hell's gon' break loose.
Either way.
Mama show up.
Mama don't show up.
One hour
then all hell
just like that day
you played that trick on me
Member?
All hell breakin' loose.
I put **that**
in that play
I keep talking about
I'm gonna write
but never seem
to do.

TWO.

A Scene from *The Crystal Stair* by
LORRAINE.

The **conspicuous** portrait of
OBAMA is now that of **JESSE
JACKSON's** 1988 Presidential
Campaign whose caption reads
"KEEP HOPE ALIVE"

A **23 YEAR OLD LORRAINE.**

TRAVIS stares at her.

Silence.

LORRAINE.

What's the problem?

TRAVIS.

You tell me.

LORRAINE.

What's the problem Daddy?

TRAVIS.

The Po'lice just left.

LORRAINE.

What did they want?

TRAVIS.

There's been an accident

LORRAINE.
(panic)

Where's Mama?

TRAVIS.

Asleep.

LORRAINE.

Something with your Bus?

TRAVIS.

No.

Silence.

LORRAINE.

Okay.

TRAVIS.

What's going on?

LORRAINE.

"What's going on??"

TRAVIS.

Yeah, what's going on with you Lorraine?

LORRAINE.

I don't know what you're talking about Daddy

TRAVIS.

They found your ID in that car.

Silence.

LORRAINE.

What ID?

TRAVIS.

What ID you thank? Your Medical School ID.

LORRAINE.

What car?

TRAVIS.

That car what was in that accident.

LORRAINE.

What **accident**, Daddy, why are you talking like I already know what you're talking about?!

TRAVIS.

That po'lice man said that he found your ID on the **drivers** side of that car.

LORRAINE.

What??

Silence.

TRAVIS.

Do it sound like a joke?

LORRAINE.

Is this a joke?

LORRAINE.

Yes.

TRAVIS.

They didn't find the Driver. They found **your** ID. Lying there next to the dead bodies. Dead . . . Graveyard Dead.

LORRAINE.
(laughing)

That's impossible.

TRAVIS.

Why is that?

LORRAINE.

Because it is.

TRAVIS holds her ID up to her.

She stops laughing.

Silence.

TRAVIS.

You wanna explain this to me young lady?

Silence.

LORRAINE.

I must have lost it.

TRAVIS.

Where was the last time you used it?

LORRAINE.

I don't remember.

TRAVIS.

Try.

LORRAINE.

I can't remem—

TRAVIS.

Try. Harder.

LORRAINE.

I guess on my way to some party on campus . . . I must have dropped it.

Silence.

TRAVIS begins to laugh.

LORRAINE.

This is a joke!!??!!

TRAVIS.

It came in the mail today . . . some lady found it. Said she thought you might need it and since you still have our address on it, it came here.

LORRAINE.

. . . Daddy you had me come all the way out here in the middle of the night just so you can play some trick?

TRAVIS.

You don't visit anymore.

Beat.

LORRAINE.

I don't visit anymore?? I'm in medical school—

TRAVIS.

You don't call and you don't visit.

LORRAINE.

I don't have time for games.

TRAVIS.

Awww

LORRAINE.

I don't.

TRAVIS.

I was just having a little fun with you girl, calm down.

LORRAINE.

Fun.

TRAVIS.

Like when we useta make up new endings to them old movies.

LORRAINE.

This is not fun.

TRAVIS.

What's **not** fun is you **not** visiting your old folks who's paying for you
to go—

LORRAINE.

I'm on scholarship, so don't start.

TRAVIS.

I'm still paying on them damn Loans from your Undergraduate, so
don't you start.

LORRAINE.

I told you, you could have had those **deferred.**

TRAVIS.

I told **you,** that deferrin' just means **"pay mo' later."**

LORRAINE.

It takes me an hour to get here—

TRAVIS.

So?

LORRAINE.

So I can't just get up and visit on a whim!

TRAVIS.

What we do so wrong you don't want to see us no more?

LORRAINE.

I'm busy—

TRAVIS.

Don't wear yourself out Lorraine.

LORRAINE.

I won't.

TRAVIS.

Granddaddy wore hisself out.

LORRAINE.

I know.

TRAVIS.

Grandmama wore herself out.

LORRAINE.

I know.

TRAVIS.

But **you** ain't gotta wear yourself out Lorraine.

LORRAINE.

I gotta get back.

TRAVIS.

Pay more attention to what you do at them parties, you hear me?

LORRAINE.

I hear you daddy.

TRAVIS.

If you doin' something that makes you forget to call your folks—

LORRAINE.

I didn't **forget**—

TRAVIS.

—Makes you forget what's going on around you and not remember you dropped your ID and whatnot, then soon that ain't gonna be no more **fun**. That's gonna be a problem. And you come from a long line of folks with problems. You know that. Runs in your blood. So all I'm saying is, don't let your fun become your problem.

LORRAINE.

. . . I won't daddy.

TRAVIS.

Good . . .

LORRAINE.

. . . Now can I go back to School?

TRAVIS.

You might as well stay the night.

Silence.

LORRAINE.

I can't.

TRAVIS.

You can.

LORRAINE.

I can't.

TRAVIS.

You **can.**

LORRAINE.

I can't—

TRAVIS.

You. **Can** . . . Remember . . .

(mantra)

You. Can.

Silence.

LORRAINE.
(sigh)

I. can.

TRAVIS.
(fatherly order)

. . . Good. So sit down.

She does. TRAVIS pours himself
another drink.

TRAVIS.

Guess who's coming to dinner?

LORRAINE.
(unhappy)

. . . Who?

TRAVIS.

"Guess Who's Coming To Dinner" . . . It's coming on soon. I got the
Jiffy Pop

LORRAINE.

Jiffy Pop.

TRAVIS.

Your favorite.

LORRAINE relents . . . She gets up
and goes to the Kitchen. We hear the
sound of a Microwave starting.

She returns.

TRAVIS.
So. Tell me somethin' about somethin' . . .
LORRAINE.
Daddy, the last thing I wanna do is talk to you about medical school.
TRAVIS.
What you wanna talk about?
LORRAINE.
Why are you smiling like that?
TRAVIS.
I got somethin' to smile about.
LORRAINE.
What?
TRAVIS.
You.
LORRAINE.
. . . Daddy let's watch this movie please
(she smiles)
You're **already** drunk???
TRAVIS.
(smiling)
What makes you say that?
LORRAINE.
The drink in your hand. The smile on your face. The lie you told about my ID. The Jiffy.
TRAVIS.
(playful)
Maybe I had a few.
LORRAINE.
(just as playful)
How many is a few.
TRAVIS.
I'm the daddy. You're the little girl.
LORRAINE.
Daddys don't have to answer little girl's questions anymore?

TRAVIS.

Not if little girls don't wanna talk about medical school.

They smile.

TRAVIS.

Maybe I just wanted to have a movie date with my little girl.

LORRAINE.

I'm not so little anymore daddy.

She goes to the Bar.

He looks on incredulously.

LORRAINE.

You got me all the way out here now I need me a drink.

She makes a Drink As The
Microwave beeps from off stage.

LORRAINE.

You wanna get that Daddy?

After a quick moment. He starts off.
They smile at each other as he exits.

Soon he returns with Popcorn.

LORRAINE.

. . . Mama called me the other day.

TRAVIS.

Did she?

LORRAINE.

Yeah.

TRAVIS.

What she say?

LORRAINE.

Nothing much.

TRAVIS.

Nothing much about what?

LORRAINE.

. . . She was worried about me.

TRAVIS.

There something she needs to be worried about?

LORRAINE.

. . . I'm thinking about dropping out.

TRAVIS.

Like hell.

LORRAINE.

You see this is why I called mama, and not you, because I knew—

TRAVIS.

So **you** called **her**? She didn't call you. She wasn't worried about nothing but you decided to make her worry.

LORRAINE.

No I didn't.

TRAVIS.

Your mother ain't never told me she was worried about you dropping out.

LORRAINE.

Because she knows you would react the way you're acting right now.

TRAVIS.

The answer is No.

LORRAINE.
(simple)

The answer is not yours to give me, Daddy, it has nothing to do with you—I mean . . . I didn't mean it like that.

TRAVIS.

What did you mean it like?

LORRAINE.

I don't wanna be a Doctor.

TRAVIS.

You have brains girl—you're gifted—

LORRAINE.
(fact)

I don't like it.

TRAVIS.
(father)

Maybe you ain't suppose to like it. Maybe that's part of the point. Maybe it's suppose to help you push through stuff you don't like. Come out the other side a better person.

LORRAINE.

A better person who **hates** being a Doctor.

TRAVIS.
(dragon)

You are **not** Dropping OUT!!!

Silence.

They look off . . .

Silence.

LORRAINE.

I've tried everything I can to make it happen but I don't want it.

TRAVIS.

You don't want it?

LORRAINE.

I never wanted it for me. I only wanted it for you. And that isn't enough of a reason for me.

TRAVIS.

Think about what you're saying, Lorraine—

LORRAINE.

I can't keep this up . . .

TRAVIS.

You just started!

LORRAINE.

I'm not good at it.

TRAVIS.

You got a **Scholarship**.

LORRAINE.

I'm **not** . . . **good** at it.

TRAVIS.

You can get better!

LORRAINE.

I don't want to get better!

TRAVIS.

Lower your voice.

LORRAINE.

I hate it. I hate pretending I'm interested.

TRAVIS.

You are the **first** person in this family—

LORRAINE.

I hate pretending I give a damn about **that** as well!

Silence. TRAVIS Stunned.

LORRAINE.

I didn't ask for any of this. I didn't ask to grow up here. I didn't ask to be the first in the family to go to—

TRAVIS.

Are you on drugs?

LORRAINE.

No. I am not on drugs.

TRAVIS.

Then you should be.

LORRAINE.

Daddy

TRAVIS.

Who do you think you are?

LORRAINE.

I haven't had a chance to find that out!

He looks off.

She does not.

Silence.

LORRAINE.

Maybe I just need some time off.

TRAVIS.

"Time off?"

LORRAINE.

I just finished college.

TRAVIS.

What the hell is "Time off"?

Beat.

TRAVIS.

Didn't your advisor say the first semester of medical school is always the toughest?

LORRAINE.

Yes.

TRAVIS.

Then toughen up!

LORRAINE.

What if I don't want to toughen up??? What if I have something **else** inside me that I want to express.

TRAVIS.

Express??? . . . Is that what they taught you up at that college fo' four years? To "take time off" and "express."

LORRAINE.

What if I want to be—

TRAVIS.

You think this is funny—

LORRAINE.

From day one you have been pushing me—

TRAVIS.

I'm your father I'm suppose to push you!

LORRAINE.

I want you to stop right now daddy . . . stop **pushing** me . . . I want to stand **still** for a moment. I want to take a breath—

TRAVIS.
Take a breath when you're dead!!!

Silence.

He points to the Jesse Jackson
picture.

TRAVIS.
Do you think he's taking a Breath? . . . Lorraine?

LORRAINE.
Daddy—

TRAVIS.
He is running to be the **FIRST** and do you think he has time to
BREATHE???? To Stand **Still** for a moment . . . To take "Time
Off" . . .

LORRAINE.
It's not the same—

TRAVIS.
Do you know what granny and gramps—

LORRAINE.
I know.

TRAVIS.
Went through to be the **first black family** here—

LORRAINE.
I know—

TRAVIS.
Then you **know** you must be crazy to come bringing me some "I'm
thinkin' about dropping out"—You think I went to sleep as a little boy
and dreamt about driving a gatdamn bus—You think I wanted to do
that for the rest of my life? You are the only one in this family that has
a chance—

LORRAINE.
(final)
I've already stopped going to classes . . . I haven't been to one this entire
month . . . I didn't lose that ID . . . I threw it away.

Silence.

TRAVIS.
(stone)

. . . You threw it away.

LORRAINE.

Yes, sir.

TRAVIS.

You dropped out.

LORRAINE.

Yes, sir.

TRAVIS.

Just like that.

LORRAINE.

Just like that.

TRAVIS.

Threw it away and dropped out.

LORRAINE.

Start from Scratch.

TRAVIS.

Like a gatdamn cake.

LORRAINE.

. . . Yes sir.

Silence.

TRAVIS.

How you come to think that you can walk up into this house and tell
me to my face that I ain't got nuthin' to do with it . . .

LORRAINE.

I said I didn't mean—

TRAVIS.

Look in there and see those damn sallie mae perkins and whatsinever
other damn loans we got piling up on that damn kitchen table.

LORRAINE.

I've seen them—

TRAVIS.

You have the nerve to strut in here with your chin in the air chest poked out talking out the side of yo' neck about how you done up and threw away your ID and done dropped out!!!

LORRAINE.

It's my life Daddy.

TRAVIS.

Then why them damn loans in there got **MY NAME** on 'em?!!

Silence.

TRAVIS.

. . . You gon' pay me back? . . .

Silence.

TRAVIS.

Answer Me Gatdammit! . . . Is you gon' pay me back for them damn loans in there since it's **your** life with **my** name on the bill!

LORRAINE.

I can't pay you back.

TRAVIS.

Why not? What you planning on doing with yourself? Walkin' the street?

LORRAINE.

Of course not.

TRAVIS.

Then what the hell have you **been** doing since you up and threw your ID away?

LORRAINE.

I'm going to write.

TRAVIS.

Write what?! Write a letter to Sallie Mae and ask her to take my damn name off them damn Loans in there?

LORRAINE.

I'm going to be a Playwright daddy.

Silence.

TRAVIS stifles a laugh. Then he finds
he can't hold it in and bursts into a fit
of laughter.

LORRAINE, oddly enough, sees the
humor and laughs a little herself.

LORRAINE.

I'm gonna write plays . . .

TRAVIS now fully guffaws.

TRAVIS.

What I look like to you Lorraine . . . I look like one of them damn
Professors up there at that school that you can just say whatever come to
your mind when it come to your mind?

LORRAINE.

No. You don't look like one of them, Daddy.

TRAVIS.

Get out this house . . . I don't want to see you. In this house. Again.
You don't deserve to be in **this** house. With what Mama and Daddy
went through . . . to keep us in **this** house . . . and you go and **spit**
at it . . .

Silence.

LORRAINE is devastated. She looks to
her Father . . .

He clicks a Remote.

The sounds of **"Guess Who's
Coming to Dinner"** is heard.

TRAVIS sits as a stone.

LORRAINE.

... I'm ... I'm gonna write—

TRAVIS.
(stone)

And don't come back.

LORRAINE takes another brief
moment to accept the change that her
words have wrought.

Slowly, she leaves.

THREE.

OBAMA has replaced JACKSON.

TRAVIS is sitting, watching an
OLD Movie (which we can hear,
not see) as LORRAINE stands,
watching him.

They Drink.

Silence.

LORRAINE.

Did the check come today?

TRAVIS doesn't Answer.

LORRAINE clicks remote. The
Television sounds cease.

LORRAINE.

Daddy
you gon' answer my question.

TRAVIS.

What check?

LORRAINE.

You know what check
I'm talking about.
Did it come or not?

TRAVIS.

Not.

LORRAINE.

Isn't it suppose to be here
by now?

TRAVIS.

I don't know where it's suppose to be
by now.

LORRAINE.

That man downtown said
it suppose to be here
by now.

TRAVIS.

. . . What man?

LORRAINE.

That man I spoke to
down at the CTA.

TRAVIS.

What man you spoke to
down at the CTA?

LORRAINE.

Some man.

Silence.

TRAVIS.

What you go down there for?

LORRAINE.

Why can't I go down there?

TRAVIS.

What you go down there for Lorraine?
You know there's an investigation
down there.
You know there's an investigation into—

LORRAINE.

I know.

TRAVIS.
(seethe)

Then what you go down there for?

Silence.

TRAVIS.

You ain't got no business to be going

LORRAINE.

I went down there looking for you
The man down at the CTA
tells me that you haven't been to work
for going on a **month**
He says
it's almost like you just done
upped
and
dropped out.

Silence.

TRAVIS.

That's not what he told you—

LORRAINE.

He said
Mama has been making excuses

TRAVIS.

You stay from
down there.

LORRAINE.

Why?

TRAVIS.

Because I said so.

LORRAINE.

And what if I don't?

TRAVIS.

You won't see no part of
no check.

Silence.

TRAVIS.

That's what you want ain't it.
That's what you here fo'.

LORRAINE.

I came here because
I heard the threats on the Television.
I wanted to make sure you were alright

TRAVIS.

Bullshit.

LORRAINE.

I tried to call you
you didn't answer

TRAVIS.

You want that check.

LORRAINE.

I came here

TRAVIS.

You got that look in your eye.

LORRAINE.

What **look**?

TRAVIS.

That look
that my daddy had in his eyes.
When he come in asking
'bout a check
that 'pose to be comin'.
I want you to say it.

LORRAINE.

You're wrong—

TRAVIS.

That's not what I want you to say.

LORRAINE.

I don't know what you want me to say

TRAVIS.

"I want that money."
Say that.
"I came for that money."
Say **that**.
But don't tell me again
that you came to see
if I was alright.

Silence.

They Drink.

Silence.

LORRAINE.
(low)

I need
that money.

TRAVIS.

What money?

Silence.

LORRAINE.

The money from
that check.

TRAVIS.

What check?

He goes to make another Drink.

Silence.

LORRAINE.

I owe somebody
something.

TRAVIS.

If you the one owe
somebody
something
then why you asking me
for it?

LORRAINE.

He threaten me . . .

TRAVIS.

He did???

LORRAINE.

Yes sir.

TRAVIS.

Then you need to
call the po'lice.

LORRAINE.

I can't do that.

TRAVIS.

Press **CALL**
the number will pop right back up
ain't that how these new finger phones work?

LORRAINE.

I just can't do that.

TRAVIS.

9-1-1.

LORRAINE.

Daddy
I need that money.

TRAVIS.

You think
that after twenty years
of watching you walk into this house
with all different shades of lies
schemes
who shot johns
after giving you money
over
over
over
again
only to find
you didn't pay your rent with it
you didn't pay your car note
the light bill
the cable
the whatever
you was beggin' for it for

after all these years
you showing up
at the crack of dawn
like a gatdamn vampire
creepin' back to yo' coffin
you think
after all that
I believe a **syllable**
that comes cross
your lips?

Silence.

LORRAINE.

I ran
into a problem.

TRAVIS.

You gonna have to come
better than that
Lorraine baby
seeing that
I've heard
that one befo'.

LORRAINE.

I'm telling you
the truth
daddy

TRAVIS.

And that one too.

Silence.

LORRAINE.

He said
he'd kill you
and Mama

TRAVIS.

Now **that's** good.
That's a good openin'
Say that one again
Put some bass
in your voice
cause that's a
good one.

LORRAINE.
(deadly serious)

He is going to kill you
and Mama,
if I don't bring him
his money
Daddy.

TRAVIS.

That has a rang to it.
Say it one more time for me
Lorraine, baby.
Run in
like you normally do and
say it

LORRAINE.

. . .

TRAVIS.

Run In
Like the vampire
you are
And Say it!

Silence.

Slowly LORRAINE exits.

She Runs in.

Silence.

LORRAINE.
(deadly)

Daddy.
This man that I owe
is gonna kill you both.
If I don't bring him his money
by the end of the week.

Silence.

LORRAINE.

I'm in trouble.

TRAVIS.

Everybody's in trouble.

TRAVIS Drinks.

Silence.

LORRAINE.

I needed money
to do
my Play.

Dead. Silence.

TRAVIS.

Oh
this is gonna be
REAL
good!

LORRAINE.

I needed to rent a theater
pay the actors
the designers
print the—

TRAVIS.

This will be one

for the **books**!
You borrowed money
to put on yo' play
from a Drug Dealer

          LORRAINE.
          (fact)

He was the only one
I knew
with money

          Silence.

          TRAVIS.

At the end of this conversation Lorraine
I'm going to laugh
in your face
long and loud
but
right now
I'm gonna give you a shovel

          LORRAINE.

. . .

          TRAVIS.

What's **this** play about, Lorraine?

          LORRAINE.

Family.

          TRAVIS.

The same one you been writing for
10 years?

          LORRAINE.

I finished it.

          TRAVIS.

You haven't even had the good graces
to let me
and your mama
read it?

LORRAINE.

I wanted you to show up
see it
without knowing
anything

TRAVIS.

You said it was about
Family.

LORRAINE.

It is.

TRAVIS.

Then we already know

LORRAINE.

Not exactly

TRAVIS.
(fairy tale)

Oh yes **exactly**.
That story is a
simple one.
Mother and Father worked and bled their entire life
so that we could be the first black family
to move into this neighborhood.
Went through a hell called the 1960s
then
I married your mother
We moved in here
with Mother and Father
Had a baby named
Lorraine
glorious name
Lorraine
name fit for a title to it
name fit to throw its weight around
about somethin'
Lorraine
Lorraine became the first person in our family
to go to college

after that
medical school
She **drop out**
on **scholarship**
drop out
to write
plays
but
unfortunately
Lorraine
became

                        LORRAINE.

That's not the play

                        TRAVIS.

It isn't?

                        LORRAINE.

No.

                        TRAVIS.

What part did you leave out?

                        LORRAINE.

The play I wrote
Is about a Father
who pushes his daughter
away
she ends up
lost
and alone . . .

                        Silence.

                        LORRAINE.

Until one day
the Daughter returns
to find her Father
lost . . .
and alone . . .

Silence.

TRAVIS.
(quiet)

You ain't write no play
like that.

LORRAINE.

Yes I did.

TRAVIS.

No you didn't.

LORRAINE.

I sent a copy to Mama.

TRAVIS.

Yousa lie
and the truth ain't in you.

LORRAINE.

I read a book
You send a copy
to yourself
write your name over its seal
send it to yourself
never open it.
The date the post office stamps on it
is your
Copyright.

TRAVIS.

What are you going on about Lorraine???

LORRAINE.

I sent it to Mama.
Called her
told her not to open it
Just put it away.
That way you
and Mama
would have my
Copyright.

Silence.

TRAVIS.

You wrote that play about me?

LORRAINE.

About us.

TRAVIS.

You do know those people
came into this house Lorraine
took a bunch of stuff out with them?

LORRAINE.

I didn't know that

TRAVIS.

Boxes of stuff.
They came in here
took a bunch of boxes
of stuff
what you done up and wrote about me??

LORRAINE.

It's **just** a play

TRAVIS.

Just a play!
Right now the last thing I need
is for them folks to get
"just a play"
from my crazy
gatdamn

LORRAINE.

I am not

TRAVIS.

You take
10 YEARS
to write
ONE PLAY
then you seal it up
send it to **this** house
tell us

NEVER TO OPEN IT!
That ain't crazy?!

Silence.

TRAVIS.

. . . Lorraine . . .
what . . .
is in that **play?**

FOUR.

A Scene from *The Crystal Stair* by
LORRAINE.

A 1984 Official Jesse Jackson
Campaign poster Hangs where the
others were.

17 Year Old LORRAINE, holds
Popcorn in one hand and a Glass of
Whiskey in the Other.

She gives the glass of Whiskey to
TRAVIS.

They've just finished watching an
Old Movie.

TRAVIS.

You want this house Lorraine?

LORRAINE.

What I'm suppose to do with this old house?

TRAVIS.

Fix it up.

LORRAINE.

For what?

TRAVIS.

Make it nice.

LORRAINE.

For what?

TRAVIS.

Live in it.

LORRAINE.

Live in it?

TRAVIS.

You could fix this house up and make it nice for you to live in after.

LORRAINE.

Daddy I'm just about to like start college.

TRAVIS.

I know, but this house don't mean nothing to you?

LORRAINE.

I wouldn't say that it means "nothing" to me, it obviously means like more to **you** than it does to me.

TRAVIS.

I slept on my Grandmama's couch in the Southside projects until I was ten.

LORRAINE.

Here we go.

TRAVIS.

What you say?

LORRAINE.
(droning)

You slept on granny's couch. Mama and daddy slept in the dining room. You had to share a bathroom with like 5 other families, which I still think is like the nastiest thing I have ever heard. You finally moved here and got a room with a view that wasn't some piss smelling side of a project building. Had trees to climb instead of just plants on the windowsill. You've told me this like a thousand—

TRAVIS.

Mean I had some space to grow up . . . stretch out.

LORRAINE.
(drone)

"Nothing but white folks for miles around" blah blah blah

TRAVIS.

Blah blah blah?

LORRAINE.

Daddy that bedroom back there is not that big.

TRAVIS.

When I was 10 it was big.

LORRAINE.

I'm not 10.

TRAVIS.

So what should we do, knock out a wall?

LORRAINE.
(laughing)

No, you just sound like a broken record . . . Especially when you've had like your fifth bourbon, you start going on and on about how our family was like the first this and like the first that—

TRAVIS.

Why you counting how many bourbons I done had.

LORRAINE.

I'm the one that has been getting up and down making them for you.

TRAVIS.

You young kids don't appreciate nothing.

LORRAINE.

I don't need to hear you repeat over and over how bad it was and what Granny and Grandpa had to go through—

TRAVIS.

You have no idea.

LORRAINE.

I read about the '50s and '60s in school—

TRAVIS.

You read about it.

LORRAINE.

In like social studies class.

TRAVIS.

My father had to walk me to school every morning—

LORRAINE.

Yes daddy.

TRAVIS.

With spit and rocks and all kinds of nastiness raining down on us—

LORRAINE.

Well I wouldn't have been married with like a 10 year old kid and still living in my Mama and Daddy's house.

TRAVIS.

What?

LORRAINE.
(quick)

Nothing.

Beat.

TRAVIS.

Nawl, you got something to say, say it.

LORRAINE.

Y'all had a $10,000 dollar check daddy.

TRAVIS.

And?

LORRAINE.

Y'all could have moved anywhere. Ya'll didn't have to move into an all white neighborhood.

TRAVIS.

That's right.

LORRAINE.

Y'all coulda found a better apartment in like the same neighborhood you were already living in. Probably with like two baths of your own. And you wouldn't have to sleep on the living room couch.

TRAVIS.

We'd still be in the projects.

LORRAINE.

The projects down the street aren't so bad.

TRAVIS.

What you know about them projects down the street?

LORRAINE.

Nothing.

TRAVIS.

I told you to stay out from around down there.

LORRAINE.

So I'm not suppose to like visit any of my friends that live in the Projects?

TRAVIS.

I don't want you making a habit of hanging out down there.

LORRAINE.

Daddy "down there" is like 5 blocks away from here. No way I can avoid the projects. ALL my friends live "down there."

TRAVIS.

Why don't you invite them up here.

LORRAINE.

To do what?

TRAVIS.

Play in the backyard.

LORRAINE.

I'm 17 daddy.

TRAVIS.

I know how old you are.

LORRAINE.

I gotta be in by like midnight.

TRAVIS.

And rightly so.

LORRAINE.

I can't play my music loud.

TRAVIS.

Hell naw you can't play no loud music this ain't no disco.

LORRAINE.

I can't invite like a boy over.

TRAVIS.

"Like" A boy over? What you got to invite "like" a boy over for? To do "like" what?

LORRAINE.

I can't be like on the phone like after 10pm.

TRAVIS.

When you start paying "like" the phone bill you can be on it for as long as you **like**.

LORRAINE.

I can't drive your car.

TRAVIS.

Hell naw.

LORRAINE.

I can't go out to the clubs.

TRAVIS.

You can go to the Boys and Girls Club of America.

Beat.

LORRAINE.

Then you see my point. I can't like hang out. Like everybody else.
Period.

TRAVIS.

. . . Poor you.

LORRAINE.

That's right. Poor me.

TRAVIS.

You live in a house. A **house**, Lorraine. Not a Section 8 project. You
got such a tough life. Even gotta force yourself to sit still for a few hours
once a week to watch an old movie with your old man. I bet you just
can't wait to fly the coop. Just gon' get buck wild and act a fool, ain't
cha'? Is that what you waiting for? Is that what we gonna be giving up
our life saving for you to do up there at that college?

LORRAINE.

Yeah I can't wait to be a Bad Girl!!!

> She dances like a "Bad Girl" . . . They
> laugh.

TRAVIS.

Gone run and show your mama that move, see what she say . . .

LORRAINE.

I'm not gonna wake her up—she don't even want me on campus. She
want me to like commute! Don't even play with her like that.

TRAVIS.

Nawl you wanna be a Bad Girl. Gon' tell yo' mama you wanna be a bad
girl insteada a Doctor.

LORRAINE.

Shh Daddy, Please!!

> TRAVIS does a "Bad Girls" dance.

TRAVIS.

You grown Bad Girl, com' on—

LORRAINE.

Daddy—

TRAVIS.

What?

LORRAINE.

I changed my mind.

TRAVIS.

That quick?

LORRAINE.

I'm gonna be a good girl.

TRAVIS.

You gonna be a what?

LORRAINE.

A Good Girl.

TRAVIS.

. . . That's what I thought.

Silence. They smile.

He hands her his now Empty Glass.
She starts making another.

LORRAINE.

Have you ever even been down there daddy? How do you even know
what **these** projects are like?

TRAVIS.

Because I came out of them . . .

LORRAINE.

That was like 30 years ago! These are not the same projects you
remember—

TRAVIS.

No you're right. These ones gat **bigger** waterbugs.

Laughter.

TRAVIS.

Lorraine you lived in this house all your life, you could have made
friends around here—

LORRAINE.

You didn't . . .

TRAVIS.

Yes I did.

LORRAINE.

Waving hello to the folks next door while you're watering your lawn does not make them your friends, Daddy.

TRAVIS.

I had a friend . . . Ralph Lincoln.

LORRAINE.

Who was that?

TRAVIS.

Friend of mine, use to live over on Claremont.

LORRAINE.

You never said anything about a Ralph Lincoln . . .

TRAVIS.

They ran him over.

LORRAINE.

Who ran him over?

TRAVIS.

The folks next door . . .

LORRAINE.

What???

TRAVIS.

They said he ran out in front of their car going after his Ball.

LORRAINE.

And they didn't see him?

TRAVIS.

They saw him. They saw us both. The only colored kids in this whole damn neighborhood you could not help but SEE us.

LORRAINE.

Was it a hit and run?

TRAVIS.

Nawl, where they gon' run to? Next door? . . . We were playing in the street. I wasn't use to no backyard yet. I was 11 no 12 . . . I just turned 12. I'd only played stick ball in the street. That game was made for the street . . . They saw us. And ran him over. Looked me in my eye as they passed and rolled over my best friend. Turned into their driveway. Got out and walked into their damn house.

LORRAINE.

What the police say?

TRAVIS.

"What was this nigga doin' in this neighborhood in the first place?"

Silence.

LORRAINE.

You never told me that story, daddy.

TRAVIS.

There's lots of stories that I ain't never told you . . . lots of stuff you can't read about in "like" no social studies book . . .

Silence.

LORRAINE.

. . . Tell me another one.

Silence.

TRAVIS.

One night. Not too long after Ralph Lincoln's funeral. And just a couple days after his family up and moved away. I woke up to this house rattlin' . . . I walked out my bedroom . . . I met Mama runnin' down the hall . . . I got to the living room . . . and there wasn't a living room no more . . . there was a **hole** where I remember there being a living room . . . right here . . . a hole . . . somebody had bombed our house . . .

LORRAINE.

A bomb??? Here???!!!

TRAVIS.

Daddy got him a gun.

LORRAINE.

What???

TRAVIS.

One of them German lugers . . . On the night of that bombing . . . after
all the po'lice . . . and the preachers . . . and news cameras . . . after
everybody had left that night . . . I found **scraps** . . . in all the commotion
they'd been overlooked . . . but I'd found them . . . after mama and
daddy went to bed . . . little metallic pieces of something . . . wires . . .
scattered in the cracks of the corners . . . I picked them up . . . kept them
in my room for a bit . . . that little bit turned into a few months . . . then
one night . . . I woke up again . . . I went back down that hallway . . . I
saw my Daddy . . . **there** . . . mumblin' . . . to nobody . . . speakin' to a
covered hole in the floor . . . carrying his German luger . . .

LORRAINE.

. . . What was he sayin'?

TRAVIS.

. . . "They think I blew it up . . ."

Silence.

LORRAINE.

You showed it to him didn't you? You told him you found scraps, didn't
you Daddy?

TRAVIS.

I told Mama. I was too afraid to tell Daddy. Turns out she was too . . .
Mama said that after so long . . . and they hadn't found nothing new . . .
if all of a sudden they found . . . something new . . . It would be worse
. . . For all of us . . . So it's best, to say nothing. Let folks thank what
they wanna thank. She said . . . She wasn't sure . . . that Daddy didn't
have nuthin' to do with it . . . He knew we couldn't afford this house . . .
And he wanted him a liquor store.

LORRAINE.

A liquor store??? I thought you said this house was always like
granddaddy's **Dream**. And when he got that Check—

TRAVIS.

This house wasn't his Dream and that wasn't his check. That was
Grandmama's check. From Granddaddy's Life Insurance policy. She
gave my Daddy half the money from that check to buy him a liquor

store. My daddy gave that money to a friend of his to put down on the store and that friend left town with it. Granny took what was left over . . . and moved us all here.

Silence.

LORRAINE.

Daddy—

TRAVIS.

My father was a **failure**. You hear me Lorraine. Your granddaddy was a failure. In just about everything somebody could be a failure at. And my Mama. Your Grandmother. My Mama aborted what would have been my little brother. Because her husband was a failure . . . I promised myself when I had a child. She wouldn't be a failure. That's what this house means to me. That's what I want it to mean to you.

FIVE.

OBAMA hovers.

Both TRAVIS and LORRAINE are
sufficiently lit from their boozing.

TRAVIS stares at his Daughter.

TRAVIS.

That's what you wrote?

LORRAINE.

I took some Artistic License.

TRAVIS.

You took what?

LORRAINE.

A Writer
bends the truth
in order to—

TRAVIS.

Lie.
I never called my father
a **failure**.

LORRAINE.

Not in so many words.

TRAVIS.

Not ever.
In any words.

LORRAINE.

That's why it's called Artistic—

TRAVIS.

You making it sound like
he was a failure because
he wanted money
for a liquor store
Ain't nothin' wrong
with wanting to

own
something.
Even if it was a
gatdamn
liquor store.

LORRAINE.

It wasn't his money.

TRAVIS.

It was **his Daddy's** money.
He had a right

LORRAINE.

His Daddy was **dead.**

TRAVIS.

So what!
Dead White folks leave they kids
money all the damn time.

LORRAINE.

He didn't leave that money.
It was Great Gram's money
to do what she
wanted
to do with it.

TRAVIS.

And she
wanted
to give half of it
to my damn daddy
for a
gatdamn
liquor store!

LORRAINE.

It's a **play**.

TRAVIS.

A **play**
where you have me saying
my father
bombed

his own gatdamn house!
That my mama
and me
kept the pieces of that
bomb
away from the po'lice.

                                        LORRAINE.

Your character doesn't

                                        TRAVIS.

My **character?**
What the hell do **you** know about
my Character??

                                        LORRAINE.

Your character
doesn't
say your father blew up his house
he says that your father
was tormented
by the fact that everybody
THINKS
he blew up his house.

                                        TRAVIS.

And what the hell
do you thank the
FB gatdamn I
is gonna
thank
when they read
THAT?

                        Silence.

                        LORRAINE.

You don't know
for sure
that they found it.

TRAVIS.

It was in a
sealed envelope
hidden in this gatdamn house
somewhere.
Trust me.
They **found** it!
They took **boxes!**
They was here for 20 hours **straight**.
Loading shit up.
The FB gatdamn I
is use to putting
2 and 2
together
getting 5.
They investigatin' me
and you go and write

LORRAINE.

They ain't investigating you
they investigating the bombing

TRAVIS.

I told people Lorraine!

LORRAINE.

Told people what?

TRAVIS.

All these damn folks walking around
down there
scared to death
because somebody
FINALLY
blew up a Bus.
Like they didn't see this coming!

LORRAINE.

What did you tell people, Daddy?

TRAVIS.

I told them folks
when they knocked those

two damn buildings
down
up there
in New York City
they was COMIN'
for the Buses next!

LORRAINE.
(scared)

You said that to folks
down at the CTA??

TRAVIS.

Been tellin' them that for years!!
Didn't nobody wanna listen to me.
Not your mama
Not the folks down at the CTA
Not even the FB gatdamn I.
Those same folks that didn't
give a damn when
Bombs
were being put on Busses
when **IIII** was a kid
Running around **now**
scared as all hell
that somebody
has come over here
and started blowing up shit
They think this the first time
somebody
blew up a **Bus**??!!
They have the **nerve** to
INVESTIGATE ME???!!!!

LORRAINE.

Daddy—

TRAVIS.

YOU
done up and gave them
Proof!!

Silence.

Silence.

TRAVIS Reaches for the Bottle.

LORRAINE grabs it out of his reach.

Silence.

LORRAINE.

How it feel?

TRAVIS.

How what feel?

LORRAINE.

Drankin' ya'self to death.
How that feel?

TRAVIS.

Give me that bottle Lorraine.
I bought that damn liquor
I'm gonna drank just as much as I like.

LORRAINE.

You done set you up a pretty picture.
Mama come home and find you bent over

TRAVIS.

Give me that drank!

LORRAINE.

. . .

TRAVIS.

LORRAINE!!!

LORRAINE.

. . .

TRAVIS.

You give me that drank
or
I'll take that damn check
rip it to shreds.

Silence.

LORRAINE slowly pours him a Drink.

TRAVIS.

More.

She pours More.

TRAVIS.

More Gatdammit!

She pours him even more.

He drinks.

Silence.

Silence.

LORRAINE.

PTSD.

TRAVIS.

What?

LORRAINE.

Post Traumatic Stress Disorder.
That's what you got.

TRAVIS.

Hell you talkin' 'bout?

LORRAINE.

Born in the ghetto
Moved to an all white suburb at 10
Just when you think all the wars are over
They blow up your Bus
You got a post traumatic stress disorder
if there ever was one.
Your whole life has been
one big disorder, Daddy.

TRAVIS.

I got a Disorder
then you and all these
gatdamn signs
color codes
give it to me.

LORRAINE.

How I give it to you?

TRAVIS.

You were the one
suppose to go all the way
Mama and Daddy
left the projects and came here.
You left here and went to the Projects
They thought this house
would put this family
on the right road
Instead
it tore us apart
left a hole in the center.
You.
You the hole, Lorraine.
In the center of this family.

LORRAINE.

Maybe it's genetic.
Maybe you passed
your hole
down to me, Daddy.

TRAVIS.
(dark)

When your Mama and me gone.
Ain't gonna be nothing left
but a hole.

Silence.

Silence.

LORRAINE.

Why did Granddaddy leave you
and Granny
a year after you moved in?

Silence.

TRAVIS.

He didn't leave us.

LORRAINE.

That's not what mama told me.

TRAVIS.

I don't give a hot damn what she told you.
My daddy didn't leave me.

LORRAINE.

What he do?
Take a coffee break?

TRAVIS.

Yeah.

LORRAINE.

That coffee musta had some liquor in it cuz
he never came back

TRAVIS.

He came back!

LORRAINE.

Now who's taking **Artistic License**, Daddy?

TRAVIS.

My daddy did not leave us and
he wasn't a **failure**!

LORRAINE.

You ain't even read the play—

TRAVIS.

The FB gatdamn I
is the one that's doing the reading.

LORRAINE.

Well then I wonder if they've gotten to the part
about that woman I met down
in the projects.

TRAVIS.

What woman?

LORRAINE.

I meet a lot women
in the projects.

TRAVIS.

I bet you do.

LORRAINE.

You told me you'd
never
been down there.

TRAVIS.

I haven't.

LORRAINE.

I met **her**, Daddy.

TRAVIS.

You ain't meet nobody!

LORRAINE.

Said her name was
Ruth.

TRAVIS.

. . .

LORRAINE.

You gave her Granny's name . . .

Silence.

LORRAINE.

There's a nice little scene
in my play
where I tell you I met her.
Where I finally gather up enough courage
to stand in your face
tell you **I met her**.
When I was **14**
I met her.
I didn't have the courage to tell you then.
I do now.

TRAVIS suffers.

LORRAINE.

She looked like I look . . .
Same crook in the eyeline.
Same bend to the lips.

TRAVIS.

. . .

LORRAINE.

How many more out there?
How many more I gotta run up on
after you gone?

Silence.

LORRAINE.

How many

TRAVIS.

Two.

LORRAINE.

Only two?

TRAVIS.

Two! . . . Gatdammit.

LORRAINE.

Does Mama know?

TRAVIS.

Yes.

LORRAINE.

You got yo' mouth wet
let somethin' **slip** out

Silence.

LORRAINE.

Them other two
you sure they ain't gonna come
for this house
when you gone?

TRAVIS.

This ain't they house
this your house, Lorraine.

LORRAINE.
(deadly)

So I can burn it down
if I want.

TRAVIS.

You know how many folks
down there
wish they had something
like this?

LORRAINE.

I know of at least
one
named
Ruth
that do

TRAVIS.

White picket fence
Backyard
swing set
garage
Lorraine
you don't even know
you sitting here on top of
the gatdamn
American Dream.

LORRAINE.

Daddy
you don't even know
you **stuck**
inside it.

Silence.

LORRAINE.

They got a reward out

TRAVIS.

So what.

LORRAINE.

For any information
leads to the arrest

TRAVIS.

I know

LORRAINE.

I was thinking
of making
something
up

TRAVIS.

Something
like what?

LORRAINE.

How many drinks did you have
before you got behind
the wheel of that Bus?

TRAVIS.

Wasn't nothing wrong with **ME**
or
that bus when
I got in it that morning.

LORRAINE.

How many dranks, Daddy?

TRAVIS.

Who you think you talking to, Lorraine?

LORRAINE.

I'm thinking about making me up
a nice new scene for my play.

TRAVIS.

With yo' track record
I'll be dead by the time
you finish.

LORRAINE.

This is going to be
a very short scene, Daddy.
In fact
I just might use it as my
epilogue.

TRAVIS.

As yo' what?

LORRAINE.

Epilogue.

TRAVIS.

And what's that?

LORRAINE.
(dark)

**it's what happens
when you come
to the end of it all.**

Silence.

LORRAINE.

Tell me about that morning.

TRAVIS.

. . .

LORRAINE.

If you don't
I'll take some more
Artistic Licenses.

Silence.

He holds his glass out to her. An
Offer.

Slowly She fills his glass. An
Acceptance.

SIX.

A Scene from *The Crystal Stair* by
LORRAINE.

There is an Empty Frame where
OBAMA had been.

Static from the Television.

TRAVIS has passed out with a Glass
of Bourbon in his hands.

A 14 Year Old LORRAINE is next
to him holding a Bottle.

She takes in Her Father for a
Moment.

She screws the top back on the
Bottle and Removes the Glass from
TRAVIS' hand.

She finds the remote. Click.

She returns the items to the BAR.

TRAVIS.
(waking. quiet. drunk)

. . . Where you been?

Beat.

LORRAINE.

. . . Down the street.

TRAVIS.

. . . What time is it?

LORRAINE.

Not that late.

TRAVIS.

You know what your curfew is on a School night.

LORRAINE.

Daddy.

TRAVIS.

Don't Daddy me Lorraine. I done told you about side steppin' out this damn house.

LORRAINE.

Mama said I could.

TRAVIS.

She say you can stay out to all hours of night down there runnin' the streets?

LORRAINE.

I wasn't runnin' the streets, Daddy.

TRAVIS.

Then where the hell have you . . .

He stops Himself.

Silence.

TRAVIS.

. . . I ain't forget.

LORRAINE.

It's alright daddy.

Silence.

TRAVIS finally sits fully up out of his stupor.

TRAVIS.

Did your uh . . . Did your mama give you that uh . . .

LORRAINE.

She gave it to me . . . Thank you . . .

TRAVIS.

Was it the right size?

LORRAINE.

I'm wearing it daddy.

TRAVIS.

Oh . . . okay . . . yeah that's nice . . . Let me have a look at you . . .

She moves closer.

TRAVIS.

. . . That's the one you wanted right?

LORRAINE.

Yes sir.

TRAVIS.

You like it?

LORRAINE.

I like it.

TRAVIS.

Happy Birthday.

Beat.

LORRAINE.

. . . Thank you daddy.

TRAVIS.

You bout grown ain't cha?

LORRAINE.

I'm 14.

TRAVIS.

You **Old**.

LORRAINE.
(smile)

No I'm not.

TRAVIS.

Yes you is. Look at cha'. You bout ta bust outta here ain't cha?

LORRAINE.

Daddy you silly.

> TRAVIS.

You the one silly.

> Silence.

> TRAVIS.

You have a good time with your friends.

> LORRAINE.

Yes sir.

> TRAVIS.

What movie y'all see?

> LORRAINE.

. . . We ended up not seeing anything.

> TRAVIS.

Then what you do?

> LORRAINE.

We just hung out . . . nuthin' much.

> He notices the silent Television.

> TRAVIS.

Why you turn the TV off? I was watchin' something.

> LORRAINE.

You passed out.

> TRAVIS.

I ain't pass out . . . hell you talkin' bout . . . just resting my eyes . . . Turn the TV back on . . .

> She notices the Empty Frame.

> LORRAINE.

What happened to the Poster?

> TRAVIS.

It was old. Bout time for a new one . . . Plus I tripped into it.

> LORRAINE.

Its just an empty frame now . . . that looks weird.

TRAVIS.

Well . . . Ain't it about time we had a place to put your awards and stuff.

LORRAINE.

I don't have any awards and stuff.

TRAVIS.

Your . . . diplomas.

LORRAINE.

I don't have any diplomas, Daddy.

TRAVIS.

Just wanted to make some space for when you do.

LORRAINE.

(laughing)

Daddy, diplomas don't come that big.

TRAVIS.

(laughing)

They don't?

LORRAINE.

No they don't.

TRAVIS.

. . . Oh . . .

Silence. He nods off.

LORRAINE.

I'm going to bed. You okay?

TRAVIS.

Yeah I'm fine. I told you I was just resting my eyes . . .

Beat.

LORRAINE.

Good night Daddy.

TRAVIS looks around the couch.

She lets him search for a bit.

LORRAINE.
(indicating Bottle and Glass)

I put it back on the Bar.

TRAVIS.

What you do that fo'?

Silence.

LORRAINE goes back to the BAR and retrieves the Bottle and Glass.

She holds his glass out to him. An Offer.

He takes it.

Slowly She fills his glass. An Acceptance.

SEVEN.

OBAMA has Returned.

TRAVIS speaks. LORRAINE
listens.

TRAVIS.

I got to the station
same time
I get there every morning.

Got on my bus . . .
Started out on Beaumont Dr.
Picked up my usuals.
Everybody tryin' to
beat back that wind.
Kids started to get on.
Chatter.
Cellphones.
Laughter. Long. Loud.
Trying to stay warm.
Heat just kickin' in
Once I'm full I'm full.
I don't play that mess
stuffin' everybody up in there
like sardines
or something.
Folks know on my route
I'm full
you wait for the next one.
I fly pass a few stops
angry faces
cussin' me out
Then I feel it.

LORRAINE.

Feel what?

TRAVIS.

When I gotta go I gotta go.
Folks use to it with me.
Ask any of them folks
on that bus they'd say . . .

Silence.

LORRAINE.

What would they say?

Silence.

TRAVIS.

When I gotta go
I gotta go

I pull up alongside the BP
Cashier tossed me the keys
to the men's room
I do my bizness
next thing
I know

I'm standing outside again
holdin' myself in my hands

the whole buildin' just lifted up

there I stood

nuthin' but flat grey specks
floatin' 'round me

like god done dirtied up
a snow storm . . .

Silence.

Silence.

He looks directly at LORRAINE
now . . .

TRAVIS.
(barely)

Your Mama
She give me 3 days
To come to the end of that

To come to my
. . . epilogue

Said when she gets back
she wants me at work

Or back
down there

Telling them folks
what they want to know

But

I can't get them children
out my head

they knew me

Silence.

TRAVIS.

That was the **FBI**
I was speaking to when you

showed up
I called them on the folks
next door.

LORRAINE.

For what?

TRAVIS.

Because they **Muslims** . . .

LORRAINE.

So you gonna do to them
what the white folks tried
to do to you
Run 'em off.

TRAVIS.

they live next door
they know where I work
they know my comings and goings
who knows what else they know

the signs say
if you see something
say something.

LORRAINE.

What did you see?

TRAVIS.

Something

Something
seem lak I will never
stop seeing.

Silence.

TRAVIS.

Pour me another drank, Lorraine.

LORRAINE pauses.

She does. She hands the drink to
him.

He doesn't take it.

Instead he looks at her for a long
moment.

He takes the Check out of his pocket.

TRAVIS.
He really threaten to kill us, Lorraine?

Silence.

LORRAINE.
No sir.
I need that money
To put on my play.
TRAVIS.
They took up a collection
they know the family of them kids
probably gon' sue
But this check
This check got **blood** on it.

Silence.

He hands the Check to her.

Slowly. They exchange items.

LORRAINE.
I'll get this back to you Daddy.

Silence.

Slowly, having gotten what she came
for . . .

LORRAINE begins to leave.

TRAVIS.

I should have walked you to school.

LORRAINE stops.

TRAVIS.

No matter where Daddy was
Even after he left us
he would show up
walk me to school

LORRAINE.

I took the bus.

TRAVIS.

We should have walked
held your hand
walked
could have told me
your dreams

I kept you locked up
a princess
moment I let you out
fell apart

LORRAINE.

Falling apart
was easier than you think.

TRAVIS.

I saw it coming
I looked out that window
saw
white folks moving out

heard
projects moving in

that place down there

                 LORRAINE.

That place **saved** me.

                 TRAVIS.

That place gave you somewhere
to be nothing

                 Silence.

                 LORRAINE.

I'm not nothing

                 TRAVIS.

I ain't mean it like that.

                 LORRAINE.

I'm depressed

Most of my life
I've been depressed

                 TRAVIS.

Lorraine—

                 LORRAINE.

I'm a drunk.

                 TRAVIS.

. . .

                 LORRAINE.

You're a drunk.

                 Silence.

                 LORRAINE.

Granddaddy
was a drunk.

                 Silence.

LORRAINE.

I've had suicidal thoughts and stuff

TRAVIS.

Why didn't you ever tell
somebody

LORRAINE.

I told Mama

TRAVIS.

When?

LORRAINE.

I was . . .
I told her.

Silence.

TRAVIS.

What did she say?

LORRAINE.

"Black people don't get depressed.
We don't have time for all that."

TRAVIS.

We could have gotten you help

LORRAINE.

You ever wonder
why Mama
would always go to bed early?

TRAVIS.

I don't remember her
always going to bed early.

LORRAINE.

She was never around, Daddy.
At night.
She was always asleep early
it was always just you
and me
making up new endings
to old movies.

She was always
too tired

LORRAINE.

. . .

Silence. She looks off.

TRAVIS.

Down there . . .
I didn't have to be the first
the best
down there
I could sit out
in the sun

day dream

They have this big
round
square
in the middle
deep in the middle of the projects
they have this circle
square
Beautiful tall trees all around
you'd never know from the outside
right smack in the middle
something so beautiful
sunlight stream down
I use to sit there.

TRAVIS.

day dreaming . . .

LORRAINE.
(glorious)

Day dreaming
Daddy
every open window a plot line

every piece of music a sound track
little scratches of conversations
smells from the kitchens
everywhere you looked
adventures
dramas
love stories

middle of the projects

open myself up
new things
anything
everything

I knew
I was a writer
Never had been to a play in my life
but I was going to be a
Playwright

down there

every time I try
put something down
make something
concrete
another
Tall Tale
pop up
I'd follow that down
the hole
start all
over
over
over again

one day

on the news
this man
Black man
standing in the middle of a square
sunlight
beaming
down on him
somewhere close
television said he was
close
standing there at a microphone
wanted to be
President
a few train stops away from me
standing **there**
wife
two little girls
by his side
wanted to be

President

this Black man
I said
If **he** won
If **he** stuck in
finished the race

I would **finish**
my play

everyday
turn on the tv
he still there

still in the race

I write

next week
he stuck in
I **write**

next month
He stuck in

I **WRITE**
It **STUCK**

He finished the race
Daddy

I finished
that very day
I finished

on my way down to
Grant Park
made a copy
signed my name over the seal
put it in a mailbox
sent it

here

home

one play

10 years.

                                        Silence.

Silence.

TRAVIS takes her in his arms.

TRAVIS.

How does it begin, Lorraine?
Tell me how your play begins

LORRAINE.

with you
holding me
in your arms

EIGHT.

A Scene from *The Crystal Stair* by
LORRAINE.

A Portrait of MLK hangs in the place
of all the others.

TRAVIS holds an Infant in his
Arms, in the moonlight of the Living
Room.

LORRAINE watches from the
Wings.

END.

INTERVIEW WITH ROBERT O'HARA

Robert O'Hara is a director and playwright. His Antebellum *won the 2010 Helen Hayes Award for Outstanding New Play, produced at the Woolly Mammoth Theatre Company.* Insurrection: Holding History *received the Oppenheimer Award for Best New American Play in its world premiere at the New York Shakespeare Festival, which he also directed. His other widely produced works include* Booty Candy, Good Breeding, Brave Brood, *and* American Maul. *He also rewrote* The Wiz *for its revival at La Jolla Playhouse, directed by Des McAnuff.*

Rebecca Rugg: Tell me about the origins of your play *Etiquette of Vigilance*—where does it arise from for you?

Robert O'Hara: La Jolla Playhouse asked me to consider the state of African Americans at this point in history. That seemed to me to be too big of a question to tackle and not really that interesting for a play for me to write . . . But I've always wanted to do something with *A Raisin in the Sun* . . . A play that I think is truly amazing . . . I was always struck by how people think the play's ending is uplifting. A broken family moving into a house they CANNOT afford (they only have enough for a down payment).

Why on earth would anyone think that this fucked-up family would make it through the sixties segregated Chicago suburbs intact . . . And what of the young boy . . . ? Travis is ten at the end of *Raisin* . . . He has slept all those ten years on the couch in a living room of chaos . . . And at the end of the play he is thrust into one of the most brutally racist and violent points in our history in one of the most brutally racist cities in our country . . .

[Martin Luther] King famously moved into an apartment on the West Side of Chicago to protest the vicious segregation in that city, and he had several of his most violent encounters on the marches through the white suburbs of Chicago . . .

How would the historical reality play into the lives of the dysfunctional family we are left with at the end of *Raisin* . . . So I thought I'd play with that idea in mind . . . What is the legacy of segregation . . . the legacy of *A Raisin in the Sun* . . . And what might be the legacy of the first black president . . . on African Americans . . .

Those are all questions around which I've created this play and which have no answers, but what feels very resonant to me is the way that we look at domestic terrorism NOW as opposed to the church bombing, house bombing, lynching, and brutalization of African Americans that has been a part of American history . . .

How does that history affect a person's sleep, can you have a post-traumatic stress disorder from simply LIVING in America today . . . Those are the ramblings surrounding the creation of this play . . .

Finally, how does one become an artist today . . . What if you don't have an MFA, or have never seen a play before . . . How does one tap into their creative expression in such a hostile environment . . . And so you have Lorraine . . . a woman caught inside the deferred dreams of her father and his family's legacy . . .

RR: **Why turn to questions of neighbors and neighborhoods today in the age of Obama?**

RO: Well, I live in Fort Green, Brooklyn. When I moved to the neighborhood, there were barely any white people around me. There were certain streets and corners that I would not really venture into, and I lived there! I'd walk in the opposite direction. It's really amazing . . . after all these years in the neighborhood . . . now we've got white folks here.

My neighborhood has definitely changed, and now it's a very, very different place. There are low-income houses, but now there are also these million-dollar condos. Where, eventually, are these low-income houses going to go? And why would anyone pay a million dollars to live across from a project? Laundromats, grocery stores, have all been replaced by various gourmet places that many people can't afford. If I can't walk across the street to do my laundry because it's been turned into a parking lot for folks in the condo who have a washing machine inside their apartment, then I'm going to have to walk further to do my laundry, and that's the cycle, and eventually I'm going to have to move. It's a weird thing . . . whether it has to do with the play, I don't know.

And I think Obama's election colors all different types of things: how we talk to each other, how we disagree with each other.

RR: **Neighborhoods are a good place for investigating these ideas just because, as you say, they're a template for how people live side by side.**

RO: *If* they live side by side. It's very weird because we're about to buy a condo at the edge of the neighborhood, and it's really amazing because the front of the building looks off into Manhattan and the Brooklyn and Manhattan Bridges, and the back of the building overlooks the projects. It's the same building. The people who are coming in are very, very different people than the people who've lived in Fort Green for a long time. Including gay couples. So, there's some sense that we can be an openly gay couple in this neighborhood now. So a gay couple, if you have enough money and they build the right building, will bring other gay people into the neighborhood, and that's basically what's happened. I even had one broker in a condo tell me that she "always likes to help out my gay people" . . . she was THAT forward in trying to get us into her building.

RR: Is there a lot of tension in Fort Green around the gentrification?

RO: You know, I don't think so, I don't think there's a lot of tension because people were expecting it. It happens all over New York and very often . . . For me, it feels like a very, very safe place now. I don't think it was ever like a really dangerous place, because I would never move into a very dangerous place, but the *idea* of it was dangerous because it was "Brooklyn," and I'd lived all my time thus far in Manhattan. And there are as many streetlights; there weren't as many places where you could go have a drink in a lounge. There were bodegas and liquor stores and check cashing places. Now, it's all changed. Now, Chase is here. Bank of America is here, Doggy Spas, etc.

I'm disconnected because as a playwright, I live a very solitary life. I'm not often walking the streets. When I do, it's usually in other cities where my work is being done or where I'm directing something. My relationship to my neighborhood is usually grocery stores, BAM, or the movies. I don't really participate in the day-to-day activity of my neighborhood. As for laundry . . . we have our own machines in our apartment, and our own pool, gym, and even movie theater, inside the building. So basically, I don't have to go out. I've created a neighborhood inside of a neighborhood.

RR: Inside of your building! With that in mind, it doesn't seem strange at all that one of the things *Etiquette* investigates is neighborhoods.

It also, obviously, is in dialogue with theater history. Where do you place your play in the genealogy of theater, and particularly African American theater history?

RO: In a crazy way, there are neighborhoods in theater as well. And I haven't really found anyone like me in my neighborhood, and nor do I want to. I like being around people who are completely different. And so my work is usually to investigate the places where I am not.

This is a one-set play, which is not something that I normally do. And it's also a two-person play, which is also not something I normally do. I mean, I have written a two-person play before called *The Living Room,* about the last two white people on earth who happen to be trapped in their living room, but it wasn't set in a real place.

Etiquette takes account of the historical reality. When I was writing it, I was wondering what was going on with African Americans, as that's what the original commission was for. But I realized, "I have no idea, you'd have to ask somebody else." We've come to this idea that one person can speak for a community, just as, for instance, if one neighborhood is bad, or one neighborhood has issues, then every neighborhood like that has the same issues. This is not okay.

I don't know what's happening with African Americans. I only know what's happening with me. But there's a monolithic idea that if I write about it, it's saying something about the minds of African Americans, and that's limiting to me.

As I said, I like to investigate where I'm not. I like to investigate where we think we've been. *A Raisin in the Sun* is a huge, brilliant, iconic piece of work. It's gotten a lot of scholarly attention. There's a lot of protection surrounding it, and my interest is to go in and just break into the protected walls of neighborhoods called black theater or *A Raisin in the Sun* or so-called "one-set plays" or "two-person plays" and see how I can wiggle my way into a window and break in.

RR: I love the idea of your play as itself an act of neighborhood integration, or transgression.

RO: It's vandalism in a way. I'm taking things. I'm going into someone's house—theater is someone's house—and I'm changing the furniture around. And stealing what I need from *Raisin,* and sitting around and eating dinner. But I know when they're coming home. And I'll just hide in the closet.

RR: That's such a great image—the writer Robert O'Hara hiding out in the closet, rewriting the scene on a laptop as it's happening. Fantastic.

RO: I was a kid who grew up in a sort of mad way . . . my parents didn't take me to the theater, they didn't walk me to school, it wasn't a "let's all sit together and read a book" upbringing. My cultural education came from my own nosiness. I think often of this kid, Travis, who was the heart of *A Raisin in the Sun,* for me at least. We never really deal with him or his situation in the play or with what happens after *A Raisin in the Sun.* So, I always think, where is that kid? What has not been investigated about him? Where is he for the majority of *A Raisin in the Sun*? It's a three-hour play, and we see him maybe a few times? Is he in the street? Where is he? Where is your ten-year-old kid, who sleeps on your couch, at 9:00 at night? Where is he?!! Because I always had to be at home in bed at like 8:00 P.M. when I was a kid.

RR: And you also ask what happens to his kid? Your play captures and investigates the whole idea of generational legacy.

RO: Yes. How fixing Dad a drink turns into fixing yourself a drink. How having to listen to Mom and Dad talk about the fact that "we don't need a baby" turns into how I deal with having a baby. Or a liquor store. Or a grandma. How waiting for a check turns into something really big, a check that no one worked for. What's your entitlement? Where does a sense of entitlement come from? And Travis—who's teaching Travis how to be a man, if there is such a thing? The world is in 1959. Shut the door on the play, and we're in 1960s suburbs of Chicago.

RR: One of the most racially incendiary cities in the country.

RO: Right, it's ridiculous. And the play takes Travis from the couch, and now he has a room to himself, but we know that outside there is a mob. He's in a wonderful spacious bedroom with a mob outside!

RR: You have so much compassion for Travis and attachment to him.

RO: Well, I was completely isolated as a kid. I was one person in school and another when I was at home, and they were just completely different, and no one seemed to care. It was just sort of expected that I would adjust and be fine, and, unfortunately, I didn't adjust. I became a playwright and director. I never really feel comfortable anywhere.

RR: Why do you think there are so many plays right now that are reflecting on *A Raisin in the Sun* in particular? It's curious.

RO: I think that every now and then people turn back to certain classics. Obama's election was a historical event. Those people in *Raisin* could not imagine an Obama. Now there's an examination of that generation before Obama, who could not imagine an Obama, and the feelings we have for them. Also, I think that every now and then, people want to look back and stick a knife into something. I know, as an African American, there's this mental annihilation that I feel, especially as an artist when I see white artists getting more exposure, more opportunities, so we place a sort of limit on ourselves. So that we don't get our emotions up too much or that we don't invest too much into getting a production because the disappointment when you look at the season schedules of the American theaters can be heartbreaking. That's an artist's life . . . Rejection has very little to do with being black; being black just makes us better able to adjust to it afterwards, I think.

RR: It's a crowded, small room.

RO: Exactly, it's crowded, and we're suspect of each other. You have to kill five of us to get one of us in the room. And so with Obama, there's a knowledge that now we're in the room, and not only are we in the room, but we have every right to be in the room. I've always felt that way . . . it's something that George C. Wolfe taught me . . . While we always thought we had a right to be here, now we can openly WRITE about being in the room, and we can kill off those other rooms. In a way, I love *A Raisin in the Sun* so much that I want to kill it. I want to strangle it to death because I love it so much.

RR: George C. Wolfe uses similar language in talking about *The Colored Museum*, of killing off his theatrical forebears.

RO: I think it's the restless role we're so attached to that makes us want to slit their throat, and take a knife in the air and shout, "Look at me" or "Let's stop going to that well, and let's build a new well!" You put poison in the water so that now you have to find some other source. And because there's a sense that certain things like race or *Raisin* is sacred, there's been a sense that "It's hot, don't touch it!" Now, I just think people are ready: "I'm going to touch it!" He wasn't supposed to run for president . . . well he did. We're not supposed to vote for a black person . . . well, we did. Now what?

RR: Also in the group of people investigating *Raisin* is Bruce Norris, who's a white guy. I wonder about the different resonance it has for him to poke around that house.

RO: Bruce Norris will get a lot more opportunities for his play than mine, I mean it's obvious. People are more likely to produce a nine-person play by a white person than a two-person play by a black person. You know? It's just a fact. So, you can follow that rabbit hole and become a crazy person or you can appreciate the people who are actually looking in your direction.

RR: I'm also interested in how you are all looking at each other, in how it feels like there is a conversation between the plays themselves or maybe between all of you as writers.

RO: Bruce and I had a conversation because we were both writing our plays at the same time . . . We were just in shock that we were both writing about the same period. *A Raisin in the Sun* came up, and we both talked about how we were approaching it. I was very excited to see how he pursued it because I loved *The Pain and the Itch*—it was such an incredibly mad play, so I wanted to see what he would do, like how he would see it, how he would touch the chord of *A Raisin in the Sun*. And I thought that mine was going to be a very, very small sort of look into a window, and not really at *A Raisin in the Sun* but a look at its aftereffects. So that was our conversation. I think we were a little bit wary of revealing too much to each other because as writers we want to keep the mystery to ourselves sometimes. It was wonderful because I'm a big fan of his, actually. And, having seen *Clybourne Park,* I felt what was wonderful was the audacity behind the play. I think that's so exciting. And so necessary.

RR: What about *Neighbors*? In some ways, it feels more like a play I would expect from you than the one you've written—it's big and messy, and, in those respects, has some great similarities to your play *Insurrection*.

RO: Well, I've gone down the rabbit hole. I'm going to other people's houses now. *Neighbors* feels like it was written by someone with something "hot on the tongue" to say. And I love that about the play . . . it feels like Branden was getting something out, throwing something up and OUT . . . just like I did with *Insurrection* . . . folks told me that there was just too much stuff happening in *Insurrection* and it was trying to deal with a whole lot of stuff at the same time—slavery, homosexuality, family, race, history, musicals, love, revolution—and my response has always been, YES . . . it is all that and MORE . . . it was an "Insurrection" against all of the educational training I'd had in the theater . . . I said to myself, I want to put it alllll up there . . . I had something HOT on my tongue . . . just like Branden seems to have with *Neighbors* . . . I don't have that hot on my tongue anymore . . . I have other tastes now . . . let someone else be spicy . . . so like *Clybourne Park,* I loved the audacity of *Neighbors* . . .

LIVING GREEN

Gloria Bond Clunie

PRODUCTION HISTORY

Living Green was first presented by Victory Gardens at the Biograph Theater in Chicago in February 2009. It was directed by Andrea J. Dymond, with set design by Mary Griswold, costume design by Judith Lundberg, lighting by Mary Badger, sound by Mikhail Fiksel, and production dramaturgy by Aaron Carter. Cast was as follows:

Angela Freeman . . . . Ann Joseph
Frank Freeman . . . . Kenn E. Head
Dempsey Freeman . . . . Samuel G. Roberson Jr.
Carol Freeman . . . . Aurelia Clunie
Mr. Parks . . . . Cedric Young
Shondra Davidson . . . . Melanie Brezill
Buddy Davidson . . . . Corey Marshaun Cantrell

CHARACTERS

(in order of appearance)

(3 females, 4 males)

Frank Freeman, early forties, successful corporate businessman, Angela's husband, father of Dempsey and Carol

Angela Freeman, early forties, successful corporate businesswoman, mother of Dempsey and Carol

Carol Freeman, seventeen, intelligent, good kid—slightly spoiled

Dempsey Freeman, fifteen, bright, struggling student

Mr. Parks, late sixties, down home, from "the old neighborhood," janitor, neighborhood leader

Shondra Davidson, sixteen, smart, shy, raised in the projects

Buddy Davidson, seventeen, Shondra's brother, "West Side" street, loves his sister

Note: All characters are African Americans.

STAGING

The family room of Frank and Angela's tastefully decorated, upper middle-class home reflects their appreciation for European culture as well as their African American heritage. This spacious, work-entertainment area is graced with a state-of-the-art television, a computer, a leather couch, and other expensive modern furniture. The space includes a small ultra-modern kitchen with a comfortable eating area. There is a back door in the kitchen, a door leading to the family room bathroom, and the suggestion of a front door and formal living room just offstage. Upstage, there are additional exits or a raised area suggesting a second level. On the upper level, we see another bathroom door and exits leading to the bedrooms of Frank and Angela, Carol, and Dempsey. In short, we are aware that there are three bathrooms in the house: 1. a bathroom on the upper level; 2. an unseen, to-be-remodeled private bath in Angela and Frank's bedroom; and 3. the family room bathroom on the lower level.

ACT 1

SCENE 1

[*It's early morning on a work/school day.* ANGELA, *an attractive mother and businesswoman, enters from her bedroom. She moves through the house with purpose, picking up her suit jacket and buttoning her skirt and blouse. As if a matter of habit, she steps over the partially boxed, new blue toilet and construction material in the hallway. She stops, turns around, stares at it, shakes her head, and continues into the kitchen.*]

ANGELA [*shouting*]: Frank! Dempsey!

[*Pause.*]

CAROL! If you miss that bus!

[ANGELA *checks her date book, packs her briefcase and laptop, pours coffee, and sets out plates, muffins, and juice for her family. She moves with speed and practiced precision, as if she is no longer capable of doing one thing at a time.* ANGELA *stops when she sees "the plant." It was a small, green potted plant. When she picks it up, the poor thing is limp—very limp. She tries to revive it, but it is dead—very dead. She hesitates then sadly drops the pathetic plant in the garbage can.*]

ANGELA [*calling upstairs*]: People! Get moving!

[*Pause.*]

　Now!

[DEMPSEY, *fifteen, wearing pajamas, enters from upstage right, half asleep.* CAROL, *seventeen, in a robe with a towel, enters upstage left. She sleepwalks until she sees* DEMPSEY. *Shouting, they both race to the bathroom on the upper level.* DEMPSEY *bangs his toe on the blue toilet, trips on the construction material, pulls himself up, but loses the race.*]

DEMPSEY: Carol!

[DEMPSEY *bangs on the bathroom door.*]

　Mommmm!?!

ANGELA: You want bathrooms? Kirby? The plumber? Four-thirty—let him in.

[DEMPSEY *limps to the kitchen.*]

DEMPSEY: How come I always get stuck with . . . ?

[ANGELA *cross-checks the color-coded refrigerator calendar with her personal date book.*]

ANGELA: Dad's got an appointment. Carol's got SAT class, and you've got no Spanish Club, play rehearsal tomorrow, and piano's not until 6:00. One measurement and he's gone. *Again!* So, four-thirty or "Run, Dempsey, run!" for another month?

DEMPSEY [*reluctantly*]: Okay, okay.

[DEMPSEY *sees the dead plant in the garbage can.*]

Yes!

[DEMPSEY *pulls the dead plant from the garbage and does a "touchdown dance."*]

Victory is mine!

[ANGELA *takes the plant and tosses it back into the trash.* DEMPSEY *grabs the Grandma Pot—a beautifully hand-painted flowerless flowerpot—from the shelf and removes eight dollars.*]

ANGELA: If you break my pot . . .

[ANGELA *snatches the Grandma Pot from* DEMPSEY *and puts it back on the shelf.* DEMPSEY *exits into the lower-level family room bathroom as* CAROL, *wrapped in a towel, pokes her head out of the upper-level bathroom; seeing no competition, she races toward her room and exits as* FRANK, *a confident, successful businessman, enters the front door in suit pants, an open dress shirt, and an untied tie. He reads the* Chicago Tribune.]

FRANK: Well, Father. Fuhrman took the fifth. Got to be lying on O. J. if he took the fifth.

[FRANK *tries the doorknob, then bangs on the downstairs bathroom door.*]

Hurry up in there. Says here, Johnny C's got the tapes to prove it. Man said in ten years hadn't called anybody a nigger. And Johnny's got that white boy saying it forty-two times. Forty-two times on the same tape. [*Referring to bathroom*] Who's in there?

ANGELA: Go upstairs.

FRANK: The glove does not fit. Don't care if O. J. wins, but would love to see Cochran take the day!

[FRANK *hits the bathroom door.*]

Carol? Dempsey?

[FRANK, Tribune *in hand, stops on his way to the upper-level bathroom.*]

So. What happened to you last night?

ANGELA: Shubert deal. Long story. Long night.

FRANK: Angie, you gonna come home one day to a big FOR SALE sign out front.

ANGELA: Call me at the office and we can . . .

FRANK: We can't sell a house between meetings.

[CAROL, *still wrapped in a towel, enters hallway carrying toilet items and clothes.* FRANK *sees* CAROL, *just as* CAROL *sees* FRANK.]

Hey! I'm in there.

[CAROL *races* FRANK *for the upper-level bathroom.*]

FRANK: Carol!

[FRANK *trips on the blue toilet in the hall as* CAROL *slams the bathroom door.*]

God bless America! They ever gonna finish this thing? Tear up a perfectly good bathroom—my perfectly good bathroom, then got to wait four damn weeks for a part. [*Shouting*] Carol! In thirty seconds—I'm headed for the tree out front.

[DEMPSEY *appears from the lower-level bathroom.*]

DEMPSEY: Daddy really gonna pee on a tree?

FRANK: Out.

[FRANK *enters lower-level bathroom.*]

ANGELA: Go put some clothes on.

[DEMPSEY *exits to his room.* CAROL *enters from the upper-level bathroom, wrapped in a towel, waving a shirt.*]

CAROL [*outraged*]: Mommy! You washed it! You ruined it! It's a
    Tommy . . .
ANGELA: If the bus leaves you—Mr. Hilf-nigger won't give two cents.
CAROL: Everything else is dirty.
ANGELA: Then put on the cleanest, dirty-thing you've got. Go naked.
    But don't miss that bus!

[CAROL *grabs her backpack and, still dressed in the towel, heads for the front door.*]

    Girl, don't even try me.
CAROL: I HAVE NOTHING TO WEAR!
ANGELA: I told you to do the laundry.
CAROL: Honor Roll assembly's *today* and I HAVE NOTHING TO
    WEAR! Nada.

[*Beat.*]

ANGELA: Top drawer. The pink one.
CAROL: Pink?
ANGELA: Naked?
CAROL: Right.

[SOUND: *Bathroom flush.* FRANK *enters from bathroom and gives a final spray of air freshener.*]

    Mom?
ANGELA: Dad'll be there.
FRANK: Two o'clock? Right, Doc?
CAROL: But Mom.

[ANGELA *gives* CAROL *"a look."*]

    Never mind.

[CAROL *goes upstairs.* DEMPSEY *enters and catches* CAROL *in the hall.*]

DEMPSEY [*whispering as he shoves a paper and pen toward* CAROL]: Hey, Carol.

CAROL: No.

DEMPSEY: Ah, come on.

CAROL: I told you. Not again. Come conference time, Mom'll go ballistic. Just tell her.

DEMPSEY: Give you five bucks.

CAROL: No.

[CAROL *exits to bathroom.* DEMPSEY *exits to his room.* FRANK *pulls a folder from his briefcase and tosses it on the breakfast table.*]

FRANK: Helene put some figures together. House prices 'round here— through the roof. We need to move while the market's hot.

[ANGELA *tries to get around* FRANK.]

ANGELA: Frank . . .

FRANK: If you cut out early . . . ?

[FRANK *reaches for a blueberry muffin.* ANGELA *intercepts and gives him a bran muffin.*]

ANGELA: The blueberry's Dempsey's. [*Shouting upstairs as she gets her suit jacket*] Dempsey, get down here before your father eats your breakfast!

FRANK: Got proof I don't need bran.

[FRANK *puts folder by* ANGELA's *plate and switches his bran for the blueberry muffin.* ANGELA *switches muffins back, takes folder, and puts it in her briefcase.*]

ANGELA: Just eat the bran.

[*While* ANGELA *closes her briefcase and prepares to walk out the door, she doesn't notice* FRANK *switch the muffins again.* DEMPSEY *enters dressed in a school uniform with a backpack and unsigned paper. He tries to get* CAROL, *who is racing through the hall, to sign it.*]

DEMPSEY: Carol?

CAROL: No!

[CAROL *exits to her room.* DEMPSEY *heads downstairs.*]

FRANK: We talk tonight.
ANGELA: It'll be eleven—if I'm lucky.
FRANK: Ten.
ANGELA: Frank? Okay. Okay. Ten.
DEMPSEY: Will the new place have bathrooms?

[ANGELA *and* FRANK *exchange glances.*]

ANGELA: Who said anything about a new place? And where's your tie?
DEMPSEY: I look like a dork. I hate going to school with dorks wearing
    dorky ties. I'll take the demerits.
ANGELA: Frank?
FRANK: If he's willing to sit in study hall . . .
ANGELA: I don't want another phone call over some stupid mess.
FRANK: Get the tie.

[DEMPSEY *pulls the tie out of his backpack.* ANGELA *gives* DEMPSEY *a quick kiss.*]

DEMPSEY: Mom! Bran!?!
ANGELA: Frank!

[ANGELA *grabs her briefcase and gets her keys from the key basket.*]

    I'm gone, people.
FRANK: Ten o'clock!
ANGELA [*shouting*]: Carol! The bus!

[ANGELA *exits.*]

FRANK: Hey . . .

[FRANK *tosses a lunch to* DEMPSEY.]

    Get going.
DEMPSEY: Do I have to?

[FRANK *looks at* DEMPSEY *until* DEMPSEY *picks up his backpack.* DEMPSEY *trudges toward the door, gets keys from the key basket, then turns back. He slides a paper toward his dad.*]

FRANK: Mom see this?

[DEMPSEY *shakes his head.*]

DEMPSEY: She won't sign it. Last time, said she was too embarrassed to sign it, 'cause a son of hers ought to be too ashamed to make a grade like that. And I've got to get it signed.

[FRANK *signs paper.*]

FRANK: Get out of here.

[CAROL enters with a backpack, in a pink blouse, and wraps a muffin in a napkin.]

CAROL: Dad? This summer, after the college tour thing, a bunch of us want to like—fly to Jamaica.
FRANK: Girl, you can't even catch a bus.
CAROL: Seriously . . .
FRANK: Go!
CAROL: Why do I have such a wretched existence?

[CAROL *grabs her keys from the key basket and opens the front door.* SOUND: *Sound of bus.*]

Stop!

[CAROL *races out the front door.* FRANK *puts up breakfast dishes then opens the paper.*]

FRANK: Finally!

[*Seconds later,* CAROL *sticks her head in the front door.*]

CAROL: Dad?
FRANK: You didn't?
CAROL: It just—left me.
FRANK: Damn!
CAROL: If I had a car like everybody else . . .
FRANK: Girl!

[FRANK *grabs his briefcase and exits with* CAROL *as . . . lights fade out.*]

ACT 1

SCENE 2

[*Later that night. Eleven thirty* P.M. DEMPSEY *picks through a pizza box and sips pop while he attempts to study.* FRANK *(in sweatpants and a Sox T-shirt) and* CAROL *pore over maps and college brochures.* FRANK *checks Mapquest on his laptop.* CAROL *jumps up, shouting.*]

CAROL: Yes! Yes!! Yes!!!

[CAROL *is momentarily frozen in elation.*]

　No.

[CAROL *sinks onto sofa.*]

FRANK: God help us. This will be the longest road trip in history.
CAROL: I could, maybe, live without—NYU? No. Cut Howard.
FRANK: And kill Aunt Vivian?

[DEMPSEY *balances a book on his head and walks as he imitates his Great-Aunt Vivian.*]

DEMPSEY: "If it was good enough for Thurgood Marshall, Alain Locke, and me, then surely, it should be good enough for . . ."
FRANK: You. Study.

[FRANK *looks out the window.*]

DEMPSEY: Think she'll be home soon?

[CAROL *jumps up and grabs the map.*]

CAROL: Lightbulb! Step outside the box. We do the NU thing, and all the ones around here spring break, *then,* in the summer—drive east. See Carnegie Mellon, Boston U., *then* Vassar, *then* Brown and . . .
FRANK: Whoa. Whoa. Whoa. Back in that box. Back girl, back. We've worked this thing a million ways. See this? Stone! Including Howard and Clark Atlanta. Now, get out of here.
CAROL: But, Dad . . .

[FRANK *folds maps and packs up brochures.*]

FRANK: It's late.

CAROL: Can we at least . . . talk Jamaica?

FRANK: You can talk. I won't listen.

[FRANK checks the window again.]

CAROL: But, Dad! Jen and Monica are going. Just think! Jamaica! It'll be, like—a cultural experience.

DEMPSEY: Yeah. Rasta and ganja!

CAROL: Why you got to be so ig'nant?

[CAROL *swats* DEMPSEY.]

FRANK: Stop.

CAROL: You let me do Mexico.

FRANK: You were *supposed* to be learning Spanish.

CAROL: *Por favor?*

FRANK: *De nada. No pesos. Buenas noches.*

CAROL: So what do I do all summer?

FRANK: Well, you're too old for camp so . . .

DEMPSEY: Carol with a J.O.B?

FRANK: Think of it as a 9 to 5 cultural experience.

CAROL: Nine to five? But, Daddy, I won't like . . . have a life!

FRANK: Like—join the club. Now, clear out.

[CAROL *kisses* FRANK. *She is about to try again . . .*]

Night, Doc.

[CAROL *exits to bed.*]

[*To* DEMPSEY] You too.

DEMPSEY: About the test . . . Does Mom have to know?

[*Beat.*]

FRANK: Want me to tell her?

[*Beat.*]

You've got to ace the makeup.

DEMPSEY: Gotcha.

[DEMPSEY *exits.* FRANK *stares out the window.* FRANK *hums "In the Still of the Night."*]

[SOUND: *Car pulls up.* ANGELA *enters and drops her keys in key basket.*]

ANGELA: Is there a reason every light in the house is on?

[ANGELA *turns off two lights.*]

FRANK: We're pretending it's not almost midnight.
ANGELA: I tried.

[ANGELA *picks up a program near the key basket.*]

How was the assembly?
FRANK: Girl did us proud.
ANGELA: Wish I could've been there.

[ANGELA *drops her briefcase, then collapses.*]

To be on my last leg, I'd have to borrow one.
FRANK: All I got is stumps, baby. And the kids been gnawing on them.
ANGELA: Good. They ate.

[ANGELA *picks through the remains of pizza on* FRANK'S *plate.*]

And the plumber?
FRANK: Got a piece, too.

[*Yawning,* ANGELA *rises and walks toward their bedroom.* FRANK *blocks her path.*]

Oh, no you don't. I made lots of coffee. Doc's planning college tours like we own the Taj Mahal.

[ANGELA *tries to escape.*]

ANGELA: If we're headed to the poorhouse, we'll still be headed there in the morning.
FRANK: Need I remind you, her *college fund* looks like a *kitchen*?

[ANGELA *succumbs, stretching out on the sofa.* FRANK *gets them both coffee.*]

ANGELA: The stove was falling apart.

FRANK: But we did the *whole* kitchen! And the patio. And the rec room. And . . .

ANGELA: Okay. Okay. So, the money's in the house.

FRANK: And you and Bob Vila promised, "It'll pay off later." Well, it's later.

ANGELA: God, she grew up quick.

FRANK: If we sell now . . .

ANGELA: I love this house!

FRANK: Take the equity. Downsize.

ANGELA [*sarcastically*]: One bathroom, perhaps?

FRANK: It was an investment.

ANGELA: With character! And oak floors, and French doors, and . . .

FRANK: And holes in the ceiling, faucets by Niagara, shag rugs, no bushes, and whoever picked the wallpaper was on LSD.

ANGELA: But now, it's home.

FRANK: If it hadn't been a foreclosure . . .

ANGELA: I love this house.

FRANK: You loved the last one.

ANGELA: I know, I know.

FRANK: And the first one.

ANGELA: I know.

FRANK: Think. Fresh canvas!

ANGELA: Nooooo.

FRANK: Ready or not, she graduates next year. Move now, we take our time and make a killing. Wait—and we take what we get.

ANGELA: Whoever started this crap about sacrificing for your kids?

[FRANK *pulls out an old college blue book from the desk labeled "Carol's College Plan" and drops it in* ANGELA's *lap.* ANGELA *carefully opens the book.*]

Not fair.

[FRANK *kneels beside* ANGELA, *who fans through the blue book full of notes and figures.*]

FRANK: And I quote, "Not gonna be 'the scholarship kid.' Not our baby."

ANGELA: God, we were up all night. Planning that child's future! She was so tiny.

FRANK: Flip this house, plus what's left in the college fund, that's a full ride—for both of them.

[*Beat.*]

Dempsey flunked the math test.

ANGELA: I swear . . . ! How could he be an A student last year, and now . . . !

FRANK: Make-up's Tuesday.

ANGELA: Maybe we should've beaten them when they were young.

[*Beat.*]

FRANK: It's still a good plan.

ANGELA: I love this house.

FRANK: More than Carol and Dempsey?

[*Pause.*]

ANGELA: Helene will be thrilled. Thanks to us, that's a hell of a rich agent.

FRANK: So, we're moving?

ANGELA: I guess.

[*Beat.*]

Who knows. Maybe there's another sweet old lady we can bail out.

[*Beat.*]

Bay windows. I want bay windows, this time. Lots of 'em. Deep ones, with big seats. Where I can curl up and cry when the plumber pisses me off. And a mahogany staircase. That's the one thing we missed when we bought this place. Can you picture Carol, in a wedding dress, coming down . . .

FRANK: Let's pay for college first.

[FRANK *studies "the plan."*]

ANGELA: What is it, Frank?

FRANK: You feel it, Angela?

ANGELA: What? Carol? Leaving?

FRANK: No.

[*Pause.*]

ANGELA: What?

FRANK: We were so sure.

ANGELA: When?

FRANK: Once upon a time. We knew exactly where we were headed.

ANGELA: And we've arrived.

FRANK: I keep thinking about that first little walk-up.

ANGELA: The shower never worked.

[FRANK *slips his arms around* ANGELA.]

FRANK: But we had some incredible fun in that big old claw-foot tub. And the Parkses were always . . . Oh! Parks got the job. Sends love and thanks for the good word. Says he saw Carol his first day.

ANGELA: Hard to miss chocolate swimming in a bowl of cream.

FRANK: Said she didn't know him. But then, she was so small when . . .

ANGELA: We should celebrate. Invite them over.

FRANK: For real this time! Was great talking to him. Still goes to Shiloh Baptist. And said Carmen's was still around! That little grocery store? And the Bar-B-Q Shack. 'Member the South Street Laundromat?

ANGELA: You mean actin' a fool there. Y'all thought you were at the Regal.

FRANK [*singing*]: "Bo-bo-bo-bo-bo . . . bo . . . bo-bo . . . In the still of the night . . ."

[ANGELA *covers her ears.*]

Now C. J., Boo-Butt, and me could sang!

ANGELA: Nostalgia is a dangerous thang.

FRANK: Always a bunch of old guys outside philosophizing.

ANGELA: Rusty old men, conjurin' make-believe lives, from ain't-done-nothin'.

FRANK: Had to *earn* your place. Fields owned their house ten years and folks still said, "You know—The Fields. The Fields—who live over in Miz Alberta's house. Mama could quote chapter and verse who got drunk, didn't pay a bill, made soggy banana cream pie. Haven't had banana crème pie in . . .

ANGELA: If all that gossip was money.

FRANK: Some good deals in the city.

ANGELA: The city?

FRANK: Bronzeville? West Side? Talking real change over there. Some great old mansions being renovated. If we catch it at the right time . . .

ANGELA: "News flash. Back to the hood! Three people shot. Film at 10:00." Been. Done. Sold the T-shirt.

[FRANK *peeks through the curtains to see the street.*]

FRANK: Always soooo quiet, out there. Nobody walking, or hanging on the corner.

ANGELA: 'Cause they all got jobs.

[*Beat.*]

And air conditioning.

FRANK: Deathly still.

ANGELA: Exactly why we moved here. Peace.

[*Beat.*]

I got to get some sleep.

[ANGELA *picks up her briefcase.*]

I'll call Helene in the morning.

FRANK: So we talkin' Wilmette or West Side?

ANGELA: Peace, baby. We talking a great deal, mahogany staircase, and peace.

[ANGELA *exits to the bedroom as* FRANK *stares out the window singing "In the still of the night . . ." . . . lights fade out.*]

ACT 1

SCENE 3

[*Two days later. Late afternoon.* ANGELA *fusses as she changes a lightbulb.* CAROL *enters, drops her backpack, and pulls off her sweater.*]

CAROL: Hey.

[CAROL *heads to the refrigerator to get a snack.*]

ANGELA: How can a house full of intelligent people pretend, for three days, this light did not go out?

CAROL: We were waiting for true genius.

[ANGELA *gives* CAROL *the bulb. As* CAROL *changes the bulb,* ANGELA *sorts through tile samples.* FRANK *enters with* DEMPSEY. DEMPSEY *ducks back into the foyer when he sees* ANGELA. ANGELA *is not aware* DEMPSEY *has entered.*]

FRANK: Angela. You're here.

ANGELA: Well, somebody had to meet Kirby. Hard to sell a house with a toilet in the hall. Could've 'fessed up, you'd be home.

[ANGELA *checks her watch.*]

Client dinner at seven. Got to get this done and get back.

FRANK: Please tell me you're not in a mood.

ANGELA: Me? Mood? No, I'm just picking tile samples—in the dark.

[LIGHTS: CAROL *turns lamp on.*]

Thank you.

[ANGELA *holds up a tile sample.*]

Beige?

FRANK: You like everything beige.

ANGELA: Help?

CAROL: How 'bout red?

[ANGELA *gives* CAROL *a look.*]

FRANK: Just pick one.

ANGELA: See. That's how it happens. Start this all over again, and there's me, sitting in a pile of rubble with a million paint chips and a thousand tile samples and you say, "Just pick one."

FRANK: Fine! Beige.

ANGELA: But which beige? Autumn beige? Kissed by Cream? Subtle Twilight? Hint of Oak?

FRANK: That one.

ANGELA: Don't you think that's too dark?

[*Beat.*]

FRANK: I had to pick up Dempsey at school today.

[*Beat.*]

Demps.

[DEMPSEY *enters holding an ice bag over his eye.*]

ANGELA: Come here.

[ANGELA *lowers the ice bag.* DEMPSEY *has a black eye.*]

CAROL: Dag.

ANGELA [*to* DEMPSEY]: What?

DEMPSEY: You had to be there.

ANGELA: And since I wasn't?

[*Pause.*]

DEMPSEY: This new kid asked me . . . Asked me . . . was I on scholarship.

ANGELA: With the grades you've been pulling? How the hell could anybody think you're on scholarship?

[*Beat.*]

So you hit him.

[*Beat.*]

DEMPSEY: No.

[*Beat.*]

I said, "Why? 'Cause I'm black?" And he gave me this look. So I called him an ass . . . an asshole.

ANGELA: And . . . ?

DEMPSEY: He shoved me, and called me an asshole. So I shoved him back. Then, he hit me. So, I hit him.

ANGELA [*to* FRANK]: I'm gonna kill your son.

FRANK: Least he gave as good as he got.

ANGELA: Frank.

FRANK: Get your music.

[DEMPSEY *runs by* ANGELA *to get his music.*]

Carol, could you give him a lift to his lesson?

[CAROL *gets the keys from the key basket.*]

ANGELA: That boy's not going anywhere.

FRANK: We already talked.

ANGELA: Oh, we're gonna do more than talk. A lot more than . . .

FRANK: Angela, let him go. Just let him go for now.

CAROL [*whispering to* DEMPSEY]: Escape.

ANGELA [*to* CAROL]: Bring my car straight back.

[DEMPSEY *and* CAROL *exit.*]

How many days?

FRANK: Two.

ANGELA: What are we going to do with that boy?

[FRANK *hands* ANGELA *a flyer.*]

ANGELA [*reading*]: "The Million Man March"?

[*Beat.*]

Louis Farrakhan?

FRANK: A million *black* men.

ANGELA: OK?

[ANGELA *glances over the flyer.*]

FRANK: Marching to Washington.

ANGELA: Marching? Honey, you swear for an hour after five minutes on the treadmill.

FRANK: I'm serious. The brothers at work have been talking. It's like—the March on Washington. Only, all men. All black. Bus leaves on a Thursday, March on Friday.

[*Beat.*]

And I'm taking Dempsey.

ANGELA: What? Get suspended and win a free trip?

FRANK: We've got to do something.

ANGELA: When?

FRANK: In three weeks.

ANGELA: No way. Freshman project is due at the end of the month. It's half his grade.

FRANK: Two days won't kill him.

ANGELA: You mean another two days.

FRANK: He's going.

ANGELA: Gonna pack up and go off with a bunch of strange . . .

FRANK: Not strange. Black. And he's going.

ANGELA: Then I better pack my bags. 'Cause, somebody's got to make sure, for every man on your precious march, that boy finishes an index card.

FRANK: Angie, it's a million *men.*

ANGELA: After the last fiasco he called a paper, he'll need a million.

FRANK: *Men.* A million *men.*

[*Pause.*]

Sometimes we need to get together without . . .

ANGELA: Without "the sistahs"?

[ANGELA *looks more closely at the flyer.*]

Why? So "the brothas" can gather 'round the smokehouse and do a little spittin' and chawin'?

FRANK: Not appreciated.

ANGELA: And Farrakhan's just the guy to break out the spittoons.

FRANK: And Jackson, and Ben Chavis and . . . And you don't get it? Do you?

[FRANK *takes the flyer.*]

A million black men! This is big!

ANGELA: Ain't heard word the first.

FRANK: So if *Peter Jennings* said, "All you brothers, come on down!" Then, you'd be, "Frank, let me help you pack"?

ANGELA: Your son's lost his mind, almost lost an eye, and now you want to drag him halfway across the country to some he-man hoedown, nobody's heard about, when he needs to be studying for . . . He is this close to flunking out of one of the best private schools in the state.

FRANK: Dempsey hates Bayberry. And he's right. They're a bunch of snobs.

ANGELA: Connected snobs.

FRANK: But he's not. Not to us, or . . . A Jew teaches Dempsey black history.

ANGELA: I don't care if he's white, black, green, or purple—as many museums and lectures we've dragged those kids to—from Detroit to Birmingham. Got a shelf full of books up there.

FRANK: Pay your money and see how the colored folks live! My son is disappearing. Reading about and knowing—knowing in your soul, who you are—are two different things.

ANGELA: If he doesn't know who he is by now . . .

FRANK: Hell, I don't even know who I am anymore. All day long, white hands slapping my black back saying, "Way to go, Frank!" But I feel like shit. Don't tell me you don't see it in Carol, too?

ANGELA: What?

FRANK: Something . . . Something missing.

ANGELA: They're teenagers. A whole lot's missing.

FRANK: Carol's birthday? Fifteen kids. Three black—and they were cousins.

ANGELA: Little late to get religion, now.

FRANK: She got what we gave her. A white school, in a white suburb, with white friends, getting ready for a white college and a white life. Consciously or unconsciously that's what we gave her.

[*Beat.*]

What happens, if she wakes up one day and discovers she's black? Worse, what happens if she doesn't?

ANGELA: All of a sudden, we not black enough?

[*Beat.*]

If you wanted them growing up in some little "black box," then what was all this [*refers to house*] about? See, that's the difference between you and me, Frank—I don't feel guilty. We struggled hard to get where we are.

[*Beat.*]

It's alright for their lives to be different than ours.

[ANGELA *picks up the flyer.*]

Frank, I need to think about this.

FRANK: I'm not asking for permission.

[FRANK *exits.* ANGELA *studies the Million Man March flyer, balls it up, and throws it. Lights fade.*]

ACT 1

SCENE 4

[*Three weeks later. Late afternoon.* ANGELA *enters with her briefcase. She is upset. She quickly checks to see if* CAROL *is home. When she looks out the window and finally sees* CAROL *coming,* ANGELA *stands like an unmovable force.* CAROL *enters.*]

CAROL [*surprised to see* ANGELA]: You're home early.

ANGELA: And you're home late.

[CAROL *takes off her coat and backpack then heads to the kitchen to make a snack.*]

CAROL: Practice ran over.

[*Pause.*]

　They back yet?

ANGELA: Bus left Washington at six this morning. It'll be a while.

CAROL: We still gonna decorate?

ANGELA: Mr. Parks called.

CAROL: Who?

ANGELA: Mr. Parks? You know, "Mr. Parks"? Works at your school?

CAROL: The teacher?

ANGELA: He's the janitor.

CAROL: Oh. That Parks. God, he's always going on about, "Child, I knew you when—"

ANGELA: Can't believe you don't remember the Parkses.

CAROL: Now, you sound like him. So what'd he want?

ANGELA: I guess you'll know when he gets here.

CAROL: What?

ANGELA: Is there something you want to tell me?

CAROL: No. Well . . . Okay, Okay, Okay. We kind of . . .

[*Pause.*]

　. . . trashed a bathroom.

ANGELA: Oh, really?

CAROL: We didn't mean to.

ANGELA: How the hell can you not *mean* to trash a bathroom!

CAROL: We were just, like playing around, and it got out of hand.

ANGELA: Out of hand?

CAROL: We were just having fun.

ANGELA: Who the hell is "we"?

CAROL: Laura. Jen. Monica.

ANGELA: Oh, Lord! First Dempsey, now you.

CAROL: I know. It was stupid.

ANGELA: So, what're "we" gonna do about it?

CAROL: Do? Can't I, for once, forgo Ms. Goody-Two-Shoes? It was just TP and a few knocked-over trash cans?

ANGELA: But Mr. Parks had to clean up your mess. You have no clue how hard that man works, do you?

[*Beat.*]

But I think it would be a real good idea if you found out.

CAROL: About what? Life as a janitor?

ANGELA: Sounds good to me.

[ANGELA *gives* CAROL *"the look."*]

CAROL: You're kidding?

ANGELA: And those little hoodlum friends of yours are gonna help.

CAROL: What?

ANGELA: I'll arrange it. Call their parents.

CAROL: No way. Us? Walking 'round acting like some kinda "Mr. Parks"?

ANGELA: No way. 'Cause *he's* got too much class. But God willing, maybe a little will rub off so you won't turn out to be the fool you're hell-bent on being.

CAROL: But, Mom . . .

ANGELA: But? Don't "but" me! "Butt" is just your behind gettin' in the way of what you got to do! Here's the deal. Do it—or say, "*Good-bye, Toronto*"!

CAROL: Like . . . skip junior trip!?!

ANGELA: Like . . . your choice.

CAROL: Holy crap! Why you always on my case? Dempsey fights, flunks out, and does God knows what, and he gets to go to Washington. But me? A little toilet paper, and you want to cancel my life! You act like some *teacher* had to come clean up behind me. He's *just*—a *janitor*!

[ANGELA *slaps* CAROL's *face so hard she almost falls to the floor. Sound of loud slap, or a loud "AHH"—a sharp guttural exhale from* ANGELA *marks the slap.* CAROL *is shocked. She has never been slapped by her mother. She has never been slapped before.* ANGELA *is shocked. She has never hit* CAROL *before.* CAROL *sinks to the floor. Death pause.* ANGELA *slowly kneels beside* CAROL. ANGELA *takes* CAROL's *hand, and deliberately drags it across the floor.*]

ANGELA [*very quietly*]: Feel it. Oak! You know why oak survives when pine doesn't? It's harder. I'm so afraid, you got no hard stuff in you.

[ANGELA *rises from the floor.*]

When Dad and I were students, we lived on the West Side in a tiny little walk-up near Shiloh Baptist. We were crazy—with classes, work, a new marriage . . . And po'! God. I never want to be that poor again. On some nights, we'd go to this little hole-in-the-wall—the Bar-B-Q Shack. Cup of tea—fifty cents. We'd wear out the tea bag, then, order more hot water. Add salt, pepper—ketchup and *that* would be dinner. But you wouldn't know about ketchup soup, now would you? 'Cause, God forgive us, we had to save our baby from struggling. Well, one night, two plates arrived—spilling over with fried chicken, green beans, coleslaw . . . I was so hungry, I cried. Then, Mr. Parks comes over. Says, "Welcome to the neighborhood!" and goes on about how the meal "Won't no bribe or nothin' . . . but a small church needs young blood." Every Sunday the good Lord brought, he'd say, "Stick with it, chir'en." And church dinners? Always wrapped us up two, three plates. And one September evening I was sitting on the church steps wondering, "How the hell am I gonna finish grad school—taking care of a baby?" A baby I couldn't even bring myself to tell your daddy I was carrying. A baby I was going to . . .

[*Pause.*]

But Mr. Parks wiped my tears. Said, "You got to hold on, child. What's the point, if you can't pass it on. Be *just* book learnin'." Said, "God's children were all around, and they would make a way—

[ANGELA *looks at* CAROL.]

   —for you."

[*Pause.*]

   How did I let it all become . . . "just book learnin'"? Private schools
   and . . .

[ANGELA *drags* CAROL's *hand across the floor one more time.*]

   Oak or pine, baby? You got to decide one day, if you're oak or pine.

[*Pause.* SOUND: *Doorbell.*]

   That's him. Now, go in that bathroom and straighten out your face.
   When you step through that door, better act like a child we raised, or
   so help me God . . .

[CAROL *exits into bathroom.* ANGELA *opens the door for* MR. PARKS.]

ANGELA: Mr. Parks!

[MR. PARKS *hugs* ANGELA.]

MR. PARKS: Lord, Lord! Still sweet as sugar!
ANGELA: *So* good to see you!
MR. PARKS: Been too long, baby. Too long. And where's that devil you
   married?
ANGELA: Washington.
MR. PARKS: Well, praise Father.
ANGELA: Figured they might be one shy of a million, so he went.
MR. PARKS: Should've gone myself. Look glorious, glorious on the TV
   last night.
ANGELA: Come in. Come in. How's Miz Parks?
MR. PARKS: 'Livia? Oh she gettin' on. Sent this.

[ANGELA *smells then peeks into the package.*]

ANGELA: A Carolina Crunch! Nothing closer to heaven than Miz Parks's
   Carolina Crunch.
MR. PARKS: Heard tell I was comin', so last night, hopped out the bed,
   and couldn't hold her back. 'Membered how you favored it.

ANGELA: "Can cure anything with conversation, coffee, and . . .

MR. PARKS/ANGELA: "Carolina Crunch Cake!"

ANGELA: Lord knows, many a time, she patched me back together with a slice. Still got the recipe, but nobody could top Miz Parks! Ought to whip you for not bringing her.

MR. PARKS: Arthritis on her kinda bad. Blood pressure got her up one day, and down the next. Sends her love, and says y'all got to get together real soon.

[MR. PARKS *admires the house as* ANGELA *prepares coffee.*]

Lord, what a fine house.

ANGELA: Long way from the corners.

MR. PARKS: This that fixer-upper?

ANGELA: One of them. Should have seen it. Paint was peeling. Woodwork black.

MR. PARKS: Hired out?

ANGELA: Frank and I did most of it.

MR. PARKS: Y'all was always smart chir'en.

ANGELA: If you know somebody in the market?

MR. PARKS: Now, why anybody sell a home like this?

ANGELA: Time to tackle another one.

MR. PARKS: Ought to come on back to the ole neighborhood. Some nice young couples, wid money, comin' back, fixin' up some them fine old houses 'long the boulevard. Be feelin' like the old days.

ANGELA: I'm not so sure . . .

[CAROL *enters.*]

Oh. Here's . . . Carol, you know Mr. Parks?

[MR. PARKS *extends his hand.* CAROL *shakes it.*]

MR. PARKS: Hello, young lady.

CAROL: Hello, Mr. Parks.

ANGELA: Don't you have something else to say?

CAROL: Ahhh. I'm sorry. You know . . . about trashing the bathroom? I mean, I really am. Not just because Mom's making me say it. I was wrong. I didn't mean to make all that extra work for you.

MR. PARKS: Apology accepted.

ANGELA: And she's come up with a wonderful way to show you how sorry she is.

MR. PARKS: Was a heartfelt apology. Nothin' else needed.

ANGELA: Oh, yes. Tell him how you plan to make amends.

MR. PARKS: Don't have to . . .

CAROL: Well, ahhh. Mr. Parks, is it maybe all right . . . if I kinda—help you out?

MR. PARKS: How you mean?

CAROL: Follow you around and . . . Well, help you do whatever you do? At school, I mean.

ANGELA: I'll arrange it with the principal and check with the parents of the other girls. You won't have to do a thing. Why don't I get coffee while you two talk?

[ANGELA *exits to the kitchen area.*]

MR. PARKS: Carol, yo' mama come up with this scheme, didn't she?

CAROL: Oh, no . . . She ahhh . . .

MR. PARKS: Sound like her.

CAROL: Maybe she helped—a little.

MR. PARKS: Wife and me raised four of our own and seven foster. You see, you gettin' up there. Sometimes, parents, get a little crazy. Wonderin' "Did we teach her good?" "Do she know everything she need to meet the world?" Miss the fact that even a good kid, on occasion, will do something stupid. Don't mean you stopped being a good kid, just turned stupid . . . *temporarily.* Right?

CAROL: Yes, sir.

MR. PARKS: You straight in my book, but let's see if we can navigate this thing with your mama. Okay?

[ANGELA *enters with coffee.* MR. PARKS *whispers to* CAROL . . .]

Let me do the talkin'!

ANGELA: Have a nice chat?

MR. PARKS: Oh, yeah. Sweet young lady, like her mama. But taggin' behind me on a school day might be kinda cumbersome. 'Sides, child's in honors classes and . . .

ANGELA: She can sacrifice one day.

MR. PARKS: I'll agree, on one condition. It's between her and me. You don't ask, and we don't tell. Next Saturday, there's this choral competition. Kids from all over the state . . . 'cept won't be none from North Shore Prep. Could use some help then.

CAROL: I'll be there with bells on.

ANGELA: Better yet, a mop and a broom.

MR. PARKS: So, we got a date?

CAROL: Sounds good. And . . .

MR. PARKS: 'Nuff said.

[*Beat.*]

Carol, would you 'scuse us for a bit. There's a little matter, nothin' to do with you, per se . . .

CAROL: Sure.

[*Beat.*]

And thanks, Mr. Parks—for everything.

ANGELA: Go on. We'll talk, later.

[CAROL *exits.*]

You still got the touch. She's a good kid, just lately . . .

MR. PARKS: Lotta good kids in the world don't get her opportunities.

[*Pause.* CAROL *eavesdrops from the upper level.*]

There's this one little matter I wanted to . . .

ANGELA: Anything!

MR. PARKS: You might wanna hear me out first. Like I said, Miz Parks been more down than up lately.

ANGELA: Serious?

MR. PARKS: Needs rest mostly. She be back at it soon. Got to be. Anyways, we promised to take in one more young lady. Nice girl. Problems, but who ain't got problems.

ANGELA: Young lady?

MR. PARKS: Foster child. Been bounced around the system so much she got bruises. But nothin' a good home won't heal.

ANGELA: How old? Five . . . six?

MR. PARKS: Well, Shondra, that's her name. Shondra, she's past that cute stage. Most would pass her by, but the Missus just saw somethin'.

ANGELA: How old?

MR. PARKS: Sixteen.

ANGELA: She's practically grown.

MR. PARKS: That's what she think, too. Been tryin' to take care of her mama since she was six. But you know no sixteen-year-old is ready to be out raisin' they selves. And don't want her left to ruin in one of them teen houses. And not like she's a stranger. Carol knows her. Goes to North Shore Prep.

ANGELA: Oh? That new girl? Come this year?

MR. PARKS: Knew she could do better. So, when I announced to the church 'bout scholarships at North Shore, she wrote, herself, and wid Shiloh's support, got one. But poor thing, looked so tired all the time. Then 'Livia said, "We got to help that child." Just like that said, "We got to help that child."

ANGELA: So, you want us to . . . ?

MR. PARKS: Just till Miz Parks's back on her feet.

ANGELA: I know I said *anything* . . .

MR. PARKS: I'm 'fraid if the child hook up with us now, she be tryin' to do for Miz Parks, 'stead of us doin' for her. And that baby needs to concentrate on her schoolin'. Don't want her to get tired, give up. You know how it is. Sometimes you just need somebody to reach back, and say, "I got your hand." If we don't save our own . . . ? Y'all got plenty of room.

ANGELA: But, we just put the house on the market.

MR. PARKS: Then, too, I got to thinkin', if Carol was exposed to, well . . . Sometimes, you can't see how lucky you are—if all you see is luck.

ANGELA: It sounds good, but . . .

MR. PARKS: Talk to Frank. Then, put it on the Lord, and see what He say. Got to be gettin' on. See 'bout Miz Parks. I'll call you tomorrow.

ANGELA: I'm so glad you came.

MR. PARKS: Just put it in the Lord's hands. And tell Carol bye. That's quite a young lady you got.

[MR. PARKS *hugs* ANGELA *and exits. Lights fade.*]

ACT 1

SCENE 5

[*Later that night. At 2:00 a.m.* CAROL *enters with a "Welcome Home from the Million Man March" sign. She lights candles, bathing the room in a soft glow, then stands on a chair to hang the sign. She sets out food including Hecky's ribs and a Carolina Crunch.* ANGELA *enters the back door, dragging a trunk. She stops at the door.*]

ANGELA [*referring to trunk*]: Found it! It was buried in the garage. [*Referring to sign*] Looks good. [*Referring to trunk*] Help!

[CAROL *helps her drag the trunk in.*]

CAROL: What's in here?

ANGELA: My life. My life before children.

[ANGELA *opens the trunk. She hands* CAROL *a photo album from the trunk then continues to search for something.*]

CAROL: Is that Mr. Parks?

[CAROL *points to another face.*]

Mrs. Parks?

[ANGELA *nods and continues to search through the trunk.*]

Dag! You and Dad? You're—young! And your hair! Like two little bush babies.

ANGELA: Earned every one of those split ends.

[ANGELA *pulls a red, black, and green tablecloth from the trunk.*]

Yes! Hand-stitched. By me.

CAROL: I'm impressed.

ANGELA: Here, help me.

[CAROL *helps* ANGELA *spread the cloth out.*]

Red—blood—the struggle. Black—our people.

CAROL: And Green . . .?

ANGELA: Life!

CAROL: Hard to think of you "fighting for the cause."

ANGELA: I wasn't a Panther or anything, but did my share.

CAROL: So what happened?

ANGELA: You.

CAROL: Sorry.

ANGELA: I'm not.

CAROL: Were you really going to—not have me.

ANGELA: I was young. Scared.

[*Beat.*]

What you do when you're scared marks you. Good or bad, it makes you—you. Everything costs, but sometimes the payoff can be so big.

CAROL: Thank God for Mr. Parks.

ANGELA: Yeah. Otherwise, who would I have to drive me crazy?

CAROL: Dempsey?

[ANGELA *sets cloth, more food, and candles on the table.* CAROL *finds a wooden pledge paddle engraved with "Power to the People!" in the trunk.*]

CAROL: And this is . . . ?

ANGELA: Freshman year. Dad got creative pledging.

CAROL [*reading*]: "Power to the People."

ANGELA: Oh! Weak, *My Sistah!* Weak. Sound like some scruffy scrub pine. Got to get that *"Oak Thang"* goin'. [*Deep voiced chant*] "Strong like Oak. Built to last."

CAROL: "Oak Women . . ."

ANGELA [*with energy, raising fist*]: "Power . . .

CAROL [*with energy, raising fist*]: ". . . to the People!"

ANGELA: Right on, My Sistah!

[CAROL *pulls out a dashiki from the trunk.*]

CAROL: Off the hook. Very . . .

ANGELA: "Cool!"

CAROL: May I?

[CAROL *slips on the dashiki as* ANGELA *decorates the room with items from the trunk.*]

What was it like?

ANGELA: You mean when the dinosaurs roamed?

[ANGELA *strokes the cloth.*]

> *Exciting.* Everything seemed possible. Nothing sure. Mr. Parks use to say—"It's all a leap of faith! Jump!"

[CAROL *models outfit.*]

> Looks good, My Sistah.

[ANGELA *pulls African fabric out of trunk and swirls around the room.* SOUND: *Key in the door. Offstage,* FRANK *and* DEMPSEY *sing, "I don't feel no ways tired, Lord."*]

CAROL: They're here.

[CAROL *grabs a piece of fabric from the trunk and drags* ANGELA *into the bathroom.*]

> Mom. Quick.

ANGELA: Girl . . .

[FRANK *and* DEMPSEY *enter with overnight bags, wearing Million Man March T-shirts and singing.*]

FRANK/DEMPSEY: "Come too far from where I started from. Nobody told me the road would be easy . . ."

FRANK: Shhhhh.

[*Beat.*]

> Bus ate my behind up. I could sleep till next week. Will you look at this?

[*The table is set in red, black, and green and Kente cloth. "Welcome Home!" and "Million Man March" signs adorn it.* FRANK *and* DEMPSEY *taste the food.*]

DEMPSEY: Taste good. Think they really cooked it?

FRANK: Shhhhhhh. Don't wake 'em.

CAROL [*shouting from bathroom*]: We not sleep.

[CAROL *and* ANGELA *enter from the bathroom.* ANGELA *has on an African wrap.*]

ANGELA: Naw, the Sistahs are not sleeping! Tell 'em, My Sistah!

[CAROL *and* ANGELA *attempt African dance steps of welcome as* CAROL *speaks.*]

CAROL: We have prepared a feast for our warriors' return! Or rather, Hecky's did.
DEMPSEY: My Sistah, My Sistah!
CAROL: My Brother! My Brother!
DEMPSEY: I am starved!

[DEMPSEY *sits to eat then raises hands in praise.*]

Thank you, Lord. Bless this food and the hands that cooked it—or bought it!
FRANK: Amen to that!

[FRANK *smells coffee cake.*]

Is this?
ANGELA: Mr. Parks came by today. Tell you 'bout it later.

[FRANK *and* DEMPSEY *eat.*]

DEMPSEY: Where did all this stuff come from?
CAROL: Mom's old college trunk.
DEMPSEY: From back in the day?
CAROL: *Way* back in the day.
ANGELA: I beg your pardon.

[CAROL *holds up a Funkadelic album.*]

CAROL: She has everything, including the Funkadelics in this trunk. See these?

[CAROL *pulls out bell-bottom jeans with hearts and flowers.*]

I can't believe Mom was ever this small! And they're so . . . "retro."
ANGELA: Frank, we're "retro"!
FRANK: *"Salaam Aleikum."*
ANGELA: *"Waleikum Salaam."*
DEMPSEY: And for "the Sistahs" . . .

[DEMPSEY *presents Million Man March T-shirts to* ANGELA *and* CAROL.]

FRANK: Figured a million men wouldn't be nothing without "the Sistahs."
CAROL: Next year, gonna say—"The Million Women March"!
DEMPSEY: And for you . . . !

[DEMPSEY *presents an "African American Women—Our Sheroes" poster to* CAROL.]

CAROL: Snap. "Our Sheroes." Thank you, My Brotha. Bethune, Sojourner Truth—Miss Rosa Parks! Everybody. Hit it Oak Women.
ANGELA: Looking down like guardian angels.
DEMPSEY: Oak Women?
ANGELA/CAROL [*chanting, with power choreography*]: "Strong like Oak! Built to last!"
ANGELA: You had to be here.
DEMPSEY: Should've been there!
ANGELA: Menfolk didn't invite us.
FRANK: It was incredible! Start to finish—smooth! Busses from every-where. Military precision. You know, Muslims don't do shoddy. Brother XYZ had us clicking like 1 . . . 2 . . . 3.
DEMPSEY: Guys walking 'round sayin', "Hey, Brother!"
FRANK: "Hey, Black Man!"
DEMPSEY: All the speeches and stuff! Ben Chavis and Farrakhan, Cor-nel West, Jesse Jackson . . . And Rosa Parks—Live!
CAROL: 'Member the Ford Museum? We sat on the bus. The *same* seat. Third grade—my report—"Miss Rosa Parks!" And you saw her—live?
DEMPSEY: And in color. Whole thing was like a walking history book. Mr. Lefkovitz—would've thought he died and gone to black heaven.
CAROL: We saw it!
ANGELA: CNN. 24-7. Haven't felt like that since . . . since freshman year.
CAROL: And with a million men out there, could've sworn we saw *you—on TV.* Up on this pole! Hanging like a monkey! Waving and singing! Mom was yellin', "That's my, baby! That's my, baby! Don't fall!"
DEMPSEY: That was me! That was me! There was this kid, my age, Ayende Bapatist—and he went up to speak . . .

CAROL: Saw him! Cute! Capital C!

ANGELA: Great speaker.

DEMPSEY: So I climbed up on this pole to get a better look. And dag . . .

[*Beat.*]

North, south, east, west. Every direction! Singing, and praying, and drumming. Black men—helping each other—being together. And as far as I could see—a sea of black!

[*Pause.*]

For the first time in my life, I felt like, like I could see . . . *See me!*

FRANK: Praise God.

DEMPSEY: And the best thing. When I looked down, Dad was right in the middle of it.

ANGELA: Hallelujah.

FRANK: Made me feel—*like a proud Black man*

ANGELA: You always been a proud Black man.

FRANK: But yesterday, I *felt* like one.

[FRANK *puts his arm around* DEMPSEY.]

A man among men.

DEMPSEY: It was awesome!

FRANK: Like this tribal force.

DEMPSEY: Now, all that's left is to make a plan.

ANGELA: It's three in the morning.

DEMPSEY: Been sleeping too long!

ANGELA: Lord, you done brought back a militant!

[DEMPSEY *moves about the room preaching.*]

DEMPSEY: Miss Angelou said . . .
    "Nights been long,
    And deep are the wounds,
    But we got to clap hands together . . ."

[DEMPSEY *claps his hands.*]

FRANK: "And rise up!"

DEMPSEY: "Put hearts together . . .

[*They clap hands.*]

FRANK: . . . and rise!"

DEMPSEY: Atone for our wrongs.

FRANK: Move on!

DEMPSEY: Brother Farrakhan preached . . . and we took the pledge!

[FRANK *and* DEMPSEY *pull out their Million Man March Pledge Cards.* DEMPSEY *jumps on the table (or trunk) to preach.*]

To love my brother, my sistah, myself.

CAROL: All right, now!

DEMPSEY: Improve—Physically! Morally! Economically! Politically!

FRANK/CAROL: Preach, brother.

DEMPSEY: Rise up! For the good of family!

FRANK/CAROL/ANGELA: Rise up!

DEMPSEY: And respect our women!

CAROL AND ANGELA: Rise!

DEMPSEY: Quit callin' our sistuhs that "B"-nasty—dog word. You know the one I'm talkin' 'bout. Cleanse it from our minds, our mouths . . .

CAROL: Our CDs!

FRANK/CAROL/ANGELA: Rise!

DEMPSEY: Against drugs and filth!

ANGELA/CAROL: Rise!

DEMPSEY: Dispel the lies!

ALL: Rise!

DEMPSEY: Support black enterprise!

ALL: Rise!

DEMPSEY: With eyes on the prize!

ALL: Rise! Rise! Rise! Rise!

FRANK, CAROL, AND ANGELA: Amen! Hallelujah!

[ALL *clap, shake hands, and hug* DEMPSEY *as they shout "Hallelujah" and "Amen"!*]

FRANK: Boy went forth and got wisdom.

ANGELA: And a good dose of Jesse Jackson.

[*Beat.*]

DEMPSEY: So, now, what we gonna do?

ANGELA: Does "rising" mean grades?

DEMPSEY: Grades and a lot more.

ANGELA: Great! Then I'm a happy camper. Come on. Bedtime. It's three in the morning.

DEMPSEY: And later than you think. Right, Dad?

FRANK: From the mouths of babes.

ANGELA: Honey, I'm glad you're excited—but sometimes . . . Well, you spent two days with a bunch of brothas who . . .

DEMPSEY: A million brothas!

ANGELA: Even a million brothas can't change the world overnight.

DEMPSEY: Why not?

ANGELA: 'Cause we tried. And after those first bright moments, changing the world is a weary business.

DEMPSEY: Doesn't have to be. There was this old man, sitting on the ground, rocking and singing. [*Sings*] "I don't feel no ways tired, Lord." Holding on to the words like he had something real to hold on to. I don't feel "tired," Mom. I did, but I don't anymore. Don't want to sleep. Afraid to sleep. Don't want it all to disappear like some— dream. We've got to *do* something. Now! Tonight! Right, Dad?

FRANK: Ahhhh . . .

CAROL: We could take in Shondra?

ANGELA: And what do you know about . . . ?

CAROL: I kinda overheard.

FRANK: What?

CAROL: A sister at North Shore—on scholarship big time. Needs a place to stay. The Parkses were gonna take her, but Mrs. Parks is sick and . . .

ANGELA: That was a whole lot of overhearing.

FRANK: You two friends?

CAROL: Not like she hangs with my crowd, but hey—only seven of us there. She's nice. Works hard. Quiet. Clothes—wouldn't call it style, but . . .

ANGELA: We don't know this child. We're not even sure how long *we're* gonna be here. Are you really ready to share another bathroom?

DEMPSEY: We got three.

ANGELA: Two and a half.

CAROL: And a guest room.

ANGELA: Miz Parks might be sick longer than we think.

FRANK: Angie, we use to do it all the time. If there was a kid out there, somebody in the neighborhood would take them in. We didn't useta throw 'em in the trash.

CAROL: Mom, you know when Mr. Parks was talking about luck?

ANGELA: Well next time, just pull up a chair and have a sit down.

CAROL: When you think about it, don't we kinda owe him?

[*Pause.*]

DEMPSEY: Rise up!

FRANK: Rise, baby?

[*Pause.*]

ANGELA: But . . .

CAROL: But? Butt? How did you put that? So beautifully phrased. "Butt" is just your behind, gettin' in the way of what you got to do!

DEMPSEY: Whoa! Come back and slap me again!

[CAROL *and* ANGELA *exchange a look.*]

FRANK: Don't you hate it when they're right.

ANGELA: I don't know . . .

FRANK: We can do this.

ANGELA: I guess . . . Just till the Parkses can take her back.

DEMPSEY: Now, we movin'!

[*Yawning,* CAROL *rises to go.*]

CAROL: And I vote it be to bed. This Black Power stuff kinda wears you out.

ANGELA: Help put the food away. We'll clear up the rest in the morning.

[FRANK *picks up his bags as* CAROL *and* ANGELA *clear up the food.*]

DEMPSEY [*to* FRANK]: Wait! Dad? Aren't you gonna tell her about "the thing"?

FRANK: Maybe Mom and I should talk first.

ANGELA: What "thing"?

DEMPSEY: Dad and I were talking on the bus and . . .

FRANK: We were just talking . . .

DEMPSEY: We were thinking . . .

CAROL: "Danger, Will Robinson. Danger."

ANGELA: Thinking?

DEMPSEY: 'Stead of buying a house up North . . .

FRANK: We were just talking . . .

DEMPSEY: Maybe we could get one in Bronzeville. Or somewhere on the West Side.

CAROL: West Side?

FRANK: Back in the old neighborhood?

DEMPSEY: Somewhere, where there's more of us. Like a lot of us. Like— it's all us.

ANGELA: Frank?

DEMPSEY: "Rise up!"

[ANGELA and CAROL give him a look.]

ANGELA: One more person, and no more bathrooms is 'bout as high as I want to rise.

DEMPSEY: Oh, come on, Mom?

FRANK: If we catch a deal on the West Side, before stuff goes sky high . . .

ANGELA: The only thing high over there is . . .

DEMPSEY: Mom, what're you afraid of?

ANGELA: Naïveté.

[Beat.]

How 'bout Evanston? They got lots of "us" there. Even got a black mayor . . . or Skokie? Near Old Orchard?

FRANK: We were talking about a place, where . . . Where we might make a real difference.

DEMPSEY: Economically. Politically.

FRANK: Charlie just got a place on the West Side. It's not that far from the Parkses. There's a base of really good people over there. People trying to change things. Solid people.

ANGELA: And schools?

DEMPSEY: West Side Prep sounds good to me.

CAROL: And me?

FRANK: In a year—college.

CAROL: And now?

ANGELA: Carol? In an all-black school? They'd smell my baby coming.

FRANK: But a year in the old neighborhood would do her a world of good.

CAROL: And school?

DEMPSEY: You're commuting to the other side of the universe already. So, I was thinking, if she stayed at North Shore, *maybe* we can get a safe, *cheap* used car.

CAROL: A car?

ANGELA: Frank . . . ?

DEMPSEY: Least she wouldn't be missing the bus all the time. Think about it, Mom.

CAROL: Yeah! What happened to "Power to the People!" "Anything's possible!" "Faith!" And "leaping" and . . .

[FRANK *pulls a newspaper from his overnight bag.*]

FRANK: I circled a few. Look. "Mahogany staircase."

ANGELA: For that price, it's probably sitting in a pile of rubble.

DEMPSEY: I was little, but from what I remember, this place was no great shakes either.

ANGELA: Got it all worked out, huh? All worked out, except me. No.

FRANK: Give it a chance.

DEMPSEY: Ah, come on, Mom. At least look.

ANGELA: My family is crazy.

DEMPSEY: So what's new? Come on.

[*Pause.*]

CAROL: Mom, if Mr. Parks lives there, it can't be all bad. A chance to be deeply immersed in our cultural heritage—and a car. Please!

[*Beat.*]

ANGELA: No promises.

DEMPSEY: So . . . maybe?

ANGELA: I'll sleep on it.

DEMPSEY: "Lie down!"—so we can "Rise up!"

CAROL: Lie down sounds good to me.

DEMPSEY: So we can "Rise up!" "On the West Side!"

CAROL: "Rise up!" and "Drive car!"

[CAROL *and* DEMPSEY *dance, chant, and riff on "Rise up on the West Side . . . Rise up and drive car . . ."*]

ANGELA: Go to bed!

[CAROL *and* DEMPSEY *stop then quietly resume chanting as they exit.* FRANK *and* ANGELA *put food in refrigerator.* ANGELA *blows out candles.*]

FRANK: You gonna pack all this up tomorrow?

ANGELA: It belongs to another era.

FRANK: Give it a chance. I saw my son, this weekend. Our son. He started to look like the man we want him to be. We need to make this move.

ANGELA: I'm not sure.

[FRANK *hands* ANGELA *the real estate section of the newspaper with the circled house.*]

FRANK: They think they can change the world. Remember when we thought we could change the world? Maybe this time it'll really happen.

ANGELA: We'll look.

[FRANK *kisses* ANGELA *then picks up his suitcase.*]

But no promises.

[FRANK *quietly sings a refrain of "I don't feel . . . no ways tired Lord."* ANGELA *touches the red, black, and green tablecloth, glances at the real estate section, blows out the last candle, then joins* FRANK *as they exit toward the bedroom. Lights fade out. Intermission.*]

ACT 2

SCENE 1

[A week later. FRANK proudly wears a Million Man March shirt as he helps ANGELA set the table for coffee and company. ANGELA frantically rearranges the table.]

ANGELA: Don't know why I let you talk me into this.

FRANK: Can't atone for a thing sitting on our butts.

ANGELA: How come when the "brothas" start "atoning," it's always "the sistahs" who got to get down on their knees?

FRANK: Calm down. It's just for the weekend. If it doesn't work out . . .

[SOUND: *Doorbell rings.*]

They're here.

ANGELA: Carol? Dempsey? Hurry up.

[FRANK *opens the front door.* MR. PARKS *enters with a suitcase, followed by* SHONDRA, *holding a box.*]

MR. PARKS: Frank! Son of a saint!

[MR. PARKS *hugs* FRANK.]

ANGELA: Come on in!

MR. PARKS: Bless you for givin' this a chance. And praise the Lord! You coming to visit? Done Miz Parks a world a good. Why, thinkin' you might be movin' back—she 'bout as 'xcited as a bee makin' honey.

ANGELA: Mr. Parks, told you we were just looking.

MR. PARKS: Now, Edna's graystone, needs work, but not a finer piece of construction this side of Daley's own place.

ANGELA: We're looking in a lot of neighborhoods.

MR. PARKS: Need good young folk like you over there. Be like the old days. Why . . .

ANGELA: And this must be . . . ?

[FRANK *takes box from* SHONDRA, *and* MR. PARKS *sets the bag beside it.*]

MR. PARKS: Lord, my manners. Baby, come here. This here's—Shondra. Shondra, this is Mr. and Miz Freeman.

ANGELA: Welcome.
SHONDRA: Hey.

[CAROL *and* DEMPSEY *enter.*]

CAROL: Hi, Mr. Parks.
MR. PARKS: Hey, buddygirl. Shondra, this my buddygirl. Child can
   handle a broom like a pro.
CAROL: And proud to have been taught by the best. Whas'sup, Shondra?
ANGELA: And this is Dempsey.
DEMPSEY: Hey.
ANGELA: Come. Sit. Make yourself at home.

[SHONDRA *sits, while everyone else stands. She stands up, as everyone sits.
Awkwardly, they all sit down, together.*]

   Well.

[*Beat.*]

   We're so glad you're here, Shondra. Yes. Ahhh . . .

[*Beat.*]

   Carol said you made the honor roll. Congratulations.
SHONDRA: Thank you.
ANGELA: And you write for the school paper?

[SHONDRA *nods.*]

CAROL: And she's like the best artist.

[SHONDRA *smiles.*]

ANGELA: Well, we're glad you're here.
SHONDRA: So am I. Really. Oh!

[SHONDRA *jumps up, takes a brown grocery bag from her box, and gives it to*
ANGELA.]

   It's not much. I just . . .

[ANGELA *unwraps a beautiful green plant. She is delighted.*]

ANGELA: A philodendron! It's beautiful!

SHONDRA: Thanks. I mean thank you. You know, for . . .
ANGELA: Oh, you shouldn't have!

[CAROL, DEMPSEY, *and* FRANK *try not to laugh, but can hardly contain themselves.*]

Stop it, you two!
FRANK [*to* MR. PARKS]: Now, I know it's been too long.
MR. PARKS: I thought . . . She used to try so hard. And when I was over here . . . These looked so . . .

[MR. PARKS *touches a large green plant in the room.*]

Fake!?!
FRANK: "Expensive artificial."

[MR. PARKS *adjusts his glasses and looks closer.*]

ANGELA: Will you two stop. Frank.

[SHONDRA *is confused.* CAROL *and* DEMPSEY *can't contain themselves and break into fits of laughter.*]

SHONDRA: Did I do something wrong?
ANGELA: No. I just birthed two fools and married another.

[DEMPSEY *and* CAROL *crack up again.*]

DEMPSEY: We're *not* laughing at you.
FRANK: Angela, it's better for her to know now.

[PAUSE.]

ANGELA: Truth is, I haven't had much *luck* . . .
DEMPSEY: Luck?
ANGELA: I love plants. I really do. I've always wanted a house full of plants. Buy them all the time.
DEMPSEY: But give 'em a week. A month tops.
CAROL/DEMPSEY: Doomsday!
DEMPSEY: Ugly dead!
MR. PARKS: Miz Parks use to say, "Hope that child's good with money, 'cause anything else green . . ."
SHONDRA: The mums out front are beautiful.

FRANK: Lawn service.

ANGELA: Will you all just quit.

DEMPSEY: Truth is. We take bets.

FRANK: Mr. Parks started it.

CAROL: Really?

ANGELA: You didn't!

MR. PARKS: Now, you know, I was just funnin' back then.

DEMPSEY: This calls for . . .

DEMPSEY/CAROL: The Grandma Pot!

[DEMPSEY *grabs the Grandma Pot, a pencil, and paper.*]

ANGELA: If you break my pot . . .

DEMPSEY: Oh, be a sport. Winner gets whatever's in the pot. Loose change and all. Kitty starts at . . .

CAROL: Two bucks. Two weeks.

[CAROL *passes the Grandma Pot as* DEMPSEY *writes the bets down.* DEMPSEY *gives two dollars to* CAROL.]

DEMPSEY: Two weeks, five days.

[MR. PARKS *takes out his wallet.*]

MR. PARKS: I want a piece of this action. Gimme three days. Just kiddin! Three weeks. Hey. For old time sake!

FRANK: I got faith in ya', baby. A month.

[FRANK *adds two dollars.*]

ANGELA: See how they treat me?

SHONDRA: Had a room full of plants at my mom's. It's not rocket science.

ANGELA: All right, you all. Help Shondra get settled, then *she* can come down and have some cake. I might even let you have a piece, Mr. Parks. But I can't believe you started . . .

MR. PARKS: Thank you, honey, but 'Livia's got a doctor's appointment.

[MR. PARKS *hugs* SHONDRA.]

You behave now, baby. Talk to you tomorrow.

FRANK: I'll walk you.

[FRANK *and* MR. PARKS *exit.*]

CAROL: Come on, Shondra.

[DEMPSEY *grabs* SHONDRA's *bag.* ANGELA *picks up the philodendron, struggles to decide on a place, then sets it by the window.*]

SHONDRA: Uhhhhhhhh . . .
ANGELA: Yes!?!
SHONDRA: That's a . . . a new variety. Doesn't need much sunlight. Grows almost anywhere. Except—direct sunlight. Over here would be nice.

[ANGELA *picks up the plant and sets it down with a sigh of relief.*]

Except . . .
ANGELA: Yes?!?
SHONDRA: I didn't have time to get, you know—like a nice pot or anything. Everything's so, so pretty here.
DEMPSEY: Don't be silly. It'll be dead in a week.
ANGELA: I'm going to beat that child.
SHONDRA: That one might fit?
CAROL: The Grandma Pot?

[ANGELA *dumps the money from the Grandma Pot as* DEMPSEY *struggles to catch it.*]

ANGELA: Do something with this mess.

[DEMPSEY *puts the money in an empty vase as* ANGELA *tries to arrange the philodendron pot in the Grandma Pot.*]

SHONDRA: Here. Let me . . .
ANGELA: Perfect.
SHONDRA: Don't worry. Nobody can kill a philodendron.

[CAROL *and* DEMPSEY *crack up.* ANGELA *gives them a death stare.*]

That's a real nice planter.
CAROL: Was my great-grandma's.
ANGELA: Said at first, it was "just an old pot from the Raleigh mercantile."

SHONDRA: Mercantile?

ANGELA: Dry goods store? Five and Dime? [*Pronounced Tar-jay*] Target? But Grandma was gifted. Painted and shellacked it herself.

SHONDRA: She did this?

CAROL: When I was little, we named all the flowers. That pink one, just opening up—that's me. And this is Mom, and the vine is Grandma Rose.

ANGELA: Lord, that woman had a green thumb! And a backyard to prove it! Day she graduated eighth grade, *her* papa gave it to her. Man couldn't read nor write but said, "Education's like a plant. Can't let it stop growin'." She didn't go any further, but got all eight of her kids through high school. Then Granny gave it to my mom when she finished high school. Day I finished Northwestern, they all drove up for the big event. And I'm standing there, tassel to the side, purple robe flying, arms wide open . . .

DEMPSEY: But word was out.

ANGELA: Granny looked at Mama, and Mama looked at me. Then she looked at her precious pot and said, "You child, have not yet fully bloomed." I was fit to be tied. Had to struggle all the way through grad school before I could get my hands on this pot.

CAROL: Swears they'll call me "Doctor Carol"—before it's mine. But one day . . . Right?

ANGELA: That's a promise. When Mama gave it to me, it had this fabulous philodendron, rooted straight from the original.

DEMPSEY: We mostly use it for spare change, now.

[CAROL *adjusts the plant in the Grandma Pot.*]

ANGELA: And bedeviling me. But this is perfect, Shondra.

[ANGELA *admires the plant as* FRANK *enters.*]

FRANK: So? All settled?

CAROL: Come on. Grand tour a la "Doc Carol."

[DEMPSEY *grabs* SHONDRA's *bag, and* CAROL *gets her coat as they exit.*]

ANGELA: Call if you need anything.

[ANGELA *fusses with the philodendron.*]

Looks good.

FRANK: But will it live?

ANGELA: Frank . . .

[ANGELA *chases* FRANK, *trying to hit him.* DEMPSEY *enters and heads for the cake.*]

FRANK: Seems quiet.

ANGELA: Well, if you all hadn't acted a fool about the plant. Enough to scare anybody.

[SOUND: *Doorbell rings. Doorbell. Doorbell.*]

No idea.

[FRANK *answers the door. We hear* BUDDY *at the front door.*]

BUDDY: Hey. This the Freemans'?

FRANK: Yes.

[BUDDY, *seventeen, in gangbanger gear, tries to get past* FRANK.]

BUDDY: Shondra here?

FRANK: Whom should I say is calling?

[BUDDY *enters, slipping past* FRANK.]

BUDDY: I'm her brother, Buddy. Tell her *"Buddy's in the house!"*

[FRANK *blocks* BUDDY'*s path.*]

DEMPSEY [*shouting*]: Hey! Shondra!

ANGELA: Who?

DEMPSEY: Buddy. He's looking for . . .

BUDDY: Shondra. I'm her brotha. Whas' sup?

ANGELA: She's . . . ahh . . .

BUDDY: Don't get bent. Ain't gonna jack nothin'.

[FRANK *is not amused.*]

FRANK: Have a seat.

ANGELA: So, you're Shondra's brother. Didn't know she had a brother.

DEMPSEY: Are you a gangbanger?

FRANK: Dempsey.

[SHONDRA *and* CAROL *enter.*]

SHONDRA: Buddy?
BUDDY: Hey, cuz.
SHONDRA: What are you doing here?
BUDDY: Forget something?

[BUDDY *tosses an inhaler to* SHONDRA.]

SHONDRA: You didn't have to. I brought *three* with me. .
BUDDY: Well, yeah. Now you covered.
SHONDRA: How'd you get here?
BUDDY: Jacked a car.

[*Pleased with shocking* ANGELA *and* DEMPSEY.]

    Psych! Bummed Smitty's.
SHONDRA: Told you 'bout drivin' around without a license.
BUDDY: I be 'aight. Buddy-baby gone be fine.

[BUDDY *explores the room.*]

    Wow. This place be slammin'.
FRANK: You in school?
BUDDY: Tryin' to be.

[*Beat.*]

    Well, check you later.

[BUDDY *stares at the cake.*]

CAROL: We're just about to have some cake.
SHONDRA: Don't you have to get Smitty's car back?
CAROL: There's plenty of cake.
FRANK: Sounds like the boy has to return a car.
BUDDY: Carolina Crunch? Smells good!
FRANK: Mom made it from Miz Parks's recipe.
BUDDY: The Parkses? You know the . . . ? Oh, snap! Right. And Miz
    Parks? She can burn.

[CAROL *offers a plate with coffee cake on it.* BUDDY *smells the cake.*]

FRANK: We've known them a long time.

BUDDY: From back in the day, huh? Yeah, Mr. Parks say you used to live over by Miz Alberta's house.

[BUDDY *tastes the cake.*]

Tastes . . . Not quite like Miz Parks's. Got more cinnamon. Not too much. Just more. But it's way live . . . just not Miz Parks's.

[BUDDY *looks around at the house.*]

Yeah, this place is straight up. Nice you helpin' Shondra.

DEMPSEY: So, if Shondra needs a place to stay, how come you . . . ?

FRANK: Dempsey.

BUDDY: Naw. It's okay.

ANGELA: So you're . . . ?

BUDDY: Makin' ends. 'Sides, somebody got to keep an eye on Moms.

SHONDRA: You need me?

BUDDY: Done done yo' time. Check this. I be running the streets, and she be home, scrapin' Moms off the floor. One night, ma' girl has this straight up wack attack. Zip in the inhaler. Mom's so bent, couldn't dial 911. Come in, my girl's crawling down the hall to the pay phone. Reel to reel, don't come back, less you coming to tear that shit . . . My bad, I mean . . . You know what my girl's gonna be, don't cha? A architect! Dog, from the time she was a shorty, she be drawing dese pictures. You show 'em yo' pictures?

SHONDRA: Buddy, I just got here.

BUDDY: Got to see her pictures. Don't go nowhere 'less she got her pictures. Show 'em yo' pictures, Shon.

[BUDDY *grabs a small sketchbook from the back pocket of* SHONDRA'*s jeans.*]

SHONDRA: Buddy!

[BUDDY *gives* ANGELA *the open sketchbook.* ANGELA *turns through the pages.*]

BUDDY: What I tell ya'.

ANGELA: These are good!

BUDDY: Moms, all the time, use to be gettin' her drawing paper. Talkin' 'bout the big old mansion she gonna build for her one day. Pictures showin' how live stuff could look.

[BUDDY *takes the sketchbook and flips to a picture.*]

Little trees outside. Grass. Green stuff. Green stuff eat up . . . eats . . . oxygen.

SHONDRA: . . . carbon dioxide.

BUDDY: Yeah. Give off . . .

SHONDRA: Oxygen.

BUDDY: Righhhht! So you can breathe. Swear! She be droppin' knowledge.

SHONDRA: You smart, too.

BUDDY: Can't touch you.

Yeah. Oxygen. Life! So you can breathe. Can't breathe over there. But jiggy folks on the Boulevard buyin' up those big old mansions and plantin' like they in Garfield Park. One day, she gonna come back and throw down green in *my* backyard. We all be breathin' then. Be so fresh!

Yeah . . . it be so . . .

Yeah, one day, be "livin' green." Yeah.

[BUDDY *checks his watch.*]

Oh, snap. Got to bounce.

[BUDDY *gives the sketchbook back to* SHONDRA.]

Get Smitty's ride back.

DEMPSEY: Nice watch.

BUDDY: Just a little bling to make my heart sing!

[BUDDY *takes one last bite of cake.*]

SHONDRA: Where'd you get that?

BUDDY: Easy on the cinnamon, and it'll be straight up fo' sho.

[BUDDY *hugs* SHONDRA.]

Shondra . . . take care, hear?

SHONDRA: You watch yo'self. Okay?

BUDDY: Keep it on the down low, but I'm all da way live, fo' sho!

[FRANK *escorts* BUDDY *to the door.*]

Peace out. Check ya later.

[BUDDY *exits.*]

SHONDRA: He not really bad. Just runs with a rough crowd. If you don't
want him around . . . ?

ANGELA: Maybe, it would be best if . . .

FRANK: He's your brother.

CAROL: I think he's kinda cute.

[FRANK *and* ANGELA *give* CAROL *a look.*]

Must run in the family. But Shondra, you are like, hiding your light,
girl. I've got a great top for those jeans. Come on. Gonna hook you
up to some style.

SHONDRA [*hesitantly*]: Great. Yeah. Style.

[SHONDRA *heads up the stairs then turns back.*]

What I'm trying to say is . . . And don't get me wrong . . . I really
appreciate bein' here. I'd give anything to wake up in the same bed
every day, go to the same boring school, with the same boring teachers,
folks who believe I just might be there to learn. So, I hope, really hope
this, you know, works out—but . . . Well . . . Don't go feeling sorry for
me, ya hear. My life's not some kinda . . . what's that Miss Leggett's
always calling stuff? Poetic tragedy? It's a life. All that, what Buddy
said? Helped make me who I am. I got broke places. Everybody got
broke places, but I guess it's how we patch up that counts.

[*Beat.*]

Yeah.

[SHONDRA *exits.*]

DEMPSEY: Dang. She used "poetic tragedy" in a real conversation.

ANGELA: Somebody put some oak in that child.

CAROL: Don't know if I could do it.

ANGELA: What?

CAROL: Work that hard. To go to school. Work that hard for anything.

[*Beat.*]

Could you?

[ANGELA *studies* CAROL.]

ANGELA: I did.

[SOUND: *Phone rings.* DEMPSEY *answers the phone.*]

DEMPSEY: Just a sec. [*Covering the phone*] It's the real estate lady.

[ANGELA *takes the phone.*]

ANGELA: Helene? Yes. Already? Okay. Yes. Okay, okay. Call me back later.

[ANGELA *hangs up the phone.*]

They met our price.
FRANK: We just put it on the market.
ANGELA: It's a great house.
DEMPSEY: We're moving? We're moving?
CAROL: Oh, my God. Where?

[FRANK *picks up the house photographs from the desk. He shuffles through the pictures, showing one set to* ANGELA.]

FRANK: How about this one. Near the conservatory.
DEMPSEY: On the West Side?
FRANK: Look at that molding. The staircase—mahogany. That brick-work—there.
ANGELA: This is nice, but three blocks from here, and we're in the middle of . . .
FRANK: Mr. Parks's neighborhood.

[*Beat.*]

I love it.

[*Beat.*]

It's worth saving.
CAROL: But the West Side?

[ANGELA *studies* CAROL.]

ANGELA: And you and Dempsey are old enough to help this time. See. That's a nineteenth-century door with hand-turned molding. Just think, a month ago you were trashing a bathroom, and now you'll be remodeling one.

FRANK: It's got a lot of potential.

[ANGELA *looks at* CAROL]

ANGELA: And a mahogany staircase!

[*Lights fade out.*]

ACT 2

SCENE 2

[*One month later. Late Saturday afternoon. The house is full of green plants—and they are alive! Boxes are scattered everywhere.* ANGELA *packs, listens to music, and drinks wine from a crystal goblet.* SHONDRA, CAROL, *and* DEMPSEY *return from the garage—marching like soldiers.* DEMPSEY *salutes.*]

DEMPSEY: "Mission accomplished, ma'am. Boxes successfully stored in garage." Dad's stuffing boxes like a maniac. It's getting pretty full out there. Private Carol attempted escape, but we caught her.

ANGELA: At ease, soldiers. Next assignment. Linen closet. Leave one set of towels for everybody and pack the rest.

CAROL: But Mom?!?

ANGELA: Did you say "butt"?

[CAROL *salutes.*]

CAROL: Leave one set of towels for everybody and pack the rest. Ma'am.

[ANGELA *stacks folded boxes in the arms of* SHONDRA, CAROL, *and* DEMPSEY.]

ANGELA: I love ya', troops! Move out!

[SHONDRA *and* DEMPSEY *exit—marching.* CAROL *sinks on the sofa, with an empty box.*]

CAROL: We're really going to do this, aren't we? I mean, really going to do this! We're really moving!

ANGELA: No. We're boxing gifts for Marshall Fields.

CAROL: I mean, sounded great, at first. Changing the world. Leaping and jumping . . . Especially the car. Now, I just can't believe . . .

ANGELA: That's why we're having this little packing soiree. I figured, if you actually saw things go into a box, you'd stop saying five thousand times a day, "I can't believe we're moving!"

CAROL: To the other side of the world.

ANGELA: Repeat after me. Room galore, a wraparound porch, three fire-places, bay windows, and a mahogany staircase. I can't wait for you to get married.

CAROL: But half the railing is sitting in a pile at the bottom of the steps. And only two bathrooms.

ANGELA: The house fairy giveth, and the house fairy taketh away. It's not what's there, it's what you can imagine, that's exciting.

CAROL: But it's so . . . so . . . ?

ANGELA: It's not Timbuktu.

CAROL: But it's so . . .

ANGELA: Black?

CAROL: Well, it's clearly not . . . as *ethnically diverse* as . . . I just . . .

ANGELA: What? You're afraid Jen and Monica won't come a callin'?

CAROL: Can you see them hanging out with Buddy at the mall? Is there a mall?

ANGELA: Not a Rosa Parks kinda question.

CAROL: I know it's the *right thing to do . . . but . . .*

ANGELA: One of those—oak or pine moments?

[*Beat.*]

In the blink of an eye, my darling baby, you and Dempsey will be gone. Then, it's just me and Dad. It's his turn. And he's so happy. Already teamed up with Parks on this community action thing. Next week—starts tutoring. Got his company to pay for the computers. Wants to save the world again. Don't spoil it for him. We'll be fine. I promise you, we'll be fine. Now, go. They shoot deserters.

CAROL: Aye, aye, Sergeant.

[CAROL *exits.* ANGELA *continues packing.* FRANK *enters in blue jeans and a tight T-shirt. He looks great. Energized and enthused.*]

FRANK: Garage is looking—better. Boxes. I need boxes!

ANGELA: Don't pack it. Throw the stuff away.

FRANK: It's good stuff.

ANGELA: There are unpacked boxes from two houses and fifteen years ago. Throw the stuff away.

FRANK: You just can't throw good stuff away.

ANGELA: If you don't, I'm gonna go out there and mark everything Salvation Army.

[ANGELA *prepares to pack the vase that holds the betting money. Shakes it, then . . .*]

What day is it?

FRANK: Saturday.

ANGELA: The date.

[ANGELA *checks the refrigerator calendar.*]

Well, hallelujah. Victory is mine!

[ANGELA *removes eight dollars from the vase and does the "touchdown dance."*]

FRANK: Miracles never cease.

[SOUND: *Doorbell rings.* FRANK *answers the door.*]

FRANK: Hey, Buddy!

[BUDDY *enters.*]

BUDDY: Hey, Mr. Freeman. Yo'! Buddy in the house!

FRANK: Yo! Buddy in the house!

ANGELA: Yo'! Yo'! I know! Buddy in the house!

FRANK: Tutoring.

BUDDY: Next Saturday. Community center. You thought I forgot.

FRANK: Bring books.

BUDDY: Don't got books.

FRANK: Bring you.

BUDDY: Reporting for duty, ma'am!

[BUDDY *presents a flower to* ANGELA.]

For you.

ANGELA: Did this come out of my yard?

BUDDY: Last one!

[ANGELA *wraps the base of the Grandma Pot for travel. The plant—lives!*]

Look a here, look a here! All the way live. Livin' green, Miz F!

ANGELA: For you.

[ANGELA *hands* BUDDY *a plate with a big sandwich.*]

You're late, but I love ya', so head up. And pull up your pants!

[BUDDY *eats as he exits upstairs.*]

ANGELA: I love him, but, if I saw him on a dark street, I would cross to the other side.

FRANK: And if you saw Dempsey on a dark street, without that dorky tie, would you cross to the other side?

ANGELA: Shondra's smart and nice, and Buddy's so . . .

FRANK: Sweet?

ANGELA: Trouble doesn't care if you're smart, or nice, or "sweet."

FRANK: They're both good kids. If we can just keep that boy in school. Besides, this has done more for Dempsey and Carol than . . . I mean, Dempsey's really turned around.

ANGELA: I know. It's just . . .

[ANGELA *hands* FRANK *a box marked "fragile."*]

Garage. And careful.

FRANK: I'll mark it—"Salvation Army."

[FRANK *exits as* BUDDY *enters carrying a box.*]

BUDDY: Yo', Miz F? Carol wanna know what to do wid dis?

ANGELA: Gimme.

[BUDDY *hands over the box then tries to sip* ANGELA's *wine.*]

Boy!

[ANGELA *hands* BUDDY *a soda.*]

Here.

BUDDY: Saw yo' new place. Mr. Parks showed me. Could stand a little fixin' up. Maybe a bunch of fixin' up. But still straight up—boo ya. Whole block gettin' to be boo ya—cool as the other side of the pillow. Never thought I'd say that 'bout a place over by me. Like being out here, only it's like, out there. And now, you got this green thing under control, betcha gonna bring your own air.

[*Beat.*]

Yeah. Livin' green. Big-ass place, too. Real big.

Fo' sho' you gonna let me roll wid y'all at yo' new crib, right?

ANGELA: How could we survive without you!

BUDDY: Hey! Sho' you right.

[BUDDY *watches* ANGELA *pack for a minute.*]

Big old boo ya house. Maybe . . .

[CAROL *enters with a box but stops before* BUDDY *and* ANGELA *can see her.*]

Maybe . . . Maybe you let me . . . Let me . . . park my kicks?
With you, I mean. You know, like Shondra?

[CAROL *listens.*]

ANGELA: Ahhh . . .
BUDDY: Big-assed place. Lotta air. So I thought . . . maybe . . . well,
maybe, you let me live with you?

[*Long pause.*]

ANGELA: Ahh . . . Buddy . . .
BUDDY: Gottcha.
ANGELA: It's just . . . Right now . . .
BUDDY: Not a problem. We straight. I gottcha.
ANGELA: Buddy, you can always come, hang out and . . .

[BUDDY *sees* CAROL.]

BUDDY [*to* ANGELA, *referring to box he brought down*]: So you got that?
Right? [*To* CAROL] She got that.

[BUDDY *heads upstairs.*]

ANGELA: Buddy?
BUDDY: I'll tell 'em you got that.
CAROL: Buddy? Mom?

[BUDDY *bumps into* SHONDRA *and* DEMPSEY, *who march in carrying boxes.*]

DEMPSEY: Company halt. Yo' Sergeant. Linen closet's done.
ANGELA: Great. At ease.
DEMPSEY: I'm beat. Let's burn the rest. Start fresh.

[DEMPSEY *collapses on the couch.*]

Break time!

BUDDY: Yeah, break time.

SHONDRA: There's all this packing left.

DEMPSEY: Got a whole week.

BUDDY: Everybody oughta catch a break sometimes. Right Miz F?

[*Beat.*]

ANGELA: Right, Buddy. Just not . . .

BUDDY: How 'bout the mall?

[SHONDRA *gives* BUDDY *a look.*]

SHONDRA: Not the mall.

BUDDY: To see a flick, I mean.

[*Beat.*]

Yeah, see a flick. Then afterwards, drop me at the El.

CAROL: Great.

DEMPSEY: Chick-flick? Pass. Gonna commune with my pillow.

[ANGELA *points to a box.*]

ANGELA: Garage first.

[DEMPSEY *exits with the box.*]

BUDDY: Mo-vie. Mo-vie.

SHONDRA: Buddy.

ANGELA: It's okay, Shondra. Buddy's right. Movie sounds good. My treat.

[ANGELA *uses the money from the money vase.*]

Just report back by . . .

ANGELA/CAROL: Curfew.

ANGELA: And . . .

ANGELA/CAROL: Drive carefully!

ANGELA: Your dad and I have this thing later tonight, but we'll call—so be here.

[CAROL *grabs the keys from the key basket and exits with* SHONDRA *as* FRANK *enters with a box.*]

Buddy? It's not that . . .
BUDDY: Hey. Got it. Not 'nough air.

[BUDDY *exits as* ANGELA *crosses to the door.*]

FRANK: What was that all about?
ANGELA: Nothing.

[*Lights fade out.*]

ACT 2

SCENE 3

[*Later that night.* SHONDRA *enters, sucking her inhaler, followed by* CAROL. SHONDRA *is upset.* CAROL *looks around to see if anybody is there.* SHONDRA *continues to suck inhaler as* BUDDY *enters.*]

CAROL [*to* SHONDRA]: Say something.

[*Pause.*]

My bad? Okay?

[SHONDRA *uses her inhaler again.*]

You Okay?
BUDDY: So say somethin'!

[DEMPSEY *enters from upstairs. Nobody speaks.*]

DEMPSEY: Chick flick, right? Lame, huh?

[*Pause.*]

Doc? Shondra, you don't look too good.
SHONDRA: Really?

[SHONDRA *pulls a digital camcorder out of* CAROL's *pocket. The price tag dangles.* DEMPSEY *looks at the tag.*]

DEMPSEY: $800 bucks! Dag, people! You lost your friggin' minds? What happened to a movie?
BUDDY: Went shoppin' instead. Hey!

[BUDDY *pretends to make a movie of them with the camera.*]

Why see a movie when you can make one.
DEMPSEY [*to* CAROL]: This ain't trashing some prep school bathroom!
CAROL: Buddy slipped it in my pocket and I . . . It was stupid, Okay?
SHONDRA: The only thing worse than stupid—is real stupid.
BUDDY: Like yo' li'l North Side homeys don't do it 24-7.
DEMPSEY: Mom finds out, death will no longer be a concept. Suppose the cops had . . .

BUDDY: All she do is drop these numbers, they slap her wrist, and we walkin'.

SHONDRA: And when you drop yo' address? Who put you up to this? Poochie? Slick? Keep runnin' with them dogs, you gonna wake up dead.

BUDDY: I'm down wid them, 'cause they be down wid me.

SHONDRA: I'm bustin' my butt trying to get out and . . .

BUDDY: But what about me? Ain't got jack. Ain't gonna invite us all up here. Just the smart ones.

SHONDRA: This ends now.

BUDDY: Who died and made you boss?

SHONDRA: Nobody—yet. And I want to keep it that way. The Freemans find out about this, and somebody's going down, and it's not gonna be me. They find out 'bout half the stuff you been pullin' and . . . Buddy, I love you. You my brother—but you can't be coming up here stealing stuff, borrowing her car . . .

BUDDY: Her car. She can do what she want wid it.

SHONDRA [*quietly*]: Maybe, you better not come up here at all.

BUDDY: What?

SHONDRA: If somebody's on fire, and you lock arms, you burn, no matter how much you love 'em—you burn. That what you want, Buddy? That what you want for me?

BUDDY: What about me? What you want for me?

[ANGELA *enters with a grocery bag and cleaning.*]

ANGELA [*shouting*]: Hey! People! Help!

[DEMPSEY *tosses camera to* BUDDY. BUDDY *hides it in his jacket.* DEMPSEY *rushes to help with the cleaning.*]

Careful, I've got to wear that tonight.
You all are back early?

CAROL: Missed the show.

ANGELA: Thought you were going to drop Buddy at the train?

CAROL: Shondra wasn't feelin' too good.

[*Beat.*]

So we brought her back first.

ANGELA: You okay?

SHONDRA: Fine.

[SHONDRA *uses her inhaler.*]

ANGELA: Sure?

[*Pause.*]

Why don't I drop you at the station, Buddy?

BUDDY: I can walk.

ANGELA: Buddy?

BUDDY: I can walk!

[BUDDY *exits.* ANGELA *exits, following* BUDDY. DEMPSEY *exits to his room.*]

CAROL: Hey. I'm sorry. It was dumb. But you can't just cut Buddy off that way. He's your brother. I know he's got problems, but . . . I mean, if it was Dempsey . . . No matter what. He's your brother.

SHONDRA: Fifth grade. City gets this grant. Gonna plant gardens in all the vacant lots. Community gardens. I talk Moms into gettin' a plot. We plant seeds. They grow. Pretty. Green. Then she starts up again. DCFS come. I go. Get back in September. All weeds. The blink of an eye. All weeds.

[SHONDRA *exits upstairs.* ANGELA *enters.*]

CAROL: Mom, Buddy and Dempsey could share a room.

ANGELA: It's just not the right time.

[CAROL *runs upstairs behind* SHONDRA *as lights fade.*]

ACT 2

SCENE 4

[*Later that night. The family room is dark.* SOUND: *Doorbell. Urgent rings.*]

CAROL [*shouts from offstage*]: Somebody!

[CAROL *enters, turning on lights as she crosses to answer the door.*]

DEMPSEY [*shouting*]: I'm in the bathroom!

[SOUND: *Doorbell rings again.*]

CAROL: Keep your pants on.
BUDDY: Let me in.

[CAROL *opens the door.* BUDDY *enters.*]

CAROL: You look like hell.
BUDDY: Cold.
CAROL: Thought you took the train?
BUDDY: Short fiddy cent.

[*Beat.*]

   Yo' mom left?
CAROL: Yeah, with Dad.
BUDDY: Shondra?
CAROL: Taking a nap.
BUDDY: She got pillows? She breathe better wid pillows. 'Specially when she mad.
CAROL: She okay.
BUDDY: You didn't tell yo' moms, 'bout the camera? Didja? Or the bracelet?
CAROL: Naw.

[*Beat.*]

   Buddy, I heard you talking to Mom.
BUDDY: Thought yo' mom liked me.
CAROL: She does.

BUDDY: She be frontin' like she do.

Always on me 'bout my pants. She think I'm dealin'?

Just 'cause I wanna be fresh, don't mean I'm dealin'. Know what I'm sayin'? You want a fo' real contact high? Stand by yo' homies up here. Monica fo' sho'. Her eyes? Smitty say I wanna make some real cash? Deal up here. But Shondra'd kill me. Like "figurative" like, kill me.

CAROL: You mean, "literally"?

BUDDY: That with blood?

CAROL: Yeah.

BUDDY: Yeah.

[*Beat.*]

Here. You want the camera?

[BUDDY *takes out the camera.*]

CAROL: Naw, Buddy.

Mom finds out—I'm dead. Literally.

BUDDY: Naw. She be "groundin'" you. Like on TV.

[*Beat.*]

What she want? You know what she want from me?

CAROL: I'll talk to her.

BUDDY: Yeah. You talk to her.

[*Beat.*]

Gotta go. Wanna come? Come on. Drive me back. Drive me back, okay?

CAROL: I can't, Buddy.

BUDDY: Then let me touch yo' car. 'Sa cold out there.

CAROL: No.

BUDDY: Why you hatin'?

CAROL: Buddy, I'm glad you came back, but . . .

BUDDY: I'll get it back 'fo' mornin'. Fo' sho.

CAROL: Can't.

BUDDY: Thought you had my back?

CAROL: Shondra said . . .

BUDDY: Don't care what Shondra say. Shondra "livin' green" up here wid you.

But I can't come up here no mo'? Huh? Can't live in yo' new house? Ain't good enough? Huh?

CAROL: I'd drive you, but Mom would kill me.

BUDDY: The hell with her!

CAROL: Buddy, stop!

I'll get you some train fare.

[CAROL *exits.*]

BUDDY [*quietly*]: Buddy in the house.

[BUDDY *steals the keys from the key basket and exits out the back door.*]

CAROL: Buddy!

[SOUND: *Tires squeal.* CAROL *follows, screaming after* BUDDY.]

Buddy! Stop, Buddy!!!

DEMPSEY [*calling from upstairs*]: Carol, you okay?

[DEMPSEY *and* SHONDRA *race in as* CAROL *reenters.*]

Hey? What's up down there?

CAROL: Buddy . . .

SHONDRA: What is it?

CAROL: He took my car.

I said "no!" But he was mad, and acting crazy and . . .

SHONDRA: Damn him. Why he always . . . He gets so stupid when he gets mad. Probably hookin' up with that fool Poochie. Lord knows what mess they gonna make. He go to juvie one more time, he never gonna get out. God.

[SHONDRA *struggles for breath and uses her inhaler.*]

CAROL: We got to find him.

DEMPSEY: How?

[CAROL *picks up a set of car keys.*]

CAROL: Mom went with Dad. We can take her car. Come on.

DEMPSEY: We can't take Mom's car. She'll kill us!

CAROL [*to* DEMPSEY]: He's her brother!

SHONDRA [*to* DEMPSEY *and* CAROL]: I'll go, and you . . . just . . .

CAROL: You can't drive. Or breathe.

DEMPSEY: She's gonna kill you both. She gonna kill me for letting you go. There's gonna be mass murder if anyone leaves this house!

CAROL: You're always talking about rising up! Taking action!

[*The girls grab identical coats and head for the door.*]

DEMPSEY: But this is . . . this is . . .

CAROL: Shut up and come on!

[CAROL *gets* ANGELA's *keys.* SHONDRA *and* CAROL *run out.*]

DEMPSEY: Wait.

Wait, you guys. Wait for me.

[DEMPSEY *scrawls a note and leaves it on the counter.* DEMPSEY *races out as lights fade.*]

ACT 2

SCENE 5

[*Eight hours later. At 4:00 a.m. House lights are blazing.* ANGELA *and* FRANK *enter. They are dressed in evening attire.*]

ANGELA: I'm going to kill your children. It's four o'clock in the morning. And every damn light in the house is on. Dempsey? Carol? Shondra?

FRANK: You're gonna wake the dead.

ANGELA: Yes. But first I've got to kill them. Looked like a burning inferno driving up here! Could see that child's tuition money going up in flames!

[FRANK *starts to turn off a light.*]

Don't touch that! They are going to get up, march down here, and turn off every one of these.

[ANGELA *races upstairs to wake* DEMPSEY *and* CAROL.]

Dempsey! Carol!

FRANK: You're gonna drag them out of bed at four o'clock in the morning?

ANGELA: Damn straight! Three almost grown people should have enough sense, between them, to turn off the lights. Dempsey! Carol!

[ANGELA *returns.*]

Frank? They're not here.

[FRANK *reads the note.*]

FRANK: "Buddy took Carol's car. We drove Mom's to West Side."

ANGELA: What?!?

FRANK: "8:30. Please don't kill us. Back soon. Dempsey."

ANGELA: It's four o'clock in the morning.

FRANK: And they're running around on the West Side?

ANGELA: With Buddy!

[*Beat.*]

I'm calling the police.

FRANK: No. Wait. He doesn't need . . . I'll drive over there.

ANGELA: I'm going, too.

[FRANK *gets his coat.*]

FRANK: No. Stay here. I'll hook up with Parks. If I don't catch up with
'em in a couple of hours . . .
At least they're together.

ANGELA: Yeah, three times stupid.

[SOUND: *Phone rings.* ANGELA *grabs the phone.*]

ANGELA: Hello. Lieutenant Anderson? Yes . . . Yes.

[ANGELA *hangs up the phone.*]

FRANK: Angela?

ANGELA: Come on.

[FRANK *and* ANGELA *exit as lights fade.*]

ACT 2

SCENE 6

[*Four days later. After midnight.* DEMPSEY *sits, head in hands.* ANGELA *and* FRANK *enter. They are coming from the hospital and look like they haven't slept for days. Both are near the breaking point.*]

DEMPSEY: How is she?

FRANK: Sleeping.

DEMPSEY: She's been sleeping for two days.

FRANK: The drugs. They make her . . . It's normal after surgery.

[*Pause.*]

They sent us home. Said, the real battle is . . . Is when she wakes up.

ANGELA: They said . . . if.

FRANK: They said, *when. If* we're both so tired, *when* . . . she wakes up.

ANGELA: But *if* it had been an inch to the . . . or had hit her spleen . . .

FRANK: She was lucky.

ANGELA: Lucky?

FRANK [*to* DEMPSEY]: In a few weeks, she'll be as good as . . .

Aunt Ethel and Mr. Parks are there, now. Gonna put your mother to bed, then go back.

ANGELA: No. I'm changing and . . .

[SHONDRA *enters with a small box containing a plant.*]

SHONDRA: Mrs. Freeman . . .

ANGELA [*to* SHONDRA]: Thought you were at the Parks'.

[SHONDRA *takes a step toward* ANGELA.]

SHONDRA: I just . . .

ANGELA: Don't.

SHONDRA: I wanted you to know . . .

ANGELA: You have to go.

I'm sorry about Buddy, but . . .

If you hadn't come. If you and he hadn't . . .

[FRANK *reaches for* ANGELA.]

Don't.

FRANK: You've got to . . .

ANGELA: I don't have to do anything.

FRANK: Angela . . .

ANGELA: Don't make me say it.

FRANK: Say it.

[*Pause.*]

Say it!

ANGELA: Your *noble experiment* killed my daughter.

FRANK: She's not dead. She's . . .

ANGELA: —been shot!

[*Beat.*]

Had to "rise up." Didn't you. Rise up and change the goddamn world. 'Stead of saying, "Thank you, Lord, for what we got." "Thank you, Mr. Boss Man, for this house, in this place, away from that jungle." Could've hunkered down up here, and hoped that the devil didn't notice. But you had to . . .

FRANK: I just wanted . . .

ANGELA: *You* wanted!

FRANK [*quietly*]: We see it on the the news—every night. We say, "It's got to stop." Then we change the channel.

ANGELA: Well, now, it's *my* baby!

[*Pause.*]

Where were they?

FRANK: Who?

ANGELA: Your million men. Your million, goddamned men. Hell, any man? Where were they? Where were you?

[*To* FRANK] Where were you! Where were you!

SHONDRA: Trying to save me.

[*Pause.*]

But I guess, I don't count.

ANGELA: No. Because . . . *you* are *not my baby.*

[*Lights fade out.*]

ACT 2

SCENE 7

[*One month later. The night before "the move." It is late. Past midnight. The house is dark.* ANGELA *enters slowly. She turns on a single light and packs the Grandma Pot and plant in a box with tissue.* CAROL *enters with a box, holding a teddy bear and the "Sheroes" poster.*]

CAROL: The last of it.

ANGELA: You should be in bed. You take your medicine?

[CAROL *nods.* ANGELA *pulls the teddy bear out of the box.*]

Snuggles looks—loved.

[CAROL *takes the teddy bear.*]

How're you feeling?

CAROL: Okay.

ANGELA: Really?

CAROL: Can't sleep.

ANGELA: Big day tomorrow.

[CAROL *hugs the teddy bear.*]

CAROL: Keep dreaming about Buddy. I see him walking in this field. This big green field. Waving. Then he disappears.

[*Beat.*]

I'm scared, Mommy.

ANGELA: I thought you said . . .

CAROL: I know. And I meant it. I want us to move. At least try. For Buddy.

[*Beat.*]

I just . . . I needed to say it out loud.

ANGELA: Oh, baby. It'll be all right.

CAROL: I know. I'm being stupid.

ANGELA: Better get some sleep.

CAROL: Thank you, Mommy.

[ANGELA *hugs* CAROL. CAROL *exits hugging teddy bear.* ANGELA *watches* CAROL *exit then, trancelike,* ANGELA *unpacks the box she was packing and meticulously places the items back where they belong. The box that holds the Grandma Pot is next. The green of the plant peeks out. She removes the newspaper from around the base of the pot, but the pot remains in the box as she stares into space.* FRANK *enters, but* ANGELA *doesn't notice him.*]

FRANK: Angela?

[*Long pause.*]

ANGELA [*quietly*]: Our daughter is so beautiful.

[*Beat.*]

I can't do this, Frank.

FRANK: We can't unsell the house.

ANGELA: He was killed three blocks from the house you want me to move my babies into. We can't pretend that's normal. Crazy is to pile into a van and move into a war zone.

FRANK: Crazy is watching it happen, over and over again.

ANGELA: He's dead. And a million men, a million women, couldn't stop it.

FRANK: Maybe it takes a million and one.

ANGELA: Home is where you feel safe.

FRANK: We've been over this a thousand times.

[*Beat.*]

Carol wants this.

ANGELA: Carol is a child.

FRANK: Not anymore.

ANGELA: She wants it, because she feels guilty, Frank. About Buddy.

FRANK: We all feel guilty.

ANGELA: No. Frank. It's different. She overheard us. Buddy and me. He asked me if, if he could come live with us. In the new house. But we were moving, plus a new school for Dempsey, and work and . . .

[*Beat.*]

Carol tried to change my mind. Thinks if she had changed my mind . . .

FRANK: Why didn't you tell me?

[*Beat.*]

> You mean if you had said, Okay. Yes. Yes, we can. Yes, we will. Yes, we'll try. Maybe he would be alive?

ANGELA: Or maybe, they'll aim higher next time, and Carol will be dead.

[*Beat.*]

> Over and over, for what, weeks now, I've said, "No." And then somehow, you convince me . . .

FRANK: 'Cause you know I'm right.

ANGELA: My liberal, "gonna save the world," "God, I feel guilty," "let me do the right thing," was "raised to rise" corner of my brain says, "Yes, you're right." Tells me Shondra should have every advantage Carol has. That it's not Buddy's fault. That Dempsey and Carol need to tackle hard stuff. My bleeding heart says, "You're right."
But in the quiet of the night, I know the truth.
It scares me, I know. That I think it, that I feel it. Can't escape it. Got to face it.

[*Beat.*]

> We are animal, Frank.
> Animal.
> White, black, green, purple—the lot of us. Animal.
> You can dress us up, and drag us out of our caves, put us in fancy houses—but we are animal.

[*Beat.*]

> Fight or flight.

[*Beat.*]

> And every bit of me says grab my babies and run.

FRANK: We can choose to be human.

[*Beat.*]

> Dempsey and Carol . . .

ANGELA: Are blood. My blood.
FRANK: They have to know you can't run from—
ANGELA: Oh, yes we can! We can afford to.
I love you. I chose you.
But I made them.

[ANGELA *strokes the Grandma Pot.*]

Everything I am, and everything I'll be, grows out of them.
FRANK: And what do you want them to be?
ANGELA: Alive.

[*Beat.*]

FRANK: We've sold the house.
ANGELA: I'll take the kids to a hotel if I have to.
FRANK: We move in the morning.
ANGELA: No.

[ANGELA *takes the Grandma Pot out of the box.*]

No, sweetheart. We don't.

[ANGELA *exits. Lights fade.*]

ACT 2

SCENE 8

[*Morning. The next day. The house is almost packed up, except for some of the final items. A box, two suitcases, and a stack of framed paintings await departure.* DEMPSEY *and* CAROL *enter bringing belongings that will go, including the poster of "African American Women—Our Sheroes."* FRANK *tapes a box then gives the tape to* DEMPSEY.]

FRANK: I got these. Tape that and put it in the trunk.

[DEMPSEY *tapes up the box.* FRANK *grabs another carton.*]

Front seat. And see if your mom is . . . Never mind.

[FRANK *exits.*]

CAROL: Strange. The Flemings own our house now.
DEMPSEY: Is she coming? They've been screaming so much. Then it got so quiet last night. Who would you go with? I mean, if . . .
CAROL: Don't even think that.

[FRANK *enters.*]

FRANK: Anything else for the Jeep?
CAROL: Suitcases.

[SOUND: *Doorbell rings once . . . twice . . .*]

[FRANK, CAROL, *and* DEMPSEY *look at each other.*]

DEMPSEY: Got it.

[DEMPSEY *exits to open the front door.* CAROL *pulls a dead leaf from the philodendron in the Grandma Pot.*]

FRANK: You still okay with this?
CAROL: Mom's not serious, is she?

[MR. PARKS *enters. He holds a small green plant.* DEMPSEY *enters, following* MR. PARKS]

MR. PARKS: Hey, buddygirl. Miz Parks can't wait to get hold a' you. Frank?

FRANK: God, I'm glad to see you.

[DEMPSEY *exits with a box.*]

MR. PARKS: How's Angela?

FRANK: Still says she's not coming. Said she'll take the kids to a hotel before . . . The truck will be here in a minute.

MR. PARKS: I'll see what I can do.

FRANK: Angela.

CAROL: Mom. Mr. Parks is . . .

[ANGELA *enters.*]

MR. PARKS: Frank say, van'll be here in a bit.

[ANGELA *doesn't answer.*]

House looks great. Whole neighborhood pitched in. TV story got folks from all over. White, colored—from everywhere. Worked late into the night, but it's all done. That mahogany staircase never looked so . . . Shondra sent this.

[ANGELA *won't take the plant.*]

She's doin' all right, considerin' Buddy and all. Says she understands why you couldn't come to the . . . Funeral was nice. Sad, but real nice.

ANGELA: God, deliver us from *nice* funerals.

[MR. PARKS *sets the small green plant beside the Grandma Pot.*]

MR. PARKS: Plant's still green.

ANGELA: I'm a regular George Washington Carver.

[SOUND: *Moving van—sound of a large truck outside.* DEMPSEY *enters.*]

DEMPSEY: They're here.

[*Beat.*]

ANGELA: Dempsey, Carol. Put your bags in my car.

DEMPSEY: But, Mom . . .

FRANK: Angela —

ANGELA: So help me God. Don't cross me on this.
  I'm scared. And you should be, too.

FRANK: We can't be scared of our own people.

ANGELA: They are not my people!

DEMPSEY: Mom?

ANGELA: What? Claim every foul-mouthed, gun-toting, freak misfit
  walking the face of the earth 'cause their skin looks like mine!?! Who
  says I got to tote all that on my back?
  What do we do? Keep piling it on till we all fall down?

[*Beat.*]

  Dempsey, Carol! Get your things!

FRANK: No. They're coming with me.

[FRANK *grabs* DEMPSEY's *arm and blocks* CAROL's *path.*]

  Get in the Jeep.
  We are moving to *our* new house!

[FRANK *grabs a box, shoves the Grandma Pot into it, and reaches for* ANGELA.]

  And *you're* coming with us!

[ANGELA *grabs for the box holding the Grandma Pot.*]

ANGELA [*screaming*]: Noooo!

[FRANK *and* ANGELA *struggle. The box crashes to the floor. We hear the
Grandma Pot shatter.*]

FRANK: Angela . . .

[ANGELA *looks at* CAROL. CAROL *kneels by the broken Grandma Pot.*]

[*Pause.*]

[CAROL *picks up pieces of the Grandma Pot and tries to save the philodendron.
She puts them in the box that held the pot.*]

ANGELA: Let it go.

CAROL: You mean throw it away?

ANGELA: I'm . . . sorry.

CAROL: Over and over in the hospital. You. Daddy. Everybody. Sorry. Buddy in a pool of . . . "So sorry."

ANGELA: We didn't kill him.

CAROL: Didn't save him either.

[CAROL *packs a piece of the Grandma Pot in the box as she speaks.*]

He was so mad at you. So mad at you. When we found him, said, he wasn't mad anymore. Said he understood. Like picking teams. Some kids get picked. Some kids don't. Then the shooting started. Wrong place, wrong time.

ANGELA: I'm sorry, baby.

CAROL: Sorry. So much sorry. When Buddy pushed me down, the ground hit me—smack. Smacked sorry out of me. Bullets ate up Buddy. Ate up my soft stuff, Mommy. Two of us layin' there. Covered in blood. Ate up my sorry.

[*Beat.* CAROL *sees the "Sheroes" poster.*]

Must've been—Oak Women. Looking over me. 'Cause I got up. He didn't, but I got up. "Don't be no scrub pine," you said. "Don't be no sorry scrub pine." Oak Women—like Rosa Parks. Didn't say she was sorry. Said she was tired. Sat down, so we could rise up . . .

[CAROL *stands.*]

. . . and not be so damned sorry!

ANGELA: We can't all be Rosa Parks.

CAROL: What if we were?

[*Beat.*]

Got to rise up, or slip down in the blood of every Buddy we let die. Because we got picked!

ANGELA: But, baby . . .

CAROL: Butt!?! Mama?

[CAROL *grabs* ANGELA, *pulls her to her knees, and drags her mother's hand across the oak floor.*]

Oak or pine?

[CAROL *stares into her mother's eyes as she presses* ANGELA's *hand into the oak floor.* CAROL *stands.*]

ANGELA: I just wanted to save my babies.
CAROL: Oak or pine?

[ANGELA *looks up—but doesn't get up.* CAROL, DEMPSEY, FRANK, *and* MR. PARKS *wait—a long time.* ANGELA *finally rises slowly.* CAROL *hugs* ANGELA. MR. PARKS *pats* ANGELA *on the shoulder.*]

MR. PARKS: Miz Parks got a big old crunch cake waitin'.

[MR. PARKS *exits carrying a suitcase.* CAROL *picks up the box with the broken Grandma Pot.* DEMPSEY *grabs the "Sheroes" poster and a suitcase.* CAROL *and* DEMPSEY *exit together.* FRANK *picks up a suitcase and waits for* ANGELA.]

FRANK: Time to go, baby.
ANGELA: In a minute.

[FRANK *waits for* ANGELA *at the door.* ANGELA *looks around. She notices the small green plant* SHONDRA *sent her.* ANGELA *picks up the small green plant, pulls off a dead leaf, then turns back for one last look.* FRANK *and* ANGELA *exit together as lights fade to black.*]

INTERVIEW WITH GLORIA BOND CLUNIE

Gloria Bond Clunie is an original member of the Victory Gardens Theater Playwriting Ensemble and founder of Fleetwood-Jourdain Theatre in Evanston, Illinois. She is the author of numerous plays, including North Star, Shoes, Sweet Water Taste, *and* Sing, Malindy, Sing! *Born in Henderson, North Carolina, she has been a full-time drama specialist in Evanston's School District 65 since 1981.*

Harvey Young: When did you first read *A Raisin in the Sun?*

Gloria Bond Clunie: I can't remember when I read *A Raisin in the Sun* for the *first* time. It's one of those pieces—if you're an African American—that become a part of the fabric of your being. Just like home, you assume that you've always lived there. The story is part of you. Before August Wilson, it was *the black play* that everybody read.

　　Reading *Raisin* again after moving to Chicago was really great. I realized that Lake Shore Drive was the "shall we take the drive sir?" Take the drive! I love that line. Shortly after graduating from Northwestern—I was teaching at the time—I was cast in a local NBC production about Lorraine Hansberry's life. I got to play Lorraine Hansberry! And as I got to know Chicago, I realized that Clybourn Street is *"the* Clybourn Street"—the one in the play! I learned about her father and the controversy over redlining. Having grown up in the South, I understood what segregation was from a Southern perspective, but it wasn't until then that I realized how segregated Chicago was. That was part of the seeding of *Living Green.* Do you know the musical *Raisin?* We used it to open the new space at Fleetwood Jourdain—the theater.

HY: Why did you pick that show?

GBC: It had to do with getting a new home. We were moving from a space in the community center, to a real theater—newly renovated with lights and sound—so we were celebrating a new home. At first, there was a little bit of a disconnect, because I love *A Raisin in the Sun* so much—the lines—but as we worked, I got really excited about the musical, too.

HY: What else inspired you to write *Living Green*?

GBC: There came a moment of looking back and asking, "What happened to all of us who lived on the cusp between segregation and integration?" What happened to those born in a segregated world—going to a segregated first grade, second grade, etc.—who then went through the integration process? Integration happened at different stages throughout the South. Having gone through that transition and having been part of that generation of moving out of *the neighborhood*, I wondered what were the benefits? I think Aurelia, my daughter, was young, and we were living in Evanston—now that's a comfortable, very integrated suburb, right outside of Chicago—and I began asking myself, "How did we change? What did we gain? What did we lose?"

Back when I was writing *North Star*, I had a chance to go home and interview Dr. Green, our old family doctor and a childhood friend from my hometown in Henderson. By then, he was a state senator, but back in the day, he was very active in civil rights. He talked about how we gained a lot because of civil rights—but there were a lot of good things that we left behind. He could remember, in our town, when Horner Street was a *thriving* black neighborhood! Where you had black businesses . . . a black restaurant . . . where you knew the pharmacist, and he was black . . . and you'd get ice cream from him instead of Walgreens. You would see him, and your doctor, at your church. The same thing for teachers. If you had a problem at school, you didn't have to wait for a "parent conference"—you knew your teachers would see your parents at church or the grocery store. And the die was cast at that point! What did we gain as we moved out of our neighborhoods? But also, what did we lose? Then two, without that economic and social mix, how did the neighborhoods change?

There was an article that was in the [*Chicago*] *Tribune*, I think. It was about a friend who had graduated from Northwestern, who, though grateful for his business success, talked about his sense of loss, of missing something, of the alienation that he felt after spending years in corporate America. In *Living Green*, this notion is reflected in the father who goes off to his high-paying job and says, "I go, I'm successful, I've got white hands slapping my black back," but he keeps wondering, "What have I lost?" What kinds of connections to my community have I lost?

I began to wonder, when we're raising African American children in today's world, what do we need to put in them to make them strong? Are we assuming that that strength "to overcome" is there because of what *we* have gone through? That kind of assumption, that this strength from ages past is in our DNA, that it's automatically part of the black mind, is not necessarily valid. Like the old folks say, "Can't get to heaven on your mama's religion, you gotta have your own. God bless the child who has got his own."

That question of what happened to us personally over that period of time is really a question of what happened to our neighborhoods. When I was growing up, it was an African American neighborhood that I was born into. Though there were outside forces that may have been very challenging, you had a cocoon that nurtured. Someone would say, "You are wonderful." Now, at the same time, they'd say, "you've got to be twice as good," because they knew what awaited in the outside world. That combination bred a certain kind of grit, or strength, that is worth preserving, but how do we do that within the dynamics of today's world?

HY: As part of this collection, I interviewed George C. Wolfe, and he said something similar. He went from growing up in a predominantly black community to being the only black student—or one of a few black students—at his high school. It was his childhood and the black community that steeled him for life outside that community.

GBC: I went to Virginia to a wonderful boarding school, Chatham Hall. There were only two of us there for quite some time. It was a period when the doors to white institutions swung open for blacks. Like, there was the ABC program . . . my brother went to Governor Dummer Academy, and then on to Harvard. My mom, she went to Howard. They used to call it "the black Harvard," and Dad went to St. Augustine. Do you know the Delany sisters? Lived until they were one hundred and wrote this great book—became a play called *Having Our Say.* They went to St. Aug. While she was at Howard, Mom worked in Mordecai Johnson's office. Mordecai Johnson was the first African American president of Howard University.

In the forties, when Mom was there, she was going to school, but she was also his secretary. It was a wonderful opportunity because she got to meet all of these great people like Mrs. Roosevelt and Mary McLeod Bethune. All of these people connected to Mordecai Johnson. Alain Locke was one of Mom's teachers. Thurgood Marshall graduated from there and was often on campus. There was a cocoon of extraordinary talent in that African American university. Mordecai Johnson used to call my mother "daughter." "Daughter, could you . . ." Though I never met him, he was my brother's godfather—so there was always that assumption I would go to Howard or perhaps St. Aug.

When the sixties and seventies occurred, there was a *swoosh,* and these brain trusts were dispersed across the country. A host of talented blacks who would normally be concentrated in the Howards, or St. Augs, or Spellmans were now given scholarships and scattered across the country in white schools that wanted to integrate. We've got to ask ourselves, with these broader opportunities, who didn't go to Howard? What concentration of black minds *weren't* pooled together, because they were now scattered across the country?

Who *didn't go,* from that Henderson neighborhood, where I lived growing up, where the doctors lived next to the janitors, and all sorts of different strata lived together? Think about it. If you didn't have a force within your family that propelled you to believe and achieve, there was somebody next door. That whole cocoon of a neighborhood . . . what does it create? How does it affect your local society, and how does it impact the world when you look at Thurgood Marshall and all the people who were at Howard, and all of the things that have changed in relation to our history and culture—dramatic changes *because* of *that* history, *that* collection of people, *that* mind trust. What about the mind trusts on the Chicago South Side, in the theaters, like the Regal, and the cultural clubs and social institutions.

I think this awareness was a very strong inspiration for *Living Green.* It forced me to ask, what happens to us as we disperse? What are our obligations and responsibilities in a redefined, broader world? How do we address them? And at the same time, when you have a child, you're trying to figure out what is the best decision for him or her. Do you go back to the old neighborhood where the cocooning occurred? But the neighborhood has changed. Do you try to recapture it? Can you go back in time?

When *Living Green* was done at Victory Gardens, there was a wide range of audiences in terms of ages and cultures. Responses came from all different races—Polish, Chinese, to whatever. Comments began with, "Oh, I used to live . . ." "I lived . . ." That whole idea of "can you go back again?" was debated. Can you go *back* to a community? Back in time? Should you go back? Is there any value in it?

HY: For Frank, it's the Million Man March that shows him the power of community again and gets his desire to go back to his old neighborhood.

GBC: Notice, that it's in response to the behavior of his son. That's why he goes to the Million Man March.

HY: For Angela, it's the trunk. Opening the trunk and putting on clothing from her college years—the seventies—gets her thinking about the past.

GBC: Both of those are driven by a response to their children. First Carol acting the fool. Excuse my French.

HY: Trashing the bathroom.

GBC: In a girls' school, where she's "an only"—or not an only, there're three or four of them.

HY: An almost only.

GBC: That's a new category, an AO, an "almost only." And she's responding to the pressures that come with that territory. And again, the son, Dempsey, did well in his first years at a private school but is now beginning to rebel, to act out as he struggles to define himself.

When they come back from the Million Man March, Dempsey talks about looking out and "seeing me." He says, "I see me." There was a teacher from the school where I teach—Mr. Willis—he took off from school and went to the Million Man March. He teaches history and is a track coach, former military, great guy—he took the day off to go. I saw him the morning he got back. We only had a minute or two in the hall before classes, and I asked him how it was. And he

stopped, with this faraway look in his eyes, and he said, "It was wonderful! I just remember looking out, and all around me—black men!
All around me. It was like, like I could—see *me*." That resonated.

In such an integrated world—especially if you have the isolation
that this particular family in *Living Green* has, where they live in an
affluent, mostly white neighborhood, not that they don't have good
friends in the neighborhood, friends who value them—when they
look out, what they see is not a reflection of who they are. And what
they see is not what their neighbors see: which is their brownness.
They were not looking out and seeing their brownness reflected back
every day. They could not hear themselves as an echo.

I remember being in Texas once. I had a very brief but very beneficial stint with IBM. We were in Texas for this training session—and
we were down there for three or four weeks at a time. I remember
sitting in a restaurant, and there weren't many African American
marketing reps in this particular environment. I was very young. We
were sitting in a restaurant. Nice restaurant. A white coworker asked
me, "How does it make you feel to be the only one in here?" I had
not noticed, at that point, that I was *the only*. Then what concerned
me even more was I noticed that I had not noticed. That whole idea
of perception in relationship to creating identity. How much do you
need to see of you to create a strong core. Back to that philosophy—
"you can't get to heaven on your mama's religion." How much of that
core for me was created because I had grown up in my early years in an
African American kindergarten? Because second, third grade, fourth
grade, fifth grade was *all* African American? And then, after forming
a somewhat solid core, I faced integration?

My mom was a teacher. As I said, integration happened in waves
in the South. Just because *Brown v. Board of Education* said it was
so didn't mean everybody was listening. When they were integrating
in Henderson, I don't know if there were separate school districts,
but there were black schools and white schools. The superintendent
asked my mother, "Will you let Gloria go to E. M. Rollins?" Rollins was a white school on the other side of town. And so we went to
E. M. Rollins. Desiree White—now that was a smart girl and a good
friend, and her mom was a teacher, too. So eighth grade, a cab would

come pick me up, and then Desiree, and off we'd go to E. M. Rollins every day.

In the life of a child, some things don't seem strange. It just is your life. It's amazing. Even when they put KKK stuff on my desk . . . it wasn't really weird. I had been steeled—that cocoon was thick and deep. My mother was going to go to school about it, but I didn't want her to. As a middle-school teacher, I realize now that it was a middle-school response to say, "No. Don't come." Forget race. You never want your parents to come to school. Not in junior high.

HY: It's as bad as having your parents take you to school.

GBC: Yes, truly, which is why we were grateful a cab was taking us versus our parents.

Writing is a wonderful way to address issues that you sometimes don't even know you have. I must have lived a lot of life, and still do, with blinders on. It wasn't until someone pointed it out to me that I realized I often have young people in my plays. Now, this was after I had written several plays with young people in key roles, like *Living Green* and *Shoes* and *North Star*. Sometimes casting can be a challenge. "You know, you have another kid in this play?" At some point, it hit me that I must be addressing how children develop in the world—especially black children. I'd been teaching forever, and it was like (*having a eureka moment*), "That's what my plays are about!" At least some of them. About issues kids face now, and resolving issues I faced as a child. So, I sometimes write myself into a new . . . knowing, a new understanding—of myself and the world, of myself in the world. Hopefully, an audience will be stretched by this new awareness, too. Writing can provide a reflection of life that creates this new knowing. We need to see a reflection of ourselves to understand who we were at some past point in our history and who we are at this present point in time and history. We must ask, as we go into the twenty-first century, how has this reflection changed? What are our responsibilities to the community that we've left? What are our responsibilities to someone from the old community? Shondra comes from the old community, into the Freemans' community, and they have to deal with it.

HY: If Shondra's the person who has been given a chance to succeed, then who is Buddy?

GBC: Shondra can succeed. She's smart. Artistic. A good student. We accept her. We bring her in. But can we leave the Buddys behind? No, because he's going to find us. Buddy's going to find us. Why? Because he's resourceful, he's a hustler, a charming hustler we're embarrassed to know. The fact is, there are some people who find their way in and are invited to the table, and there are some people who have many talents and many skills but aren't necessarily invited to the table. When that part dies, as Buddy does, what do we lose? When we leave them out, like we leave Buddy out, what do we lose? Just like when we lose important parts of a community, when we leave it. That doesn't mean that progress does not go on. The direction of life is this way (*gesturing forward*). Forward. Actually, Buddy became the character that junior high and high school audiences most associated with. They loved Buddy. I was there when a large group of kids came to the show. They loved the whole idea of Buddy. They were in tears with, "How could you?!" when Buddy died.

HY: You killed Buddy.

GBC: I didn't kill him. The community killed him. His lifestyle killed him. It's not my fault. There was a very strong connection with Buddy—not just with young audiences. Even Angela loved Buddy. She was concerned but loved Buddy and started to incorporate Buddy into her life. But when it came down to stepping up, to really accepting him, when he asks, "Can I stay here too? Is there room in the house for me?" Well . . .

HY: The answer is no.

GBC: It wasn't even the "no" that crushed him. It was the hesitation.

HY: Before the "no."

GBC: The hesitation, when you're not secure, is worse than the "no." Especially to a child. That hesitation, even if she brought him in, would have always been the comma on his heart. So Buddy comes in—and I'm thinking through this as we talk—when Buddy comes in, even his sister says to him, "What am I supposed to do?" She doesn't want Buddy to ruin it for her. And Buddy says, "You've got all this. What about me?" And Carol is finally getting a sense, in a tangible way, that her life is not everyone's life. That's a changing point for a young person. To say people think differently, see differently, etc., than you do. We often lose that innocence that says, "everybody should have a chance." You have that when you're young. If you can hold on to that whole idea of equality, it's wonderful. I see it in my kids in middle school. That quest for the right. There're certain moments, when they're sticking up for the right; it's a very black-and-white issue . . . not a lot of gray. The gray comes when you have your own kids—there's right and wrong, and then, sometimes, there's me providing for my kids.

HY: In the end, Buddy's dead, but they're still moving to the old neighborhood. They're moving back to . . .

GBC: They're braver people than I am. That's the wonderful thing about plays—they can be very brave, or they can be very stupid, or they can be very sad people while they work out their lives and create a mirror for us.

HY: Is the lasting lesson that they're more concerned about the dangers of them staying where they are than the threat of violence where they're heading? Or, is it because the house has been sold?

GBC: Well, the house has been sold, and they are definitely moving. But Angela is saying that she'll put her kids in a hotel before she will move them to a neighborhood where Buddy was just killed. And her husband is very much for the move, for a lot of reasons, mostly in relationship to the kids and the neighborhood. He's already started working with youth groups there—he's already aligned with Mr. Parks—and sees a glimpse of what that area could be. They've already renovated the house—which is a minor detail—and the other neighbors have helped.

The crux of it is when Carol has that speech about Rosa Parks. She feels we have to stand up, we have to do this. If you don't care if Buddy dies, then the blood of every kid that dies is on our hands. Earlier, when the dad asks Angela to think about moving to the neighborhood and Angela is not so sure, he says, to paraphrase, "I see my son becoming the man that I want him to be." You want and hope a lot of things for your children. And there are moments when you look at them and maybe just for a moment say, "That looks like a grown person, a grown person I respect, that I'm proud of." For Angela, it's seeing Carol in that last speech, convincing her mom.

Before Buddy got shot, Carol was gung ho for the move because she thought that she was going to get a car. And when Carol started to have doubts, her mom teases her with "You're just worried that your buddies are not going to want to come down to the mall on the South Side or the West Side or wherever."

Then, that whole idea of Angela seeing her daughter say, "We *have* got to do this" . . . just seeing that makes Angela, with very few words, pick up her bags and go. Not knowing how it's going to turn out, but at this point, seeing her daughter grow up in those brief moments makes the journey worth it. She's seen her grow. When you're talking about living green, it's that whole idea of growth. What is "living" and what is "living green"? Buddy has that wonderful speech: "Maybe you'll come back, throw down in my backyard." Someone has to come back. Come back and plant. And grass spreads. Grass spreads, trees grow.

HY: **What are your thoughts of the Steppenwolf production of** *Etiquette of Vigilance*? *Etiquette* **is another play picking up where** *Raisin* **left off and produced a year after** *Living Green.*

GBC: I remember leaving and feeling very positive about the piece. I liked it. I definitely liked it. What stands out in my mind is how they transposed time, like with the progression of images on the door: from King to Obama.

I had very personal responses. That whole idea of fighting for your art, of wanting to write about the experiences that you lived, was significant. And that her father—because of that generation gap—had not perceived what his daughter's understanding of the world was. He had one view, of what he wanted his daughter's world to be, and she had a passion for something else.

This was the house, supposedly where the Youngers moved. The father, as a chauffeur, had worked so hard. The plight of his son,

Travis, is having to work so hard again and not having time to attend to his dreams. This was the Travis, as a little boy, who had grown up and his father had sacrificed a great deal and was continuing to sacrifice.

HY: Also becoming a chauffeur, of sorts.

GBC: *Taking the drive.* Again, the dream deferred. What happens to a raisin in the sun? At what point does one defer a dream, and at what point does one let go of a dream so that you can hold on to another one? If you're just holding on to a dream, you cannot necessarily grab on to another dream—which is her [Lorraine's] dream to create a play.

I love the monologue in the end, where he is cradling the baby. Her play, Lorraine's, has been born. *Etiquette of Vigilance.* I pondered the title. *Vigilance* really sticks. There is a sense of vigil. When you hold a vigil, you're waiting for something to happen. How different is that idea of holding a vigil for someone and the idea of vigilance, fighting for something or standing guard until something has been accomplished. I'm thinking about this as we are talking. How does that word *etiquette* come in? I associate *etiquette* with manners. *Etiquette of Vigilance.* What is the proper way to fight for something? What is the way that we fight for or hold on to or keep a dream? As I think through the play, maybe that's what it is exploring. The way that he cradles the baby—just the visual image. You know the Langston Hughes poem:

> Bring me all your dreams,
> You dreamer,
> Bring me all your
> Heart melodies
> That I may wrap them
> In a blue cloud-cloth
> Away from the too-rough fingers
> Of the world.

It's in *The Dream Keeper*, which is in the same book that has "Dream Deferred." When he was holding that baby, that image, I got the sense of holding a baby in the "blue cloud-cloth away from the too-rough fingers of the world." I have no idea whether it relates to the speech that he was giving, but the image was very vivid on stage and made me think of the Langston Hughes poem—and dreams. What are we if we don't have our dreams?

NEIGHBORS

Branden Jacobs-Jenkins

PRODUCTION HISTORY

Neighbors was developed with the assistance of the Public Theater (Public LAB series), Oskar Eustis, artistic director, and Andrew D. Hamingson, executive director, in New York City in February 2010. It was directed by Niegel Smith, with set design by Mimi Lien, costume design by Gabrielle Berry, lighting by Peter West, and sound by Ryan Rumery. Emily Park Smith was the production stage manager. Cast was as follows:

Richard Patterson	Chris McKinney
Jean Patterson	Birgit Huppuch
Melody Patterson	Danielle Davenport
Mammy	Tonye Patano
Zip Coon	Eric Jordan Young
Sambo	Okieriete Onadowan
Jim	Brandon Gill
Topsy	Jocelyn Boh

The play was subsequently developed and produced by The Matrix Theatre Company at the Matrix Theatre in Los Angeles, Joseph Stern, producing/artistic director, in October 2010. It was directed by Nataki Garrett, with set design by John Iacovelli, costume design by Naila Aladdin Sanders, lighting by J. Kent Inasy, sound by John Zalewski, and choreography by Ayana Carr. Cast was as follows:

Richard Patterson	Derek Webster
Jean Patterson	Julia Campbell
Melody Patterson	Rachae Thomas
Mammy	Baadja-Lyne
Zip Coon	Leith Burke
Sambo	Keith Arthur Bolden
Jim	James Edward Skippy

Topsy . . . . Daniele Watts

Note: At the time of this manuscript going to press, *Neighbors* was set to receive a revised production at the Mixed Blood Theatre in Minneapolis, MN, Jake Reuler, producer/artistic director with Nataki Garrett as director, during which the playscript may have undergone changes that are not reflected here.

CHARACTERS

Richard, 39, father, black
Jean, 39, mother, white   } THE PATTERSONS
Melody, 15, daughter, biracial

Mammy, mother, in blackface
Zip Coon, uncle, in blackface
Sambo, oldest, in blackface   } THE CROWS
Jim, middle, in blackface
Topsy, youngest, in blackface

SETTING

A distorted present.

Note: The ethnicity and/or gender of the actors playing the Crows is not specified.

A "—" connotes a revised or broken thought if it comes within a line or an interruption if it comes at the end.
A ". . ." connotes a slight pause or "searching" if it comes within a line or a trailing off if it comes at the end.
A "/" is where the next line, spoken by whoever speaks next, begins, creating an overlap.

OVERTURE

[*A barely, barely lit stage. Almost black.*

Almost.

And totally silent. (You can't even hear me.)

Five people—a family—enter the near emptiness, suddenly and from every direction, toting boxes, carrying furniture, moving in. They communicate in a hundred thousand ways as they converge and traverse the space: talking, hooting, hollering, joking, fighting, scolding, laughing, gossiping—and whatever they're saying, it's funny. If only we could see them.

Amidst the noise, a deep amber light comes up somewhere, revealing RICHARD, *who stands behind a window, watching the family wander about as though he were watching himself have a bad dream. Also barely seen through the window is* JEAN, *his wife, who busies herself with unseen tasks in the darkness behind him.*

The family seems to be just on their way out, when its last and smallest member, a young girl, drops something out of her box and falls behind to retrieve it. The family is gone by the time she gets to it, and when she's alone and bent over to grab it, a bright-ass spotlight KATHUNKS! on overhead, revealing:

TOPSY, *a picaninny in blackface—sackcloth dress, nest of pigtails, big juicy red lips—reaching for a white baby doll.*

Startled, little TOPSY *looks up at the light. Annoyed, she sucks her teef, rolls her eyes. She looks around for someone messing with the lights. Finding no one, she attempts to move on, stepping out of her spotlight and into—KATHUNK!— another one.*

TOPSY sucks her teef again, half-mutters something to herself. She tries stepping in another direction and—KATHUNK!—the same thing happens again— KATHUNK!—and again—KATHUNK!—and again—KATHUNK!— and again.

Defeated, TOPSY *heaves a sigh, rolls her eyes, puts down her box and takes her position. She cues somebody, and a simple version of "Dixie" begins playing.*

Suddenly possessed by some spirit, TOPSY *begins jesting, emoting, grinning, and grimacing, all the while dancing something that looked like a jig and a tap dance had a baby that was slow.*

At some point, TOPSY *turns around: the hem of her skirt is tucked into a watermelon-print thong. At some other point, she overturns her box, emptying its contents—which is like a hundred white baby dolls—onto the floor. She sort of dances on top of them. Maybe.*

Who knows?

The dance ends with TOPSY *mooning/flashing everyone, naughtily: she curtsies deeply, too deeply, lifting her dress completely over her head, flashing the crowd with her pubescent goodies. It's cute. It's repulsive. But there is a pattering of recorded applause.* TOPSY *loves her audience. The audiences loves her.*

Frantically, she grabs her box, her baby dolls, and exits, blowing kisses.

Immediately:]

SCENE 1

[An early morning in the Patterson kitchen. RICHARD *stands at the window, tense-looking, distracted, disgusted and confused.* JEAN *still bustles about the stove and counter, brightly handling the business of a big breakfast. There is a kitchen table cluttered with books and papers:* RICHARD's *notes.]*

JEAN: What do you see? What is it?
RICHARD [*regarding what he sees*]: What?
JEAN: Richard?
RICHARD: Baby, come here.
JEAN: What?
RICHARD: Come here and look at this.

[JEAN *tosses off a sigh, wipes her hands, comes over to the window. She looks. She reacts:*]

JEAN: Okay, now . . . Oh.
RICHARD: What is this?

[*Silhouettes pass by, moving in. Silence, while the* PATTERSONS *watch.*]

JEAN: New neighbors. This is . . . great?
RICHARD: Great?

[*The teakettle screeches or something happens that summons* JEAN *back to the stove.* RICHARD *continues watching.*]

JEAN: We're not the only new face anymore. That's great.
RICHARD: Yeah, just great. [*Audibly mumbling:*] A bunch of . . . niggers.

[JEAN *freezes, maybe drops something.*]

JEAN: What?
RICHARD [*confused?*]: What?

[*They study each other across the kitchen.*]

JEAN: What did you say?
RICHARD: What? When?
JEAN: Just now.
RICHARD: Just now? Did I say something?

[*They stare at each other across the kitchen.*]

JEAN [*confused*]: I thought—

[*Beat, moving on:*]

Never mind. I think it's great they finally sold that house. It was just sitting there, empty.
RICHARD: Do you actually think they bought that house?
JEAN: I thought it was for sale, but I don't know. Maybe they're renters, too. Why do you care?
RICHARD: Because maybe we should have bought it.
JEAN: Um, we have our own house?
RICHARD: But we're renting.

JEAN: With option to buy?

RICHARD: I mean, who are these people?

JEAN: Do you want to go over and say hi?

RICHARD: What—Jean, no! No. We don't know these people.

[*Beat.*]

Now I'm worried we're paying too much.

JEAN: Richard—

RICHARD: Are we paying too much?

JEAN: Okay, now you are just making things up to stress out about! Will you sit down? I'm almost done. And I thought you were preparing.

RICHARD [*wandering back to the table*]: I am. I can't concentrate.

JEAN: I told you you need to take it easy. There's a such thing as over-preparing, you know. You're overextending yourself. You've been on edge all morning. And you, of all people, should know that you have to keep your stress levels in check. Remember what Dr. Silverman said. / Hypertension begins with your attitude.

RICHARD [*going over notes, distracted*]: Hypertension begins with my attitude, Jean, yes.

JEAN [*crossing with breakfast*]: I'm serious. It's real. It's a real thing! You need to listen to your body. I mean, look how irritable you are. And over nothing. Think of your blood pressure. I don't want you to go into that lecture hall with a nosebleed. Here. Egg white omelette. Turkey bacon. Sweet potato and kale hash. Freshly-squeezed orange juice. Chamomile tea with agave nectar. Booyah.

RICHARD: Look at you outdoing yourself.

JEAN: Well, it's somebody's big day.

RICHARD: Don't start getting too good at this housewife thing.

JEAN: Ugh, trust me. I'm not trying to.

RICHARD: Did you hear back from those people about maybe teaching freshman comp next year?

JEAN: No. But who needs someone with ten years of experience writing press releases? I'm sure that's the last thing they want these kids doing.

RICHARD: Well someone was telling me about an administrative opening in our department.

JEAN: Richard.

RICHARD: What?

JEAN: I don't want to be a secretary.

RICHARD: It's not a secretary! It's an administrative position!

JEAN: It's a secretary. Trust me. Besides, I don't want to be a secretary in my husband's office. Think about how that would look.

RICHARD [*pulling her onto his lap*]: Oh come on. What? Are you afraid of getting sexually harassed?

JEAN [*getting covered in kisses, enjoying it*]: Maybe. Or not harassed enough. All those co-eds coming in and out of your office, trying to get extensions. I would just get too jealous. I would do something rash.

RICHARD [*with a kiss*]: Rash like what?

JEAN: Like tell your wife.

RICHARD [*with another kiss*]: Tell her what?

JEAN: Tell her to—

[*Suddenly,* MELODY *enters like a cyclone with a backpack, grumpy, pubescent, prone to shrieking, maybe. She sees them and makes a very loud noise of disgust before sitting at the table and pushing her chair as far away from her parents as possible. In spite of this,* RICHARD *seems to brighten a bit in her presence. The parents disengage.*]

RICHARD: Good morning, baby!

JEAN: Good morning, sweetie.

MELODY: Don't touch me! You're disgusting!

RICHARD: Did you sleep okay?

MELODY: I slept fine!

JEAN: What would you like for breakfast, honey?

MELODY: I don't want anything! Stop being a parody of yourself!

JEAN [*becomes more of a parody of herself*]: You're eating breakfast.

MELODY: Whatever! I'll just throw it up later anyway!

RICHARD: Melody—

MELODY: Why is everyone freaking out at me?! God! I'm hideous!

[*Pause, in which* JEAN *sets some breakfast down in front of* MELODY, *who doesn't touch it.*]

JEAN: Your first day of school, honey. Are you nervous?

MELODY: Nervous? No, Mother! Nervous is for when there is actually the chance of something good happening. I am resigned! I'm resigned to my fate of becoming a social retard forever! And why? Because of you! Who does this!? Who transfers their kid sophomore year?! It's like all the hard work I did freshman year meant nothing! Nothing! Now I have to start all over again! Why didn't you just find a time machine and go back in time and convince your younger selves to just abort me while you had the chance!? I'm sure that would have been much more convenient for everyone!

[MELODY *gets up and stalks toward the door.*]

RICHARD: Where are you going?

MELODY: Where do you think I'm going? School!

RICHARD: You still have some time. Don't you want to hang out with your family a little bit longer?

MELODY: Are you people out of your minds?

RICHARD: Well, let me just get the keys, at least. I'll drop you off.

MELODY: No! I'm walking!

RICHARD: Why?

MELODY [*as she's exiting*]: Because it's like eight blocks away! And being dropped off is embarrassing! Besides, my fat ass could use the exercise!

[*The door slams. Outside,* MELODY *takes out a pack of cigarettes and wanders off to a secluded somewhere. Meanwhile, there is a long pause, in which* JEAN *and* RICHARD *look at each other.*]

JEAN: That was fun.

RICHARD: Should I—?

JEAN: No. It will only make it worse.

RICHARD [*going back to work*]: I don't understand why is she being so dramatic. Kids transfer all the time.

JEAN: Yes, but I can understand. I miss California, too.

RICHARD: So do I, but what else were we going to do?

JEAN: We could have waited.

RICHARD: The job wouldn't have waited, Jean.

JEAN: I guess. Though I still think you could have held out for something at Irvine.

RICHARD: You didn't think five years of teaching intro Greek was hold-out enough?

[*Beat of working, then frustrated:*]

Dammit!

JEAN: What?!

RICHARD: Some of Rose's notes are so old you can barely read them.

[*Frustrated,* RICHARD *gets up and goes back to the window.*]

JEAN: Stop worrying so much about Rose's notes. This is your class now.

RICHARD: This isn't my area, Jean. Rose has been teaching this for years.

[JEAN *crosses to embrace him.*]

JEAN: It's a survery course, Richard. You could teach this in your sleep. You could stand up there and just start rambling and it would be brilliant. Rose wouldn't have had you hired if she didn't think so, too. Just be yourself and you'll be great.

[*Beat.*]

RICHARD: I just haven't dealt with this drama crap since grad school.

[ZIP COON *enters the space, carrying boxes.* RICHARD, *still in* JEAN'*s embrace, sees him out of the corner of his eye.*]

JEAN [*playfully grandiose, disengaging, crossing to stove*]: But it's not just drama, Richard! It's tragedy! Greek tragedy!

RICHARD: That's Rose's thing. I'm just an Aristotelian.

JEAN [*fixing her own breakfast*]: Well it's all Greek to me!

RICHARD: I hate when you make that joke.

JEAN: Speaking of, how is Rose? You saw her yesterday, didn't you?

RICHARD [*out the window*]: She's hanging in there. Chemo's got her totally bald now. Walking around in these terrible wigs and with her eyebrows painted up to here.

JEAN: Rose has always painted her eyebrows.

RICHARD [*not hearing her*]: It's so sad. She's really sick.

[ZIP *has set his boxes down to pull up his pants and tie his shoes, which takes a while. Maybe he waves his big ass in the air in* RICHARD's *general direction?* RICHARD *watches him, getting more distracted over the following.*]

JEAN: Poor thing. [*suddenly exclamatory*] "Oh, Rose, thou art sick!" Who is that? Is that Yeats?

RICHARD [*unhearing, to himself, regarding ass-wiggling* ZIP]: Are you kidding me?

JEAN: Well, I don't know, Richard. I haven't read Yeats in ages.

RICHARD: What?

JEAN: I said I haven't read Yeats in ages.

RICHARD [*out the window, distracted*]: Read what?

JEAN [*giving up*]: Never mind. [*To herself*] "Oh Rose, thou art sick!" Sounds like Yeats.

[JEAN *takes a seat at the table and starts reading something—*RICHARD's *notes—just as* ZIP *is jauntily crossing the stage with a box in his hands.* ZIP *stops and sees* RICHARD. RICHARD *sees him seeing him.* ZIP *gives a spritely nod or wave.* RICHARD, *disgusted, not wanting to engage, abruptly closes the blinds.* ZIP *reacts, gives a shrug, keeps walking, and immediately:*]

SCENE 2

[*Outside.* MELODY, *finishing up a quick pre-school cigarette is finally on her way to school, just as* JIM CROW *enters from the other direction, his view obstructed by a box he carries full of banjos and tap shoes and stuffed chickens and thangs. When* MELODY *has stopped to discreetly put the cigarette out,* JIM *bumps into her, dropping all the boxes.*]

MELODY: Oh my God! / I am so sor . . .

[MELODY *sees* JIM *and trails off.*]

JIM [*collecting his things*]: It's all right. I should watch where—

[JIM *sees* MELODY *and trails off. A super pregnant pause, before they catch themselves staring.*]

Hi.

MELODY: Hi.

[*Long beat, in which they kind of keep staring at each other.*]

JIM [*sensing he should explain himself*]: I'm new here. I just moved here.
MELODY: Moved where?
JIM [*pointing*]: Here.
MELODY: Really? I live next door. I've never seen you before.

[*Small beat, in which they look at each other.*]

JIM: That's cause I just . . . moved here. Are you smoking?
MELODY: Yes.
JIM: Oh.

[*Beat, extending his hand.*]

I'm Jim.
MELODY: Melody.

[*Pause.*]

JIM: I'm sorry. You were in a hurry.
MELODY: Yeah, school.
JIM: Oh, cool, there's a school around here?
MELODY: Yup . . . You gonna go?
JIM: Oh, uh, I don't know. Maybe?
MELODY: What do you mean maybe?
JIM: I've been to school before so . . .
MELODY: What? You, like, home-schooled or something?
JIM: Yeah. Sort of. Well, no, actually. My family and I—we're usually on
    tour, so I've never—
MELODY: On tour? Doing what?
JIM: Oh, um, you know, singing, slash acting, slash dancing. My family,
    I mean. Not me. I'm just the stage manager. And we've actually been
    on hiatus for a while so maybe I will . . . go to . . . school . . .

[JIM CROW *has noticed something on* MELODY'*s face.*]

MELODY: What?
JIM: Don't move.
MELODY: Oh my God, what?! Is there something on my face? Oh my
    God is it a bug!? / Oh my God!

[JIM *retrieves it, showing it to her.*]

JIM: Shhh! Calm down. Look: it's an eyelash. Make a wish.
MELODY: What?

[JIM *sticks his finger gently in her face.*]

JIM: You're supposed to make a wish and blow it away.
MELODY: This is weird.
JIM: Just do it.

[MELODY *closes her eyes, makes a wish, blows the eyelash off his finger, and opens her eyes to find him staring into her face. They freeze for a nanosecond, trapped in its tender awkwardness: she's just sort of standing there, leaned over, breathing softly onto his fingertips. The sound of a passing car snaps them out of it.*]

MELODY [*seeing the car, double take*]: Ahh, fuck! Are you kidding me?
JIM: What?
MELODY: My dad. Did he just see me with this?
JIM: Who?
MELODY: Fuck! Shit! I have to go!

[MELODY *takes off running.*]

JIM: Um, nice to meet you!

[MELODY *exits, glancing back.*]

MELODY: Likewise! See you around, neighbor!
JIM: See you around . . . neighbor.

[*Smiling,* JIM *looks in her direction for a while then he looks at the car, which slows down and stops next to him. He raises his hand to give a timid wave. The car takes off, screeching. Confused,* JIM *frowns slightly, but then he takes up his boxes and keeps moving, right into:*]

SCENE 3

[*The Crow residence. With some struggle,* JIM *enters his new house. There are cardboard boxes everywhere.* MAMMY *is hanging up some family portraits.* TOPSY *is making curtains in a fancy watermelon print.* ZIP *is tuning a big piano.* SAMBO *is assembling furniture.*]

TOPSY: Here dis nigga is.

JIM: Topsy, please.

[SAMBO *takes a toolbox from* JIM.]

SAMBO: Damn, nigga, wut took yuh so lawng?

JIM: I ran into somebody.

SAMBO: Who you runnin' into when we just got che'ah?

TOPSY: Yeah, nigga. We don't know nobody jus yit.

JIM: This girl who lives next door.

TOPSY: Aww, shucks! Jim Crow already done founds him a galfriend. / Ooooh!

SAMBO: Aw, Topsy, don't make fun.

[SAMBO *humps* JIM.]

You know this nigga don't know the first thang to do wit a galfriend.

JIM: Shut up, you guys!

TOPSY AND SAMBO: Ooooh!

[*They continue to tease and dry-hump* JIM.]

MAMMY [*breaking that shit up*]: Hey! Y'all quit! I ain't got nerves fo y'all jolly nigga games rat nah!

TOPSY AND SAMBO: Yes, Mammy.

MAMMY: Akkin like a buncha field hands. Jimmy, you got yo' daddy's ashes witchu?

JIM: Right here, Mammy.

[JIM *reaches in the box and pulls out a ceramic cookie jar fashioned into the shape of a black tramp biting into a huge slice of watermelon or maybe stealing a chicken. I don't know. He hands it to* MAMMY.]

MAMMY: Thank you, baby. This is gonna go right che'ah. So he can always be watching ovah us.

[MAMMY *sets the cookie jar on the mantel, takes a step back, considers it. Satisfied, she clasps her hands together, looks around, takes in a whiff of her new surroundings, gets a little emotional.*]

Woo! Lawd! Ooh wee, I miss y'alls daddy so much! To think he had to die for us to see this, for us to be able to own such a nice, big ole home in such a fine, fancy neighborhood? It's lak a dream. I feel laks I'se in a dream, but I pray to Lord Jesus that I never wake up. No, no! Praise Jesus! Praise him! We made it, Jesus. Jimmy, senior, we made it! We made it, Jesus! We made it, Jim Crow! Jim Crow! Jesus! Jesus! Jim Crow! We made it, Jesus and Jim Crow!

[MAMMY *goes on and on with her spiritual melodrama, speaking in tongues, and swooning and stuff, talking about Jim Crow and Jesus, maybe improvising a little story about Jim Crow and Jesus hanging out together in heaven and watching TV or something, and the rest of the family eventually grabs tambourines and adds on to the backbone of her chanting with their own music, swooning, testifying, etc. Everyone sans* JIM, *of course, who just kind of sits there, embarrassed and stunned and excluded, arms crossed, eyes rolling. This happens all the time. Eventually,* MAMMY *catches the spirit. Everyone sans* JIM *goes crazy with their tambourines and testifying, fanning her, helping her up. Eventually it dies down as, one by one, everyone catches* JIM *sort of staring into space with his arms crossed. He catches himself and sees them.*]

JIM: What?

SAMBO: What?

JIM: What?

TOPSY: What?

JIM: What?

SAMBO: What?

JIM: What?

TOPSY: Ain't nobody said nuthin! Shit!

MAMMY: Chil'ren, why don't y'all go and heat up some uh dem collard greens and fried chicken and waffles and cornbread and candied yams with marshmallows and pigs feet and oxtails and turkey necks and black-eyed peas and biscuits and gravy and popcorn shrimp and chitlins and peach cobbler and ice pops fo' lunch? Mammy too tired to cook.

TOPSY: But, Mammy, I wanna sing!

MAMMY: Later, girl.

TOPSY: But that's what you always say, Mammy! I got some new ideas for our comeback show! I wanna show everyone!

JIM: Comeback show? / What comeback show?

MAMMY [*through gritted teeth*]: Girl! I said, git!

JIM: What's Topsy talking about? / A comeback show?

MAMMY [*regarding* SAMBO]: And take yo nappy-headed brother witchu!

[SAMBO *and* TOPSY, *with a cross of her arms, pout of her mouth, and stomp of her feet, exit, but maybe they actually just find somewhere to eavesdrop.* ZIP *stays at the piano, maybe underscores some of the following.*]

JIM: Mammy, what's Topsy talking about?

MAMMY [*as if none of that actually just happened*]: Jimmy, we coming back!

JIM: What?!

MAMMY: We booked a show at a little theater in the city! A comeback show!

JIM: Coming back when?

ZIP: Coming back this Wednesday.

JIM: Mammy, that is two days! What happened to our hiatus?! I thought we were on hiatus!

MAMMY: Yes, and hi—hiya—hia—break is over. Jimmy, it's been over a year since yo' daddy died. And we can mourn and mourn all we want to, but eventually we gotta get back into the swing of thangs! What? You did think we was just gonna be sittin' up in here in big ole fancy house just watching Tyler Perry movies and doing the Electric Slide all day? Nuh-uh, baby. We still gotta eat. We still got bills to pay.

JIM [*after a beat of consideration, with a minor sigh*]: Mammy, you should have given me more notice! You know, I have to get the space measurements and get in touch with the tech staff and—wait, let me grab my binder—and we got to put out an open call to fill Daddy's part.

MAMMY: No, you ain't gotta do that. We already found somebody.

JIM: You did? That's great, Mammy. [*Poised to write something down*] What's his name, so I can get started on his paperwork.

MAMMY: Of course, baby. His name is James . . .

JIM [*writing*]: Uh-huh.

MAMMY: Crow.

JIM [*writing/realizing*]: Uh . . . huh . . .

MAMMY: Junior.

[*Long pause.*]

JIM: Mammy, no! What are you talking about? I already told you guys, no! I can't!

[MAMMY *suddenly smacks* JIM.]

/ Ow!

MAMMY: Jim, dis fambly's been doin' what we'se been doing fo' generations now. Evvybody's done it. Yo daddy. His daddy befo' him. His
daddy's daddy. Evvybody. It's in yo' blood, Jimmy. Dat ear for pitch.
Dat innate rhythm. Dat natchral proclivity fo' mimicry. You can't
waste those gifts, Jimmy. It's yo' destiny.

ZIP: And there ain't no family act without a family in it.

[*Beat.*]

JIM: But why can't we just remake the show around Daddy's part?!

[MAMMY *smacks* JIM.]

/ OW, MAMMY!

MAMMY: Jimmy, how you gonna remake the show around the frontman?

JIM: But why can't Sambo do it?

[MAMMY *smacks* JIM.]

WHY ARE YOU / SLAPPING ME!?

MAMMY: Because Sambo got his own part.

[JIM *removes himself from* MAMMY'*s reach.*]

JIM: Mammy, I can't do this! I'm not like Sambo and Topsy! You know,
I've never been onstage in my entire life!

MAMMY: Nobody sayin' you got to be like Sambo and Topsy! You could
be your sweet self!

JIM: But *I'm* just not built for this!

MAMMY: Well, then, what is you built fo'?

JIM [*pleading, rhapsodic*]: I don't know, Mammy. I'm built for stage
managing. I'm—maybe I'm built for school! Maybe! I heard there's
a school around here. I was thinking—Maybe I can go to school,
finally—I'm really curious about—

[MAMMY *runs up and smacks* JIM *really fucking hard. It's loud and painful-
looking and* JIM *sort of falls to the floor with a shout.*]

MAMMY [*overemoting*]: Not in my house!

JIM [*deeply confused about the rules of what is happening*]: WHAT?!
MAMMY [*suddenly, to the sky, eyes closed*]: Strength, Jesus! STRENGTH!

[*Long pause, in which* JIM *is stunned,* MAMMY *sort of rocks herself, mumbling "Jesus," with her fists cocked above her shoulders, and* ZIP *is just like, La-dee-da-da-da I'm not here.*]

JIM: But, Mammy—

[MAMMY *embraces* JIM *so deep in her bosom that he can't talk or breathe.*]

MAMMY: Jimmy, shh! Calm down. You'll be great.

[MAMMY *holds* JIM *there so long, it's like a sleeper hold, and* JIM *struggles to breathe. Just before he loses consciousness, she lets him go, and he more or less collapses, gasping for air.*]

Brush up is tomorrow morning. Don't be late.

[MAMMY *looks at him, getting a little verklempt.*]

Oooh, my baby getting so big.

[MAMMY *drops the act to exit, shouting offstage, as she exits.*]

Sambo, mow the damn lawn like I ast you!

[MAMMY *exits.* JIM *and* ZIP *are alone.* ZIP *drops a bunch of sheet music onto the floor in front of* JIM. JIM *looks up at* ZIP *pleadingly.*]

ZIP: You can't fight, Jimmy, so just try it. See how you like it.
JIM: And what if I don't?

[ZIP *doesn't respond. In fact, he just stands there awkwardly as if* JIM *hadn't said anything before awkwardly exiting, dandily.* JIM *is alone. He stares at the pile of sheet music in front of him, full of dread, and lights fade, as immediately:*]

SCENE 4

[*A podium in a noisy college lecture hall.* RICHARD *rushes in hurriedly with his briefcase and stands behind it. The lecture hall begins to quiet itself down.* RICHARD *is rifling through his briefcase, looking for his notes, realizing he's left them at home.*]

RICHARD: Good morning, everyone. Good morning. You'll have to excuse me. I ran into a bit of traffic on the way from my daughter's . . . school . . . and I've left my notes . . . at home . . .

[*Beat, as it dawns on him.*]

Great.

[*Beat, during which it looks like he might have a meltdown, then closes his briefcase.*]

Um, but that's okay! All right: Good morning! Um.

[*Beat, during which he takes in the vastness of the room again.*]

I know many of you were expecting Professor Wexler, but unfortunately she had to take a last-minute leave, but due to the class's popularity and the fact of its being overenrolled! . . . I have been asked by the department to fill in for her, though we will still go ahead and use her syllabus. So, um, my name is Professor Patterson, Richard Patterson, I guess, and, um, we should start off with . . . we should start off with . . . um . . .

[*Long beat.*]

What the fuck am I doing? . . .
[*Recovering*] Here—uh—you here—doing—uh—What the fuck are we doing here?

[*The class is a little scandalized.*]

Oh, come on now. We're all adults here. Sometimes I'm just going to curse. I'm just going to keep "real" like that. Anyone? Now, come on. This is about the easiest question I'll ask you all semester: What the . . . heck are we doing here?

VOICE OF A STUDENT: Uh . . . we're here to learn?

RICHARD [*making it up as he goes, but finding his footing*]: Okay. Yeah . . . that's . . . that's true, but there's actually a bigger question that I'm trying to get at, which is, uh . . . What, uh, is the meaning of your existence? Uh, what are we all doing right now in this room in this moment here together? How did we get here? What is it, in your life, that brings you to where we are right now, in this room, together? To this class? On Greek tragedy?

[*Beat.*]

No? Too deep? Okay, well let's try something else: Tragedy! What is it? Anyone? Nope? Did I scare you guys away? Okay, well, say this: a tragedy . . . is a play. A sad play. A tragedy is a play about suffering. A play about someone who suffers. That's it. And why do they suffer? A person suffers because they lose . . . something. Sufferers are losers and when we are watching a tragedy, we are bearing witness to basically the worst day in a person's life, yes? But, you know, where does the worst day in someone's life come from? Where does loss begin? Say you're having a horrible day—if you trace back every single event, decision, or thing that took you to that day—if you count up and assess and scrutinize and probe every single day that came before it— where does it take you? For instance, just as a silly example: my notes! I forgot them! What a tragedy! Boo hoo hoo! Now you all think I'm a terrible professor! But where did that moment of forgetfulness begin? Where could my mind have been while packing my briefcase? Maybe I didn't get enough sleep because I've been up all night? Maybe because my wife made a weird breakfast? Maybe because my daughter threw a little tantrum at the kitchen table this morning and threw me off? Or maybe because we have new . . . neigh . . . new neighbors. Who have moved in. But I digress! What I mean to say is it might be helpful for us to keep this in mind: the power of tragedy goes beyond the events of the drama itself. Tragedies are about something bigger than simply the worst day or hours or even minutes of someone's life. Tragedies are about the breadth of life in its entirety, the very experience of living, the terror of it—of the not knowing—and how the simplest and most innocent choices we make—and occasionally the choices of others thrust upon us in the most innocuous stretches of our past—can have such disastrous effects, can follow us, haunting us, deep into our very present . . . into this present even . . . and this present . . . and this present . . . and this present . . . and this present . . . and this present . . . and this present . . .

[RICHARD *seems more and more pleased with himself, as lights change immediately:*]

SCENE 5

[*Lights up on the Patterson kitchen.* JEAN *is still sitting at the table, drinking tea, staring into space with a big, thick book splayed open in front of her. Is she thinking about something she just read? Or is she just zoning out? Suddenly,* ZIP *is at the door. He knocks and* JEAN *jumps a bit, startled. A little disoriented, she gets up to go open the door. They are both surprised by each other's appearance.* ZIP *carries a jar of something.*]

ZIP: Oh. Good morning. I'm looking for the . . . lady . . . of the house . . . ?

JEAN: Yes, um. Speaking. Um—

ZIP: Oh! Hi. Uh, my family and I just moved in next / next door.

JEAN: Yes. Yes yes yes yes yes!

ZIP: Zip Coon Crow.

JEAN: Mr. Coon Crow.

ZIP: The last name is just Crow.

JEAN: Just Crow.

ZIP: But you can call me Zip.

JEAN: Zip.

[*Pause.*]

JEAN [*almost shouting*]: Oh! Jean! I'm Jean! Patterson!

ZIP: Jean.

[*Pause.*]

Well, I just thought I'd come over and introduce myself and drop off a little "howdy neighbor" gift. Pickled pig intestines! A special recipe.

[ZIP *hands her the jar. It's heavy.*]

JEAN: Oh! . . . Yum. Thank you!

ZIP: Oh, please. Just being neighborly.

[*Pause, in which they stare at each other.* ZIP *wants to be invited in.*]

JEAN [*embarrassed, frantic*]: Oh, I'm sorry—would you like to come in for a bit? Would you like some tea?

ZIP: Why, I'd be delighted.

JEAN [*rushing to make tea*]: We only have chamomile right now. I hope that's okay.

[ZIP *enters.*]

ZIP: Girl, I only do herbal.

[*Beat.* ZIP *notices* JEAN's *big-ass book.*]

A little light reading?
JEAN: Oh, psh, no. I was just looking something up.
ZIP: What?
JEAN: A poem. Couldn't find it, though.
ZIP: Ah, po-e-try! I love po-e-try!

[ZIP *turns the book over, confidently trying to read the cover.*]

[*Sounds like*] "Yeets"?

[JEAN *brings tea over.*]

JEAN: Uh, it's actually pronounced "Yates."
ZIP: Are you sure? 'Cuz that look like "Yeets."
JEAN: Uh, I'm sure.

[*Awkward pause, then sipping.*]

So! Hey!
ZIP: Hey!
JEAN: Welcome to the neighborhood.
ZIP: Thank you!
JEAN: Where the heck did you guys come from—I mean, where are you from?
ZIP: Oh, here and there. Everywhere. Nowhere, really. Gypsies, mostly, been on tour for about as long as I can remember, but we thought it might be time to settle down.
JEAN: On tour?
ZIP: Yes. My family and I, we're performers. Maybe you've heard of us? The Crow Family Coon-A-Palooza? [*Makes a crazy face, with outlandish accent*] "Mo' Coon Than A Little Bit!"

[*He breaks it.*]

No?

JEAN: No. Never.

ZIP: That's weird. Though we have been off the grid for a while.

JEAN: Ah. What exactly is it that you guys do?

ZIP: Oh, you know.

[*Beat.*]

And what do *you* do for a living?!

JEAN: Me? Oh, I don't—I don't really work. Not right now, at least. I mean, I used to. Work, I mean. PR. But I'm looking. I have an MFA. So, you know . . . it's hard . . . But my husband, Richard, is a professor! At the college. In the Classics Department. Adjunct-soon-to-be-assistant-professor! Fingers crossed! We'll see how it goes today. Or, actually—

[JEAN *looks at a clock/watch.*]

We'll see how it goes three minutes ago!

ZIP: What happened three minutes ago?

JEAN [*motormouth*]: His first lecture is today—was today—was now—We're actually sort of new here ourselves—I should have said that earlier—We moved here the end last Spring, from San Francisco. Richard was hired last minute to fill in for this lecture class at the last minute—because the department chair, who usually teaches the class, one of his old teachers actually, from grad school—this incredibly sweet woman who's actually sort of a mentor to him—she found out she has throat cancer! Which is the worst! But also great! I'm sorry, not the cancer—the cancer's not great—the cancer's worst—We love Rose—but, anyway, the opportunity—it's great for Richard, because, you know, I think Rose's been planning to . . . retire soon, and he thinks—you know, if Richard does a good job with this class, they might actually hire him full-time, as Rose's replacement, which would . . . you know, which would make a difference! So, you know, this is a big day for him! For us!

ZIP: Is your husband a tall man, sort of . . .

[ZIP *makes a very quick, very small, not-completely-obvious gesture meaning "black"—like swiping his hand across his face—which* JEAN *immediately picks up on without much thought or notice.*]

JEAN: Yes! Have you met him?

ZIP: No no. I think I just I caught a glance at him through your window or something. These houses are close together.

[*Lull, in which he slurps his tea slowly.*]

But a professor, you say? Impressive. And an MFA for you.

JEAN: Yes, in creative writing. Kill me, right?

ZIP [*gasping*]: A poet!

JEAN [*genuinely shocked by* ZIP's *seeming clairvoyance*]: Oh my God, how did you know?

[ZIP *nods toward the big poetry volume.*]

Of course. I'm such an idiot.

ZIP: No, you're not! You're a poet! I love poets!

JEAN: Well, used to be.

ZIP: Oh, no! What happened?

JEAN: Oh, nothing happened. That time in my life has totally passed, thank God. I'm just a mother now. And a wife. Who's learning how to cook healthier. And who reads. Sometimes. Did I mention I'm looking for a job?

ZIP: A mother?

JEAN: Yes! I have a daughter! Melody. She's just turned fifteen.

ZIP: Fifteen!

JEAN: I know. Just when you thought it was safe, there's suddenly a personality in there. Threatening to throw up all the time, coming and going as she pleases. It's great. Do you have any kids?

ZIP: Oh, no, no. Just two nephews and a niece, but I'm helping my sister-in-law take care of them. My brother recently passed.

JEAN: Oh, no. I'm sorry.

ZIP: Thank you, but it's been . . . it's been a while.

JEAN: But still . . . All teenagers?

ZIP: Yes.

JEAN [*easing the conversation into lighter territory*]: Oh, wow. So three times as bad, huh?

[JEAN *sips her tea.*]

ZIP: Oh, yes. Ha ha ha ha. But you—

[ZIP *sips his tea.*]

You've got the black husband!

[JEAN *sort of chokes on her tea.*]

I'm sorry—that's not what I / mea—
JEAN [*clearing her throat, awkwardly*]: No, no, no it's fine. It just went down the wrong way.

[JEAN *clears her throat more.*]

Um. Yes. I do. I've got him. [*Recovering,*] Ugh, you know, sometimes I just forget.
ZIP [*skeptical*]: You forget?
JEAN [*self-conscious*]: Yeah. Well, I mean, I don't *forget.* I just don't necessarily walk around being like, you know, "Woohoo, I have a black husband!"

[*Small beat.*]

It's more like . . . I have a husband who happens to be black.
ZIP: Wait. What's the difference?
JEAN: Uh, you know. Like, he's my husband. But he's also black.
ZIP [*confused, skeptical, but polite*]: Oh . . . okay . . .

[*Vastly awkward lull.* JEAN *starts to say something before* ZIP *interrupts.*]

Well, I should really be getting back to unpacking. We still got a lot of boxes in that van out front, but I hope we can do this again!
JEAN: Oh, definitely!
ZIP [*kind of just blurting it out*]: So glad I'm not the only lonely nobody in this neighborhood.
JEAN: Absolu—I'm sorry, what?
ZIP: I'm—Excuse me, I mean—was I—?

[*Beat.*]

Wow, I should go.
JEAN: No, no. What ever would give you the impression I'm lonely?
ZIP: Ohhhhhhhhhhhhhhhhhh, it's just your eyes. Those pretty eyes. You can tell a lot from someone's eyes. I think. And the way they talk.

[*Beat.*]

And you talk a lot. A lot. You know: like you don't have enough people to talk to. It all just comes flooding out, doesn't it? I read somewhere it's actually a sign of depression. Imagine that.

[*Beat.*]

[*Whisper*] But it takes one to know one, right?

[*Pause, in which* JEAN *just sort of stares at him and he holds it.*]

[*Suddenly*] All right, I'm gonna go! Have a good day!

[ZIP *exits.* JEAN *just sort of stands there dazed for a second. She looks at the jar of pickled pig intestines on her counter. She puts them somewhere. She looks at her eyes in the teapot. What just happened? Something's changing, and it's not just the lights:*]

ZIP COON'S INTERLUDE

[*Music plays.* ZIP *is there, arms filled with musical instruments—a tuba, a violin, a viola, a trumpet, a bugle, a tambourine, a banjo—just a ton of instruments. He has so many that for every step he takes, he drops one and has to bend over to grab it, and every time he bends over to pick up an instrument and takes another step, his pants—which are ill-fitting and held up by a rope—fall down, lower and lower, so he has to continually stop and hike up his pants in between picking up the instruments that keep falling; but the lower his pants are, the harder it gets to hike them up without dropping something. Quickly, it gets to the point where his pants are around his ankles and he bends down to pick them up, but he drops everything. Pissed off, he takes the pants off, holds them in his hands, picks up all the instruments—just barely—because now he has his pants in his hands. But he manages, takes a couple of steps, and then it's his underwear that start falling down. It gets to the point where they are around his ankles, and he's just flashing the goodies to the audience. He picks up his underwear, sniffs them for no reason, recoils, holds them, but now he has so much stuff in his hands he can't pick up all the instruments. He tries anyway and fails a few times. Eventually he looks at his buttocks, which are clenched tightly, and he looks at a bugle, which is one of his largest and most ungainly instruments, and then he looks at his buttocks and gets an idea. He walks over to the horn, lowers himself over the horn, inserting the skinny part of the bugle into his anus, clenches, and picks it up. It looks like he might be a success, takes a few steps, but then it slips right out. It might be too heavy for his sphincter! He tries again, lowering himself even further, rolling his eyes in an odd mixture of pleasure and pain. He has it for a second, but then he drops it again. He tries one more time, lowering himself on the horn EVEN further, rolling his eyes EVEN bigger in that crazy mixture of pleasure and pain that comes with a stimulated prostate. And it sticks! He is a success! Now that he has room enough for everything,* ZIP *bends over to collect his remaining belongings and walks proudly offstage with his clothes and his instruments and the bugle sticking out of his ass, swaying back and forth like a rooster's tail. At some point, as in the beginning, a deep amber light has come up, illuminating* RICHARD, *who stands in the window, looking on with utter disgust. Music keeps playing, but it's fading, fading, fading, until it fades into a weird bugle solo, reminiscent of passing gas, and immediately:*]

SCENE 6

[*The Patterson kitchen, later in the day.* RICHARD, *home from work, is standing there, fuming and disgusted at the sight.* JEAN *is handling dinner business, though something is on her mind.*]

JEAN: And then what happened?

RICHARD: What?

JEAN: Richard, stop being so nosey. Let those people move in and finish your story.

RICHARD [*back to reality, shaking off what he's just seen*]: What? Oh, right, well, so, I couldn't find my notes.

JEAN: Yes, you left them on the table over there.

RICHARD: I can see that now, Jean, thank you. Anyway, I'm standing up there. And I'm really starting to panic. I can sort of feel my blood pressure rising. I'm on the verge of being just like "Fuck it!" and walking out and just—I don't know. But then, Jean—you'll like this part—I heard your voice. From this morning. "Just be yourself," you were saying. "Just be yourself. Just be yourself." And then I blacked out.

[*Faintly, at some point, a small shrieking is heard in the background that grows and grows and grows, coming closer and closer, over the following:*]

JEAN: What!?

RICHARD: Well, not like passed out, but just sort of blacked out for a second and suddenly, the next thing I know, I'm . . . talking. I'm like lecturing, Jean. All these things are coming out of my mouth—smart things, like from the lizard part of my brain or something—and I kind of catch up with myself and I just *wing it*, basically, and before I know it, the hour has just flown by and we've gone over by ten minutes, but no one has moved. I can't explain it, but, there was this . . . this energy in the air. You could feel it. And that's when I actually really look up and out over that pale sea of college students and guess who I see sitting all the way in the back of the auditorium?

JEAN [*a little gasp*]: Rose!?

RICHARD: Rose.

JEAN [*heartened*]: No! She came and sat in on your first lecture? Oh my God.

RICHARD: I know. And this poor woman, after I've dismissed everyone, she hobbles up to me in her crazy wig with these eyebrows that are like up to here and she puts her arm on my shoulder and leans into me and she says—

[*The kitchen door flies open and* MELODY *enters, more like a whirlwind than ever before, and just shrieking, nonstop. She bursts in, shrieking. She stalks around the room, shrieking. It's like durational performance art or something, how much she's freaking out. Her parents just watch her, dumbfounded by the display. At some point, still shrieking, she opens up her backpack and angrily empties it onto the floor, making a mess.*]

JEAN: / Melody!

[MELODY *stops shrieking and zeroes in on* RICHARD.]

MELODY: I HATE YOU!
RICHARD: / Melody—
JEAN: *What* is going on?
RICHARD: She's / mad at me.
MELODY: MY LIFE IS OVER!
JEAN: What?
RICHARD: I was trying to make sure she was okay!
MELODY: He followed me *into* school!
JEAN: What?!
MELODY: This douche monster followed me into my first period biology class with this huge bitch of a teacher, Mrs. Chow, who clearly already hates me because she's Asian and I'm late on the first day of school, because I'm such a fat cow, so I'm a slow walker, and I'm not even in my chair good when Dad stalks in out of nowhere, doesn't even say anything, just marches right up to my seat, grabs me by my arm like I'm some sort of prostitute, and yanks me out of the classroom where he starts *yelling* at me, Mom, in the hallway with this terrible echo so the whole school can just hear him screaming about rape and crack and self-respect and People Trying to Pull You Down!
JEAN: Rich / ard!
RICHARD: Melody, you are exaggerating! I spoke with the teacher, Jean—

MELODY: *Spoke* with her? This woman like stumbles out into the hallway with this look on her face like: "Oh my God. Angry man just come in and kidnap one of my studeehh!"

JEAN: Melody!

MELODY: And then he starts shouting at her!

RICHARD: Why would I *shout* at your biology teacher?

MELODY: I don't know! Because you are a freak!? Do you understand what you've done?! You have just ruined the entire rest of high school for me! Everyone thinks I've been raped! And that I'm on crack! And I can't go back to that place! I can't go back ever again, because you are a monster and I hate you and if I could I would kill you for doing this! I would kill you and then I would kill myself!

[MELODY *runs out.* JEAN *and* RICHARD *are left alone.* JEAN *is still dumbfounded. What just happened?*]

JEAN: You followed her into class?!

RICHARD [*seriously*]: I saw some boy threatening her and I was trying to see if she was okay!

JEAN: What!?

RICHARD: When I left for work today, I passed her at the end of the block and he was standing there, in her face, like this.

[RICHARD *demonstrates on* JEAN, *points his finger.*]

Pointing at her like she's some sort of—I don't know. Harassing her.

JEAN: Harassing her?

RICHARD: Yes! Probably propositioning her with some lewd ghetto sex act.

JEAN: Richard!

RICHARD: I couldn't hear what he was saying, but she had this look on her face like she was afraid for her life before she just burst into a sprint. [*Forgetting who he's talking to for a sec, reliving it*] And of course, you know, I snap into reverse and pull right up to this little country nigger and look him dead in the face, and the son of a bitch had the nerve to give me this little wave.

[*He imitates.*]

JEAN [*fighting her incredulity*]: Richard, was this boy one of our new neighbors?

RICHARD: Yes. I mean, I don't know. Probably. He had a bunch of boxes.

JEAN: Well, for your information, Richard, our new neighbors are . . . a professional family act of trained actors slash performers, who've been on tour for the last few years. They are not from the ghetto, or the country, or the . . . country-ghetto. What is wrong / with you?

RICHARD: What? How do you know?

JEAN: Know what?

RICHARD: That they're a "professional family act of trained performers"? What?

JEAN: Oh. Because one of them came over today and introduced himself.

RICHARD: Which one?

JEAN: His name is Zip.

RICHARD: Zip?

JEAN: Yes, the one with the top hat. A very well-dressed, articulate, friendly man. He lives with his sister-in-law and her three kids. He recently lost his brother. We had tea.

RICHARD: You mean to tell me you let one of those people in this house?

JEAN: Yes, Richard. Is something wrong with that? With being neighborly?

RICHARD: Yes, Jean. Do you know who lives on this block!?

JEAN: How should I know? We've never / met them.

RICHARD: The Dean of Faculty. And around the corner? The Academic Provost.

JEAN: So?

RICHARD: So Jean, do you have any idea how close we are? Haven't I been busting my ass trying to publish as much as possible these past three years? My dissertation is finally about to go to press, I am struggling to make a good impression, and things are just finally starting to line up for us. They are just starting to pay off! And I just cannot—I will not stand to have a bunch of . . . bumpkins move in next door and fuck my shit up, okay? I'm too old to go through this again! I'm tired!

JEAN: How, Richard? How are they going to fuck your shit up?

RICHARD: People, Jean—People will see them and . . . think we're related! Somehow!

JEAN: What?

[*No response.*]

Richard, what are you talking about?

RICHARD: They're going to look at them and they're going to look at us and they're going to compare us.

JEAN: How are they going to compare us!?

RICHARD: Jean, they just will! They just will!

JEAN: Listen. These new neighbors—I mean, they're—they're certainly a . . . you know, they're different, obviously. They're not, you know, they don't look like . . . you know, but different is good. Different is good for this stupid neighborhood. I would think you would be excited we weren't the only new faces. I mean, we weren't invited to a single barbecue all summer. And I know they're having barbecues, Richard! I can smell them! No one has paid us a single visit once. No one even says hi in the supermarket.

RICHARD: Jean, this is exactly my point.

JEAN: What?

RICHARD: These older people are just not used to us. Okay? They've only been around each other for like a hundred years and they're old and w . . . they're territorial and they just have to know that we are safe first and then they come. Then they will accept us, okay? But they will not accept us if they see us cavorting with . . . with . . .

JEAN: Black people?

RICHARD: Jean, what!?

JEAN: I mean—I don't know!

RICHARD: What are you—Jean, I'm black!? Did you forget that?

JEAN: I know, but you were calling them . . . calling them . . . n-words . . .

RICHARD: Jean, no I wasn't . . .

JEAN: You—you did. You just called the boy an n-word.

[*Beat.*]

I heard you. And you called them that this morning.

[*Pause, in which they consider each other.*]

RICHARD [*guiltily but defiant*]: And . . . ?

JEAN [*flustered*]: And, well, I don't . . . I don't / really know.

RICHARD: I'm allowed to do that sometimes. I mean, so / are you, if you really want.

JEAN: I just—I just don't understand.

RICHARD [*annoyed*]: Well, Jean, I don't know how I can help you understand! So just leave it alone, please. Leave them alone. Now I have work to do, if you don't mind.

[*Beat, as* RICHARD *goes back to work.* JEAN *meanders back to the stove, but she's clearly preoccupied with other thoughts. Eventually* JEAN *speaks up.*]

JEAN: Richard, can I just ask you a question?

RICHARD: What, Jean?

JEAN: When you look at me, do you see me as your white wife? Or do you see me as your wife who happens to be white?

RICHARD: Well, is that a stupid question or a question that happens to be stupid?

JEAN: Excuse me?

RICHARD [*sighs, stopping work*]: Jean, do you look at a green apple and think, is that a green apple or an apple that happens to be green?

JEAN: So you do think of me as your white wife?!

RICHARD: No, that's not what I'm saying! I'm saying a green apple and a red apple aren't the same thing!

JEAN: Why not?

RICHARD: Because it's just not the same fucking apple, dammit, it tastes different!

[*Beat, calms down.*]

Jean, why you would want to reduce us to—to—I don't know—to wordplay? Don't you think we're beyond this? I don't think of you as either of those things. I look at you and I see you, my wife. Isn't that enough?

JEAN: But would you agree I'm white?

RICHARD: Well, yes, Jean, unless there's something you're not telling me.

JEAN: Okay . . . so . . . like . . . where . . . does that . . . come into the equation?

RICHARD: What?

JEAN: Like . . . where do you . . . like . . . see that . . . when you look at me?

RICHARD [*incredulous*]: Where do I see that you're white when I look at you?

[JEAN *nods. A hella long beat.* RICHARD *stands up.*]

RICHARD [*calmly, gathering his things*]: I think you need to get a job. I know you've been having a hard time finding something that suits you, but I think you just need to get a job, any job. Take what you can get, whatever you can get, even if you have to volunteer or something, because I think you're right: all this time you're spending at home all day is really taking its toll. You are thinking all these crazy thoughts and I just think you need something to occupy yourself with.

[*Beat.*]

JEAN: That was not an answer to my question.

[*Beat before* RICHARD *finishes gathering his things and exiting.*]

Wha—where are you going?
RICHARD: I'm going upstairs.
JEAN: Why?
RICHARD: Because I can't focus down here.
JEAN: Why not?
RICHARD [*stops*]: Because you're embarrassing me.

[RICHARD *exits, leaving* JEAN *alone, who just stands there a while. She goes to pick up her daughter's things, puts them back in the backpack, but there's something sad about it. She's just doing her job, as lights change and immediately:*]

SCENE 7

[*The Crow family living room.* JIM *is at the piano, poking around. His voice is all right, but also not great. A light illuminates the window and* MELODY *is there. She is smoking a cigarette, watching him.*]

JIM [*singing, his voice cracking on the last "Crow"*]: *Come listen all you gals and guys, I'm just from Tuckyhoe; I'm gwine to sing a little song, my name's Jim Crow.* [*Not singing, frustrated*] Ugh! I hate this. [*Singing, trying to hit the note*] *Crow.*
MELODY [*startling him*]: Boo! What are you doing?

JIM: Uh, nothing.

MELODY: Liar. What were you just singing?

JIM: Nothing.

MELODY [*after a beat, exiting the window*]: Then come outside. Since you're doing nothing.

[*He grabs a coat or something and exits through the side door. Lights go down on his home. Lights up on the lawn between the two homes. They assess each other.*]

You want a cigarette?

JIM: No thanks.

MELODY: Have one.

JIM: No thanks.

MELODY: Come on!

JIM: I'm cool. How was school?

MELODY: Ugh, it was my asshole.

JIM: Uh . . . what?

MELODY: It was the worst.

JIM: Oh. Why?

MELODY: I don't want to talk about it. But, just FYI, my dad thinks you're trying to rape me.

JIM: What?

MELODY: He saw you earlier. I mean you *were* really aggressive with that eyelash.

JIM: I'm sorry—

MELODY: I'm kidding. It was a frickin' eyelash. My father is just an asshole.

[*Beat.*]

Is your father an asshole?

JIM: Uh, well, my dad is dead.

MELODY: Oh! I'm so sorry.

JIM: It's fine.

[*Beat.*]

[*Politely changing subject*] So did your wish come true, or?

MELODY: What? Oh. No. Of course not.

JIM: What did you wish for?

MELODY: I can't tell you that!

JIM: Why not?

MELODY: Because then it will never come true.

JIM [*surprisingly suave*]: Well, maybe if you tell me, I can make it come true.

MELODY [*saccharine rebuff*]: Awww. A cornball!

[*Noting* JIM*'s insecurity, a peace offering of cigarettes.*]

You sure you don't want one?

JIM: No. Smoking's bad for you.

[MELODY *lights a new one.*]

MELODY: Not if you quit before you turn 26. [*Exhaling*] Anyway, we just moved here, too.

JIM: Oh yeah? How do you like it?

MELODY: Ugh, I hate it. I'm a Cali girl. This place is for the birds. There's nothing to do here.

JIM: Nothing?

MELODY: Well, I mean, there's like hiking trails and shit, if you're the kind of moron who likes to hike. And, like, the campus, which is almost fun, in the summer at least, when it's empty. And there's a Whole Foods.

JIM [*rapt*]: Uh-huh . . .

MELODY [*noticing how strung along he is*]: And a playground, over by the hiking trail. Sometimes, I'll hang out there long enough and this guy will drive up in a BMW and offer me twenty bucks to get in the car with him.

JIM: Wow. Twenty dollars just for that?

MELODY: Well, I mean, that and a blowjob.

JIM: A what?

MELODY: A blowjob. I suck his dick? I put his penis into my mouth and move it around until—

JIM: Oh my God, Melody. That's called a what?

MELODY: A blowjob. And then, of course, if the money's right, I like let him have sex with me. But I'm still a virgin, so I only let him put it in my butt . . .

[*Pause.*]

Oh my God, I'm totally kidding.

JIM: So that doesn't really happen?

MELODY: Of course not! Do I look like a child whore? God, your sense of humor is like so off.

JIM: You're really crazy. And a really good liar. You could be an actress.

MELODY: Ugh, please. Not with this fat face.

JIM: Oh, stop, you know you're very pretty.

MELODY [*meek, no one's ever said anything like this to her before*]: I'm not pretty.

JIM: Uh, yes you are.

MELODY: No, I'm not. I'm fat and I talk too much and I'm / fugly.

JIM: And you're super-pretty. Shut up.

[*Long pause. Check.*]

MELODY: Well, you are like this huge corn machine. It's like you open your mouth and all this corn falls out.

[*Beat, in which she studies him.*]

Have you ever kissed a girl before?

JIM: No. Have you?

MELODY: Yes.

[MELODY *kisses him suddenly. He is, at first, completely taken off guard and very uncomfortable, but eventually he relaxes into it. It's sweet. It's electric. It's a first kiss. They eventually disengage each other and share a slightly giddy pause.*]

MELODY [*playing it off*]: All right. I'm going to go back inside now.

JIM: Okay. Uh, I hope you have a better day at school tomorrow.

MELODY: I'm not going to school tomorrow.

JIM: Don't you have to?

MELODY: Not if I don't want to. So watch out.

[*Turning to exit, she stops herself.*]

Hey, wait, did you write that song?

JIM: What song?

MELODY: "Come listen all your gals and girls . . ."

JIM: Oh. No, no, no. It's a song my dad used to sing.

MELODY [*touched*]: Oh. Well, you got a decent voice. You could be on *American Idol*.

JIM: Shut up.

MELODY: No, you shut up.

[*Beat, smiling.*]

Good night.

[JIM *waves awkwardly as she carefully sneaks back inside the house.* JIM *stands at his door, watching her, before he starts to go back inside. A small blackout, in which a screeching starts.*]

SCENE 8

[*The Patterson kitchen the next morning.* JEAN *sits at the table alone, reading the newspaper, circling things. She looks through it unhappily, despondently, to the sound track of* MELODY'S *distant screeching again, to which* JEAN *now seems immune. At some point,* JEAN's *eyes wander on to the book of Yeats poems. She opens it up and starts reading it, skimming it, thumbing through it, absently, sadly. The screeching gets closer and closer and closer and closer until here's* MELODY, *walking in. She sees her mother sitting alone at the table and stops screeching.*]

MELODY [*a little disappointed, confused*]: Where is Asshole?

JEAN: He—I mean your father left early this morning.

MELODY: Oh.

[*Beat.*]

I don't want any breakfast.

JEAN: Okay, honey. You're almost an adult.

[*Beat.*]

MELODY: Is something wrong?

JEAN: What? No.

MELODY: You look . . . upset or something.

JEAN: Oh. I'm just tired. I didn't sleep very well.

[MELODY *heads toward the door.*]

MELODY: Okay. Well, I'm going to school now.

JEAN: Good. I'm glad you're going to school. [*Stopping her*] Wait, Melody. What exactly did that boy do to you yesterday?

MELODY: Nothing. He just took an eyelash off my face.

JEAN: What?

MELODY: He took an eyelash off my face and made me blow it away.

JEAN: Oh. That's . . . weird . . . but sweet.

MELODY: Yeah. It was actually kind of gay.

JEAN: He seems like a nice boy.

MELODY: He is. Well . . . I'm going to go to school now.

JEAN: Okay.

[MELODY *starts to exit then stops herself.*]

MELODY: What are you going to do?

JEAN: What?

MELODY: What do you do all day when Daddy and I are gone?

JEAN: Um . . . a lot of stuff. You know, read. Cook dinner. Go to Whole Foods.

[*Holding up the newspaper*] Mommy's looking for a job.

[*Beat.*]

MELODY: Do you have any friends?

JEAN [*back in the Yeats*]: What? Of course! I have you. I have your daddy.

MELODY: I was afraid you were going to say that.

[MELODY *exits, leaving* JEAN *alone.*]

JEAN [*finally hearing her daughter, looking up from her book*]: Wait, what?

[*Light change and immediately:*]

SCENE 9

[*The Crow household, the next day. Different members of the family are running in and out and about, preparing for rehearsal, sans* JIM. TOPSY *walks around, stretching exaggeratedly, doing weird vocal warm-ups.* ZIP *is at the piano tinkering around, doing scales.* SAMBO *is pacing the room, going over music, maybe picking his 'fro.* MAMMY *is running around tweaking people's costuming or something. Suddenly the doorbell chimes to the tune of "Dixie." Everyone sort of stops what they're doing and looks around. They all seem mildly terrified.*]

MAMMY: What the hell was that?

ZIP: The doorbell? You'se expecting visitors, Mammy?

[*The doorbell chimes again. Everyone drops to the ground, maybe someone a little in fear.*]

MAMMY: Sambo, get the do'.

TOPSY: I'll gets it.

SAMBO: No I'll gets it.

[*They both scuffle a bit, each trying to get to the door first. They eventually open it.* MELODY *is standing there. She is kind of shocked, kind of.*]

MELODY: Um, hi.

SAMBO: Damn, shorty. Who you is?

MELODY: I, um, live next door.

TOPSY: It's Jim's new galfriend!

[SAMBO *takes* MELODY*'s hand and kisses it.*]

SAMBO: Jim? What'cho fine self comin' ova heah lookin' fo' that chump nigga when you got Sambo Crow at yo' service, gurl.

[MAMMY *pushes past* TOPSY *and* SAMBO, *making her way to the door.*]

MAMMY: Chile, hush. [*To* MELODY] Well, lookit che'ah at this purty thang.

[MAMMY *ushers* MELODY *in.* JIM *has just returned from the bathroom. He freezes on the stairs.*]

ZIP: You must be Melody, right? Y'all, this is the neighbors' daughter.

MAMMY: Ooooh! Jimmy said you was purty, but he ain't tell us we was livin' next do' to a byurty quane!

[JIM *rushes past* MAMMY *toward* MELODY—*or tries to, but you don't rush past* MAMMY.]

JIM [*embarrassed*]: Mammy! I never said—

MAMMY [*loud whisper*]: Boy, shut up. I'm tryna help you out. [*To everybody*] Oooh, look y'all, she got that good hair.

TOPSY AND SAMBO: Oooooh.

[*Everyone starts touching* MELODY*'s hair.* JIM *pushes both of them away from* MELODY.]

JIM: Excuse us!

[JIM *takes* MELODY *into a corner, the entire family watching.*]

    I'm so sorry! My family is so— / wait, should you be at school?

MELODY: No, I'm sorry. I don't know why I thought you'd be the only / one home.

MAMMY: I don't mean to intuhrupt you two, but Jimmy has a rehearsal should be warming up fo'!

MELODY: Warming up? I thought you were just a stage manager?

MAMMY: Ackchally, Jimmy Jr. here just joint the act.

JIM: / Mammy!

MELODY: Is that what you what you were / doing last night?

MAMMY: He taking ova fo' his dead daddy. Is you coming to see the show?

MELODY: Show? I didn't know you had a show coming up!

MAMMY: Yes. It's our big comeback special.

TOPSY: We opens tamarra!

JIM: This is a nightmare.

MAMMY: You mean to tells me Jim Crow ain't invited you?

JIM: I am in a nightmare.

MELODY: I guess not.

SAMBO: Nigga! Why ain't you invited her? Don't you know a purty girl always attracksin a crowd.

JIM: Okay, can we just stop please! Can we stop!

MELODY: Jim, it's fine. Look, I'll go—

JIM: I'm sorry—

[MAMMY *takes* MELODY *by the arm and sits her down.*]

MAMMY: Naw, naw, chile. You ain't got to go nowhere! We ain't got no closed rehearsals. Sit yo' skinny little behind down. Please. It's been so long since we've had an urdience. You'd be doin' us a flavor. Girl, you know, you so purty, you could be an actress.

[MAMMY *winks at* JIM, *who, in return, dies a little on the inside.*]

MELODY: That's funny, Jim said the same / thing . . .

MAMMY: Well that's 'cuz Jimmy Jr.'s got good taste! And, besides, this is his big debutt! Maybe you'll inspire him? What's da word fuh dat, Zip? Moose? You can be his moose.

ZIP: Muse, mammy.

MAMMY: Whateva. [*Rallying the troops*] All right, y'all, warm up is ova!

[*Everyone gathers around the piano, except for* JIM, *who is just standing there in his stage manager outfit, staring at the scene, shaking.*]

MAMMY: Come on, Jim.

SAMBO: Come on, nigga! Shit!

TOPSY: Yeah! We'se only doin' dis fa' yo' ass. We knows ourn lines.

[*Long pause, in which* JIM *does not move. For a minute, it looks like he might kill everyone and run away to Alaska and live out the rest of his life canning fish or something.*]

MELODY [*in a small way enjoying seeing* JIM *like this, sweet, encouraging*]: Go on, Jim.

[*At the twinkle of her encouragement,* JIM *kind of shuffles over to the piano.* MAMMY *seems pleased.*]

MAMMY: All right, now, we all just gonna skip the overture and go rite to da top of scene 1, from the group song. Mark the choreo. Topsy, you wanna cue us in?

TOPSY: Yes, Mammy.

[*"Acting"*]

"Whew! I thought massa would *neva* leave! Everybody can come out now!"

[*The playing begins. It is a rearrangement of "We Are Family" by Sister Sledge, that feels like a jazzy Broadway number, slowed down at first and building. They split up the verses and share the choruses, except replace the word "sis-*]

tabs" with "niggas." Everyone is having an incredibly fun time—sans JIM, *of course—doing the "bump," etc.* MELODY's *also kind of into it.* JIM *continues to want to die and sings quietly on his verses until he just can't do it anymore, missing his cue, fucking up everyone's energy. Everyone looks at him.* MAMMY *tries to feed him his line, but he just explodes.*]

JIM [*out of embarrassment, throwing the sheet music to the floor*]: STOP!!!

[*Everything comes to a screeching halt, and everyone watches him.*]

MAMMY: / Jimmy.
MELODY: Jim.
JIM: MAMMY, I ALREADY TOLD YOU I CAN'T DO THIS! I CAN'T DO THIS AND I DON'T WANT TO! I DON'T WANT TO! I CAN'T!

[*There is a very long, very awkward pause, in which* MAMMY *starts breathing heavy, slowly raising her trembling slapping hand, and then suddenly takes off after* JIM. *It becomes a crazy commotion—*MAMMY *swatting at the air most recently vacated by a fleeing* JIM *(maybe with sound effects),* ZIP *maybe providing some sort of chase-scene underscoring,* SAMBO *and* TOPSY *looking on, maybe shrieking and catcalling, while* MELODY *just sits there taking the whole scene in. It's like a whole thing. Eventually,* JIM *somehow makes it out the front door and flees. Things get quiet.* ZIP *is at the piano, minding his business.* TOPSY *and* SAMBO *are sort of giddy.* MAMMY *is out of breath. Eventually, everyone sort of remembers* MELODY *is there and turn to look at her. A beat.*]

MAMMY: I'm sorry you had to see that.
MELODY: Uh, I'm sorry. That was probably my fault.
TOPSY [*sassy-sarcastic*]: Oh you think!?
MAMMY: Aw, naw, Jimmy Jr.'s just a nervous person. But maybe it was too urly for an urdience. [*To* ZIP] Now what are we gonna do?
MELODY: Maybe I could go talk to him. I could try to bring him back. It's the least I could do.
TOPSY [*always got something to say*]: The least.
MAMMY: Aww, baby, that's sweet. He does seem to listen to you. Why don't you do that?
MELODY: Okay.

MAMMY: But take your time. Take all day if you got to. He only need to come back when he good and ready. I'm not gon' have all that negative energy fuckin' wit our shit, now. I brought him in this world, I'll take him out!

MELODY: Okay . . . [*Starts to leave, stops at the door, to everyone*] That was totally great, you guys!

MAMMY: Thank you, baby.

[MELODY *smiles at this and exits.*]

[*To the sky, taking a moment*] Strength, Jesus! STRENGTH!

[MAMMY *says a little silent prayer, opens her eyes, turns around to look at the rest of the family.*]

All right, y'all, well, I guess rehearsal's over. Come on, Zip.

[TOPSY *sucks her teeth, exiting with stomps and shrieks.*]

TOPSY: Ugh! This is unprofessional!

SAMBO: Mammy—

MAMMY: What, boy?

SAMBO: How come you ain't ask me to sing Daddy's song?

MAMMY: Is yo' name Jim Crow?

SAMBO: No . . .

MAMMY: Okay, then. Now mow the damn lawn like I ast you!

[MAMMY *walks away from* SAMBO, *exits with* ZIP.]

SAMBO [*confused—wait, what are the rules?*]: Wait. What?

[SAMBO *stands there and looks around sadly. He looks at his daddy's ashes, crosses his arms, and pouts. Poor* SAMBO! *Lights change and immediately:*]

SCENE 10

[*The Patterson kitchen.* JEAN *stares into space, thinking. The book of Yeats is probably somewhere within arm's reach, but it's not open.* ZIP *knocks on the door, snapping her out of reverie. She answers.*]

ZIP: / Hi

JEAN: Oh, hi!/ I was just—

ZIP: I just wanted—
JEAN: I'm / sorry—
ZIP: No—
JEAN: Go ahead—
ZIP: What / were you—
JEAN: Go ahead.
ZIP: Well, Jean, I just came over to quickly apologize for yesterday. I
  didn't mean for it to end on such an awkward note.
JEAN: Oh, Zip— / don't—
ZIP: No, no. It was just so rude and I've just been feeling completely ter-
  rible about it and I feel like I've—I just feel like I've messed something
  up, because I . . . I really want us to be friends.
JEAN: Really?
ZIP: Is that—is that weird?
JEAN: No, no. It's just that—I just haven't heard that in a while.

[*Beat, as* ZIP *takes in* JEAN's *bashful reaction.*]

ZIP: Oh. So do you accept my apology?
JEAN: Well—yes, of cour—I mean, yes! Ack, this is awkward! Yes!
ZIP: Yay!

[*Do they jump up and down a little bit?*]

  Okay. Now, you go.
JEAN: What?
ZIP: What were you going to say?
JEAN: Oh, I was . . . going to ask you how the move was going! Wait, do
  you want some tea or something?
ZIP: Well, I guess I have a little time to kill . . . friend.
JEAN: Great . . . friend.

[ZIP *enters, sitting down.*]

ZIP: Moving's mostly done. Right now, we're just focusing on the show.
JEAN: What show?
ZIP: Oh, I forgot to tell you. We booked a show in town! A little coming
  out as suburbanites, so to speak.
JEAN: That's great! When is it?

ZIP: It actually opens tomorrow.

JEAN: Oh my God, that's tomorrow!

ZIP: It is. You'll have to come. Are you free? It's the opening.

JEAN: Oh! I think so. I have to check with my husband.

ZIP: Oh well please check with him.

JEAN [*uneasy*]: I will.

ZIP: Worst-case scenario, you can just come without him.

JEAN [*uneasier*]: Right.

ZIP: I'll leave the comps under your name.

JEAN [*insurance*]: Oh you don't have to comp us. We can just get our tickets at the door, right?

ZIP: Oh, please, girl. It's what neighbors do.

JEAN: Well, then you'll have to let me return the favor sometime.

ZIP [*slightly lascivious*]: Oh, Jean, please. That's gonna be the easy part.

JEAN [*after a beat*]: Uh, I'm sorry?

ZIP: Your poetry. I'm dying to read it.

JEAN: Uh . . .

ZIP: Oh, don't be coy.

JEAN: It's not that I'm coy—I just, I haven't written anything new in years.

ZIP: So something old. I don't care. You must have something around here?

JEAN: Yes, but, I—

ZIP: Great. Then go get it. I won't take no for an answer.

JEAN: Uh . . .

ZIP: Go!

[JEAN *exits, running.* ZIP *just kind of sits there, waiting, sipping his tea. Maybe he waves at somebody in the audience. I don't know. At some point, the phone begins ringing. A small change takes place.*]

ZIP [*shouting*]: Do you want me to get that?

JEAN [*offstage*]: What?

ZIP [*shouting*]: The phone! Do you want me to get it?

JEAN [*offstage*]: Oh! No, it's fine! It's probably Richard. It'll go to voice mail!

[*The phone stops ringing.* JEAN *returns with a bunch of loose pieces of paper in her hand. She is out of breath. She puts the papers down on the table in front of* ZIP.]

    This is my thesis.

ZIP: What a treat! [*Reading the title*] "The Spirit Rapist."

JEAN [*humiliated*]: I know. I don't know what I was thinking with that title. I was young.

ZIP: How young?

JEAN: I, jeez—how old is my daughter? 15? I wrote this right after she was born. So I was twenty-three? Twenty-four? No, twenty-three.

ZIP: Oh wow. And when did you marry Richard?

JEAN: Twenty-four.

ZIP [*doing the math*]: Oh.

JEAN: Yeah.

[*A slightly uncomfortable beat, which* ZIP *handles.*]

ZIP: I just got a crazy idea.

JEAN: What?

ZIP: I want to hear you read.

JEAN: What?

ZIP: I want to hear you read one of your poems. Do you have a minute?

JEAN: Yes, but—

ZIP: Then come on, girl. It'll be fun! Let's go back in time! I wanna meet Miss Wildchild California Coffeehouse Poetess. [*Delivered like a choreopoem*] I wanna see Jean / from Fifteen / Years Ago / that Mr. Classics Professor got to know / and fell in love with.

JEAN: Hahah, oh, no. I'm afraid you've got me mistaken. I wasn't some sort of like—I was actually really quite shy. I mean, if anyone was the wild one, it was Richard. He was the—he was the big intellectual with all the ideas, the big geeky classics major activist philosopher man. And he was a poet for a short while, too, you know—a much better poet than me. It's how we met at Dartmouth. We met in a poetry class, three times a week. He used to say the most amazing things. He had the most interesting thoughts—they always felt so . . . dense and so new. He really had that effect on people where people always wanted to be around him, isn't that funny? He was so inspiring, had so much energy. But he was really feeding off the times, too. It was a different time. Things seemed to be changing—they were changing. You could feel the change. Even at our wedding you could feel it. You know, our parents didn't really want to come—or they came reluctantly—but we just had this beautiful ceremony on the Bay—we were in San Francisco at this point—and I remember gazing out over this crowd of faces, all of our friends, and seeing our parents' faces and you could see they were moved, too. I mean . . . our marriage really meant something, you know? Our marriage really meant something.

[*Beat.*]

ZIP: Because he was black?
JEAN [*taken off guard*]: What? No!
ZIP: Oh, / I'm sorry, I—
JEAN: I mean, not really. Not exactly, or—

[*Long beat, recovers from awkwardness, bravely.*]

Did I miss like a memo or something? What happened? I mean, is there suddenly something wrong with thinking of someone as your husband first and then as a . . . member of their . . . race second?

[*Beat.*]

ZIP: Well, Jean, that's a complicated question. I mean, I don't *think* so, but I also don't know what difference that makes? I mean, it's not like one day he's going to wake up and be your husband and not be black? If anything, one day he could wake up black and not be your husband, am I right? But that's a whole other conversation and certainly not something we're going to begin to answer right now, in your kitchen, over tea.
JEAN [*lightly*]: Oh, of course!
ZIP [*jovial*]: I mean, it's not like you have some sort of a thing for black men, right?
JEAN [*laughing*]: Of course not!
ZIP [*deadly serious*]: Are you sure?

[*Long pause,* JEAN *stops laughing.*]

[*Brightly*] Girl, I'm just kidding.

[ZIP *laughs.* JEAN *laughs, too, uneasily.*]

Okay. Okay. Go ahead and read. I'm ready now.

[ZIP *closes his eyes to listen and there is a beat, as* JEAN *processes what just happened but then compensates for her easiness by getting really serious.*]

JEAN: This is the title-poem of the collection. "The Spirit Rapist."

[JEAN *clears her throat and begins.*]

"Dear Daddy, it's me—"

[*Lights change and immediately:*]

SCENE 11

[RICHARD'S *office. He is sitting at a desk, finishing something up. Someone, the audience, has just walked in on him.*]

RICHARD: Be right with you. Go ahead and take a seat.

[*He finishes whatever he was doing.*]

Okay. What can I help you with?

[*Whoever it is has a really long-winded question, to which* RICHARD *listens patiently.*]

Uh-huh. Uh-huh . . . Uh-huh . . . Well, those are some very intelligent questions, though I do want to remind you that this is a class on tragedy, so there's no need to have too many anxieties about . . . No, no, I understand—No, it's fine . . . Okay, well, the way it was taught to me is this: if you're ever confused about a tragedy versus a comedy, you just gotta look at the ending. In our first lecture, we talked about tragedies being about loss, remember? Oedipus loses his sight and his mother slash wife and his crown. *Medea*—well, it's the tragedy of Jason, who loses both his loves and his children. There is change because there is absence, there is sacrifice. Whereas comedies, most people don't realize, are fairly conservative. They're about restoration. They move in circles, reaffirming a community's values. Evil is punished and the lovers marry. Or the fool finds his fortune. Or the slaves are freed, etc. etc. So, in the end, I think, the difference is about the ending . . . but like I said, there's no real need to be too worried about that with this class, seeing how it's about tragedy . . . uh huh . . .

[RICHARD *listens, getting progressively annoyed; it's in his face, and he heaves a sigh.*]

Well, okay, "tragicomedy," "dramedy," whatever—between you and me—no, no, I understand—personally I think the category is . . . questionable. Tragedy can make you laugh. I mean, if you're laughing at the right thing. And, likewise, comedy can make you . . . sad . . . But, ultimately, tragedy is defined by loss. Loss. Change. Comedy? Restoration. Tragicomedy—it doesn't exist.

[RICHARD *listens, firmly.*]

Right, but either there is change or there isn't, there is no in between. I don't care how likeable or unlikeable your protagonist is. But like I said, there's no need for you to worry, because this is definitely a class on tragedy . . .

[*Lights change and immediately:*]

SAMBO'S INTERLUDE

[*Finally,* SAMBO *comes outside with the goddamned lawn mower—a Tiger 3000.* SAMBO *fills the lawn mower with gas. He tries over and over to start it, scratching his head like an ape when he can't figure it out. He eventually starts it. It runs for a second before stopping again. He starts it again. It runs again and stops. He starts it a third time, more comically than before, and the lawn mower runs. He tries to get behind it, but the lawn mower swivels out of his grasp. He reaches again, and it swivels out of his grasp.* SAMBO *starts whistling and pretends to ignore the running lawn mower. Suddenly, he dives for it, but the lawn mower skids away to the other side of the stage.* SAMBO *begins to chase after it, lifting his knees high into the air. He chases it offstage. There is a weird crash.* SAMBO *reenters, being chased by the lawn mower. He exits, he reenters, still being chased, over and over, until eventually the lawn mower steps out of the chase, waits for* SAMBO, *who still runs, ignorant to the fact he isn't being chased. The lawn mower, at the right moment, grabs him and sucks off his entire grass skirt before running offstage.* SAMBO *stands in the middle of the stage, completely naked, holding his privates. He blushes to the audience. He sees someone in the audience. He waves, moving one of his hands, and this enormous fire-hose–esque phallus unravels from his groin into offstage.* SAMBO *blushes again, tries to pull it back, but it's stuck on something.* SAMBO *works hard to pull his penis back and whatever object it is stuck on. When he finally gets it back onstage, he realizes that it's roped a watermelon.* SAMBO *preens. He goes up to the watermelon, tries to untie his penis from around the watermelon. He fails at the knot. Frustrated, he pouts for a bit before he gets an idea and then proceeds to chew through the shaft of his penis. With half of a penis and a watermelon, he is a success. He poses, pats himself on the back, preens. Then he licks his lips, looks around, to make sure no one is looking at him. He looks at the watermelon. He looks at his half of a fire-hose penis, which is now, I guess, the size of a semi-normal penis, and he gets an idea. He pokes a hole in the watermelon, and then inserts his penis into the watermelon, and proceeds to make wild, passionate, savage love with the watermelon. He ejaculates. He pulls out. He's exhausted, doesn't know what to do. He looks around again, to make sure no one's looking, before he breaks the watermelon over his knee. He starts eating it hungrily. He smiles the biggest smile he can at the audience. His face is dripping with watermelon juice and*

maybe semen, but that might be too much. At this point, the music is at its loud-
est. Like in the first scene, the window is illuminated slowly by the stark amber
light, revealing JEAN, *who now stands in* RICHARD's *place, with a look on her*
face like, "Uhmmm." The living lawn mower comes back onstage. The music
stops. It chases SAMBO *offstage. Lights change, and immediately:*]

SCENE 12

[*The Patterson kitchen.* JEAN *stands at the window, looking shocked and*
worried and aroused and compliant and distant. ZIP *is gone, but her thesis*
remains, as well as more books of poetry. RICHARD *enters from the living*
room, carrying his briefcase, etc. He's just come from work.]

RICHARD [*sees* JEAN *at the window, stops, concerned*]: Jean?
JEAN [*startled, covering up guilt with exuberance*]: Richard!

[*They study each other across the room for a moment and the chemistry in the*
room seems to shift, as JEAN *remembers that they are technically still fighting.*]

[*A little passive-aggressive*] You left early this morning. I woke up and
you were already gone.
RICHARD: Oh, yes. I thought I told you? I had office hours.
JEAN: You didn't tell me anything last night.
RICHARD: Yes, well, I had office hours. Rose said it's better to have
office hours as early as possible. That way you avoid all the slackers
looking for excuses and extensions who can't get up before twelve.
JEAN: Uh-huh . . .
RICHARD [*trying to make conversation*]: Though what she didn't tell me
is that instead you get the overachievers and there's nothing worse
than an overachieving classics major. A bunch of brainiac, contradic-
tory punks. Some kid came in today actually asking about comedy. I
was like, Do you realize that you're taking a class on tragedy? Then
he proceeded to have a debate with me about it. I think they come in
because they have no one else to talk to—these lonely pathetic kids.
It's like, I don't have time for this. Did I tell you I'm reworking on my
lecture for tomorrow? You inspired me to—I'm gonna abandon Rose's
notes and just do my own thing from now on.
JEAN [*icy*]: Great.

[*Beat.*]

RICHARD: What's for dinner?

JEAN [*remembering that she's forgotten dinner staring out the window all day, embarrassed*]: Oh God, dinner! Oh God, what time is it?

RICHARD: It's six.

JEAN [*scrambling, quickly assessing what's possible in the cabinets*]: Oh God. I forgot to go to Whole Foods. How is it six already?

RICHARD [*gaining a little power with his disappointment*]: What have you been doing all day?

JEAN [*slamming cabinets, agitated with guilt, seems aggressive toward* RICHARD]: Nothing. What have you been doing all day?

[*They study each other across the kitchen.*]

RICHARD [*a concession, guiltily*]: Are we still fighting?

JEAN: I don't know. Are we?

RICHARD: Listen, Jean. I have been thinking a lot about last night. Maybe I did overreact yesterday. Maybe I didn't have to follow Melody *into* school after that boy did or said whatever he did or said to her, but I need you to understand where I was coming from. I was thinking about her. It was coming from a place of protection and love for my—our daughter. I have taken this job for a reason. We have made the decision to move here and start over for a reason. And that reason is her, isn't it? That reason is to insure she has the best chance at the best future possible? The chance that we never had, right? So just trust me. This is all for her.

JEAN: He was removing an eyelash from her face.

RICHARD: What?

JEAN: I asked Melody what happened this morning at breakfast and she said the boy from next door was just removing an eyelash from our daughter's face. He wasn't harassing her. He wasn't trying to rape her. He was removing an eyelash from her face. Which actually sounds very gay.

[*Beat.*]

RICHARD: Okay and I'm supposed to believe that?

JEAN: Why would she be lying, Richard?

RICHARD: Who said anything about lying? She's fifteen years old. She didn't know what was going on. I know what I saw.

JEAN: And how do you know what you saw is what you saw?

RICHARD: Because I know, Jean! Godammit, I know these people. And you don't!

JEAN: Well, I want to get to know them!

RICHARD [*exasperated*]: Okay, Jean. Just stop—just stop right there. Please. Just stop.

[*Beat.*]

JEAN: Can I ask you a question?

RICHARD: Is it about how white you are?

JEAN: No.

RICHARD: Then go ahead.

JEAN: Can you look into my eyes for a second?

RICHARD: Okay, now what?

JEAN: Do you see anything weird?

RICHARD: Like a sty or something? No.

JEAN: Do I talk too much?

RICHARD [*genuinely confused by his wife's behavior*]: Jean, what is this?

JEAN: Do I?

RICHARD [*a little off the cuff*]: I don't know. Sometimes?

[JEAN *is hurt.*]

What? I still love you?

JEAN: Am I a lonely person?

RICHARD: I don't know. Are you?

[*Beat.*]

JEAN: I don't know.

RICHARD: Jean, what does this have to do with anything we're talking about?

JEAN: I don't know.

RICHARD: How is your job search going?

[RICHARD *shuffles through the papers on the table, as though they're unfamiliar bills.*]

What the hell is all this? How am I supposed to work here?

JEAN [*quickly collecting the papers*]: It's my poetry.

RICHARD [*with distaste, but hiding his own vulnerability*]: Your poetry? You're still writing poetry?

JEAN [*a little offended*]: It's my thesis. I was reading my thesis.

RICHARD: Why?

JEAN [*pointed*]: Because our neighbor came over today and asked to read it.

RICHARD: What? You mean to tell me you let that man back in the house, after I expressly forbade—wait, you mean to tell me that while I'm trapped in my office all day doing actual work, you're sitting up in my kitchen having Def Poetry Jam with another man?!

JEAN: You know, sometimes I just wonder why you actually married me!

RICHARD: What in the—

[*Beat.* RICHARD *sees the two teacups, turns one around, revealing red.*]

Oh. Oh, shit. Okay, wow. This top-hatted nigger is just coming over here to mess with me.

JEAN: Oh God, now you are just being paranoid!

RICHARD: Paranoid? Paranoid about what?

JEAN: You tell me.

[*Beat.*]

RICHARD: You know, Jean, you're only paranoid when you're wrong. But when you're right, you have good instincts.

JEAN: Oh, what is that supposed to mean?

RICHARD: All I'm saying is don't let me have good instincts, Jean, because this is some suspicious shit and you're blind if you don't see it.

JEAN: What, Richard! What am I not seeing?!

RICHARD [*pointing in her face, like she's some sort of . . . I don't know*]: Okay, Jean, you know what? Just fucking keep that man out of my house!

JEAN: I can't believe this. Are you actually *forbidding* me from having a friend!?

RICHARD: Yes, Jean! That man is not your friend!

JEAN: How do you know?

RICHARD [*peak of fury*]: BECAUSE I KNOW!

[*Something happens, and* RICHARD *gets light-headed suddenly.*]

Whoa.

JEAN: Richard? What's wrong? What's happening?

RICHARD: My blood pressure just—I just—

JEAN [*going to him, panicking, a little annoying*]: Oh God, Richard! Oh God! Have you taken your medication? Have you taken your medication?

RICHARD: Yes!

[RICHARD, *still irritated from the fight, sort of shakes her off a little aggressively, instinctively. He realizes what he's done, just as she realizes it and they look at each other for a beat.* RICHARD *stands up.*]

[*Exiting*] I just need to—I think I just need to lie down. I'm going to go lie down.

JEAN [*shouting after him*]: But what about dinner?!

RICHARD [*exited*]: What dinner?!

[*Zing.* JEAN *stands there. She looks around, exhausted, somewhat despondent, somewhat angry, generally confused. She looks in the cabinets again, this time not so wholeheartedly. She sees the jar of pig intestines. She takes it down from wherever it is, opens it up, sniffs it, is a little disgusted. After a hesitation, she reaches in anyway and plucks out a pig intestine. It looks sick. She eyes it, curiously, takes a bite. She chews. She swallows. It isn't half bad. She takes another bite, chews, and considers the many complexities of its flavors.*]

[*If you have to take an intermission, I guess you can take it here.*]

SCENE 13

[*Outside. It is early, early, early the next morning, and almost completely dark—well before sunrise. Hand in hand,* MELODY *and* JIM *are just now coming back from their long walk. The only light is a small pool of street light that it takes a while for them to find.*]

JIM: . . . It has nothing to do with confidence. I just don't want to play Daddy's parts.

MELODY: Why not?

JIM: Because . . . I don't . . . want to . . . be like him? I mean, I love him, but I don't want to be like him.

MELODY: Who's saying you have to be like him?

JIM: Everybody. Mammy. It feels weird just doing all the things he did. I just feel like . . . I don't feel like myself, when I'm doing all the things my daddy did.

MELODY: What is being yourself supposed to feel like?

JIM: I don't know. I like being with you. Maybe it's supposed to feel like that. A little bit.

[*Beat.*]

Did I just say something really corny?

MELODY: Yes.

JIM [*yawning*]: I must be tired. What time is it?

MELODY [*checking her watch*]: 2 A.M.

JIM: What? Mammy's going to kill me.

MELODY: No, she won't. Just blame it on me. I think she likes me.

JIM: I think she does, too. And Mammy doesn't like anybody. What will I tell her?

MELODY: Tell her I kept you out.

JIM: Kept you out doing what?

MELODY: I don't know. What did I keep you out doing?

[*As she says this, she steps into the light, revealing her face covered in splotches of black and red, and instantly we know what they've been doing. JIM notices and is, for a second, really taken aback. He makes a motion to wipe it away, similar to the eyelash moment in scene 2.*]

JIM: Whoa, uh!

MELODY: What?

JIM: You have, um—

MELODY: Another eyelash?

JIM: No, um, it's—

MELODY [*reaching for her face*]: Oh my God, what is it?!

[*She looks at her finger.*]

Oh?

[*She looks at* JIM.]

Oh.

JIM: I'm sorry.

MELODY: Oh, no, no. It's fine. I don't mind . . .

[*She doesn't finish the thought, studying the paint on her fingers before continuing.*]

You know, when I was little, I used to not wash my face.

JIM: Really?

MELODY: Yeah. Like, when I was little, my skin was like really light, like milk and I would go into the bathroom sometimes and climb on the sink and put on my mom's makeup, and then, you know, one day, her foundation—Alabaster Lilly—I put it on and for the first time, it streaks. It doesn't go on like it used to. It's white. And so I think to myself, there must have been dirt on my face—days and days of dirty had accumulated on my face—so I took the makeup off and I washed my face and I reapplied and it was still streaking. And I washed my face so many times and so hard until I'd basically rubbed my face raw and finally was like whatever and put the makeup on anyway, but when I looked in the mirror, I didn't see my mother anymore. I saw this clown, basically. So I run to my mother, crying because my face is stinging because I've chafed it and covered it in all these like fucked-up chemicals, and she's sort of confused for a second and then she sort of figures out what's happening and is trying to calm me down and she says to me, "Your skin is changing color!" But, of course, I'm like five, so it doesn't occur to me that this has anything to do with my father, you know. I still think it's because I'm not like . . . washing my face . . . and I guess I was just like so traumatized that I resolved that, rather than wash my face, I was going to let it get so dirty that I was just black—like totally black. I don't think I washed my face for weeks, maybe even months. Not until I got chicken pox. Then I sort of forgot all about it.

JIM: Whoa.

MELODY: I know, right? That just came back to me pretty recently. I wonder where that memory went.

[*Beat.*]

Ugh, but listen to me. I must sound like a total freak.

JIM: Yeah. You do.

MELODY: Shut up!

JIM: Just kidding. Well, I have a choreography intensive with Mammy in four hours.

[*Sweet beat.*]

I had fun today.

MELODY: Me, too. Maybe I'll see you tomorrow?

JIM: Ha ha ha maybe you will. So watch out.

[JIM *waves and disappears inside.* MELODY *crosses the lawn to her home and is about to go inside when she decides, instead, to have a quick cigarette.* MAMMY *emerges from the shadows.*]

MAMMY: Hey, girl.

MELODY [*hiding her face*]: Oh! Hi, Mammy. You scared me!

MAMMY: I'm sorry, baby. Can Mammy bum a cigarette offa you, girl? I'm all outta my Newports.

MELODY: Um, sure.

[MELODY *gives* MAMMY *a cigarette and helps her light it.*]

MAMMY: What's yo' brand?

MELODY: Um . . . Marlboro?

MAMMY: Mmm, girl. Mammy need to get you into Newports.

[MELODY *doesn't respond, they smoke for one second.*]

How was your walk? Y'all were out for a minute.

MELODY: I think it went well.

MAMMY: Good.

MELODY: It's so late. You're still up?

MAMMY: Yes, girl. You think this house clean itself? Don't you know Mammy don't sleep? Mammy don't never sleep. Plus I still gotta warsh everybody's costumes for tamarra.

[*Beat, in which they smoke.*]

Has I ever told you that you look ezzakly like one-a my aunties? It's like lookin' at a ghost.

MELODY: Really?

MAMMY: Yes. You purty just like her. Her name was Eliza, but we called her Aunt Zoe. Had that good hair—like you. How you get good hair like that? What you be puttin' in it?

MELODY: Oh. Well, my mom is actually white, so . . .

MAMMY: Oh! So was Auntie Zoe's!

MELODY: Really?

MAMMY: Well, no, wait, I'se sorry. It was they daddies who was white. She used to be in the show wit us, you know. I was only a little Mammy at that point, but I remember: she was such a beautiful, amazin' actress. She had all the dramatic parts—all the monologues and the dramatic scenes, jumping across rivers, getting chased by dogs. Ugh! Them was the days! After her scenes, the mens used to be lining up on the lip of the stage, tossing they booqwets of fla'hs, shouting, "Zoe! Zoe! We loves you!"

MELODY: What happened?

MAMMY: You know. I don't even remember.

MELODY: Hm.

[*Silence, in which they finish smoking their cigarettes, sort of assessing each other out of the corner of each other's eyes.*]

MAMMY: Gosh them was the days. Back when we had real drama, huh? Now all we got is palooza.

[MAMMY *looks at* MELODY.]

But obviously you're too young to remember that, huh?

MELODY: Yeah.

MAMMY [*finishing her cigarette*]: Well, Mammy gots to go back to work. Hope I be seein' you tomorrow?

MELODY: Tomorrow.

MAMMY: Yeah, girl. I like yo' energy. And we gotta get little Jimmy over his stage fright somehow, right?

MELODY: Right.

MAMMY: And you betta quit that smoking! 'Fore you end up looking like me.

[MAMMY *guffaws.* MELODY *laughs along nervously.*]

Bye, chile.

[MAMMY *exits, leaving* MELODY *alone outside, who sits there with the black paint on her face. She touches it again. She studies it on her fingertips. She looks from one house to another and back again before a sudden, small blackout.*]

SCENE 14

[*The Patterson kitchen.* RICHARD, JEAN, *and* MELODY *are all sitting around the table, eating in perfect silence.* JEAN *looks very anxious, staring into* RICHARD's *face.* RICHARD *is very intensely going over his lecture notes. He occasionally meets her glance uncomfortably. The only one not sore is* MELODY, *who eats her Cheerios and her grapefruit and her Pop-Tart with a relish we've never seen from her. She smiles the entire time, maybe hums to herself. Maybe she gets more Cheerios. This goes on for a while. Eventually,* MELODY *gets up, takes her time putting her dishes in the sink, grabs her bag.* RICHARD *and* JEAN *watch her the entire time.* MELODY *exits without a word, and* RICHARD *and* JEAN *look at each other, a little confused, but go back to their business. Suddenly,* JEAN *speaks up.*]

JEAN: I wanna know if you ever dated any other white girls before me.

RICHARD: Oh my God!

JEAN: Did those white girls ever have a thing for black men? Did you date other types of girls too? Did you date any Asian women? Or black women? Did you? Latinas? Eskimos? Did you only date white women?

[*Pause.*]

RICHARD: Don't you see how uninteresting and didactic and unproductive this conversation is? Nobody wants to hear this! Nobody!

[*Pause, in which they look out at the audience with disconcerting faces, taking in any empty seats. When they are done, they look at each other.*]

JEAN: Think of your blood pressure!

[*Lights change and immediately:*]

SCENE 15

[*Lights come up on the Crow residence. Everyone, sans* JIM, *is gathered in the living room.* MELODY *is sitting on the couch. Everyone looks offstage in eager anticipation.*]

MAMMY: Jim, you betta come on and get cho behind out che'ah! We ain't got all day!

[*After a moment,* JIM *enters slowly, totally unhappily, and in costume—straw hat, striped suit, and enormous bowtie. He kind of looks ridiculous. He also kind of looks amazing. Also, he is humiliated. Everyone reacts—*TOPSY *and* SAMBO *pejoratively. It is a moment.*]

MELODY: Jim, you look great!
SAMBO: Like a great big ole biatch.

[MAMMY *smacks* SAMBO *to the floor.*]

SAMBO: OW!!!
MAMMY [*without missing a beat*]: Strength, Jesus, strength—[*Business*] All right, Zip, we ain't got too much time, so let's just take it from Jim Crow's entrance.
ZIP: / All right.
TOPSY: Ugh, Mammy!
MAMMY: What, little girl?
TOPSY: Me and Sambo, we need to practice ourn numbers, too!
MAMMY: Hush up. I told you we ain't got too much time.

[*Beat.*]

Girl, stop pouting. Just mark yo' damn lines.
ZIP: Let's take it from Topsy.
TOPSY [*sucks her teeth, but still self-indulgently "acting" full-out*]: Sambo, you done took my watermelon!
SAMBO [*taking his cue from* TOPSY, *also "acting"*]: Topsy, you ain't never had no watermelon! You stole my chicken!
TOPSY: I ain't steal yo' chicken! You ain't had no chicken—
MAMMY: I said mark it, girl!

[TOPSY *sucks her teeth again, rolling her eyes, pretending to do her nails, half-assed.*]

TOPSY: You ain't had no chicken. Coon coon coon. Das de massa's chicken!

SAMBO [*also half-assed, quick "marking"*]: Massa coon coon nigga coon coon coon watermelon!

TOPSY: Chicken nigga coon coon coon Jemima!

SAMBO: Coon coon coon coon ooga booga, ooga booga!

TOPSY: Coon coon coon coon yassah!

SAMBO: No massa coon coon coon Kuntakente!

TOPSY [*marking a dance, very professional*]: Dance, dance, dance.

[*Stop marking dance.*]

Coon nappy coon—

SAMBO: Coon malt liquor coon coon—

TOPSY: Jigaboo coon coon—

SAMBO: Jim Crow coon—

TOPSY: Coon coon coon—

SAMBO: Coon coon coon—

MAMMY: Coon!

TOPSY: And here come Jim Crow now!

[*Music starts.* JIM *is fuming, staring at* MELODY, *humiliated, so he misses his cue.* ZIP *plays it again.* JIM *misses it.*]

ZIP [*whispering*]: Jim.

[ZIP *plays again.*]

JIM [*singing timidly, terribly, softly*]: Come, listen, all you gals and boys, I'm just from Tuckyhoe;
I'm gwine to sing a little song, My name's Jim Crow.
I went down to de river, I didn't mean to stay,
But there I see so many gals, I couldn't get away.

[*Entire family joins in the chorus.*]

FAMILY: Wheel about, an' turn about, an' do jis so!

MAMMY: Wait, cut, cut. Stop it, Zip.

[ZIP *stops playing. Everyone is all bothered by it.*]

TOPSY: Come own!

MAMMY: Jimmy, where's de choreography I spent awl mo'nin teachin' you?

JIMMY [*through gritted teeth*]: Mammy, I told you I can't do this—

MAMMY: And I told you you'se an African. Not a African't. [*To* ZIP] Take it from "I went down to de river."

ZIP: All right.

[*Music starts again.* JIM *heaves a big sigh. He is a little stronger, but still sucks. And there's half-assed choreo!*]

JIM [*singing*]: *I went down to de river, I didn't mean to stay,*
   But there I see so many gals, I couldn't get away.

FAMILY: *Wheel about, an' turn about, an' do jis so!*

JIM: *Eb'ry time I wheel about, I jump Jim Crow.*

SAMBO: This is ridiculous!

JIM: *I'm rorer on de fiddle, an' down in ole Virginny,*

[SAMBO *joins in now, subtly at first but builds to the point that he is kind of out-cooning* JIM. *He also gets so bold as to start performing to* MELODY, *which upsets* JIM.]

SAMBO AND JIM: *Dey say I play de skientific, like massa Pagganninny.*
   I cut so many munky shines, I dance de galloppade;
   An' w'en I done, I res' my head, on shubble, hoe, or spade.

FAMILY: *Wheel about, an' turn about, an' do jis so!*

SAMBO AND JIM: *Eb'ry time I wheel about, I jump SAM-BO/JIM CROW.*

[SAMBO *does the Jim Crow jig for four bars. Meanwhile,* JIM *is stunned. He looks to the rest of the* FAMILY, *who act as though nothing out of the ordinary is actually happening.*]

SAMBO [*amazing, at times even taunting* JIM]: *I met Miss Dina Scrub one day, I gib her sich a buss;*
   An' den she turn an' slap my face, an' make a mighty fuss.
   De udder gals dey 'gin to fight, I tel'd dem wait a bit;
   I'd hab dem all, jis one by one, as I tourt fit.

FAMILY [*sans* JIM]: *Wheel about, an' turn about, an' do jis so!*

SAMBO: *Eb'ry time I wheel about, I jump Sam-bo!*
JIM [*overlapping with* "*Sam-bo*"]: Jim Crow!

[*A small hoedown happens involving everyone. Lots of hooting and hollering. Meanwhile, something insane snaps inside of* JIM, *like a hurricane unleashed as he begins to take back his song from* SAMBO. *Progressively, but quickly, he becomes, simply put, the most incredible thing you have ever seen in your entire life. It's a* JIM *we have never ever seen, almost like a man possessed—eyes bugged out, limbs loose, moving, dancing, mo' coon than a little bit. It becomes like this savage contest of manhood, and* JIM *wins in the end. Of course, he wins in the end.* SAMBO *drops out halfway through, shamed, and just stares for the last line or two. Meanwhile,* MELODY *is getting all heated and starry-eyed.*]

SAMBO AND JIM: *I wip de lion ob de west, I eat de alligator;*
JIM: *I put more water in my mouf, den boil ten load ob 'tator.*
    De way dey bake de hoe cake, Virginny nebber tire;
    Dey put de doe upon de foot, an' stick 'em in de fire.

[*Even the* FAMILY *is kind of stunned. It's like his father is back from the grave.*]

FAMILY [*stunned, but working with it*]: *Wheel about, an' turn about, an' do jis so!*
JIM [*ending in a huge flourish, holding the last note, riffing, whatever needs to happen*]: *Eb'ry time I wheel about, I jump Jim Crow!*

[JIM *holds this really incredible note for such a long fucking time that the cookie jar containing his father's ashes just kind of explodes, releasing an enormous cloud of ash, like a haze, that should remain present and perhaps spread like a haze for the rest of the play. When the explosion happens, everyone except* JIM *and* MELODY *turn to watch it.* TOPSY *freaks out, as she was standing too close and is now covered in her dead father's remains.* MAMMY *immediately reaches over and covers her mouth. There is a hella long pause, in which everyone just sort of stares at* JIM. *Slowly, he seems to realize what has just happened. He stands up, as he has been on his knees, at least in my head.*]

MAMMY: Jim?

[*Pause. The atmosphere is weird.* TOPSY *is still screaming, or at least sobbing.*]

ZIP: You okay, Jimmy?

JIM: Yes, I'm—I'm fine.

MAMMY: I think that's enough rehearsing for now. I think—

[MAMMY *looks at* ZIP, *smirking, proud.*]

I think we're gonna be just fine for tonight.

ZIP: I think so, too.

SAMBO: But Mammy!

MAMMY: What?

SAMBO: But me and Topsy ain't even pracktus ourn sawngs!

MAMMY: Y'all can practice by yo'self. In yo' room. Go. And take yo' sister wit you.

[SAMBO *exits angrily with* TOPSY, *who is still crying.*]

Well, I guess Imma go head and start dinnah now.

[MAMMY *winks, cordially.*]

I sho' hope you come tonite, Melody.

MELODY: Oh, definitely.

MAMMY: And if you evuh thank you'se be int'rested in a life of the stage, girl, you let Mammy know. Cause Mammy can hook you up. [*Regarding the mess*] I'll clean this up later. [*To the ashes, darkly*] Shame on you, Jimmy Sr. [*To* ZIP] Come on, Zip.

[MAMMY *exits with* ZIP.]

JIM [*in a daze*]: I—I can't believe that just happened—

MELODY: Jim—

JIM: I don't know what—what just came—I felt for a second like—

MELODY: Jim—

JIM: Like I was outside of myself—

MELODY: Jim—

JIM: Outside of my body—but—

MELODY: Jim—

JIM: Is something on fire?

MELODY: Jim—

JIM: You must think—

MELODY: Jim, shut up.

[JIM *shuts up.*]

MELODY: That was amazing. You are amazing, you—your whole family's thing it's—it's amazing. It's wow. Wow.

JIM: What? You liked that?

MELODY [*heated*]: I've never seen anything like that before it was—I feel so—I don't know I feel so—Was Mammy serious? Oh my, I feel—I didn't know you could do that—I—

[*Pause.*]

Let's go outside.

JIM: Why?

MELODY: I need to show you something.

JIM: Well, uh, let me change.

MELODY: No! Leave it on!

[MELODY *drags him out the door and around the corner of the house. Lights change, and immediately:*]

SCENE 16

[RICHARD *is at the podium. He arranges his papers.*]

RICHARD: All right, everyone. Let's settle down. Settle down, please, and let's begin.

[*Beat.*]

Iphigenia at Aulis by Euripides.

[*Small beat.*]

What a play, huh? So, just a quick summary for those who haven't read it—

[*Gives a look like, "I'm disappointed in anyone who didn't do their work."*]

On his way to battle the Trojans, Agamemnon's ships are halted at Aulis by a sudden ceasing of wind. As a result, he seeks out the oracle Calchas, who informs him that it is Artemis who has stopped the wind because many years ago he was hunting in the forest, killed a deer, and boasted to his companion that he was a better hunter than she

was, you know, which sort of pissed her off, because she was the goddess of the hunt and you don't go around saying shit like that. Calchas
tells him that in order to placate the goddess and continue with the
war, he must sacrifice his daughter Iphigenia. And Agamemnon, you
know, must seriously consider this because his crazy, bloodthirsty soldiers are stuck at the port and are getting drunk and anxious and are
about to rebel if something doesn't happen so he's sent a message to
his wife, telling her to bring Iphigenia to Aulis under the pretense of
marrying her off to Achilles. And so the play, as we all know, or as
we all should know, is about Agamemnon's struggle over whether or
not to kill his daughter and appease his troops and the gods, or to not
kill his daughter and "screw everything up." And in the end, as we
all know—and spoiler alert to those who don't—he sacrifices her. He
kills her. Sad story, yes?

[*Beat, in which he thinks about something.*]

For today's lecture, I want to, uh, I want us to take a look at some of
what's going on in this play, and really interrogate what Euripides
seems to be saying. I think it might be helpful here for us to remember Euripides was an interesting cat, obsessed with the circulation of
power, authority, and authenticity and deconstructing a society's values, and I want us to think through this triangulation of Agamemnon
and the gods and the soldiers. Let's start by tracing back to the origi-
nary event. Now, as I've just said, this whole thing is triggered by
Agamemnon's boast in the forest. This whole ordeal is triggered by
the fact that Agamemnon has the gall to get "uppity" and tell the
gods, "Hey! I am just as good as you are!" Now most professors
would stand up here and tell you that this was hubris, you know this
really dated idea of the tragic flaw, a kind of arrogance that results
in one's downfall, but I actually believe Euripides was after something else—and this is gonna be kinda crazy—but it's my reading that
Agamemnon, for Euripides, was actually an embodiment of lapsed
courage. Not arrogance. Courage. The true loss here is the loss of
courage. Agamemnon, as a military man, who was brought up among
the lowly, ignorant "soldiers" believed he was and may have been just
as good as the "gods." And he had the nerve to believe in himself and

tell them that. And, for that, he was punished? And with what? No wind? Okay.

[*Gradually, lights start coming up so so so slowly on two separate sides of the stage. By the end of this lecture/tirade, we can just barely see, in one spot, MEL-ODY giving JIM a blowjob, the sounds of her going at it kind of amplified, and, in the other spot, JEAN sitting at her kitchen table, nibbling on her nails, sipping tea, looking crazy-eyed, occasionally glancing at her door, and looking like a total wreck. At some point, in JEAN's area, we hear a phone ringing faintly. She looks off into the direction of the noise absently but doesn't answer it.*]

RICHARD [*continued*]: So scary, right? Not really, right? But then you got these soldiers, these crazy, uncouth, country-ass soldiers sitting in the port raping women and drinking all the time and ain't got no jobs and don't talk Greek good and it's just a mess and they're actually the ones who fuck him up. In the end, it isn't even the pressure from the gods that forces him to sacrifice his sweet, beautiful, intelligent, lovely daughter. No, uh-uh, it's the soldiers and their base, greedy appetites that he thinks need to be appeased! So that's his first mistake: giving a damn about what these people thought in the first place. And then Iphigenia, when she realizes what's going on, she has this change of heart and is suddenly talking about "honor," the "honor of sacrifice," and what kind of bullshit is that, right? "Honor of sacrifice"? That's soldier talk! Obviously that is stupid soldier talk, and in the end Agamemnon sacrifices her because of her soldier talk and that shit is crazy. Honor? Honor?! These suckers just spent the last few weeks getting drunk and whoring and hanging out in a damn port! And that is not honor! That's not honor at all! They aren't real soldiers! They're hooligans! And they want him to kill *his* daughter? Everyone trying to tell him how to raise—I mean, what to do with *his* daughter?

[*Beat.*]

It's just sad, because, you see, Agamemnon was a new breed of Achaean, all right? He was a god among soldiers, a soldier among gods, neither yet both. He was the answer! He was the future! He was the change! He fucked up the whole system, and you could tell because those ignorant hooligan soldiers, them bitter gods—they was threatened. That's why they weren't gonna let him be! They're trying to get him to sacrifice his daughter 'cause they want to stop the change! And, really, I think Euripides is saying, Agamemnon should have trusted himself, trusted his instincts, and just been like, Why do they want my daughter? Okay? Why won't they just leave Agamemnon and my daughter alone?

[*Beat.*]

Yes, you have a question?

VOICE OF STUDENT: Um, the syllabus said *Iphigenia at Tauris* and we all read that?

RICHARD: I—I'm sorry what? No, no, no, my notes say you guys were reading *Iphigenia at Aulis*? You—you all read *Iphigenia at Tauris*?

VOICE OF STUDENT: At Tauris. Aulis is next week.

[*Lights go down suddenly on* JIM, MELODY, *and* JEAN. RICHARD *shuffles his notes, really nervous.*]

RICHARD: *Iphigenia at Tauris* . . . What happens in that one again?

[*His nose starts bleeding a little bit.*]

Uh-oh. Oh.

[RICHARD *dabs at it with his finger, pulls it away. There is a little bit of blood.*]

Oh, excuse me.

[RICHARD *rushes out, lights change, and immediately:*]

SCENE 17

[*The Patterson kitchen.* JEAN *sits at the table, drinking tea, staring into space with her crazy eyes, thinking hard about something. A phone rings somewhere in the house, but she doesn't notice until the last ring. She springs up to get the phone but doesn't make it in time. She sits back down, keeps thinking. She finishes her tea. She gets up to put more water in the teakettle and then the teakettle on the flame. She sits back down at the table, same crazy look in her eyes. There is a knock at the door. She jumps up, rushes over to it, opens it. It's* ZIP, *of course. He holds some mail.*]

ZIP: Hi, Jean!

JEAN: Zip!

ZIP: I just came by to drop off some of your mail. It got delivered to our place by accident.

JEAN: Thank you! Our postman has a substance abuse problem.

[*A beat, in which* JEAN *just sort of stares.*]

ZIP: Are you doing all right? You don't look so well.

JEAN: Oh, I'm fine! I'm fine!

[*Long beat, in which that is clearly not true.*]

Actually, Zip, you know, can I be honest with you?

ZIP [*worried*]: Sure . . .

JEAN: You know, something came up in our conversation yesterday—You asked me this question—

ZIP: I did?

JEAN: YOU know: do, I um, do I have a quote-unquote "thing" for black men?

ZIP [*awkward, maybe a tad revealing*]: Oh, I didn't mean to offend—

JEAN: No, no! It wasn't—I wasn't *offended*. Weirdly, for some reason, it's just really gotten under my skin.

ZIP: Well, it was just a joke.

JEAN [*flustered, nervously trying to lighten the mood*]: Yeah, I feel so silly. I shouldn't be taking this so seriously. You know it's a joke. It was just a joke. You don't really think I have a thing for black men, do I?

ZIP: No. Do you?

JEAN: No. No, I don't.

ZIP: Okay . . .

JEAN [*building to a frenzy, thoughts racing*]: Because I mean, my husband, I mean I love my husband, but you know I don't think I really walk around like . . . you know, like *lusting* after black men. I think. I mean to say, my husband is the only black man I've ever slept with and since I have been married to my husband I haven't noticed any proclivities toward men in general, much less black men. Wait, this is coming out wrong. Okay: I didn't have very many boyfriends before I dated Richard, but I had some and they were all white, but then Richard came along and he was just so—he was just very *different*. And I don't know—I don't think that has anything to do with his being black.

[*Minuscule beat, preemptive.*]

Because, like, okay I know that there are these like, "supposedly" there are like these women who harbor these psychological fantasies, where they want to be—you know fucked by like a big, strapping, muscled sort of black man with like a gigantic Mandingo *dick*—like you know that fantasy?

ZIP: Uh, I'm familiar.

[JEAN *takes this in, starts to shift gears. Around this time, the teakettle starts whistling quietly. Its whistling builds with her intensity until, by the end of her monologue, it's basically screeching.*]

JEAN: Yeah, me, too. And, um, you know, I was recently—recently asking myself how do I—how do I know about that fantasy, you know? Like where did I learn about that fantasy because—I mean, it didn't just come from nowhere, right? Or did it? But then I remembered— Okay, so there's this romance novel I read a long, a long long time ago, you know and those things are always trashy and don't ask me why I was reading it, my grandmother used to read them, I was young, I was really young—I barely remember what it was about—but there was this plantation owner's daughter with like long, fair curls and the plantation was like suffering during the war and her father just sort of dies and leaves her in charge of the plantation and it just sort of falls apart and this is signified by her ripped dress that she had to wear all the time. But that's beside the point, the point is she's really mean to this one slave, this you know big Mandingo buck slave and then all this stuff happens and then like in the penultimate scene the slave just kind of creeps into her room and takes her, you know? He just sort of fucks her brains out and then the like final image of the book is her like sitting on her porch in her dress like watching the sunset over all her slaves picking cotton or whatever in the cotton field and for just a second she makes eye contact with the slave—the buck Mandingo slave who just raped her basically!—and she sort of like—she sort of like smiles? Or something? And that recently came back to me and I was like, "WHAT?!?!?!"

[*Beat.*]

I mean, I just started thinking of this again, because you know—what was I doing reading that so young?! And like I'm thinking about now, you know, like after all my feminist theory and cultural studies classes just thinking like, like, like—those power dynamics are just so vague! Like, you know, who's fucking who here? I mean the slave is fucking the plantation owner's daughter, but like maybe he's actually fucking the plantation owner? And like she's fucking him, but like maybe she's also like fucking her dad, because it's his property? Or like maybe she's just fucking herself, you know? Like, you know, the power dynamics are so vague and like I sort of realized like, what was I doing reading that so young?! Because, you know, that's not love! You know! And I'm not one of these women, because I *love* my husband, and love is very different. Love is—you know—love is different from a "thing"! I think! Right? I mean, it's different from a self-conscious thing, by which I mean to say that aren't real "things," I mean, real things—real "things" are like deep—so deep—like suppressed, right? And so, it's like, how can you ever even know what your "things" are, you know? Are you supposed to care? And that's really scary, because how do you even know who you *are,* much less what your *"things"* are you know? And if you can't even figure that stuff out about yourself, how are you expected to even get to know other people, you know? I mean, or does it even matter?

[*Long pause. The kettle is screeching.* ZIP *just sort of looks at her.*]

ZIP: I think your tea's ready.
JEAN: Oh yes, the tea.

[JEAN *springs to take the tea off the boil, starts talking, but remembers* RICHARD.]

Would you like some—
ZIP [*seeing her discomfort*]: No, I'm fine.

[*Beat.*]

JEAN: I'm sorry if that came across as a bit manic.
ZIP: Oh do not apologize. I didn't mean to make you go so deep.

[*Beat.*]

JEAN: Ugh, it's not just you. This all just started with this stupid fight I got into with my husband last night, you know. It's just so weird that—that this hasn't been an issue for us ever, until now.

ZIP: Until now? Has something happened?

JEAN [*lying, then not lying*]: No! No. He's just—his job's—it's something at his job. Or maybe it's me or I don't know. Maybe he's right. Maybe I do need a job. Maybe I just need a job. I don't know. But would a job make it go away? I don't know.

[*A beat of consideration.*]

ZIP: Do you . . . need a job, Jean?

JEAN: Yes. Things are getting a little tight.

ZIP: Well, you know, we actually need a house manager for tonight. I mean, it's nothing really. Just ushering and taking tickets and selling concessions. It's not like a lot of money, but it's something, if you think it will help.

JEAN: Oh, Zip, that is so . . . that is so sweet. You don't have to do that.

ZIP: Oh, please, Jean, this isn't about you, honey. We really need the help.

JEAN: Well, thank you. I have . . . I'd have to check with my husband first.

ZIP: Of course. Just let me know if there's anything. Anything I can do.

[ZIP *grabs her hand, kind of tenderly—too tenderly.*]

Neighbors are there for each other. Neighbors help each other out.

[*Small pause in which* JEAN *looks at her hand in his, gets kind of nervous.*]

JEAN: Zip, can I ask you a personal question?

[ZIP *removes his hand.*]

ZIP: Absolutely.

JEAN [*she wants to know if he's gay*]: You're . . . you're . . . right?

ZIP: I'm what?

JEAN: You're . . .

[*Beat.*]

ZIP [*super-ambiguous*]: Oh! Yes! Yes, of course. Girl, yes.
JEAN: Great! I mean, great. I mean, that's great.
ZIP: Yes.

[*Beat.*]

Well, I must get going.

[*At some point,* RICHARD *enters the space, crossing toward the doorway. His nostrils are stuffed with bloody tissues, and he looks panicked.* JEAN *and* ZIP *don't see him.*]

Just let me know about tonight, okay?

[RICHARD *doesn't say anything. He stands there glowering.*]

Richard?
JEAN: Richard! This is—this is our new neighbor. Zip!

[ZIP *stands, extending his hand.*]

ZIP: Zip, Coon.
RICHARD [*not taking his hand*]: What!?
ZIP: I actually think we might have seen each other the other morning. You were standing at the window. I waved, but you probably didn't see. / You're bleed—
RICHARD: Yes, I probably didn't. If you'll excuse me, I need to have a talk with my wife about some important family matters.
ZIP: Oh I understand. I certainly didn't mean to intrude.
RICHARD: Well, you certainly did.
ZIP: My apologies.

[*Beat.*]

[To JEAN] Well, I hope to see you tonight!

[ZIP *winks at* JEAN. RICHARD *sees this and seethes.*]

JEAN [*conflicted about what she should be showing*]: Yes!
ZIP [*standing in the threshold, to* RICHARD, *maybe a tiny bit sinister*]: And, Richard, it's a pleasure to finally—

[RICHARD *slams the door in* ZIP's *face and turns to his wife.*]

JEAN [*concerned*]: What happened? Is that blood?

[RICHARD *sits at the table, puts his head on the table or in his hand, defeated.*]

RICHARD: ARE YOU FOR REAL?

JEAN: He was just dropping off our mail!

RICHARD: THAT'S FUNNY BECAUSE HE DOESN'T LOOK LIKE OUR METH-HEAD POSTMAN! I THOUGHT I TOLD YOU I DID NOT WANT TO SEE THAT MAN IN MY HOUSE.

JEAN: He wasn't in our house.

RICHARD: Excuse me?

JEAN: He was standing outside the door, dropping off the mail. He offered me a job.

RICHARD: What kind of a job?!

JEAN: House-managing his family's show!

RICHARD: House-managing his fam—What—/ Oh hell no!

JEAN [*building to a snap*]: And, also! Are you actually *forbidding me* from making a *friend*—

RICHARD: Friend?

JEAN: When all I do is sit around the fucking house all day waiting for *you* and *Melody* to come back to make me *useful* again?! Sit around this fucking house we don't even *own*, this fucking house you basically *dragged me by my hair across the country to live in*, to go crazy all day in this neighborhood full of old rich WASPs who won't even look me in the face or even hire me because I'm married to you—*because I married you*?

[*There is a long pause, in which* JEAN *tries to regain her composure. It takes a while.* RICHARD *watches her and tries to calm himself down.*]

RICHARD: What is that supposed to mean? Do you think this is easy for me too, Jean? But this is the deal we made, Jean! We're on our way to somewhere—we're trying to get somewhere and we struggle now so the struggling will stop. Right? Right? Isn't that how it works. So I'm sorry you're unhappy! I'm sorry you're lonely! But, goddammit, when I'm sitting in that office reading nonsense and doing all this shit I never thought I would be doing, I'm feeling unhappy and lonely, too! I, too, am wishing I could go back to that crappy Mission loft and live off our granola and our coffee grounds, our "poetry" and our "good intentions," but we can't because everything is different! We're different! We can't live on my Greek instructor and your bookstore and coffeehouse salary with no health insurance! That's not what we want, right? We just have to keep moving, Jean! We have to move forward. Keep moving—

JEAN: But, Richard, what does this have to do with our neighbors!?

RICHARD: Jean, this has nothing to do with them! / WHAT IS WRONG WITH YOU?

JEAN: Yes it does! Somehow! [*Excruciating*] You're . . . somehow you're . . . having issues . . . with our neighbors, because they're . . .

RICHARD: Because they're what? Because they're black? Say it.

JEAN [*unsure, not right*]: Because they're . . . black?

RICHARD: You know what? Yes, I am having issues with our neighbors. I am having issues with the kind of people they are and where they came from and how that will reflect upon us, in the eyes of people who aren't us, because of those other people's own issues. And, if I could, Jean, I would change everything! If I could, I'd get rid of those other people's issues, but I can't, Jean. I can only hold on to everything I've got and try and put my head down and keep moving because, someday, if we're lucky, we will look up and those people and those issues and those neighbors, they will be gone! And that has nothing to do with the fact that they are *black*. But you wouldn't understand that, Jean.

JEAN: Why couldn't I?

[*Beat.*]

Because I'm white? Because I'm your white wife?

[*Beat.*]

RICHARD: You know, it occurs to me now, maybe it's *you* who is having the issue with our neighbors, because they're, what do you call it? "Black." Is that what's going on, Jean? Are you having issues with our neighbors because they're "black"?

[*No response.*]

No? No answer? Are you stuck? Jean, I think you're stuck. You should be moving. [*Changing the subject*] Where is our daughter?

JEAN: What?

RICHARD: Melody. Where is she?

JEAN: At school.

RICHARD [*getting up, suddenly upset*]: No. She's not.

JEAN: How do you know?

RICHARD: Because I got a call telling me she hasn't been to school in two days, and they only called me because no one has been picking up here. And what exactly were you doing all day when these calls came in? Sitting around reading poetry? Meditating on the race problem in America?

[RICHARD *is leaving.*]

JEAN: What are you doing?

RICHARD: I'm going out to find her. What are you doing?

JEAN: Waiting here for her . . . I guess?

RICHARD: Best idea you've had all day.

[RICHARD *exits, slamming the door.* JEAN *is alone. Again. Lights change and immediately:*]

MAMMY'S INTERLUDE

[*A brassy big-band sort of music starts playing and builds with the scene.* MAMMY *is outside, cleaning clothes on a washboard. She looks exhausted. She lights a cigarette and begins to smoke. It relaxes her. She leans back against the doorframe, nods off a little, but then catches herself. She takes another drag of the cigarette and nods off halfway into the drag. She drops the cigarette onto her ample, ample, ample bosom, where it gets lost. Her breasts start smoking.* MAMMY *snaps up, half awake, goes for the cigarette, which she thinks is in her finger. She doesn't know where it is. Has she dropped it? She looks around on the ground around her, can't seem to find it. All the while her breasts are smoking more and more. Eventually she stands up straight. She smells smoke. She sniffs around comically, before she realizes that the smoke is coming from her breasts. She goes bug-eyed. She runs around, miming like she's screaming. She starts pushing her breasts together, trying to get the cigarette out. Eventually it pops out and flies all the way across the stage into a pile of leaves, which immediately go up in flames. She stares at the growing pile of flames, goes bug-eyed again, starts running around again, mimes like she's screaming again. Eventually, she gets an idea. She opens up her shirt, takes out her behemoth breasts—which are probably not real breasts—and proceeds to put out the fire with an ungodly amount of breast milk. It works. She turns to the audience, breasts hanging out—maybe the music turns to that of an African folk documentary—and then wipes her brow. Boy, is she tired. And thirsty too. She takes one of her huge breasts and proceeds to drink her own breast milk. Yum! A woman (obviously played by* MELODY) *with the big mask of a white woman runs onstage. She is pregnant. She is freaking out. She runs up to* MAMMY, *who is still suckling on her own breasts, and gestures to her stomach.* MAMMY *shakes her head. The woman gestures again.* MAMMY *shakes her head.* "No." *The pregnant white woman slaps* MAMMY *across the face.* MAMMY *nods her head.* "Yes." *The pregnant white woman gets down on the ground, spreads her legs. Lots of fake blood and silly string fly out from between her legs, yet* MAMMY *pushes through it like some sort of Eskimo pushing through an ice storm or something. Eventually, she births two babies. Twins. She holds them both, one on each arm, and holds them out to the pregnant lady. The pregnant lady jumps up and runs offstage, abandoning* MAMMY *with the two children.* MAMMY *goes bug-eyed. She runs around in circles, as before, miming like she's screaming. Eventually, as before, she stops. She notices her breasts hanging out. She takes her huge breasts and attaches one baby to each nipple. They suckle. They start to hurt her. She tries to pry them off, but they're stuck. She lets go and they sort of hang there. She tries to shake them off, but they hang there. This shaking gets more and more extreme until eventually she is doing a Mata Hari–esque belly dance, putting her hands behind her head and twirling the babies clamped to her nipples like tassels on a bra. She does jazz hands. Deep amber lighting, as before, come up on* MELODY, *now at the window, a look of total confusion on her face. The music is at its loudest.* MAMMY *dances around the stage, shimmying, twirling, maybe she pops into a split, and then she dances right offstage as the music fades into recorded applause and immediately:*]

SCENE 18

[*Lights come up dim on the Patterson kitchen. It is dusk.* MELODY *has just sneaked home from her rendezvous with* JIM. *There is a silhouette figure huddled at the dinner table.* MELODY *shakes off the shock of seeing* MAMMY *do whatever* MAMMY *was doing on the lawn and quietly closes the door, which is just barely ajar. It closes with a small click. She turns and tries to sneak toward the doorway that leads to the living room. The silhouetted figure rustles a bit and then speaks. It is* RICHARD. *He is pissed. No one turns on a light just yet.*]

RICHARD: Do you know your principal called me at work?

MELODY [*gasps, after a pause*]: Dad?

RICHARD: But I was in class, so she left me a message. Said you haven't been to school in two days, wanted to know if you were ill. And, I thought to myself, now, I saw my daughter this morning. At breakfast. Before she left. Has something happened to her on her walk between here and school? Because we both know what happened last time. Maybe she got sick or something and came home? I come home. No one's here. Mom's here, though, chatting it up with the new neighbor, little faggoty asshole in a top hat, and I'm thinking, Not here? Where could she be? I drove around for three hours looking for you, peered up every little ass crack that stupid town's got and: nothing. So, of course, I'm starting to freak out. I'm starting to imagine the worst, like that stupid nigger boy next door and that look of his—that look of his that I saw him give you. I've seen that look. That's the look of calculation. That is the look a predator gives before he preys. And I knew that's what that boy was doing to you, just as I was circling the block in my old Honda—I could see his mouth dripping with blood, you with your belly torn open, laying helplessly prostrate before him, and he's preying on you. And at that point, my only option is to head to the police station, to file a missing person's report, but they don't let you do that until somebody's been missing for forty-eight hours. But! Then! I remembered your principal's voice mail to me. Two days, she said. She's been missing for two days. Which means you didn't go to school the day before either, but you came on home, though, didn't you? You were home for breakfast. But two days. Two days of missing school. So, I thought to myself, just let me come home and wait. Let me just come home and wait and see what decides to show up.

MELODY: I'm going upstairs.

RICHARD: No, you are not! Not before you tell me where the hell you've been!

MELODY: None of your business! Why can't you just leave me alone!

[*In the darkness,* RICHARD *jumps up from the table and grabs her arm before she can exit.*]

RICHARD: Nuh-uh, girl, 'cause when I leave you alone, when I don't drive your little ass to school every morning, you get lost.

MELODY: Stop grabbing me! Who do you think you are!

RICHARD: Your father, that's who! And you're not going to talk to me like that in my house!

MELODY: Then I'm going to leave this stupid house and I'm going to be an actress and you can't stop me!

RICHARD [*scoffing*]: Oh, right! Okay! Like that's going to happen!

MELODY: Oh, right! Like I'm going to take life advice from a bastard like you! You call yourself a father! You're not a father! You're not a husband—leaving Mom in the house all day to sit and rot like a crazy person! You're a nothing! You're a nobody! You're a joke! You're a failure!

[*Pause, before* RICHARD *starts shaking her violently.*]

RICHARD: Who do you think you are talking to! Don't you know I could snap your little ass neck!

MELODY [*shrieking*]: Get off of me! Get off of me!

[JEAN *enters from the living room.*]

JEAN: What is going on!? Why is everyone screaming!?

[JEAN *flips on a light switch, and everything is revealed, and most importantly the fact that* MELODY *is smeared all over with blackface, especially on the palm of her right hand and around her mouth. There's kind of, you know, some penis-shaped smears here and there.* RICHARD *stops, stunned. He stares at her, but the stare transforms quickly into something else, into a tremor, which in turn blossoms into anger, shock, and disbelief, and* MELODY *is ashamed.* JEAN *is also shocked.*]

RICHARD: What the fuck!

MELODY [*trying to pull away*]: I'm going upstairs!

RICHARD [*stopping her*]: No, you are not!

[*He tries to lift up* MELODY'*s shirt.*]

MELODY: Stop it!

JEAN: Richard!

[*He successfully lifts up her shirt. Her stomach is smeared with black paint. Handprints disappear into the waist of her jeans.*]

RICHARD [*raising his hand*]: You little slut!

JEAN [*shouting, going to pull him away*]: RICHARD!

[JEAN *pulls him away. He is restrained. Only because something is happening to him. He is weakened. His nose starts bleeding.*]

RICHARD [*discombobulated, under attack*]: You—Jean, get off of me—
    Jean—I—fucking—I, fucking—

MELODY: You don't know anything about me!

RICHARD: JEAN, GET THE HELL OFF OF ME!

MELODY: FUCK. YOU.

[MELODY *spits in his face before fleeing the house, causing* RICHARD *to flip his shit.* MELODY *exits running, slamming the door.* JEAN *is still restraining* RICHARD, *who looks like he might be having a borderline stroke.*]

RICHARD [*almost crying*]: JEAN, WHAT ARE YOU DOING!?

JEAN: Richard, you need to calm down! Your blood pressure! Your /
blood pressure!

RICHARD: She just—Jean, fuck my blood pressure—Go after her!

JEAN: Richard, you have to calm down! You're bleeding everywhere—

[RICHARD *breaks free. He kind of stumbles to the door. The rage in him is stronger than himself. He opens the door, he looks out.*]

RICHARD [*out of breath*]: Come. Back here. Come. Back here. You. You—

[RICHARD *sinks down to the floor.*]

Oh my God. Oh my God. Oh my God.

[JEAN *brings him pills and some water.*]

JEAN: Take these pills. Take these. And drink this.

RICHARD [*in shock*]: Oh my God.

JEAN [*very scared, but trying to be responsible*]: Drink, drink, Richard. Please, drink! I hate this! I hate this!

[RICHARD *drinks. He gets a little of his strength back. Long pause.*]

RICHARD [*out of it*]: Something has happened. Something is wrong. I wasn't even thinking—

JEAN: Richard, keep—

RICHARD: Go after her—

JEAN: She'll come back! She's coming back! I need to—I'm calling an ambulance!

RICHARD: JEAN, SHUT THE HELL UP! SHE IS CLEARLY NOT COMING BACK AND SHE'S NOT COMING BACK BECAUSE YOU FUCKED UP! YOU SAT AROUND ALL DAY BEING AUTISTIC AND SELF-INVOLVED WHEN YOU SHOULD HAVE BEEN STOPPING THIS—WHAT DID I TELL YOU!? NOW LOOK! NOW LOOK WHAT IS HAPPENING! WILL YOU PLEASE JUST GO AFTER HER!?

[JEAN *is stunned. She stands up. She backs away, pretends to be clearing up some sort of a mess.*]

RICHARD: They won't stop—I knew—I knew it—They're trying to take you and they're trying to take her. But they can't—they can't have—no, this is—I've worked too hard—they can't.

JEAN: It wasn't Yeats, Richard.

RICHARD: What?

JEAN: "Oh Rose, thou art sick!" It was Blake. William Blake. Not William Butler Yeats. I was such an idiot. "O Rose, thou art sick! / The invisible worm / That flies in the night, / In the howling storm—." Finish it. Can you finish it, Richard?

RICHARD: What the hell are you talking about?

JEAN: What a shame. How could I have been so stupid? William Butler Yeats. How could I have forgotten? I could identify a poet within the first two lines, isn't that crazy? I used to have so many poems memorized. Don't you remember? In those early days together—after we'd made love—we would roll over and I could—I could start reciting a poem and you would finish it. Remember? Like that Carl Sandburg one, "Bricklayer Love." "I thought of killing myself because I am only a bricklayer / and you a woman who loves the man who runs a drug store." I love that poem. That's one of my favorite poems—our favorite poems. Can you finish that one? I was just remembering discovering that poem for the first time on my dorm room floor in college. I was just remembering sharing it with you—how we surrounded ourselves, our lives, with verse and beauty and feelings, Richard. I was actually trying to remember what I imagined my future would look like back then—back when all I wanted was to be a part of something big and fall in love. This isn't my life. This isn't what my life is supposed to look like. I don't even know—I don't even know how I got here. Is that funny? I don't even remember why I thought giving up my passion, and my poetry, and my life to care for you and care for our daughter even made any sense, you know? I don't even remember. But now, look, look at this. I'm in my bathrobe. My daughter is roaming the streets. And you—look at you—you—in the corner, huddled in a corner, shaking, pitiful. I just don't get why suddenly—suddenly everything is so hard. I mean, it was hard in the beginning. My parents—even they were calling me saying "It's going to be so hard, Jean," but I didn't care. I thought—we could figure it out. And we would. And it would all be so easy, right? And we'd be happy! And we would show them! And I thought that we had! But now's it . . . it's still hard!? But it's a different hard? Or maybe it's just harder? And I don't understand why I—we—why no one can figure it out!

RICHARD: Jean, this is no time for you to start soliloquizing—

JEAN [*really angry*]: No, Richard, I don't understand! Or at least that's what you keep telling me. Jean, you don't understand! Jean, you don't get it! Because you're white! Jean you're white, white, white, white, white. WHAT, RICHARD?! WHEN DID I SUDDENLY BECOME THIS WHITE? I thought it didn't matter! I thought that was the whole point! I don't understand how suddenly this is a problem.

RICHARD: Jean, your fucking fixation is the only problem. Race is an illusion! If you ignore it, it will go away! This is not about race!

JEAN: Yes, this is about race. Somehow. That's why I don't get it. I don't get race. But how come I can't get it? How come you won't help me get it?

RICHARD: Jean, what am I supposed to help you get?!

JEAN: Why can't you just tell me things, Richard? Why can't I know what you're thinking and feeling?

RICHARD: Jean, I have been telling you! And you haven't been listening!

JEAN: No, you haven't!—Not what you really feel!

RICHARD: JEAN, HOW THE FUCK WOULD YOU KNOW THAT?

[*Beat.*]

JEAN: WHY DON'T YOU TRUST ME!?
RICHARD: WHY DON'T YOU TRUST ME?!
JEAN: WHAT?
RICHARD: WHAT?
JEAN: STOP REPEATING WHAT I SAY!
RICHARD: STOP REPEATING WHAT I SAY!
JEAN: STOP ACTING LIKE A CHILD!
RICHARD: STOP ACTING LIKE A CHILD!

[*A very long pause, in which they stare deeply into each other's eyes, having hit a brick wall. They hold this stare for an impossibly long time, struggling to connect without words, but ultimately, somehow, failing—a failure which frustrates, a frustration which turns to anger.*]

JEAN [*with a reluctant, sad venom*]: You're a . . . you're a . . . a . . . a beast.

RICHARD [*with a reluctant, sad venom*]: You're a cunt. A white cunt.

[JEAN *gasps. Long, purposeful pause.*]

Is that what / you wanted to hear?

JEAN: Well, the only nigger in this neighborhood is you, Richard! Nigger! NIGGER!

[*Long pause, nothing happens. Nothing is resolved. They both seem confused and angry and out of breath.* JEAN *goes over and slaps* RICHARD, *lightly.*]

RICHARD: Jean, I was—

[JEAN *slaps* RICHARD *again.*]

JEAN!

[JEAN *tries to slap* RICHARD *again. He grabs her hand.*]

Jean, I swear to God—

[JEAN *slaps him again.* RICHARD *grabs* JEAN *by the neck, almost like he's about to strangle her, but then he doesn't. Instead, he punches her. He punches her square in the face. She falls backward. She holds her eye. She scrambles to get up.* RICHARD *is just sort of standing there. Fuming, breathing hard, like he's about to explode. He can barely catch his breath. Suddenly, he kind of half-collapses, grabbing his head.* JEAN *takes a long look at him, looks at him bent over, before exiting through the kitchen door.*]

Oh my God. Jean—

[*He collapses and starts to seize as lights change and immediately:*]

TOPSY'S INTERLUDE/INTERRUPTION

[*A spot comes up on a bare space and we can hear* TOPSY *entering before we ever see her. She makes her way calmly to the center of the spot, decked out in an obvious Josephine Baker knockoff—a revealing halter studded with diamonds and a banana skirt. Around her ankles, neck, and wrists are strings of gypsy bells and a shit ton of other jewelry that makes a lot of noise when she moves. Stagehands wheel a big standing harp out on stage.* TOPSY *dabs carefully at her made-up eyes, which are still a little wet from her freak-out earlier, before she addresses the audience.*]

TOPSY: Um, hey y'all. Um, so—Topsy. Hi. Hi! How y'all doing? Y'all doin' all right? Y'all enjoying the show? Yes? No? No, you not? Okay, yikes. Well, anyway: I'm sure y'all have noticed that all throughout this evening, members of my family have been coming out here from time to time and delighting y'all with some of ourn classics antics, and I wuz lak watchin' Sambo's wawtamellon bit and Mammy's *Gone with the Wind* tribute, and lak, kindsa feeling emburrassed cuz, you know, I don't think that tap dance at the beginning really represents me as uh artist. You see, recently I been having a few new ideas about the show and my role in it and um, well durin' tha intamission, I was having a talk wit Massa [Name of the Artistic Director], and I convinced him ta let me come out cheah and take this opportunity or whatever to show y'all that I'm not, you know, like the rest of my family. I mean, as an artist. It's not that I don't respect what we be doin' or whateva, but lak, I think I just have diffuhnt ideas and the work I really want to be doing maybe isn't exactly as commercial as all this. See, I'm really tryna make work about the shared human experiamentience, because, ta me, das de real definition of Art. So, uh, because y'all have really just been an amazing audience and because I thank we're running just a little bit under, I just wawnted to show y'all summa the stuff I been warkin' on. I hope that's okay? Is that okay? Great. I hope y'alls likes it.

[TOPSY *gets in place behind the harp and holds the pose, as the music cues up, maybe "Crazy in Love" by Beyonce. What follows is the most insane and brilliant spectacle anyone can dream up, during which she doesn't play the harp*] once but crams the history of African Americans onstage into three minutes. Music, video projections everywhere, dance, lasers, disco balls, fog, backup dancers, whatever might be totally unexpected, and it is absolutely nothing less than utter, utter TRANSCENDENCE. And maybe it ends with her masturbating with a banana. In front of a strobe light. She continues to do so, even as everything fades up and it is just her on the stage, completely exhausted. Recorded applause, even if the real audience is applauding, which it probably isn't. Dozens of roses begin to people the stage. A stage manager comes out to drape TOPSY in some sort of robe. She is weak, but she still loves the audience and the audience still loves her.]

TOPSY [blowing kisses and exiting]: Thank y'alls! Thank y'alls fo' believin' in me!

[Of course, at some point, as before, a stark amber light has come up somewhere on the stage, illuminating the Patterson window, but this time, the window is empty. Lights change and immediately:]

SCENE 19

[The Patterson kitchen. RICHARD is alone, drinking water and just shoveling handfuls of pills into his mouth. He is covered in blood, but he is alert. He looks like he's been stripped to a core, and you can't tell whether he's recovering or dying. He looks like complete, complete shit. He shudders and struggles to speak and breathe, slurring his words.]

RICHARD [exhausted, struggling to speak, almost unaware of himself]: O Rose, thou art sick / The invisible worm / That flies in the night, / In the howling storm, / Has found out thy bed / Of crimson joy: /And his dark secret love / Does thy life destroy.

[Beat.]

I thought of killing myself . . . because I am only a bricklayer and you . . . and you a woman who loves the man who runs a drug store . . . I don't care like I used to; I lay bricks . . . straighter than I used to . . . and I sing slower handling the trowel afternoons . . . When the sun is in my eyes . . . and the ladders are shaky . . . and the mortar boards go wrong . . . I think of you.

[*Beat.*]

Of course I remember. I gave you that poem. But I didn't write it. Some dead man wrote it, Jean. Some dead white man.

[*Beat, really upset.*]

I told you you wouldn't get it, Jean. I told you you wouldn't understand. But I don't know how to help you to understand. I don't even know if I understand.

[*He straightens up.*]

No, I do. I do. I do I do I do I do I do.

[*Beat.*]

I don't.

[*Beat.*]

I do.

[*Beat.*]

I thought of killing myself . . . because I am only a bricklayer and you . . . a woman who loved the man who runs the drug store . . . I don't care like I used to . . . I don't care like I used to . . . Like I used to . . .

[*Beat.*]

Jean, where are you? Where am I?

[*The door opens.* RICHARD *half-staggers, half-jumps up.*]

RICHARD [*almost shouting*]: Jean, baby, I'm sorr—

[*It's* ZIP *at the door.*]

RICHARD: Wha?
ZIP: Jean told me the door would be open.
RICHARD: Where is she?
ZIP: She's with me. She's—
RICHARD: What the FUCK?
ZIP: Richard.

RICHARD: Don't call me by my name! You don't know me!

[*Beat. He half-collects himself.*]

Where is my wife?

ZIP: Your wife is with me. She's fine. She's calming down.

RICHARD: She what? What?

ZIP: She sent me over here to see if you were okay.

RICHARD: Oh.

ZIP: And get her stuff.

RICHARD: For what?

ZIP: You know, I'm not sure. She just wants me to get a suitcase.

RICHARD: And do what with it?

ZIP: Well, I think she—

RICHARD: What?

ZIP: I think Jean needs a bit of time to herself. I—

RICHARD: And where is she going to go?

[ZIP *shrugs.*]

Oh. Okay. Okay. Okay okay okay okay okay okay. I see what's happening. I see what's going on!

ZIP: Listen, Brother—

[RICHARD *picks up a chair and flings it. Almost suddenly his strength is almost back.*]

RICHARD: NIGGA, I AM NOT YOUR BROTHER!

ZIP: Listen, Mister . . . You look like shit. I am going to call / an ambulance.

RICHARD: I DON'T NEED YOUR MOTHERFUCKING HELP MOTHERFUCKER!

ZIP: I really don't think there is any need for any sort of altercation. I gotta show I'm supposed to be at—

RICHARD [*mocking*]: Yo' muthafuckin' show! Oooh, my little show, my little show.

ZIP: But I didn't go 'cause I got a woman running into my house telling me her husband has gone berserk, all right? This is a favor, man. I am doing this as a favor to Jean, who we both know, and both love—

RICHARD: Love? Motherfucker, you just moved in three days ago! You
don't love her!

ZIP: Jean is a good friend—

RICHARD: Friend, my black ass. You. Just. Got. Here.

ZIP: No, Richard! We are friends! We are friends because we are
both lo—

RICHARD: Aww, cut this shit out!

[*Beat.*]

Man, why don't you just say it? Why don't you just come out and fucking saying it?

ZIP: Say what?

RICHARD: You just want to fuck my wife. You just want to fuck my
pretty white wife, because you're jealous. Jealous like all the rest of
you stupid niggers who couldn't get it together enough to change your
own life!

[*Pause.* ZIP *smirks a bit. He has been taking a kind of pleasure in seeing* RICH-
ARD *like this, subtle but sinister.*]

ZIP: Suppose I did.

RICHARD [*wasn't really expecting that*]: What?

ZIP: Suppose I did want to fuck your wife, as you say. Then what?

[RICHARD *doesn't respond.*]

Supposed I did notice you not wave back that morning. Suppose I
saw your snarl that said, Don't Come Here. I recognize that snarl,
Richard. I've seen it before. And suppose I did come over in spite
of that, to meet your lovely, beautiful, sexy, intelligent, lonely, frustrated, insecure little white snowflake of a wife and your sweet, pretty
little girl, who just wants a little attention. Your family, who you've
always taken for granted. And suppose I saw something in Jean that
you did, too, at least at one point, and suppose I knew I could take it.
Suppose I knew how to take it. Supposed I've been wanting to take it
ever since I saw her—no, ever since I saw you.

RICHARD [*another spell coming on*]: You shut up!

ZIP: And suppose I've been sitting in your house every minute you haven't
been here, listening to her poetry, stroking her hair, charming her,

whispering all kind of nice things into her ear, telling her to lie to you, telling her she can *trust* me, and she knows she can trust me, because she sees something in me that's not in you. Anymore. And suppose I been doing this for the past few days, before I even moved in, building something up inside of her, inside of both of you, something so intricate and crazy that I knew it could come to this.

RICHARD [*fainter*]: You shut your fucking mouth!

ZIP: And suppose I've been waiting. Suppose I've been sitting in my house waiting, waiting for her to come across and bang on my door, screaming, yelling, HE HIT ME! HE HIT ME!

RICHARD [*weak*]: Fuck! You!

ZIP: And suppose the first arms she runs into are mine, and suppose I grin and suppose I whisper to her, Yes, it's fine, baby girl. Zip Coon here now. Zip Coon here. And suppose I take her, and she stays wit' me.

[*A different* ZIP, *or maybe the same* ZIP, *or maybe a different* ZIP.]

So what then, nigga? So what then?

RICHARD [*so weak*]: Shut—

ZIP [*taunting*]: I know you, nigga. I seen you before. I grew up around some-a you. I ain't even have to talk to you, before I knew you.

RICHARD: You don't know me.

ZIP: Oh, but I do, son. I do.

RICHARD [*real spitty!*]: You don't know me!

ZIP: No, baby, I do, because, guess what? We'se da same!

RICHARD: No, I'm not! I'm nothing like you, you coon. You're just a fucking nigger whose clothes don't fit! A fuckin'—a fuckin' wannabe . . . no good . . . nigger. . .

ZIP: Like you?

RICHARD: Like me . . . Not like . . . me . . . You are not like me! You are not me!

ZIP: Nigga! Who is this "me" you keep talking about? This "you." Who is "you"? Where is he?

RICHARD: He's me.

ZIP: Is he? Tell me, nigga. Have your "you" tell "me": where does this "you" that is "you" even begin to "you"?! Is he you?

[RICHARD *can't find the answer, but he's trying, he's trying, he's trying.*]

Or. Is. He.

[*Makes a big show of starting to point to himself.*]

Me?

[*Before* ZIP *can point to himself, something rushes into* RICHARD, *adrenaline maybe, the dying man's last fight. He springs up and onto* ZIP, *grabbing his throat. At first,* ZIP *is startled, but then he starts to return the fire. It's really not clear who has the upper hand, but it is violent. Things are getting overturned. Cups and saucers and plates are breaking. Glass is breaking.* RICHARD *periodically shouts NIGGER! at the top of his lungs, almost to God. We hear canned sounds of an auditorium in waiting, whispers, murmurs, an orchestra. Lights go to half on the brawl, which is so scary in its violence. Lights come up on the Crow family, sans* ZIP, *in the "backstage" area.* JIM *looks nervous. The following happens over the cacophony of noises—the sounds of the kitchen being destroyed, the noisy auditorium.*]

MAMMY: Is everybody ready?
TOPSY: Yes, ma'am.
SAMBO: Yep.
MAMMY: Jimmy?
JIM: Where's Uncle Zip?
MAMMY: He's on his way.
JIM: Should we wait?
MAMMY: Naw, baby. It's okay. He ain't in the overture anyway.
JIM [*nervous*]: Okay.

[JIM *goes into a corner and tries to shake off his nerves.* SAMBO *notices.*]

SAMBO: Don't be nervous.
TOPSY: Don't be nervous, Jimmy.
MAMMY: Yeah. Whatchu gots to be nervous about?
JIM: What if they don't like me? What if they don't laugh? What if they don't think I'm interesting? What if they boo?
MAMMY: Oh, please. Is that all you're nervous about? Boy, don't you know they luvs us. They luvs evathang we does.
TOPSY: They luvs when we dance.
SAMBO: They luvs it when we shuffles.
TOPSY: When we shucks.

MAMMY: When we jives.

SAMBO: When we gets out our banjos and we plays 'em lak dis.

TOPSY: And when get out our drums and play 'em lak dis.

MAMMY: They luvs it when we laffs.

TOPSY: When we chuckles lak dis.

SAMBO: When we guffaws and slaps our thighs lak dis.

TOPSY: They luvs it when talk crazy-like.

MAMMY: And we smacks our lips.

TOPSY: And sucks our teefeses.

SAMBO: When we be misprunoudenencing wards wrongs en stuff.

TOPSY: When we make our eyes big and rolls em lak dis.

MAMMY: And roll our necks and be lak, "I know you di-in't!"

SAMBO: And when we acts all gay and vogue and be like "You go, gurl."

MAMMY: When we be hummin' in church and wear big hats and be like, "Mmmm! Testify!"

TOPSY: When we ax all sad and be like, "Dat's de bluez."

SAMBO: When we say stuff lak, "My baby mama!"

TOPSY: When we ax like we on crack lak dis.

SAMBO: When we stomps our feet lak dis.

TOPSY: When we drop it lak it's hot lak dis.

SAMBO [singing]: When we be singin' like lak dis.

MAMMY: They luvs it when we be like, "Black people like this. White people like that."

SAMBO: They luvs it when we soliloquizing like, "The white maaann!"

MAMMY: "The white man done done me wrong!"

SAMBO: "The white man put me in jail!"

MAMMY: "The white man has done took my home!"

SAMBO: "The white man has emasculated me!"

TOPSY: "The white man made me wanna be white!"

SAMBO: "I can't get out the ghettooooo!"

MAMMY: "I hates myself!"

SAMBO: "I hates the white man!"

MAMMY: "I hates the world!"

TOPSY: "But I can't break these chains!"

MAMMY: "These white man chains!"

SAMBO: "Even though I'm a human, dammit! I am human!"

TOPSY: "Respect me, white maaaaan!"

SAMBO: "'Cause I'm so angrrryyyy!"

MAMMY: They luvs when we be lak dat.

TOPSY: So if you get nervus, just do dat.

SAMBO: Do any uh dat.

MAMMY: And you be fine, baby. Be yo'self. It's just a show.

JIM: You right. Okay. Okay. I can do this. Okay.

MAMMY: Good. So you ready, Jimmy?

JIM: Yes. I think so. I'm ready.

[*Everyone prepares. The fighting in the kitchen is still happening.*]

ANNOUNCER'S VOICE: Now presenting . . . THE CROW FAMILY
  MINSTRELS

[*Recorded applause. The kitchen continues to be destroyed. The atmosphere is soaked in the ash cloud that is Jim Crow Sr. The* CROW FAMILY *sans* ZIP *take their place on "stage," standing in a straight line. Minstrel music plays, but they don't move. Instead, they simply look into every face in the room.* ZIP *and* RICHARD *are still fighting in half-light, and they are the only sound we hear, as the entire family looks the entire audience over. The minstrel music finishes, and there is silence before the entire theater, stage and all, is ever so slowly and completely washed in amber light. It is awkward and goes on forever. We watch them. They watch us. Occasionally, they point to people in the audience and whisper to each other, sometimes mockingly, sometimes out of concern. Occasionally, they giggle.*]

SUDDEN BLACKOUT.

Silence before lights come back up for curtain call. Only the CROW FAMILY *takes a bow, and we see in the front row of the audience* MELODY, *who gives the most exuberant standing ovation you have ever seen. There are even tears of joy in her eyes. She's there for her boyfriend. The* CROW FAMILY *bows and exits the empty stage.*

Preferably there is no "real" curtain call, and MELODY *leaves with the audience. She goes outside and has a cigarette. She doesn't talk to anyone, waiting at the stage door, maybe with her mother. She looks different now, maybe, less like herself.*

Eventually JIM *comes out of the stage door to greet her. They hug and kiss. Maybe she gives him a cigarette, which he smokes. Maybe people catch this, maybe they don't.*]

MELODY: How do you feel?

[*"We Are Family" is heard blasting away over the speakers back in the empty theater, as* THE ACTOR PLAYING JIM CROW *starts to tell her how he really feels.*]

INTERVIEW WITH BRANDEN JACOBS-JENKINS

Branden Jacobs-Jenkins is a Brooklyn-based playwright, dramaturg, and performer. His work has been seen at The Public Theater, New York Theatre Workshop, PS122, Soho Rep, New Dramatists, The Matrix Theatre, Theater Bielefeld in Bielefeld, Germany, and the National Theatre in London. His plays include The Change, Zoo, *and* The Octoroon.

Rebecca Rugg: This anthology frames *Clybourne Park, Etiquette of Vigilance, Living Green,* and *Neighbors* as responses to *A Raisin in the Sun.* Yours is the most oblique in this. The others all explicitly call themselves responses to *Raisin,* while yours does not. Do you feel that this frame fits? Is there a line you would draw from *A Raisin in the Sun* to your play?

Branden Jacobs-Jenkins: *A Raisin in the Sun* was the only play about "black people" that I ever had to read for a playwriting class, which meant that it was supposed to teach me something about "good form." So I guess—given my occasional preoccupation with theatrical form and blackness in the theater—in some weird, subconscious way I'm probably always responding to *A Raisin in the Sun.* But my most overt reference to the play in *Neighbors,* which is full of references to a bunch of stuff, is through *The Colored Museum,* which is probably a more obvious influence. I try to remake the "Last Mama on the Couch," to a greater or lesser extent, through the character of Mammy, and especially in scene 3.

I mean, obviously, there are also any number of plot and thematic overlaps, but that just speaks to *A Raisin*'s own influence, though, historically speaking, narratives involving blackness and/or Americanness have always flirted with the idea of moving and home ownership (both figuratively and literally), since the general project, from the beginning, has been about finding homes for a historically displaced "people" or these "people" finding homes for "themselves." But then I think, sometime in the middle of the last century (and more interestingly to me) the question "Where is my home?" refined itself to "Where is the home I deserve?" This had something to do with African Americans suddenly realizing, for the first time, that they could be economically mobile. And that's where *A Raisin* stepped in.

So if the narrative of my parents' generation (who were just children when *A Raisin* premiered) was one of moving or movement that *A Raisin* seemed to be either articulating or presaging—the struggle to arrive to the place you *deserved*—I think the question for me now as this like . . . post-integration baby . . . is "Are we there yet?" or "Are we coming or are we going?" And if we've already arrived—which everyone seems to be saying, now that we've seen Jesse Jackson cry on television [in response to the election of Barack Obama]—"What's supposed to happen now?" Essentially, what is the step after *A Raisin in the Sun*? They moved. Great. Okay that happened, but now what? (I think it's worth mentioning that fifteen years after *A Raisin* premiered, *The Jeffersons* premiered—which coined the phrase "movin' on up" and became (and still is) the longest-running "black show" in television history. Maybe that was the "now what?")

That is why I love *Clybourne Park*. (Though I guess Bruce Norris skips over the "now what?" and goes straight to "but then what?" which is its own bag of interesting.) It was actually running in New York at the same time as *Neighbors,* and there was a certain amount of comparison happening among audiences, and when I finally skipped my show one night to see it, I lost my mind. I thought the two plays were eerily in conversation with each other and overlapped in all sorts of odd ways—like even down to certain gentrification jokes, many of which have been consequently written out of *Neighbors*—but maybe I'm just flattering myself. Basically all I wanted to do after the show was stalk Bruce Norris everywhere and eat the things he ate and read the things he was reading and wear his clothes when he wasn't looking and try to figure out how he pulled it off. In fact, I still do.

RR: I love that your plays were running at the same time. It would be great to have all the plays in this book produced together!

BJJ: I'm thrilled to be in this company. Robert O'Hara's first play, *Insurrection: Holding History,* is one of my favorite plays ever. I remember finishing it on the floor of my little apartment back in 2006 and thinking, "Where has this play been all my life?!" I can't believe people aren't reviving that play like all the time.

RR: *A Raisin in the Sun* comes to stand in for a certain line of realism.

BJJ: Yeah. It was a brilliant moment in theater history, wasn't it? The play made "African American drama" palatable to a mainstream theater-going audience by grafting this story of black frustration onto this already familiar form of the well-made social realist drama, with its attendant hints of melodrama and "all-American" themes of upward mobility and the economic power of the family unit. Formally, Hansberry sort of wedged herself onto a lineage of "recognized dramatists" like Arthur Miller and Clifford Odets and John Osborne and even Ibsen. It's similar to the way August Wilson basically rewrote *Death of a Salesman* through *Fences* and everyone was like "Bravo!" She figured out a kind of formula. She made it legible somehow. She also managed to write a pseudosympathetic white character, who was bad but not *that* bad, just misunderstanding and a little condescending.

And a lot of people are going to get mad at me for having just said that, but even Hansberry admits a lot of its canonization has to do with how successfully it played for predominantly white audiences, which in turn has to do with appealing to the acquired tastes of a pretty much entirely white critical apparatus. But it's an example of a moment in which it was necessary to be the Good Capable Negro, because, at the time, blackness was publicly synonymous with *bad* and *inept,* and the job of any black artist was debunking that. And *A Raisin* accomplished that. Artistically and economically, it was a success. But then I guess the question became, "What next?" Blacks can be good. Blacks can be bad. So what does blackness have to do with either of those things?

And, if you want to gauge things uncritically and in terms of canonical success, the answer to that question came in the form of August Wilson. He's the one that comes next in the syllabus, unless you make a mildly confusing avant-garde detour through *Dutchman, Funnyhouse of a Negro,* and maybe an Ed Bullins play, if you're feeling nasty.

RR: And now?

BJJ: Right. What exactly did August Wilson leave the conversation? Obviously, I had to go through a vaguely Oedipal, anti–August Wilson moment to become the playwright I am. And one part of that was being so annoyed by the idea constantly being shoved down my throat that he somehow successfully catalogued, through the theater, mind you, "the black American experience in the twentieth century."

Now, aside from the fact that the idea of anthropological theater makes me queasy—the idea that drama, this incredibly artificial form full of made-up people and situations was going to reveal anything about anyone "real" other than the man who wrote it and his audience—and the fact that Pittsburgh was in no way a microcosm (economically, culturally, or otherwise) of black life in America, broadly speaking, if you look at the characters in his plays, there's not a single one that's born after 1975. I was very disturbed by this. So does my experience not count? Or does my experience not start until I'm thirty? Has my experience somehow been "less black"? Now, this is not something I wouldn't even be taking August Wilson to task for, if I wasn't being told every five seconds that this was his greatest achievement, delivering some sort of definitive account.

Incidentally, I've been screamed at a lot about *Neighbors,* and one woman in the discussion after the LA workshop of *Neighbors* (at The Matrix Theatre, where it subsequently received production) was very vocal and kind of out to get us—even the producer had warned us beforehand to watch out for her—and, when she finally spoke up, she went through a lot of typical criticism I (and Niegel Smith, my director) had gotten about how "we weren't there," "we don't know what they [meaning her generation] went through," and then there was this interesting moment where she got kind of wistful and internal and a little defensive and was like, "We really thought we were raising our children to be citizens of the world." And this echoed a similar conversation I had had with my mother years ago where she concluded, "I always wonder if my generation failed you guys."

There is a strange anxiety in pockets of that generation about what they did or didn't do right. There was some torch they were carrying, and they don't know where the torch went or whether the torch was worth it. That anxiety is superfascinating to me. But when I tried to respond, this woman in LA, she just shut me down. And it was like, Okay, lady, I am one of those children you're talking about, and I'm telling you right now I don't feel like a citizen of the world, and I don't know anyone who does, and rather than listening, you're shutting down the conversation. And her defense for this was, "I don't need to hear it. I don't need you to sit up there and tell me this." And it was just like, "What?" Suddenly, it was like I had no right to have questions for her. *Because* I was a generation (or maybe two) younger, there was no longer grounds for exchange. And it's like, What was the point? Who were you doing all this work for if I was just expected to shut up once I learned to speak? Was it all just for you?

RR: The play makes a show of its relationship to theater history. So let's talk about that. Your stage directions have their own voice and explore a virtuosity in their descriptions. In particular, how do the interludes function?

BJJ: I'm very interested in the life of a script. I sort of come out of academia and wanted to write a play that was maybe partly a thesis and was also a performance text and also a text that somehow performed on its own. I was also completely convinced that this play would never be produced ever, so I was perfectly content with making something that was simply a very vivid reading experience. In *Neighbors*, there is something about the voice (if we want to call it that—the stage directions, or whatever . . .) that is very unsure. It's kind of passive-aggressive, and also kind of coy and self-effacing, with all the "if you wants" and "I don't knows." There's a weird, awkward flirtation happening. That has to do with the play itself, which is purposely very unsure about something. At least, initially. Is that virtuosic? I don't know. But it definitely is constantly trying to impress the reader, somehow.

Formally, my initial impulse was to smash together these two historical poles of black dramatic representation. The very beginnings—minstrelsy, e.g., nonblacks performing an idea of blacks for other nonblacks—and what I then thought was the "next step," post–August Wilson, e.g., an interracial social family drama . . . mostly because I was a little obsessed with the fact that Wilson was biracial and no one talked about that. And I was having a hard time thinking of how to mix the two so I eventually (and quite lazily) decided upon this ladder structure: Minstrelsy—Dramatic Scene—Minstrelsy—Dramatic Scene. Whatever those things meant. The idea is that we would be constantly moving back and forth between two very different types of dramaturgy, both having to do with "race" but with very different relationships to the audience, and maybe at some point they'd synthesize into something else—maybe I'd find the continuous thread. And the shifting back and forth for the audience would create a kind of weird destabilization, an alertness of some sort.

RR: Speaking of the experience of the play as a reader—the final moments of the play are fairly opaque to me. What are you after? How did that play out in practice?

BJJ: Something that came to me very early . . . one of the first images was of the Crow family on the lip of the stage facing out and in the background hearing a really incredibly violent fight happening. And I remember feeling the sensation of trying to see the fight but there were people in the way, who were in turn looking at me. That image came very early, and in a lot of ways I started writing toward that. What didn't come early was Jim and Melody outside the theater. And what came even later was the whole olio of "they love it when we do this, they love it when we do that." All these things arrived at different times. Because one of the things I knew was that part of the experiment I'd made for myself was to smash together minstrelsy and comedy and tragedy. And the difference I was taught between the two was about endings. Like *The Merchant of Venice* is a comedy because there's a restoration.

RR: Marriage!

BJJ: Exactly. I was also really interested, at the time, in places where laughter, melancholia, and black performance intersected, triggered mostly by [comedian Dave] Chappelle's cancelling his show and having a sort of nervous breakdown after hearing what he thought was "wrong laughter." I became obsessed with this idea of the "wrong laughter." I could just write and write and write about my obsession with the "wrong laughter." And also I was super into vaudeville for a while and Bert Williams, and there's a famous description of Bert Williams from, I think, W. C. Fields that's like, "He was the funniest man I ever saw and the saddest man I ever knew," and I was just obsessed with that—with the difference there between seeing and knowing and where funniness and sadness lived in relationship to either. And I was watching a lot of Richard Pryor, of course—also an amazing figure in this regard. Something about the truth of this play lived in my obsession with these things and these people, with this intersection. It lived in the trying to articulate or describe this weird space where tragedy and comedy exist together around blackness. And so it seemed to me the play had to evade the resolution of an ending that would identify it clearly as one or the other.

So there are two endings at once. Or several endings. Or staggered endings. I don't know. I just knew I had to create a sense of jamming or of a machine not being able to function or breaking and part of that machine rolling out the door. I don't know. There's the minstrel show and then simultaneously there's this tragedy of Richard also happening. But after a while, it all slows down to one image. If the whole play was about the effects of images, of the power of the visual, of race as a visual construction, I wanted to see if I could turn both of these weird arcs in the play into one image, and then to find out how much this one image could contain. So the arc of Richard's tragedy becomes this extended fight which becomes a feat of endurance for these actors and the arc of the family becomes just them performing in the most basic sense, watching an audience watch them. The whole play just kind of calcifies into this installation or a sculpture or performance art. At some point, without us even paying attention, the play has stopped being a play and become something else. It's hard to explain.

And of course, a common misinterpretation for the ending is that the family is standing there kind of defiantly, aggressively staring down the audience in this weird sort of living theateresque moment of castigation that's like, "How dare you! Here's who I really am!" which is my personal hell. Or a director will have them looking really sad and victimized and beaten down, as if the audience had forced them to do this, which I don't like, because I actually think the Crows are much savvier than that. The whole joke is that they're self-aware. The whole thing is about how they know what you want and they know what they want. For me the ending is simply about the audience experiencing the sensation of being watched. I don't think the Crows really give a crap about having a relationship with the audience at this point. They've been relating to the audience the whole night. Now they just want to relate with each other and see a show. The lights just come on, the dark anonymity an audience gets to hide behind is gone, and they want to see who's there, who they've been sharing this space with for two hours, and what they're gonna do.

It worked well at the Public because we were in the Shiva, which is such a long space, and the fight traveled along the length of it. And what you saw, which was perfect, was people looking at the actors, who were looking at them, or people trying to see this fight that was going on behind them. And it's a fight that's gone on for so long that nothing new is being revealed, it's just two actors grappling with each other, safely. But still, it was amazing to watch audience members have to make this choice between what they wanted to see, and either they wanted to see actors in blackface looking back, or two guys fighting with no identifiable resolution. Sometimes, they wind up watching each other.

RR: And what about the very very end?

BJJ: Oh, right! Well, I thought a lot about Melody and Jim in this play, and Melody . . . I always knew I wanted to play with this tragic mulatto figure, because she was the one archetype who was so present in history, and I couldn't find a place for her, and I found her in Melody, and initially there was going to be more of a back-and-forth, and she was going to be the thing that was really at stake. But there was something about Jim Crow that really came to life over the writing of the play. And the two of them make this odd pair, there's a sense that they don't fit in anywhere, just by the nature of history, of when they were born, and of how they literally . . . look. There's just something different happening and I knew there was something important about the fact they really didn't blend, like they hadn't figured out a category for what they were yet, and that newness was going to make it likely that an audience was going to attach a lot of hope to them. But I didn't like the idea that I would somehow . . . I hate it when teenage characters in plays somehow provide for us The Answer. Like "the children are the future," the children always come forward and say these naively "right" things that are supposed to save us. I am interested in how actually people that age have no idea what is going on and the last thing they want/can do is save us. People that age are searching, or beginning some search that will ultimately be very valuable, but mostly for them, and I would be full of shit if I acted like I knew what a biracial fifteen-year-old was going through right now. So I was interested in handing over the authority of the Author's Voice to someone who might actually know what was going on, not resolving their arc within the room of the play, which would be insincere, but letting the actors playing them, who are theoretically people their age, have a conversation. If they wanted to and outside. And it should just feel like something else, like honesty, like the theater thing is dissolving slowly and these people are just caught in the storm.

RR: And did people watch them have their conversation?

BJJ: The dream was that this conversation would happen outside the theater, in an alleyway next to the theater or somewhere unnoticeable but noticeable if you were really paying attention. But at the Public, because of the architecture, where outside the theater there are more theaters and an actual lobby—which has its own energy as a place where conversations are happening anyway—the two actors were really on display, and so people did come up to them but didn't really understand that the show was still happening. Inevitably, the conversations were always like, "Y'all were so great," because of the absence of a curtain call. The thing that really infuriates people is the absence of a curtain call. People want their curtain calls, even if actors *do not give a shit*, which this play has taught me they don't. I think curtain calls are such a creepy display of power. But, anyway, I guess these two young actors can be overshadowed by their older colleagues' performances in the play, which are pretty significantly more intense . . . so I guess it's lovely for them to be the vessels for all that audience energy and gratitude and attention.

RR: *Neighbors* is so explicitly in conversation with the theatrical past, and histories of representation, but also with these other contemporary plays. Which brings me to Obama. It feels like Obama's residency in the White House must have to do with a proliferation of plays where people live side by side across race. With the Obamas' move into the White House, it seemed like something major had shifted in this country relative to history. In the playing out of his presidency, it's unclear exactly what the lasting meaning is. These plays intersect with this, and seem to do so in particular through the lens of neighborliness. Not only the plays in this book, but also Lisa D'Amour's play *Detroit*, Thomas Bradshaw's *Mary*, and others. Do you have ideas about where *Neighbors* sits in a landscape that also has Obama in it as president?

BJJ: I wrote this play in December of 2007, well before the Obama presidency, but I remember during the primaries thinking about a class I'd taken on performance and the law at NYU, where someone theorized—or I suppose made the observation—that throughout American history, one surefire way to expose riffs in American popular opinion has been to pit a black male against a white female, which is sort of surreal in how convincing it is. Consider the O. J. Simpson trial, the Scottsboro Nine, not to mention the whole era of lynch mobs, and then Clinton and Obama—they all become national dramas, exhausting and traumatic, and, whether you like it or not, you found yourself having to pick sides, but you were also nervous about picking sides, because what side you picked seemed to be saying something about you and your relationship to your identity and desire and history and all that mania just leads to a collective breakdown.

The campaign drama specifically gave people permission to have conversations openly that hadn't been happening since the early nineties. Race was suddenly up for discussion again—a lot of things were actually up for discussion, because we were at the tail end of eight years post-9/11 that were all about suppression and silence. But race specifically was there because it's one of the longest discussions we've been having as a country. People suddenly had a lot to say about it and, consequently, revealed their own clumsiness and inarticulateness and naïveté with regards to the subject, black and white. Terms and concepts had changed. Certain ideas and words had fallen out of fashion and lost meaning without anyone noticing, because we were too busy trying to keep a straight face as Americans in the glare of an entire world that basically hated us because of the actions of this regime the populus didn't even elect initially. But now that hope was on its way and we could all take a break from being a big happy patriotic family, suddenly people you've known—or thought you knew—were saying stuff about "history needs to be history" and "postrace" and you were like, "Wait, who are you, again? And where did you just come from with that dated, dated thinking?"

But also, on a related note—and no one really talks about this anymore, which is weird—I think a lot of us were terrified by how real the possibility was that we would be living under a McCain/Palin presidency, because there were *people* who were actually about to *vote* for them, in spite of how obviously nuts they appeared to be. I mean, I just remember my jaw falling to the floor every time there was some televised Republican town hall in like Kansas City, where some biddy would stand up and be like, "Obama's a Muslim!" There were folks who didn't think like "us" and there were *a lot* of them. And this happened over and over again. We were just *not* on the same page. There was a sudden reconsideration of community, of home in the face of all that craziness. A realization of living next to people that you didn't know were there or you thought had left. And they had just as much say as you did, it seemed like. In most cases, you had just as much political power as they did, e.g., one vote. Or at least that's what it seemed like. But maybe that's always been the case.

I mean, look at Chekhov. It's all about people realizing that there are new people in the neighborhood who actually aren't that new, after all. They were there all along—you just never noticed because you never felt threatened or vulnerable. Maybe this is a trend in drama in times of extreme political and economic upheaval. Especially when it falls so cleanly in between generations. Obama was supposed to be all about this mysterious youth vote, this previously voiceless faction coming up and saying something, suddenly powerful, and folks didn't know what to do. Time did its thing and messed with everyone's sense of self. I think that's always a really fruitful dramatic territory. One that always makes sense in the context of national turmoil.

AFTERWORD: INTERVIEW WITH GEORGE C. WOLFE

Harvey Young

George C. Wolfe is a writer, director, and producer. He has won two Tony Awards, for directing Angels in America *and* Bring in 'da Noise, Bring in 'da Funk. *He is the author of* The Colored Museum, Spunk, Jelly's Last Jam, *and from 1992 to 2004 was the producer of The Public Theater/New York Shakespeare Festival.*

Harvey Young: Becca Rugg and I are working on a project about artists revisiting *A Raisin in the Sun.* What does it mean to have Bruce Norris's *Clybourne Park,* Branden Jacobs-Jenkins's *Neighbors,* Gloria Bond Clunie's *Living Green,* and Robert O'Hara's *Etiquette of Vigilance* reengaging with the work that Hansberry did fifty years ago? As part of that conversation, we both agreed that their plays were inspired or enabled by *The Colored Museum*—so we wanted to engage you and talk with you about that, noting that *The Colored Museum* is now approaching its twenty-fifth anniversary.

George C. Wolfe: Jesus. (*Laughter*)

HY: In interviews in the mideighties, you frequently noted that you were tired of seeing *A Raisin in the Sun* staged every Black History Month. Every February, there would be a local, regional theater producing *A Raisin in the Sun.* It was black theater under glass: something that you pull out, put on show, and then put away again [for another year]. Now that we're fifty years past the premiere of *Raisin,* I'd like to get your thoughts on the relevance of *A Raisin in the Sun* today.

GCW: First off it's a resoundingly smart play. In the recent [Broadway] revival it was fun rediscovering how it operates very successfully as this melodrama—will the overbearing Mama allow her children to come into their own, will the son assert himself and claim his manhood, will they move into the white neighborhood—while simultaneously engaging the audience in this very sophisticated dialogue about race and identity. Also I was struck by how brilliant the language was, how it crackled. And the inclusion of the African character, which is clearly reflective of Lorraine Hansberry's sophisticated worldview. And so in some respects my comments back then were less about the play and more so about the laziness of some white producers declaring, "*A Raisin In The Sun.* This is what it means to be Negro. This is what it means to be Black. We need look no further, the search is done."

I wrote *Colored Museum* so that I could write any play I wanted to after that. I was creatively and psychologically liberating myself from that which had gone before—claiming, celebrating, and disregarding it all at the exact same time, so that my theatrical brain could feel free to say and do whatever it wanted.

I originally gave a copy of *Git on Board* to a black producer in New York, and he wanted Miss Pat to come back at the end of the play and say, "I was wrong. I shouldn't have done what I did to those slaves." Interestingly enough, I got a lot of flak when the play was first produced because certain people weren't used to satire, didn't know how to process it. Also, given the preponderance of offensive images handed down via popular culture, black people have been programmed to have an almost Pavlovian response to certain silhouettes. If the silhouette is objectionable, don't bother listening to what it's saying.

HY: Right, because the moment that you see it, then—

GCW: It's a violation. I was deliberately trafficking in dangerous silhouettes in part because I'm drawn to things which are provocative but also because I wasn't interested in defining myself in defiance of anything, mainly because it's giving something else or someone else power over who you are. I was working on *The Colored Museum* while at NYU, and I remember this teacher saying, "I don't understand why Miss Pat isn't white." And I said without even thinking, "The only thing that's going to be white in this play are the walls." And, I was like [as if in a moment of revelation], "The only thing that's going to be white are the walls." I was interested in racism as an energy force coming at me, not racism as my definition. If that makes sense.

HY: It makes complete sense.

GCW: Plus it was a chance to both exorcise and explore the various definitions I'd been negotiating a relationship with since day one: black, Negro, and colored. I was born colored—my birth certificate says "col"—but then spent a huge chunk of my early life being a Negro, which I translate as being acutely aware of the figure, the silhouette that you cut in public. I was indoctrinated to believe that every single thing that I said or did was being judged by white people as reflective of the entire race. And then black was in defiance of that imprisonment. And then at one point I grew to view colored as an irreverent, unapologetic celebration of self. Betsy Smith is colored to me. Richard Pryor is colored to me. They're doing what they're doing—the good, the bad, the ugly—claiming it all and spitting it out and not waiting for anybody to approve or accept. And that's why the play isn't called *The Black Museum* or *The Negro Museum* but *The Colored Museum*.

HY: Birth certificates in a lot of states no longer have racial check boxes. They don't entirely exist anymore. Going back to Hansberry, her father crossed out "Negro" and put in "Black" on her birth certificate. That reminds me of something else that you said in an interview, which is that you grew up and spent the first ten years of your life in a black community and described it as "twelve years of being extraordinary." It was that experience that you took everywhere you went.

GCW: Exactly. Not for one second, growing up, was there ever any feelings of inferiority or being less than. I went to this private all-black grade school, and we're talking borderline *Manchurian Candidate*—total indoctrination. "A black man invented the traffic light. A Negro did this . . . a Negro did that . . ." I was celebrated for being smart and creative and then I went to a public, predominantly white high school, where for the first time I encountered someone looking at me as less than.

My town was segregated until I was about eight years old. Martin Luther King Jr. marched in Frankfort, Kentucky, and my grandmother took me out of school, and we marched with him. I had this forceful, very powerful grandmother who would defend me against the entire universe. I grew up in this very protected environment. At the same time, I felt this overwhelming pressure from my family and my community. "Everybody is watching you. You are representing the entire race so every single thing you say or do matters." It's the most exhausting thing in the world. Exhausting.

HY: How much of that sense of being watched, being responsible, representing where you are from inspires the work that you have created?

GCW: Oh no, I had to kill it. I had to kill that off. That kind of thought process is the antithesis of being an artist. There are many incredible survival skills and manipulation skills and agenda skills to be extracted from being raised a Negro, but that exaggerated awareness of how you are perceived is suffocating. I had to kill that off, because it was not going to allow me to become an artist, less none a semihealthy, functioning human being.

HY: It seems to me that there is a collision there. That moment where everything you know and every part of your being is being embraced, being celebrated by the community in which you live, and yet an awareness of being called a name, being seen a certain way, having a history chained to you . . .

GCW: All of that was going on, but I was protected from it.

HY: Right, it was all going on but you were protected from it. I wonder about that part of it. How much of that part of being protected comes in—not the weight of the history and the stereotypes and the caricatures that you're always having to fight through but the realization that if you ever surrender to them, then they will stifle your ability to think outside of a box.

GCW: The stories that I was told growing up were the stories of survival. I was told about my mother graduating from college and walking into a jewelry store in downtown Frankfort and this white woman saying, "Anna, it's nice you have your degree but you should come be my maid" and my grandmother going in there and telling that woman off. Those were the stories I was told, of people taking a stand, not letting folks get away with shit. I didn't hear the cowering in the corner stories.

I'm sure they happened, but that wasn't the legacy that was passed on to me.

HY: It also means that what you were surrounded by—at an early age—was strength.

GCW: Strength. And because I was so protected, I was able to live inside my imagination for a very long time. Consequently, I didn't have any authentic, personal survival skills 'cause I didn't need them. But then all of a sudden, it was like, "Wait. I don't know how to defend myself in the world."

When I went to high school, there was this initial impression that I was stupid and dismissible because I stuttered really badly. And so here I am, going from one environment where everybody knew I was smart to one where they thought I was not because of a speech impediment. And then, interestingly enough, it was theater—my mother was away getting her doctorate at Miami University so I went with her and joined this summer theater program that was part of the university, and that experience gave me the confidence to become who I was. It was theater that gave me language, gave me humor, gave me edge, and that fall when I went back to high school, I started conquering so that by the time I left I was president of this club and the head of this organization. Theater as a weapon. Language as a weapon. Language and humor as a means of defending and defining myself was instantly fused to my growth—to me coming into my power as a presence in the world.

HY: In terms of the work that you create, let's say *The Colored Museum*, was it rooted in the belief that social realism within drama tends to skew toward stereotype?

GCW: I don't think it was that. I just think that my brain, my creative brain, just didn't get social realism. In college I directed *The Fabulous Miss Marie*, a play by Ed Bullins, whose work I greatly admired. I knew, read, and respected the whole NEC social realism canon (*The River Niger, Ceremonies in Dark Old Men*, etc.), but when I wrote my first play, *Up for Grabs*, it was stylistically about as far from that type of theater as you can get.

In *Up for Grabs*, the main character, Joe Thomas, who's been locked inside a soundproof booth since the day he was born and only had cereal boxes and TV commercials to forge an identity, is suddenly at age twenty-one set free into the seemingly real world, but in actuality it's a game show called *Up for Grabs*. He ventures into four worlds/four doors. Behind door number one is the corporate world, where he achieves success by becoming congenial and banal. Behind door number two he becomes Heavy Harry Hard, a black exploitation star, and behind door number three he joins the revolution of a militant called Baba Z. In each of these worlds he and his newly claimed identity are shattered. He then enters door number four and discovers that when he was born his parents went on a game show and traded him in for a brand new washer and dryer.

I wrote this play when I was twenty, during my last year of college, so very early on in my career, hell, before I even had a career; my theatrical brain wasn't drawn to no couch with doilies. It just wasn't. I felt more at home inside of Kabuki or Brecht than social realism. My brain just went, "No, I ain't goin' in that room." It wasn't that I hated it. I admired it and was respectful of it. It just didn't appeal to me creatively.

HY: Was part of it having a visceral reaction to seeing it—to seeing social realism onstage—and seeing *Raisin* being brought out?

GCW: Growing up, I was obsessed with two things. I was obsessed with Walt Disney, with Disneyland and his movies, most of which were musicals, which oddly enough I believe was crucial to my being drawn to a more heightened theatrical aesthetic. The other: I had all these little . . . I wouldn't call them action figures because they were these small plastic toys, and I would never play with just the cowboys and Indians. I would have the cowboys mixed in with the dinosaurs and the safari figures. As soon as I got a new set, I would break it up, put medieval knights with jungle animals and pirates; all these little figures that didn't belong together I'd put together. I think it's just how my brain operated. If there was an order, I felt a compelling urge to defy it.

I also think that going to the college I went to, it wasn't about the practical application of doing theater. This was the 1970s. I graduated in 1976, and the ambition of the time was less about how to do theater and more, so what is theater, how do you make theater vital to the world we live in? We staged plays with giant puppets in a rock quarry, studied Grotowski, Brecht. And so this, combined with the way my imagination was already operating, didn't exactly put me on a path toward social realism.

Plus, I've always been fascinated by the minstrel show. Not the racial content but its structure, its fragmentation. There's something about fragments/scenes, or in the case of *The Colored Museum*, exhibits, in juxtaposition to one another, telling a story that I find exhilarating and challenging. I've always been drawn by that minstrel/vaudeville/commedia structure.

HY: Is there a desire to spotlight a person who writes in a realistic style as *the* person who represents black culture in that moment?

GCW: I'm sure that's the case, but I don't think that's what motivated the writers. For Hansberry, I believe there was a very specific O'Casey model operating. There is always a predecessor. No artist springs forth full-grown. You can't discuss Suzan-Lori [Parks] without discussing Adrienne Kennedy. It's not possible. In some respects, the plays of the black nationalist arts movement were putting the protest novel on-stage, fueled with another level of rage. Somebody always spawns the energy.

The realistic "well-made play" carries with it all these connotations: serious, viable, important. The vaudeville/minstrel structure is fundamentally a populist form and is therefore dismissible as not possessing any redeeming social value. But what I wanted to do, and have spent my entire career doing so, is bring an intellectual and cultural sophistication to the populist form. That's why I love doing musicals. I wasn't interested in embodying the form unto itself because then that's pastiche. But how do you take a populist form and imbue it with another level of intellectual rigor. That's what I was doing with *The Colored Museum*, taking a populist vaudeville structure and imploding it with sophistication and rigor and dangerous silhouettes and madness and rage. Let's have a stewardess in a hot pink miniskirt teach the audience/slaves how to put on their shackles and sing "Go Down Moses."

I remember shortly after *The Colored Museum* opened, I was on a panel with Ntozake [Shange] and Gil Moses at La MaMa, and in

Frank Rich's review in the *New York Times* he said something about "the playwright takes no prisoners" and someone in the audience, stupidly—let me point out—construed that to mean that I did not attack anybody. And all of these people started asking me all these loaded questions—people who were part of the New York black theater community—and the next day, I woke up and I was like, "Wow, they were attacking me." It was so bizarre. And there was this actress who I really loved—and when she came in for her *Colored Museum* audition, lifted up the script and defiantly declared, "I CAN NOT AUDITION FOR THIS PLAY." I got a lot of that. "Why did the character have to be putting on a wig to go break up with her man? Why couldn't she be putting on her wig to go off on her boss?"

I found it all very confusing, because this sort of thought process was not where I was coming from, at all! I wasn't operating in defiance of a white power structure. I was operating in celebration of the brilliance and the damage and the horror and the ridiculousness and the extraordinariness—the contradictions and potency that was/is Black American culture.

HY: **How much of the reception was attributed to the structure and the content of *The Colored Museum* and how much of it was "here's a person who is considered to be an outsider who is now attracting national attention"?**

GCW: Very much so. Many artists of color had already passed through the door of the Public Theater. Joe Papp had been a great champion of Ntozake's work and Ed Bullins's work and Richard Wesley's work and now me, except I had literally come from nowhere. I went to school in California, worked at a theater in LA called The Inner City Cultural Center, moved to New York, was teaching acting at City College and The Children's Art Carnival, went to NYU, did a musical off-Broadway that got clobbered by the critics, and then I did this show out at Crossroads called *The Colored Museum,* which then came into town and overnight it's this big hit. I didn't come from the New Federal Theatre. I didn't come from the Frederick Douglass Center. I didn't work my way up the ranks of the Negro Ensemble Company. I didn't come from any of those places, and all of a sudden I'm at the Public and I'm doing this odd kind of theater and saying startling things and trafficking in loaded silhouettes and using satire which was not part and parcel of the current crop of black plays being done in New York at that time. It was just too much that was new. I label those people who attacked me and my play the self-appointed guardians of black culture. Nobody voted for them. They voted for themselves.

Because of the rave review in the *Times*, the show's initial run was sold out and the audiences were primarily white. It was fascinating watching the show then, because all the white people would look over at however many black people there were in the audience to see if it was all right to laugh. And then when we moved into a larger theater inside of the Public, the audiences became half black and half white, and those performances were really charged. I remember a few times people from the audience got into confrontations with the characters. Once somebody actually climbed up on stage ready to attack a character. And then just before we moved to London, the audiences became predominately black and those performances were like a mad circus, with the audience laughing and shouting out in response to what was happening onstage. The real black folks completely embraced the show and totally got it. It was the self-appointed guardians—they were the people who took issue with it. They tried to stop it but couldn't. They tried to lead boycotts, all kinds of stuff, but none of it was able to gain traction because there's no self-loathing in that material. None. It's celebratory. It's a celebration of insanity.

HY: When you took over the Public Theater, was there an opportunity for you to make amends with those who critiqued you or for them to make amends with you?

GCW: Most of the animosity vanished comparatively quickly. If anything remained, jealously remained. But then my next project was *Spunk*, which was completely different, totally celebratory. Truth be told, after my initial hurt feelings of being attacked, I didn't really think about it too much. You just do what you do and eventually people realize you ain't goin' nowhere, and they figure out how to embrace you or they don't.

I remember at one point I won an Audelco (black theater) Award and instead of using the stairs, I just jumped up onto the stage with my mop of wild hair—this is when people didn't have mops of wild hair . . . I'd walk down the street and people would cross the street as if I was some sort of insane person. And I guess me not taking the stairs and having wild hair allowed one of the self-appointed guardians to say to me, "Oh now I understand you." I guess she got that I was unapologetically what I was and so all the crap just started to vanish and rather quickly I was claimed.

HY: One of the things that Becca and I have been talking about is artistic genealogy. Not only those who inspired you but also those who found inspiration in you. Are there people who you look at and say they were assisted in some way by *The Colored Museum* and your ability to shift the conversation away from expectations of the "Mother on the Couch" or heavy social realism to thinking of theater as a place where communities come together?

GCW: I think very probably everybody since except August Wilson (*laughter*). Robert O'Hara, Tracey Scott Wilson, bunches of folks. You should really ask them because this feels a bit Jelly Roll Mortonish to me. Morton would stop people in a bar and tell them, "You stole your music from me." I remember there was this guy, Jerome Hardison, and I saw this play he wrote when he was sixteen; it was in the Young Playwright's Festival, and I thought, "I could get hit by a bus now," because my work gave him permission to write what he wrote. I remember feeling quite wonderful about him and his play, very emotional. And very early on, Robert O'Hara wrote me a very generous letter when he was still a student at Columbia, and I went to see his play *Insurrection*, which I loved and, yes, I saw pieces of me in it, but so much more. A gifted writer. This whole question is making me feel like Jelly Roll Morton.

HY: Or like Little Richard.

GCW: Exactly. (*Imitating Little Richard*) "I did that. You didn't do that. You stole that from me."

HY: How do you see your role on [Barack Obama's] President's Committee on the Arts and the Humanities enhancing the visual arts and arts outreach to communities?

GCW: I spent twelve years at the Public Theater in service to and in service of other artists and the various communities the Public served. And because of both the scale of the job and the vision I had for the institution, I ended up suspending my own personal artistic journey so that I could go on another kind of journey, which was connected very specifically to how I was raised: "Be the nice, bright, charming Negro boy who gets in the room and then once inside, go open up all the side doors and windows so your cousins can get in as well."

After I did my first Broadway show, *Jelly's Last Jam*, I was like, "Wow, this shit's hard." I happen to be blessed with a very forceful personality that just doesn't give up. Unfortunately a lot of the gifted theater artists I knew at the time didn't have the same warrior skill set, so I thought, maybe I should become a producer and help these artists navigate their way through the oftentimes treacherous landscape. And just as I was figuring out how to implement these impulses, right in the middle of directing my second Broadway show, *Angels in America*, I got asked to run the Public.

Many years earlier, when I was in residence at the Public, Joe [Papp] offered me the chance to run a black theater inside of the Public, but I wasn't interested in running a "black" theater. I was more interested in how cultures collide with one another, the fault lines between black and white or straight and gay, and so for twelve years that's what I tried to do. I tried to put inside of one building as many of the fragments of American culture as I possibly could. I wanted to trade in the "or" for an "and," so that we were doing black plays AND white plays AND gay plays AND Asian plays AND Latin plays AND plays written by women.

Another one of my agendas was very specifically about empowering artists, feeding artists and not pressuring them to come up with hits. I took on that responsibility. Let me worry about giving the building hits. Come here and be brilliant and play and grow and acquire the information necessary to survive the systems of making theater that are currently dominating the not-for-profit and commercial landscape. I believed that if they could acquire this information, they would be able to flourish and thrive and have great careers, because without this information to back up your talent, you get devoured.

That was a very hard, very amazing twelve-year journey, but after a while I was desperate to go back to being an artist again and so I left. Leaving the Public was me reclaiming myself as a writer, reclaiming myself as an artist. And inasmuch as it was necessary for me to do this, I was not totally satisfied just being a careerist, so the President's Committee on the Arts and the Humanities is one of the ways I get to feed the need inside of me to be connected to a larger agenda. I'm also helping to craft a civil and human rights museum in Atlanta, and I'm on this Broadway Theatre Subdistrict Council, appointed by the mayor, and it's our responsibility to give a bunch of money to various arts organizations around the city.

HY: There often seems like there's a tension between arts and politics. Not that the two are equal—the former tends to be overlooked by the latter. To have a seat, to be in the room with this commission, it seems like—not to say that they (art and politics) blur together—a door gets opened in a way that hasn't really happened in the past.

GCW: Last year, at a time when people were really hurting, we gave grants totaling close to two million dollars to various arts organizations. I felt this incredible high, this amazing thrill, giving grants for $20,000, $60,000, $100,000. To me it's all about empowerment and information, and I feel very fortunate that my career visibility has afforded me the chance to be in rooms where this kind of giving is taking place. I get very excited when information is being passed on, when money is being passed on so that other people can do what they need to do.

HY: What goals do you have left for yourself?

GCW: I'm really intrigued by film. I want to do more of that. I think that film is fundamentally fascistic in that it costs a tremendous amount of money and you generally have to navigate your way past a number of complicated personalities, but at the end of the day you end up with a product that is fiscally democratic because more people can afford to see it. On the other hand, theater is fundamentally democratic in how it's put together, but given the cost, especially on Broadway, you end up with something that is economically fascistic. To me this is criminal. Horrifying. I remember when I first moved to New York and choosing to not eat so that I could go to the TKTS line and spend sixteen dollars to get a half-priced ticket to go see a show. Seeing a Broadway show for that kind of money has become totally obsolete, and I find that appalling. This populist art form that I love is going the way of opera: an economically elitist event for three people in capes to sit in an audience and applaud. I will continue to do theater, but my main goal is to work all over the world as a film artist and, whenever I can, put myself inside of structures where I can pass on information.

HY: Since it has been twenty-five years since *The Colored Museum* premiered, what do you think is its legacy?

GCW: I'd love to see a really, really good high-profile production in New York City so that a whole new generation can discover the play. I'm also fascinated and quite proud that the play is being taught in high schools and universities. I remember looking online and coming across some paper/dissertation written by this white woman director who had done a production at Smith or Sarah Lawrence, one of those places—and women played all the roles, which I thought was great. But in the paper she said that fundamentally, and I might add in a rather clueless, arrogant manner, that the play was totally apolitical.

HY: Really?

GCW: Oh yeah! The last year I was at the Public, we did a reading of the play as part of a series of presentations of "landmark productions" from the past twenty-five seasons. We brought back Vickilynn Reynolds and Loretta Devine, two of the original cast (the other three, Tommy Hollace, Reggie Montgomery, and Danitra Vance, have unfortunately passed away), and the energy exchange between performers and text and audience achieved a level of lunacy—and I use that word very specifically: a cultural, political, spiritual lunacy—that was truly astonishing.

I remember at one point when the play was first produced at Crossroads, these two women who had no context of *A Raisin in the Sun* came up to me after seeing "The Last Mama on the Couch" exhibit and said, "We just about died laughing because we had a mama just like that. If you didn't wipe your feet, she would hit you." They completely and totally responded to it as if it were reflective of their reality, whereas someone who brings a cultural context to the play gets the piece on a whole other level. So, in part, I think the legacy is informed by the receiver.

HY: The play has circulated and inspired other less-successful versions. You can imagine a person watching *The Colored Museum* and being

aware of the references that are rooted in the original production but also of all of the other things that came in afterward.

GCW: Exactly. I remember at one point—and I got over this very quickly—I went to see a production in a city that shall remain nameless at a theater that shall remain nameless, and it was one of the worst things I'd ever seen in my entire life. I was horrified. I was embarrassed. I was offended. But then afterward the cast all came rushing toward me, gushing testimonials. "Working on this play changed me. It liberated me." And I instantly understood that I didn't have a right to be horrified, because it wasn't mine anymore. It was theirs. I remember the actor playing Miss Roj sat on a stool and, at the end of "The Gospel According to Miss Roj," proceeded to cry and moan, "So dance and snap." It was clichéd and tragic, something straight out of *The Boys in the Band*, as opposed to this raging, Cassandra-like shaman in patio pants spewing doom. I wanted to stand up and scream, "Wrong, wrong, wrong," but they found themselves in it. They were liberated and empowered by it. So . . . my snobbism/judgment? Who gives a crap? You find what you find in it. Smith girl didn't find anything in it. The folks who put on this bad production did. I didn't like the end product, but they found themselves in it. You want it to be what you want it to be—but then a part of you goes (*matter-of-factly*), "It's joined the popular culture," but then another part of you goes (*with exuberance*), "It's joined the popular culture," and so you get all that comes with that.

At the end of the day, what really matters as an artist is that your work empowers either someone sitting in the audience watching it, or it empowers other artists to do something different because they were inspired by your bravery or your vision. And that's how you're a part of the continuum.

For Ntozake, for Lorraine, for Ed Bullins, for Brecht, for Stanley Crouch, for C. Bernard Jackson, for Richard Pryor, for Walt Disney (fascist though he was), for Jerome Robbins, for Arthur Laurents, for Peter Stone, for Minnie J. Hitch—for all those artists who helped me free a piece of my creative brain so that I could become the artist that I am. Hopefully in my work, as a writer, as a director, as a producer, as a cultural thinking person, hopefully I've done the same for others as well.